JAINISM

An Indian Religion of Salvation

LALA SUNDAR LAL JAIN RESEARCH SERIES

VOLUME XIV

HELMUTH VON GLASENAPP

JAINISM

An Indian Religion of Salvation

An English Translation of

DER JAINISMUS

Eine Indische Erlösungsreligion

by

SHRIDHAR B. SHROTRI

SINCE 1901

MOTILAL BANARSIDASS
PUBLISHING HOUSE

*Reprint: Delhi, **2026***
First Edition: Delhi, 1999

Also available at:
MOTILAL BANARSIDASS PUBLISHING HOUSE

- 4637/20, F-2, Hari Sadan, First Floor, Ansari Road, Darya Ganj Delhi–110 002 *Tel.*: (+91-11) 4559 7999
- 1st Floor, 1/2 Rathnavilas Road, Basvanagudi, Next to Pai Vista Convention Hall, South End Circle, Bengaluru–560004 (India) *Tel.*: +91-80-41275911

ISBN: 978-93-5903-635-9 (Hardcover)
ISBN: 978-93-5903-636-6 (Paperback)

Printed & Published by
Rajendra P Jain *for*
Motilal Banarsidass Publishing House
A-44, Naraina Industrial Area, Phase I, New Delhi–110 028 (INDIA)
Email: naraina@mlbd.in Website: www.mlbd.in
Tel.: (+91-11) 4751 1592

Foreword

It affords me immense pleasure to write a foreword to the English version of Helmuth von Glasenapp's *Jainism* which is one of the best and stimulating books ever written by scholars on Jainism. A glance at its contents will reveal the fact that Glasenapp has covered almost all the salient features of Jainism. The book is divided into seven sections, each of which is again subdivided into several parts. A complete, clean and objective picture of the origin and growth of Jainism is succinctly delineated in a historical way. The doctrines of Jainism are described in comparison with other systems of knowledge. Special attention is given to sections V and VI where the position of the Jains is penned in relation to society and Indian culture. In one word, its unique doctrines, dogmas and rites deserve the special attention of the researchers on religion.

No part of Indian history and culture can be complete without some references to Jainistic outlook and contributions. Glasenapp's *Jainism* will act as a demonstration of the truth of this assertion. He has dealt with all aspects of Jainism in a lucid way.

It gratifies me to a great extent to thank Shri Narendra Prakash Jain, Director of *Motilal Banarsidass Publishers Private Limited, Delhi,* for asking Shri Shridhar B. Shrotri to translate *Der Jainismus* into English for the benefit of the common people and researchers. I believe that this book deserves and will receive cordial welcome both in India and abroad.

25th December, 1998, **Satya Ranjan Banerjee**
Calcutta.

Acknowledgements

I am extremely grateful to Mr. N.P. Jain, Director, Motilal Banarsidass Publishers Private Limited, Indological Publishers and Distributors, Delhi for giving me an opportunity of translating this most significant work of Helmuth von Glasenapp.

My special thanks are due to Prof. S.H. Ritti, Retired Professor of Ancient Indian History and Epigraphy and Dr. S.P. Patil, Head Department of Jainology, Karnatak University, Dharwad, for helping me out with the Jaina terminology.

9-C, Garden Estate,
Aundh, Pune-411 007

SHRIDHAR B. SHROTRI

Preface

Jainism, India's third religion, in contrast to Hinduism and Buddhism, has not yet been fully introduced to the Europeans, although this religion has quite a significant influence on the history, literature and the arts of the land of the Gaṅgā; its unique dogmas and rites deserve, to a very great extent, the attention of the researchers on religion. The following pages endeavour to fill this lacuna and try to give, as far as possible, a complete, clear and objective picture of the growth and nature of Jainism of today.

I was fortunate, for I was assisted by prominent members of the Jaina sect while I was preparing this book. They helped me by providing me with several texts and by replying to my queries. I am grateful to: His Holiness Shastravisharada Jainacarya Vijaya Dharma Suri, His Holiness Itihasatattvamahodadhi Jainacarya Vijaya Indra Suri, Muni Hanasvijaya, Messrs S.K. Bhandari (Indore), Banarsi Das Jain (London), Champat Rai Jain (Hardoi), Chhote Lal Jain (Calcutta), Lakshmi Chandra Jain (Allahabad), C.S. Mallinath Jain (Madras), Panna Lal Jain (Delhi), Rai Bahadur Jogmander Lal Jain (Indore), Puran Chand Nahar (Calcutta), as also to the "All India Jaina Association" (Indore).

Privy Councillor Jacobi (Bonn) and Prof. R. Simon (Berlin) were kind enough to go through the proofs of the book; I am indebted to Prof. W. Kirfel (Bonn), Prof. Schubring (Hamburg), Prof. L. Suali (Pavia), Dr. F.W. Thomas (London) and

Herbert Warren (London) for the informations they made available to me and I thank Dr. W. Cohn (Berlin), Privy Councillor Driesch (Leipzig), Privy Councillor Jacobi (Bonn), Brooklyn Institute Museum (Brooklyn), The Indian Institute (Oxford), State Museum of Folklore (Berlin) and Victoria and Albert Museum, Indian Section (London) for the permission they granted me to reproduce the material in their possession and my father for the poetic rendering of the Jaina poems in the text.

Berlin,
20th August, 1925 HELMUTH VON GLASENAPP

Contents

SECTION I

Introduction

Jainas, as their name suggests, are the followers of Jinas, i.e., "conquerors"; they are the followers of certain great ascetics who obtained omniscience and who preached a doctrine which is said to have promised them a supermundane bliss of eternal salvation from the suffering of metempsychosis. Jainism* originated in North India, centuries before Gautama Buddha (who died around 480 B.C.) and spread gradually to the most distant parts of the South of Peninsular India. After a period of exceptional prosperity during which it dominated the religious thinking and cultural life of the people of large stretches of the land, it was gradually driven out by Hinduism which had again become stronger and by the victoriously advancing Islam from many of its territories and it lost its pre-eminence it possessed from the fifth to the twelfth century in the west and in the south; but even now, it has a sway over a small, but enterprising number of devotees, spread over the whole of India, who command quite a considerable influence on account of their education, their social status and their riches.

---

*A few German scholars write "Jinism" in analogy to Buddhism (*The Religion of the Buddha*). Jainas, in fact, Indians in general, always employ the form "Jainism" when they make use of a European language, and this practice is followed by a majority of European scholars. Since the word "Jainism" is generally accepted in the International fora, it is exclusively used in the present work; according to its form, it belongs to the names of religious movements, which are derived, not directly from the names of their founders (like Platonism, Spinozism), but from the names of their devotees, like Mohammedanism, Arianism, Kantianism, Manichaeism, the Latin "Christianism", etc.

Greeks appear to have been the first Europeans who came in contact with Jainas. They had come to India during the period of Alexander the Great and Diadochi. But we do not have any information about the Jainas from this period. The supposition of many researchers that one should understand Jaina-monks of *Digambaras* as the "Gymnosophists", the "naked wise men", is not very plausible. Christian Lassen has already observed: "As for the evidences of the classical writers, the passages in which the Τυμνοϐοφιϐέαί are mentioned, cannot be taken into consideration here, for this name denotes the Brahmanic penitents and the philosophers who have been called by this name, not on account of their complete nakedness, but on account of their scanty clothing. What then remains after we eliminate this possibility is the ironic comment of Hesychios who lived before the end of the fifth century: Τένν∂ι, οε Τυμνοϐοφτϐιαί."[1]

We do not have also more information about Jainas in the writings of a few European travellers who visited the Eastern countries during the middle ages. In fact, members of the Western Colonial powers who came to East India after Vasco da Gàma's discovery of the sea-route, give us very little information, although they noticed their individual prominent characteristics like their extensive protection of animals and the establishment of veterinary hospitals common amongst them.

The officers and the civil servants of the East India Company were the first who took keen interest in Jainas;[2] H.T. Colebrooke (1765-1837), who has done a pioneering work in so many branches of Indology, gave a brief, but a comprehensive description of their system which was based on original Indian works. Colebrooke's accounts were supplemented and complemented by Horace Hayman Wilson (1784-1860);[3] writings of these two meritorious men were for a long time almost the only reliable sources from which one could get information on Jainism during the whole first half of the 19th century. The credit of translating the first Jaina-texts goes to Otto Böhtlingk, the doyen of German-Sanskrit lexicography. He translated together with Ch. Rieu, Hemacandra's *Abhidhānacintāmaṇi* into German in 1847 and to Rev. J. Stevenson who translated *Kalpa-sūtra* and *Nava-tattva* into English. Albrecht Weber, Professor of Sanskrit in Berlin, came next with his excerpts from *Śatruñjaya-Mahātmya* in 1858 and from *Bhagavatī* in 1866. He was then the first to have taken interest in a detailed study of the canon of Śvetāmbaras. He made an impression as a pioneer in different branches of research on Jainology by writing several essays and individual articles.[4] Inspired by him, particularly, H. Jacobi, E. Leumann, J. Klatt, G. Bühler, R. Hoernle and E. Windisch, took interest in the study of Jaina-texts of different types in the following period, while L. Rice, E. Hultzsch, F. Kielhorn, P. Peterson, J. Fergusson and J. Burgess dedicated themselves to the study of Jaina-manuscripts, inscriptions and art-monuments.

Right from the beginning, the research in Jainology did not rest only in collecting and evaluating the material, but tried to determine the historical position of Jainism. The first hypotheses put forward in this connection were simply fantastic; thus one wanted to link the name "Jaina" with the patricide Cain, with the Roman god Janus or the Egyptian magician Jannes known from the Jewish tradition; the place Pālitāṇā which is full of Jaina-temples was supposed to be connected in its name with the word Palestine, etc. Scholars who tried to construe a connection between Jainism and Buddhism were nearer to truth. The views in this respect were quite divergent: while a few (like Colebrooke) liked to let Buddhism emerge from Jainism, the most like Wilson, Lassen and A. Weber were convinced that Jainas were the Buddhistic schismatists. This last-mentioned hypothesis which was based on trivial superficialities and accidental correspondences in proper names, was finally refuted by H. Jacobi in 1879. Jacobi has convincingly shown that Jainas and Bauddhas are two religious communities which are completely different from each other and their prophets Mahāvīra and Gautama Buddha were two different personalities who lived at the same time.

In spite of the propagation which the knowledge of history and literature of the Jainas experienced, thanks to the work of a series of scholars, the real heart of Jainism, its doctrine, still remained unknown in its nature to the West for a long time. This peculiar phenomenon can be explained, on the one hand, by the fact that in the case of most of the researchers their interest in antiquity and philology predominated over the one in philosophy and culture, and then, above all, in the situation that the first Jainologists wanted to obtain their knowledge on the doctrine partially from the antagonistic Brahmanic writings and partially from the canonic Jaina-works. It was an enterprise which was condemned equally to be a failure on account of the inaccuracy of the former and the unsystematic character of the latter. It signified, therefore, an epoch-making progress when H. Jacobi undertook in 1906 a translation of a systematic Jaina-dogma from a later period, Umāsvāti's *Tattvārthādhigama-Sūtra.* This work made it possible for the first time to get a clear and complete general idea of the doctrine of Jainism in its totality and thus opened a path to an appreciation of many important details which had remained so far in the dark. Jacobi's work has been continued by his pupils in several directions.

At present, research on Jainism is carried out in most of the European states, albeit in different proportions. In Germany, those who are working on it are Leumann's pupils W. Hüttemann (†), F.O. Schrader, W. Schubring, Jacobi's pupils W. Kirfel and H. von Glasenapp, then J. Hertel and his pupil Charlotte Krause, further E. Hultzsch, R. Schmidt and others; M. Winternitz and O. Stein are working in the German University in Prague. Jainology is represented by J. Charpentier in

Sweden, by Faddegon in Holland, by L.D. Barnett, J.F. Fleet, V.A. Smith, Mrs. M. Stevenson, C.H. Tawney (†), F.W. Thomas in England, by A. Guérinot, L. de Milloué, J. Vinson in France, by A. Ballini, F. Belloni-Filippe, P.E. Pavolini, F.L. Pullé, L. Suali, L. Tessitori (†) in Italy, by V. Lesny and O. Pertold in Czecho-Slovakia, by N. Mironow in Russia and by M. Bloomfield in North America.

Even Jainas themselves, since the last decades of the previous century, have started making their holy and profane texts of science available in printed editions. They also gradually began to publish books and essays on their religion in the English language to explain to their co-religionists the nature of their teachings and to win over new followers. Even Hindus took more and more interest in Jainism (R.G. Bhandarkar, Bhagavanlal Indraji, Bhau Daji, Satis Chandra Vidyabhusana, S.N. Dasgupta and others).

It is hoped for the future that Western and Indian scholars would work more and more closely together. Indian Paṇḍitas will be taught to do an unbiased and critical work by familiarizing them with the European method of textual criticism; at the same time, the European research will also be promoted in many respects by working together with the Indians. By making contacts with the Jainas, for whom the inherited tradition is a living force and not a mere historically interesting bookish knowledge, it will be prevented from losing the contact with reality and from letting their study be degenerated into endless speculation and unfruitful pettifoggery. If the co-operation between the West and the East succeeds in understanding Jainism of today in the plethora of its phenomena and in depicting it reliably, then it will be also possible, by gradually progressing from the known to the unknown, to pursue the individual phases of the process, in which the present emerged from the past, and to let the past back to its distant origins awaken to a new life before our spiritual eye.

REFERENCES

1. Chr. Lassen, *Indische Altertumskunde*, Leipzig, 1861, IV, p. 757.
2. Major C. Mackenzie, Dr. F. Buchanan and H.T. Colebrooke in *Asiatic Researches*, IX, Calcutta, 1809, J. Delamaine, F. Buchanan Hamilton, H.T. Colebrooke in *Transactions of the R.A.S.*, I, London, 1827 and Lieut.-Col. William Miles, *ibid.*, III, p. 335. Colebrooke's essays are reprinted in his *Miscellaneous Essays*, London, [1]1837, [2]1873 and his *Essays on the Religion and Philosophy of the Hindus*, Leipzig, 1858.
3. H.H. Wilson in *Asiatic Researches*, XVI, XVII, Calcutta, 1828, 1832; again reprinted in *Sketch of the Religious Sects of the Hindus*, London, 1862 by the same author.
4. Cf. E. Windisch, *Geschichte der Sanskrit-Philologie und Indischen Altertumskunde*, StraBburg, 1971, p. 346 ff.

SECTION II

History

PRELIMINARY REMARKS

The sources from which we obtain our knowledge of Jaina-history are mainly: literary works, inscriptions and antiquities of all types, like buildings, art-monuments, coins and many other things. Literary works are the most profitable for the purpose of research. Jainas themselves have tried to describe the history of their faith in the whole series of writings; the value these books have for the critical European science is really very diverse. The words said by the famous Arabian traveller Al-Bírúní (around 1030 A.D.) about the Indians apply in many respects to Jainas: "They care less for the historical sequences of events and they are careless in their enumeration of the succession of their kings. When they are forced to give an explanation and when they do not know what to say, they begin to tell fairy-tales."[1] A great part of the works written by Jainas in which the history of the Jaina-faith is discussed, has a purely mythical legendary character; it does not appear to be their duty to describe historical events; they prefer rather to present to the pious reader an hour of religious edification. Even in those writings which are supposed to depict historical facts which are chronologically close to the author, the legendary element is mostly predominant in such a way that it often strikes to a European as being strange. Many historical works of Jainas, in spite of these deficiencies, contain valuable material and offer useful information, provided they are subjected to a critical examination. Besides the real historical or pseudo-historical works, literary works of different sorts are also in many ways interesting for a writer of the history of Jaina-faith, because their contents reveal certain historical events or reflect the spirit of a certain age. Occasionally, an introduction or a colophon of a work gives also important chronological clues when the family-tree of the author, the name of his patron or such similar things are mentioned in it. The lists of the chiefs of the individual monastic orders, the so-called "Paṭṭāvalis" contain valuable material which helps in determining the lifetime of prominent personalities. Of course, they are not fully reliable, because their authors fill the lacuna present in them according to their own discretion and complete them, as far as it is possible, till they go back to Mahāvīra or even to his predecessor Pārśva. We can sometimes check and correct the information given in the literary works of the Jainas with the help of the information given in the Brahmanic, Buddhistic or other writings. These sources are, however, often of doubtful value, because the antagonists of Jainism, in their efforts to attribute all sorts of errors and offences to its followers, often distance themselves also from the truth like its enthusiastic friends and admirers.

The results of the research obtained from the inscriptions are more reliable, but also more scanty, than those obtained from literary works. Inscriptions were mostly carved immediately after a particular event. Therefore, they possess a certain freshness and nearness to reality which is lost in literary descriptions which were written later. Most of the inscriptions are the records of the foundation of temples or the idols of gods, of estates or immunities granted by a pious king or a believing layman. The names of the rulers and their ancestors, of the monks who were given gifts and of their Gurus and their predecessors provide us with a skeleton of names and dates. They are doubly valuable, because their fidelity, in most of the cases, need not be questioned.

Antiquities and art monuments of various types can also often contribute to explaining historical questions, particularly when information about the period of their origin is given on them. But their most important value is in their giving us a lively image of persons and things and an idea about the past. This helps us in getting a graphic picture of the conditions in the past periods which have been communicated to us only through words and concepts.

Although the material has been perfected by several researchers in their tenacious works in the last hundred years and although it is quite considerable, it is not even remotely sufficient to write a history of Jainism which would meet the scientific demands; it is for that purpose too fragmentary and too incomplete. It is, in fact, questionable, whether one can ever succeed in lifting the veil of darkness lying over the destinies of Jainas and the origin and development of their doctrine and cult. Few endeavours undertaken so far to describe the development of Jainism are, therefore, mostly only compilations of meagre historical facts, many problematic anecdotes and of more religious or scientific myths which are chronologically arranged. Even the present endeavour to follow the destinies of Jainas through centuries cannot claim to offer a complete history of Jainism. In fact, it has to restrict itself to giving, in a limited framework of a sketch, an approximate idea of the growth, prime and the decline of the religion of the Tīrthaṅkaras. Its task is more to impart to the reader in brief an insight into a few established facts and the most important legends dealing with the history of Jainism which are in circulation among Jainas than to give a critical explanation of minute questions or a dull enumeration of names and dates. The author would feel contented, if this brief survey which alone he is capable of giving here, would enthuse a historian to pursue individual problems which are only cursorily mentioned here and to discuss in details, in the framework of a comprehensive special work, what could be sketched here only in large outlines.

I

The Tīrthaṅkaras

1. PREHISTORY[1]

Jainas consider that religion is eternal and imperishable. It is without any beginning and it will never cease to exist. It may be, that it is forgotten from time to time. The darkness of the error enveloping the truth in certain, periodically recurring aeons clears up again and again so that the brightness of the Jaina-faith can sparkle again anew. Thus also the world-period in which we are living and we are able to enjoy the doctrine revealed to us, has come after a period in which Jainism had disappeared; and not in a distant future, it will be relieved by a period in which the real faith will become extinct. But the religion as such will never perish; it will blossom again and again in eternal youthful beauty like the spring which appears again and again in the constant change of seasons. When the time is ripe, the 24 "Tīrthaṅkaras", the prophets and the founders of holy places appear in a definite and an exactly fixed interval. They open a path for the real faith. Such 24 discoverers and prophets of salvation also appeared in our world-period. Jainas know their names and they can narrate many details from their life. But what is narrated about the most of them has quite a legendary appearance. Thus the first of these Tīrthaṅkaras, Ṛṣabha, is said to have lived for 84,00,000 Pūrva years. His height was 500 arc-lengths (about 800 ells). And although the life span and the height of each one of them decreased, it is said of the 22nd Tīrthaṅkara, Ariṣṭanemi, that he lived for 1,000 years and his height was 40 ells. Acceptable age and human dimensions are ascribed only to the last two saints of this series, Pārśva and Mahāvīra. It is taught that Pārśva, the 23rd Tīrthaṅkara, reached an age of 100, his height being 9 ells and Mahāvīra, the 24th Tīrthaṅkara, reached an age of 72 years and his height was 7 ells. Also the period ascribed by Jainas to the appearance of different Tīrthaṅkaras, agrees with our historical understanding only in the case of Pārśva and Mahāvīra: it is said that Mahāvīra died around 500 B.C., Pārśva around 700 B.C. and Ariṣṭanemi approximately 84,000 years before him. Then the other prophets must have died indeed long, long ago, partially in a period that cannot be imagined at all. In view of these circumstances, the European research, in its present condition, should do without the study of the first 22 Tīrthaṅkaras; it should deal rather with the historical personalities and it can restrict itself to carrying out research on the historicity of the last two.[2]

There is no doubt that Mahāvīra is a historical personality, because not only the Jaina-writings give convincing detailed information about him, but he is also mentioned in the works of the others who are not Jainas. The Buddhists by whom Jainas are most fiercely fought as the enemies of the true doctrine, very often mention him as a contemporary of their master Gautama Buddha and thus testify to his historical existence.[3] We don't also have to doubt the historicity of Mahāvīra's predecessor, Pārśva. It is true, we know about him only through the writings of Jainas, and much of what is narrated there about him, is doubtlessly a part of a holy legend; yet there is no reason to suppose that the cirrhus built around the personality of this man, does not conceal a historical nucleus. It is a fact that what we know about the personality and the teachings of the prophet, fits into the image we have to make of the development of the religious notions of the Indians on the basis of the results of our scientific study. This circumstance speaks for his historicity. Let us explain it with the help of a brief sketch of these developments.

There were far-reaching changes in the Indian spiritual life towards the end of the 2nd millennium B.C. The naive polytheism of the Aryan immigrants was expanded by a complicated sacrificial practice which restricted more and more the might of the gods in the concept of their worshippers, and the heavenly powers were reduced to the transcendental tools of the magically powerful priests. The position of the priest-class constantly gained thereby in significance. The more did it increase, the more prominent the idea of the caste-order became. This process was promoted by emergence of an opinion which gave, to some extent, an ethical compensation to the severity of social gradation: by the Karma-doctrine, by causality of retribution of action and by rebirth determined on account of it.

The belief that every existence is not an isolated one, but only a link in a chain of other existences had necessarily to make the profound natures think, whether the life ceaselessly repeating itself in a recurrent play of birth and death is worth living. The meditating thinking could only negate this question. It looked for a circumstance which was elevated above growth and decay, for a bliss which does not disappear after a short duration like the mundane happiness to make room for a new desire and a new suffering. In longing for an eternal, durable and a lasting happiness, every thought and desire turned away from this world with its ephemeral joys, away from a sacrificial service with its superficial rites, which being superficial, were indeed not satisfactory for the mind. Released from the worldly life, quiet thinkers searched for something higher and ethereal in the seclusion of asceticism. The yearning for knowledge was so common that it was usual, why even duty, for the upper castes that a man matured into an old age and withdrew to the solitude of the forest to meditate there on the highest questions of life. According to the Brahmanic theory of four Āśramas, the four stages of life, a Brāhmaṇa should become engrossed in Brahma, away from the world, after he had studied the Veda and founded his family, and finally roam about as a homeless beggar. It cannot be said to what extent this theoretical precept was constantly translated into reality; but it did find a serious respect and it was certainly more strictly observed by diligent people than it was demanded by law: the householder did not leave his home only after seeing his hair become grey, his skin wrinkled and seeing his grand-children play around him, but he sought homelessness even much before to dedicate all his energy to knowledge. The coming-together of the like-minded people led to the formation of ascetic communities which were bound to one another by fixed orders and which received their livelihood from the donations of benevolent pious men.

It appears that this earnest struggle for immortality had equally animated the best spirits amongst the "twice-borns". Not only the Brāhmaṇas who did austerities to fathom the force which lends power to the sacrifice and elevates the one who knows it from the world to a pure existence, but also the Kṣatriyas renounced the world, to experience in themselves the supermundane. Less restricted than the Brāhmaṇas by the tradition and the considerations for their position, the Kṣatriyas could submit themselves to yearning for the highest knowledge. It appears that the most powerful conceptions of philosophical thinking have been invented and developed by them. Even a few ancient reports inform us that

Kṣatriyas humiliated Brāhmaṇas on account of their knowledge of the imperishable and the priests had to go to them as pupils.

The speculations of the centuries after 1000 B.C. have come down to us in the Upaniṣads, the famous "secret doctrines". They form the addendum and the completion of the Vedas. Edited by priests and harmonized with their own needs and theories, they make us clearly understand in many passages of different writings that the wisdom taught here, originally contradicted sharply the doctrine of the sacrificial work upon which the position and the power of Brahmanism was established, and that the cunning priests knew to connect the new thoughts with their own conceptions and to adopt them so that they appeared later as their most diligent champions. Of course, it was not possible to strike an equilibrium everywhere, for there were doctrines which contradicted the traditions which were sanctified by the priestly origin. They opposed the claim of the Brāhmaṇa caste that it alone was the mediator between the mundane and the supermundane wisdom. We know several masters from the 6th century who opposed the assertiveness of the Brāhmaṇas and who, inimical to the Vedic sacrificial belief, went their own way without caring for the teachings of the Veda. We have to presume that even before Mahāvīra, before Gośāla and before Gautama Buddha, such prophets of salvation have appeared and gathered around them pupils who propagated their teachings. The precepts which those masters had set to their communities as canons were obviously reproduced from the Brahmanic ones. But they differed from them inasmuch as they did not acknowledge the superiority of Brāhmaṇas. As remarked by A.F.R. Hoernle,[4] this difference directed against the exclusiveness of the priestly caste, has doubtlessly contributed to aggravating the constrasts; the orders under the aegis of the clergy looked down with despise upon the heretics who believed that they could manage without the sanctions of the members of the Brāhmaṇa caste; the Kṣatriya-mendicants avoided, on the other hand, Brāhmaṇas and their ceremonies. An anti-clerical character was peculiar for the religious communities emerging from the non-Brahmanic circles; they turned against the claims of the priesthood which appeared to them to be unjustified, but they neither wanted to reform the social order as a whole, nor did they want to do away with casteism. It may be that birth and rank lost their significance within the monk-order, but their importance outside this order was neither questioned nor nullified. Thus we find that among the laymen belonging to non-Brahmanic monk-order, casteism remained without losing its force. In fact, the right of Brāhmaṇas to perform sacral rites at the time of birth, marriage, death or other occasions was so little disputed that laymen called them to do the rites, although they entrusted themselves to the guidance of the anti-Brahmanic ascetics in the decisive things of faith and way of life (a contradiction which appears to us to be strange, but which is found even now among the Śvetāmbara-Jainas).

In the focus of the philosophizing of all the orders of the ascetics was the desire for salvation, the will to free oneself from the fetters of Saṁsāra from the agonies of a recurring existence which is full of sorrows. The theoretical foundations of this belief are quite primitive in the most ancient period: the sages of the older Upaniṣads did not make a distinction between mind and matter, and the concept of a monad of a soul was still remote from their thinking. The psyche for them is—as H. Jacobi has shown on p. 8 ff. in his work *Die Entwicklung der Gottesidee bei den Indern*—not a unity, but a complex of five factors or Prāṇas: breath, speech, face, ears and mind. These five factors constitute a personality, when they are united; if a being dies, this connection is severed. An existence after death is nonetheless possible, that is, when the five Prāṇas come together again. But such a connection materializes regularly through the power of Karma, through the transcendental power of evil or good actions in an earlier existence. The cycle of birth and death ceases only for the one who has destroyed his Karma, and through it, the germ of rebirth. This happens with the help of asceticism and the knowledge of the sublime which is beyond all change. It is Brahma from which everything has emerged; it is at the bottom of everything and it takes back everything in itself. The one who merges with Brahma, will alone be free from suffering, sin and from every restriction.

The concepts of the oldest Upaniṣads (*Bṛhadāraṇyaka, Chāndogya, Taittirīya, Aitareya, Kauṣītakī*) about the nature of the psyche undergo a change in the later ones (*Kāṭhaka*, etc.) through the emergence of a new idea: the idea of an individual soul. Now mind and matter are clearly distinguished; what was psychic was not any more a bundle of different factors, but it is understood as a monad which is considered as eternal and imperishable. Every individual, whether a god or a man, an animal or a plant, possesses an immaterial self, a soul, which—burdened by the fruits of actions in earlier existences—wanders from one existence to the other as long as it is under the power of Karma. Only when the effect of Karma concealing the real nature of the soul is removed and the real knowledge of the nature of the spirit and its similarity with Brahma is attained, one gets salvation. This consists in (what is also natural) the intensive union of the individual spirit with the spirit of the world.

The new theory of the soul became prominent in the circles of the Upaniṣadic thinkers. But it also found followers among the philosophers who had little to do with the Brahma-doctrine. They made the most different Brahmanic as well as non-Brahmanic systems the foundation of their metaphysics and ethics. These doctrines representing the absolute distinction of the individual souls from one another and from matter and yet denying the existence of a supreme spiritual absolute (like Sāṁkhya, Yoga, Nyāya-Vaiśeṣika, Jainism, etc.), saw salvation only in the complete isolation of the pure soul from the impure matter; they thus swore to the individual continuity of existence of an individual being in an incorporeal, ecstatic condition in which all the infirmities and sufferings adhering to an earthly personality fall away.

Although the new idea of the presence of imperishable individual souls was acknowledged in the whole Brahmanism and even beyond it, the older idea of the complex character of the psychic continued to be extremely significant for the spiritual history of ancient India. After all—in any case, I think along with H. Jacobi and Th. Stcherbatsky that this is possible[5]—the Buddhistic doctrine is based on it. It says that there is no self, no soul and what appears as a psychic-physical individual is in fact formed by five "groups" (Skandha). Howsoever different these five Skandhas (viz., 1. the five senses and their objects, 2. feeling, 3. ideas, 4. heredity and instinct, 5. conscience) may be from the five Prāṇas of the Upaniṣads, the basic idea of both the doctrines is the same: that an individual is only a bundle of five such factors, that the connection between these elements breaks up in death and that a new unification of the same emerges on account of the power of action till salvation is attained after the destruction of Karma. But there is a long way from the primitive Prāṇa-theory of the ancient period to the profound Skandha-doctrine of Gautama Buddha, and we have to presume a long development during about five centuries which lie between the proposition of the two theories. It is a long development of which, at least, as far as our present knowledge is concerned, we do not possess any documents. And yet a high degree of probability speaks for the correctness of this hypothesis. For it is the only one which can link the grandiose Buddhistic Anattā-doctrine with the earlier, more primitive ideas and justify the existence of the precursors of Gautama, of the earlier Buddhas which is claimed by the Buddhists and which is, so far, mostly exiled into the realm of fables.[6] The assertion that between the Upaniṣadic Prāṇa-doctrine and Gautama's Skandha-theory one can suppose the pre-stages of the Buddhistic Anātmavāda is justified by a peculiar passage of the *Kāṭhaka Upaniṣad* (IV. 14) (around 800 B.C.). Th. Stcherbatsky[7] draws our attention to it and this may perhaps be conceived as a rejection of the doctrine of the psychic as the one which links the individual elements of existence (*pṛthag-dharma*). It is supposed to be the first known reference in which there is a mention of antagonism between the two philosophical points of view. Their dispute has played a prominent role in the history of Indian metaphysics for over several chiliads.

In view of the obscurity in which the early history of Indian philosophy is shrouded, it cannot be determined with certainty when and by whom the doctrine of monads of souls was first established; it must have originated in the beginning, or, in any case, in the first half of the first millennium B.C. This can be said because of the fact that it was missing in the oldest Upaniṣads, but it was generally acknowledged in the later works of this genre of literature. Jainism presupposes, for its whole philosophical conceptions, the difference between mind and matter and the theory of the existence of the eternal individual souls. It can, therefore, be presumed that it originated earliest in a period, when the new doctrine of the souls appeared. Then the first century after the year 1000 B.C. would be the higher limit for the time of its origin, if the views expressed on the difference of the psychological conceptions between the older and the later Upaniṣads are correct. But this excellently suited the doctrine of the Jainas who let their prophet Pārśva proclaim in the 8th century B.C. his doctrine of the difference between mind and matter and of salvation by the liberation of an individual soul from matter. Thus not only nothing, from the philosophical and the historical point of view, comes in the way of the supposition that Jainism was established by Pārśva around 800 B.C., but it is rather confirmed in everything that we know of the spiritual life of that period.

We are, however, not in a position to say now, whether Pārśva himself had been the first who decisively established the doctrine of existence of substances of the soul, and whether the others succeeded him in this and combined this doctrine of his with their concepts later—or whether Pārśva borrowed his theory of souls and then developed it into his own special system. Perhaps future research may succeed in solving this problem which is fundamental for the history of Jainism; we have to restrict ourselves for the present to compiling all that we know about Pārśva and to try to obtain an approximate idea of his life and his teachings from the scanty material which stands the test of a critical examination.

2. PĀRŚVA

Pārśva, according to the tradition, was born in Banāras as son of King Aśvasena from the famous Ikṣvāku family and his wife Vāmā. After a carefree youth spent in the grand-palace of his father, he was touched at his age of 30 by unsteadiness of all that was earthly, and he renounced the world and his friends and became an ascetic. He obtained the redeeming knowledge in a short time and dedicated himself immediately to the propagation of the truth found by him. When he attained the age of 100, he climbed the Sameṭa Śikhara in Bihar (which is now called Pārasnāth-hills after him), where he went into Nirvāṇa after refusing to take any food or water for a month.

It cannot, of course, be resolved whether and how these biographical facts given by Jainas in their holy books in the midst of a colourful circle of legends, correspond to the historical facts. And I think that there is no reason to question the correctness of tradition which describes to us Pārśva as a man of noble birth, who discarded all the earthly goods in the prime of his youth and sought and found the salvation of his soul in the life of a wandering ascetic, which was full of privations, but peaceful. The image of a young man from a wealthy family, who, dissatisfied with the pleasures which give him position and wealth, dedicating his life completely to the attainment and proclamation of philosophical knowledge, is not uncommon in India from the period of the Upaniṣads till our days. It may be then that the powerful position and the riches which the young ascetic had to renounce, were excessively embellished by his followers later with the means of an oriental fantasy to let the enormousness of the renunciation of their hero become extremely prominent.

The main tenets of Pārśva's doctrine, according to the accounts of Jainas, were as under: The whole, uncreated and imperishable universe is filled up in its three sections, the upper world of gods, the middle world of human beings, animals and plants and the nether world of demons and other beings in hell, with an endless number of eternal, indestructible individual souls. These souls (Jīva) as such are purely spiritual, incorporeal and blissful; they possess infinite knowledge, unlimited power, extreme moral perfection and they have the same position. But in the case of most of them, the qualities inherent to the Jīvas from their nature are not developed; most of the souls in the world are rather clothed with the bodies of more or less long-lived beings, with the bodies of gods, human beings, animals, plants and the beings in hell. They are subject to the vicissitudes of joys and sorrows, their knowledge, their power and their normal condition is imperfect, and an inescapable destiny elevates them to the heights of life, gives them pleasure, power and wealth or throws them down to the depths of misery, servitude and poverty. A complete transformation of the characteristics of the souls, or more correctly, a complete enshrouding of their natural qualities is a consequence of their combination with a different, alien element—with the matter. Subtle material objects invisible to the eye, constantly force their way into the souls, provide them with different types of bodies and organs, restrict them in their knowledge, volition and action and let them taste sometimes sweet joys and sometimes bitter sorrows. The inescapable causality of retribution of Karma, the ceaseless play of life and death, the stream of existence with its high and low tides of fortune and misfortune, in fact, the whole world-process itself is, according to Pārśva, nothing else, but a consequence of a fatal combination of the two heterogeneous substances, mind and matter. From times without any beginning, every corporeal soul moves material atoms through its thoughts, words and actions in its realm. These atoms become Karma in it; they adhere to it and they do not leave till they have exerted their more or less harmful influence and till others, the new ones replace them.

The souls remain infected with material objects till they yield themselves to their desires without any restraint and till they attract and assimilate them again and again by their unbridled action. Soiling of the soul by material objects which are metamorphosed into the Karma can only be stopped by hindering the inflow of new material objects into the souls and by destroying and expelling the matter present in them. This is only possible by complete control of all thinking and action and by transformation in the whole conduct of life. The doors of the five senses should not any more be carelessly left open to external influences; thinking should be subjected to stricter norms; the four passions: anger, pride, deceit and greed, are to be suppressed; and the will-to-live proliferating in the heart like a poisonous plant has to be completely uprooted. Observance of the four rules assists one in realizing this goal. They are the foundations of Pārśva's ethics. These rules forbid a believer from injuring a living being, from speaking falsehood, from acquiring things which were not given and from possessing property. The last includes also prohibition of sexual intercourse. Pārśva's four precepts cannot be carried out strictly by people who lead a mundane life; the presupposition for their complete observance is world-renunciation. The three precious stones of right knowledge, right belief and right conduct dazzle with full lustre on the one who has destroyed all the earthly desires. Devoted unflinchingly to strict austerities, a pious man should meditate on the real nature of the soul till all his doubts are resolved in a pious contemplation, till he recognizes the real nature of the spirit in its unstained purity. When the fire of every passion is extinguished by the water from the cloud of knowledge, then the soul does not take up new matter. It wipes out the Karma which is not materialized in it. When all the Karma burdening the soul is destroyed without any trace, when all the matter filling and surrounding it has disappeared, then the soul shines in its infinite splendour; it is then redeemed. Unburdened by all matter, it ascends the summit of the world to rest in the abode of the blissful in eternal omniscience and imperishable joy, as if on an island which is far-removed from surging waves of the ocean of Saṁsāra.

The doctrines of the tradition which Pārśva proclaims in his sermons are generally the basic doctrines of Jainism. It cannot be accurately proved, whether the views ascribed to Pārśva by the later reports were really his own. But it is quite possible that the system of the later period, in its fundamental principles, can be traced back to Pārśva. For, the theories at the basis of the Jaina-faith have as such a trace of primitive antiquity. It clearly points out to a period of origin which preceded a period of complicated concepts as they were present in Buddhism and in the classical philosophemes of Brahmanism.

Pārśva won over, according to the Kalpa-sūtra, a following of thousands for his doctrine: 1,64,000 men and 3,27,000 women joined him as lay disciples by acknowledging that his principles were true, and followed these as far as it was possible for the people leading a mundane life. But 16,000 men and 38,000 women tried to practise his ascetic ethics with all its consequences and formed the monk- and the nun-orders. The persons who threw away all the fetters of love and hatred, of family, of possession and convention and dedicated their whole life in attainment of supermundane salvation, became "Nirgranthas", i.e., the "unfettered ones". Their order was the real backbone of the community and protector of their heritage. From the main eight pupils of the master (Śubhadatta, Āryaghoṣa, Vasiṣṭha, Brahmacārī, Soma, Śrīdhara, Vīrabhadra, Yaśas), Śubhadatta took over the organization of the church; he was succeeded by Haridatta, Āryasamudra, Prabha and Keśi[8] in that order.

In the course of 250 years which are said to have passed between Pārśva's Nirvāṇa and Keśi's tenure in office, it appears that the precepts prescribed by Pārśva were not strictly adhered to, and they were interpreted in a lax manner, particularly those pertaining to the vow of celibacy. It was, therefore, a matter of great fortune to the Nirgranthas that a great personality reformed their order from its very foundations. It was Mahāvīra who is considered by Jainas as the last Tīrthaṅkara of our age.

3. MAHĀVĪRA

Vardhamāna, later also known as Mahāvīra, the "great hero", was son of a Kṣatriya called Siddhārtha. He was born in Kuṇḍagrāma, i.e., Basukuṇḍ of today. It was a suburb of Vaiśālī (now Besahr), to the north of the present city of Paṭnā in the province of Bihār. According to a legend, his father was a powerful king who was surrounded by the pomp of an oriental ruler. It is possible that the legend has exaggerated and embellished the actual situation. Siddhārtha was only a respected aristocratic big landowner, and as the head of the senate of the republic of Kṣatriya-aristocrats, he had the title Rājā. It is, of course, certain that his family was aristocratic, for he was related by marriage through his wife Triśalā to royal families. Triśalā was the sister of King Çeṭaka of Vaiśālī. Ceṭaka's daughter married later the powerful King Bimbisāra of Magadha.

The family to which Mahāvīra belonged, was called in Sanskrit Jñātri and in Prākṛta Nāya (Nāṭa). That is why the male members of the family were called Jñātriputras (Nāṭaputtas). Mahāvīra's Gotra was Kāśyapa.

Vardhamāna's life, till his age of 30, does not appear to have been different from that of the youthful sons of the aristocratic families of that period. He married a beautiful girl from a good family. Her name was Yaśodā; he had a daughter from her, Anojjā, (Priyadarśanā), who later married a nobleman Jamāli and became the mother of one daughter Śeṣavatī (Yaśovatī).

He, then 28 years old, wanted to renounce the world like Pārśva after the death of his parents, who as Pārśva's believing devotees, starved themselves to death. But Mahāvīra's family dissuaded him from doing this.* He

---

*According to the Digambara tradition, Mahāvīra had never married and had lived the life of an ascetic even as a boy and a young man. According to it, his parents were still alive, when he became a monk.

left his house and relatives only two years later after obtaining the permission of his elder brother Nandivardhana and the government of his hometown. He went into a park called Śandavana in the surroundings of Kuṇḍapura. He fasted for two and half days under an Aśoka tree, put on the garments of a monk and pulled out his hair in five tufts. He put on the clothes for a year and a month without changing them, then he even dispensed with them and roamed about as a nude penitent. As it appears, he lived at first as a member of the order of the ascetics founded by Pārśva in the proximity of his hometown, but then he severed his connections with other monks, as he thought that their precepts were not strict enough and preferred to spend an unsteady life of a wanderer.

He traversed through the land for over twelve years exposed without shelter to the inclemency of the weather. He visited desolate regions of the savage tribes and patiently endured the scorn and abuse of men who tried to disturb him in his pious exercises. He fasted, took upon himself to do all sorts of austerities, he meditated and thought about the meaning of the world and destiny. Finally after experiencing and seeing many things, he attained omniscience, the perfect clear knowledge about the nature of Saṁsāra and the path leading from it to bliss and to salvation. This happened, according to tradition, under a Śāla-tree on the bank of the river Ṛjupālikā, not far away from a place called Jṛmbhikagrāma. Vardhamāna, or as he is generally called by his honorific name, Mahāvīra ("the great hero"), became from this memorable moment Jina, a conqueror, who has conquered the world, an Arhat (a venerable person), a Tīrthaṅkara. Immediately he thought that it was his most noble duty to revive Pārśva's teachings and to proclaim the eternal truth of salvation of all creatures. He wandered about in the whole remaining period of his life with that purpose in mind and preached to gods and men, Aryans and barbarians. He traversed in his wanderings the whole region of his homeland Bihār and won over many followers. At the end of almost thirty years of preaching, he died in the chancellory of King Hastipāla of Pāvāpurī and attained Nirvāṇa.

We do not have exact information on the period of Mahāvīra's life, because Jainas give different dates of the year of his death. According to the prevalent theory, Mahāvīra died in the year 527 B.C. According to a statement in Hemacandra's *Pariśiṣṭaparva*, the prophet attained Nirvāṇa 155 years before emperor Candragupta's coronation (historical date 322 or 321 B.C.). H. Jacobi reckons accordingly the year 477 or 476 B.C. (resp. earlier 467 B.C., presuming that Hemacandra takes a different year as a basis for Candragupta's coronation.) The year 477 would approximately confirm the dates given by the Buddhists, according to which the "Nigantha Nāṭaputta" died a few years before Gautama Buddha. There is also no unanimity among European researchers; thus it is for the time being not certain when the event really took place which is so extremely important for the history of Jainas.[9]

But it is most clearly seen from what we know about Mahāvīra that he was an extremely significant man who had left a profound impression among his contemporaries by his spiritual and moral greatness. He was a great and a powerful thinker who had taken a keen interest in all the problems of his times and he knew answers to the questions with which he had become familiar. But what emerges most prominently was his most important desire to get a clear picture of the whole reality around him and to analyse and interpret everything in its last details. His endeavour to get order and overview made him one of the most prominent systematists who knew to give an exactly precise place to everything in the world and the superworld in his doctrine. He could look down upon the activity in the Saṁsāra with a royal gesture from the summit of his knowledge and show and indicate the way to all who longed for salvation.

Mahāvīra, who was not only strict with himself but also with others, was by all means a representative of ascetic conduct of life. He had himself given up a life which was full of joys and enjoyments to dedicate his whole personality to a loftier goal; he had mortified his flesh to the extreme, let all the sensuous wishes and desires be destroyed and obtained the highest self-control by the greatest will power. With stern consequences he demanded of his pupils that they followed him on this path. He became thereby the main spokesman of ascetic morality. The testimony for the strictness with which he laid down the rules of the conduct of life and adhered to them is the fact, when it is reported, that he completely cut his hair and ceased wearing any clothes, instead of being satisfied, like the most of the ascetics of his period, with just shaving the hair .and putting on the monk's cowl. Mahāvīra distinguished himself from his great contemporary Gautama Buddha by this great esteem he showed to asceticism; he preached the necessity of fasting and other types of austerities, whereas Buddha condemned them as a wrong path. This path was as much remote from the "middle path" proclaimed by Buddha as from the worldly life which chased after the pleasures and languished in them.

There is also a fundamental difference between the two great men in one more respect: in their relationship with their fellow creatures. Ernst Leumann[10] says on this: "Mahāvīra was reticent and Buddha was candid. Mahāvīra avoided social intercourse, Buddha cultivated it. This contrast is expressed partially in the fact that Buddha occasionally allowed his people to invite him for a meal, what Mahāvīra considered as a scandalous pact with the worldly life. This contrast is also partially and more significantly seen in the fact that Buddha spoke on his wanderings with one and all and influenced them with a clever consideration of their views on life and their habits in a generally educative and an elevating sense. The ascetic Mahāvīra, thanks to his shyness, could never have done such an act of the most general spiritual welfare; it never happened that he sought someone to teach him in spiritual things and to advise him, and if at all someone came to *him* for a religious discourse, he hardly knew to react to the thoughts of his visitor, but simply gave a strict answer in a rigid explanation of his own teachings."

Although Mahāvīra, as the texts describe him, did not have the affability of a Buddha, and constantly kept his distance from others with an aristocratic non-chalance, he was by no means, like the Brahmanic masters, a teacher, who communicated an esoteric science only to a small circle of the chosen few under a seal of confidentiality. Mahāvīra preached to everyone who wanted to listen to him. And in order that everyone understood him, he did not speak in Sanskrit which only the educated could understand, but in Ardhamāgadhī, the dialect of his home. The great results his teachings showed, prove that he understood to influence his listeners in an extraordinary way. The people listening to his lectures came from all stratas of the population. Princes and warriors, priests and businessmen thronged his lectures just as people from the lower strata, even non-Aryans, men and women. But the aristocrats were the first to whom the teachings of Mahāvīra, a man belonging to their class, appealed. The holy scriptures of the Jainas like to narrate with a great blaze of colours and with an epic wealth of details how kings with their harem and their courtiers and the civil servants, accompanied by innumerable warriors and servants, followed by great masses used to go to the Tīrthaṅkara to listen to the preaching of his doctrine. Not less than 23 kings are counted who joined his gospel and who were devoted to him in veneration.

However, Mahāvīra did not only know to enthrall the people by his lecture and to convert them to his doctrine, he also knew to keep them constantly on his side. He was a great organizer who gave to the members of his order laws which survived for two thousand years. If it is realized that the precepts for the monks from Mahāvīra's times, in their basic principles, have even now a binding force for all the Jaina-ascetics, then one cannot help but admire this man who lent such a solid form to Pārśva's ascetic orders which had come down to him; even the ravages of time were unable to harm them.

Although Mahāvīra was thoroughly ascetic in his views, he had an open mind to the needs of laymen. As a profound knower of human beings, he had realized that hardships of the austerities and renunciation of the world could be sustained only by a small number of the chosen ones, that many who tried to grasp the doctrine were too weak to fulfil the strict order of asceticism. Therefore, like Pārśva and other masters, he opened the doors of his community to laymen and he expected of them that they should observe the commandments in a form which could be maintained by those who were leading a worldly life. This organic adaptation of laymanship into the "Saṅgha" was extremely useful for the propagation of Jainism; the close connection between the spiritual and the layman, which was constantly maintained in Mahāvīra's religion, was doubtlessly one of the reasons why Jainism has shown that it is so full of vitality in India even down to our times, while other religions in which this contact was not so close, could not last later in the land of Gaṅgā.

The tradition agrees that Mahāvīra did not lay down any new philosophical system, but developed Pārśva's doctrine and reformed his community. As it appears, the commandments Pārśva imposed upon his followers were not strictly adhered to by them. Mahāvīra insisted with relentless energy that the moral precepts of Pārśva must be adhered to without making any changes. As we have seen, Pārśva had imposed sexual abstinence for the members of his ascetic order. However, this precept was not separately laid down, but was considered as included in the rule that one should not possess any earthly goods. Mahāvīra, to encounter wrong interpretation, emphatically demanded complete celibacy from his monks and nuns and, therefore, added this precept in the form of a special vow to the four precepts of his predecessor; it also appears that the precept of mercy to all living beings proclaimed by Pārśva was extended by the new prophet in its application. It was also an improvement that Mahāvīra used to remain naked, while Pārśva's pupils were allowed to wear upper- and under-garments. But on the other hand, there seems to be no fundamental difference between the basic philosophical views of the two Tīrthaṅkaras. Thus nothing stood in the way of Mahāvīra in winning over the members of Pārśva's order into his community. Keśi, the seniormost among Pārśva's disciples, could thus confirm in his conversation with Mahāvīra's apostle Gautama that there was complete agreement in the views of the two masters.[11]

Like Pārśva, Mahāvīra also lived in the period of religious quest and struggle. A great number of teachers roamed about in the land preaching and wooing pupils. While some of them adhered to the Vedic tradition or sought to feel it with new spirit, others strongly opposed the Brahmanic tradition. We have very little information about the majority of the masters who dominated the spiritual life in North India at that time; only the names of those who founded great communities have been preserved for us, but the information we have on them is mostly only scanty and inaccurate.[12] Among the heads of the sects of that time, Gośāla Maṅkhali-putta (in Sanskrit: Maskariputra), the founder of the sect of Ājīvikas, appears to have been the most significant besides Mahāvīra and Buddha.[13] We are interested in him in this context, because he himself was closely connected with Mahāvīra. Gośāla was a son of a professional beggar. After several experiences he had joined the Nirgrantha-order, but then left it, after being its member for six years and founded his own community. When he met Mahāvīra after sixteen years, there were animated disputes. It appears that Gośāla died soon afterwards; but his followers remained truthful to his teachings even after his death. That is why, the Ājīvikas are mentioned as a special sect even in the sixth century A.D. and then their name also appears in the thirteenth century, but this time as a name of Digambara-Jainas with whom Ājīvikas must have later got united. Gośāla was doubtlesssly a very remarkable person; it is, of course, doubtful, whether what is informed to us about his desolate life and his strange teachings by his opponents, by the Buddhists and the Jainas, is in accordance with the facts, for the inimical sects always tried to attach disreputable things to the heretics. It is evident that Gośāla proclaimed a series of doctrines which coincide with those of Jainas, it may be then that he had adopted them from Jainas, or it may be that he laid them down during his stay with Mahāvīra and moved the coreligionists of his time to accept them (this may be less probable). But on the other hand, many of his views and above all his precepts on the conduct of life deviate most strongly from those of Jainas. Besides the pronounced determinism proclaimed by him, the reanimation theory in particular, is a characteristic feature of his system. According to this theory, every soul before being able to attain salvation, after it had gone through a number of exactly determined existences in the various forms of existence, must change its body seven times in its last earthly life, i.e., enter the life of a deceased person and animate it by doing so. Only after this has happened, it is possible for it to attain salvation. Gośāla claimed of himself that he had changed the body seven times in the course of his life of 133 years. After he had changed his life six times, he had entered, for the last time, Gośāla's corpse in which he lived for sixteen years. On the basis of his theory Gośāla wanted people to believe that only in his body he was identical with Gośāla, a former pupil of Mahāvīra, while his soul had nothing to do with the one of Gośāla, since the latter had died and had been reborn in a heaven of gods.

Gośāla was not the only follower of Mahāvīra who turned away from him. Twice the disputes arose in the community, and they led to schisms; they did not, however, have great significance. We shall discuss them while discussing the sect-practices.

II

The Oldest Community

1. MAHĀVĪRA'S SUCCESSORS

According to the tradition, Mahāvīra won over 14,000 monks, 36,000 nuns, 1,59,000 laymen and 3,18,000 laywomen as his followers by his work. Each of these four groups, of these four "Tīrthas", i.e., the components of the Jaina-church, was under the supervision of trustworthy personalities.

Monks were guided by 11 Gaṇadharas or heads who each one had several hundred Munis under them. The name of the chief Gaṇadhara was Gautama Indrabhūti; others were Agnibhūti, Vāyubhūti, Akampita, Ārya Vyakta, Ārya Sudharmā, Maṇḍitaputra, Mauryaputra, Acalabhrātā, Metrāya, Prabhāsa. Chief of the nuns was Mahāvīra's cousin Candanā; lay-brothers were under Śaṅkhaśataka, lay-sisters under Sulasā and Revatī.

Nine of the eleven Gaṇadharas who were the heads of the community attained Nirvāṇa in the master's lifetime itself. Gautama Indrabhūti became omniscient in the night Mahāvīra died and, therefore, did not preside over the community as a teacher who came from the tradition of the Tīrthaṅkaras; he got salvation twelve years after his master. Thus only Sudharmā remained who could supervise the church. He held this position till Gautama Indrabhūti's death. Then he himself became Kevalī and handed the church over to his pupil Jambūsvāmī; he then lived for eight years before being released. Jambūsvāmī was the head of the church till one year after the death of his predecessor; then he also became omniscient and finally, 64 years after Mahāvīra, also attained Nirvāṇa. With him the last omniscient of the age left the world, the last saint obtained salvation. Nobody hereafter could achieve perfection.

Although the chiefs of the community succeeding the three Kevalīs did not become omniscient, they had precise knowledge of the doctrines proclaimed by the Tīrthaṅkara, as they were heard by his immediate pupil Indrabhūti and as they were recorded in words by Sudharmā. These five teachers succeeding one another are called Śrutakevalīs, i.e., knowers of all holy scriptures. The management of the church then went over from the Śrutakevalīs to the seven or eleven teachers who succeeded one another. They knew only a part of the canonic works. The management went then to those whose knowledge was still less. Most of what is narrated about the Kevalīs and their successors is very legendary. It is very difficult to find out how much of what is traditional is history and how much of it is myth, because the information on them is partially quite contradictory, and besides, Śvetāmbaras give different names from those given by Digambaras. The most important legends dealing with the Kevalīs and Śrutakevalīs will be narrated in the following pages.

2. JAINISM IN BIHĀR

Mahāvīra was closely connected with the most significant princes of his homeland. He visited the most important cities of their kingdoms in Bihār on his wanderings: Campa, Aṅga's capital, Mithilā in Videha, Rājagṛha, the capital of Magadha, etc., and he was most respectfully received everywhere. King Bimbisāra (Jainas called him by the name Śreṇika) of Magadha, the same king who also patronized Buddha, was considered by Jainas as a special admirer of their master. They, therefore, presumed that he would be born as a Tīrthaṅkara in his later existence. Even Ajātaśatru (Kūṇika), Bimbisāra's cruel son, who exposed his father to death by starvation, was well-disposed towards Jainas.* His successor Udāyī[14] was in fact a patron of their doctrine. The religion flourished even under the dynasty of the "nine Nandas" who had (at the time when Alexander the great marched into India) usurped the throne of the Śaiśunāga-kings, and there was no change in the situation even when the last unpopular Nanda-king was relieved of his throne by the great Maurya King Candragupta, the Sandrakottos of the Greeks (approx. 322-298). Jainas reckon this first historical emperor of India as also his great chancellor Cāṇakya among Jainas. Cāṇakya is said to have been a son of a Jaina-layman Caṇī and a diligent champion of their faith. He is said to have weaned Candragupta from his kindness towards the heretics in the following manner: He made him invite the teachers of all the sects into his palace and make them wait in the vicinity of the king's harem. But before he did this, he had let a fine sand be strewn around the seraglio. The lewd priests, before the king came to them, were looking at Candragupta's wives through the windows of the harem but when he appeared, they started talking to him about the significance of world-renunciation. But as soon as they had gone, Cāṇakya showed to the prince their footmarks in the vicinity of the harem and convinced him thereby that these heretics were sanctimonious hypocrites. The

*An attempt is made in the Nirayāvalī-sūtra to absolve Kūṇika of patricide by narrating that he indeed let his father be fettered and thrown into prison, but then he wanted to break the fetters of his father with an axe. The father thought that the son wanted to kill him and committed suicide to keep away the sin of patricide from the family.

next day, Cāṇakya invited Jaina-monks. They did not take notice of the harem, but sat immediately on the seats meant for them and awaited the arrival of the king. Thus Candragupta knew that they alone were the protectors of the right morals and bestowed immediately his favour only on them. It is said that he himself became a diligent Jaina, that he renounced finally his throne in accordance with the Digambara tradition, became an ascetic and went to Mysore along with Saint Bhadrabāhu and he is said to have lived and died there in Śravaṇa Beḷgoḷa in a cave.[15]

It is said that Cāṇakya's name was blackened by his envious collegue Subandhu with Candragupta's successor Bindusāra (298-273 B.C.) so that he was relieved. He, therefore, distributed his wealth among the poor, sat on a dung-hill outside the city to find there wise man's death by starvation. Bindusāra tried in vain to passify him and asked Subandhu to go to him and to excuse him. He, however, threw secretly, while he was making his obeisance to the chancellor, an incense-coal into the dung-hill so that Cāṇakya was burnt alive. Cāṇakya died in the fire and was reborn as a goddess. But the dead minister did take a fiendish revenge against his adversary. Before he left the world, he filled a basket with precious perfumes, locked it with hundred locks and left it in his house. In his search for Cāṇakya's treasures, Subandhu stumbled on the basket, opened it and found in the midst of the fragrant substances a note: "One who has smelt these perfumes and does not lead a life of a monk, would immediately invite death." Subandhu renounced all the worldly pleasures out of his fear of death and wandered about restlessly in the world.[16]

While we know the individual aspects of the relationship of the Magadha-kings with the Jaina-teachers so far only through the fabulously embellished stories of later authors and which do not sometimes harmonize with the reports coming from other sources, we are in possession of an indisputably authentic material on the connections of Bindusāra's successor Aśokavardhana (273-232 B.C.) with Jainas. Aśoka was a great and a far-sighted ruler who particularly made it a point to promote the religious and moral life in his great empire. He, therefore, supported the religious brotherhoods of his land in a liberal manner. Personally, he embraced Buddhism in his later years, and he is considered to be its "Constantine"; Jainas, however, opined that he belonged earlier to their religion.[17] In spite of his preference for the teachings of Buddha, he did not stop in showing his equal concern for the welfare of various sects and he appointed special officers who had to look after the individual orders. Aśoka speaks also of Jainas in his seventh column-edict which deals with the duties of the "Dhammamahāmātas" (law-authorities)—as far as we know, this is their first mention in any inscription. It is said in this inscription:

"Piyadasi, who is loved by the gods, spoke thus: My supervisors of law are dealing with many things connected with mercy, also with those which concern the ascetics and those which concern the householders. They deal with the religious brotherhoods as well. I have made arrangements so that they will deal with the matters of the Saṅgha (of the Buddhistic community); similarly, I have made arrangements that they will deal with the Brāhmaṇas as also with the Ājīvikas; I have also made arrangements that they will deal with the Niganthas (Jainas); I have made arrangements so that they will deal with (all) the different religious brotherhoods."

Further the pious emperor inculcates in the mind of his subjects obedience to parents and venerable persons, decent behaviour towards Brāhmaṇas and ascetics, poor and the miserable, asks them to practise charity, generosity, truthfulness, purity, humility and saintliness and reminds them of the prohibition of injury to the living beings. He concludes with the words:

"These commands are given with the intention that they may remain valid, as long as my sons and grandsons rule, as long as sun and moon shine and that human beings act according to them. If a person acts according to them, he obtains salvation in this and in the other world."[18]

Aśoka's successors on the throne of Magadha were—since his son Kuṇāla was blind—his grandsons Daśaratha and Samprati. It appears that the former ruled over the eastern, and the latter, over the western part of his empire. The Jaina-tradition mentions only Samprati who is said to have resided in Ujjain, and describes him as a patron of their faith. He is said to have been converted by the famous monk Suhastī and erected numerous temples. The later period considered him to be a founder of temples to such an extent that many buildings whose origin was forgotten, were ascribed to him. It is even said that Samprati developed a lively missionary activity and even erected Jaina-monasteries in non-Aryan regions.

Very little is known about the destiny of the Jaina-faith under the last Maurya-rulers and the dynasties which replaced them. The Chinese traveller Hiuen-Tsiang found around 629 A.D. still numerous "Nirgranthas" in Vaiśālī near Rājagṛha, Nālandā, Puṇḍravarddhana.[19] Jainism appears then to have gradually shifted, in an increasing degree, the centre of its activity from its homeland to other regions.

3. JAINISM IN ORISSĀ

Jaina-religion appears to have been propagated in the Kaliṅga-empire, for inscriptions* have been found in Udayagiri near Cuṭṭack in Orissā according to which King Khāravela had got a statue of Agra-jina (what is meant is the first Tīrthaṅkara Ṛṣabha) erected and the

*The inscription of the so-called Hāthī-Gumphā-cave is dated as composed in the 165th year of the Maurya-era. This would be the year 157-156 B.C. calculated from Candragupta's ascension to the throne. But the others dispute that the inscription gives this date.

cave-dwellings dug for the monks. It is not certain whether Khāravela himself was a convinced Jaina or only a free-thinking man who showed charity to all his different subjects; probably, the latter was the case. Kaliṅga had obviously been a cultivating ground for Jainism, since even Chinese traveller Hiuen-Tsiang (629-645) considers it to be the main seat of this religion.[20]

4. THE GREAT SCHISM

Significant changes took place in the church during the period when Jaina-faith blossomed in the Maurya-empire. There was a great famine in Bihār during Candragupta's rule. Bhadrabāhu, the head of the community at that time, realized that it was not possible either for people to feed a great number of monks under these circumstances, or for ascetics to follow all the precepts. He, therefore, thought that it was advisable to immigrate with a group of devotees to Karṇāṭaka, while the remaining monks stayed back in Magadha under the supervision of his pupil Sthūlabhadra in Magadha. The unfavourable period burdened heavily on the latter so that they could not strictly observe the holy customs any more and maintain faithfully the holy scriptures. It was, therefore, found to be necessary to acquire the canon anew. A council was called for this purpose in Pāṭalīputra. But this assembly of the church did not succeed in putting together the whole canon; the anthology published by it also remained a patchwork, and when the monks who had emigrated to Karṇāṭaka returned home, they did not approve the resolutions of the council. Besides, there was, according to the tradition, a difference in the ascetic conduct of life between those who had emigrated and those who had stayed back. As we had seen, Pārśva's followers were allowed to wear clothes, whereas Mahāvīra did not wear any clothes. Mahāvīra's pupils followed his example, but it appears that the ascetics were not generally moving around in nude; but it was regarded as particularly meritorious. Monks staying back in Magadha gave up the custom of moving around in nude and got accustomed to wearing white garments. The emigrants did not only keep to the custom practised by Mahāvīra, but it was even generally regarded as obligatory. When they returned to Magadha and found that their brothers were wearing white clothes, they had to appear to them as the people who had abandoned the whole practice, whereas those who stayed back saw in the naked emigrants fanatics who gave exaggerated interpretation to the precept bequethed by tradition. Thus there came an estrangement between the two trends, the stricter one of the "Digambaras" (those clothed in the air) and the freer one of the "Śvetāmbaras" (those clothed in white), which finally led, although much later, to a complete schism.

It is uncertain, whether the seed of the great conflict, existing even now in the Jaina-community, traces back really to the circumstances connected with the twelve-year long famine or not. It is possible that there had been since time immemorial two trends in Jainism, a stricter one, which adhered to Mahāvīra's rule and a milder one, which obeyed Pārśva's more liberal precepts. The fact that we have rules for the *nuns* from the ancient period, and of course, nakedness was forbidden to them, proves in any case that the precept of nakedness was not generally acknowledged. The gravity of the conflict between the two parties becoming more and more acute in the course of the period was doubtlessly favoured by the fact that Jainism had expanded its influence over wide regions of India, and the individual communities, separated spatially from one another, could always develop their individual characteristics. A point must have been reached in the course of this development, where it appeared that the conflicts could not any more be reconciled, and the schism appeared on its own. It cannot be said how and where a formal separation came in. What is narrated by both the parties about it, differs widely, because every side tries to show that it alone represented the ancient Jainism, and the opposite one had arisen by the secession from the pure faith. The fact that Śvetāmbaras fix the origin of Digambara-sect in the year 83 A.D., and Digambaras the origin of Śvetāmbara-sect in the year 80 A.D., suggests that the final schism followed only at the end of the 1st century according to our calendar.[21]

Each one of the two branches of Jaina-religion went their own way since that period. The differences between the two are, in spite of the schism, quite negligible. The most conspicuous of these differences concerning the garments of the ascetics does not appear to be so strict now, because the number of the naked Digambara-monks at present is quite negligible, besides they stay also in secluded places. On the other hand, there are even now important differences in the social organization of the two sects; they trace back to the original differences in faith and rites: Digambaras think that a woman can never get salvation; their cult idols show the Tīrthaṅkaras naked without a loincloth and without ornaments. Śvetāmbaras show these on their idols. The differences pertaining to the holy legend are conspicuous. Digambaras do not believe like their opponents that Mahāvīra, before being born to Queen Triśalā, was in the womb of Devānandā and that he was married before he renounced the world; they are also not of the view that a Tīrthaṅkara eats food and believe that he does not need it.

The different attitude taken by the two sects with respect to the holy tradition has a far-reaching importance. Both teach that Bhadrabāhu had been the last Śrutakevalī and that the teachers after him did not possess any knowledge of all the holy scriptures. But while Digambaras believe that the canon has been gradually completely lost so that it does not exist now,

Śvetāmbaras presume that its main part has come down to the present day. When there was a danger of the collection of the holy scriptures, as far as they had been saved through the stormy times, being lost, Śvetāmbaras called a meeting of the council in the year 980 (or 993) after Mahāvīra's Nirvāṇa under the chairmanship or Devarddhi Gaṇi in the city of Valabhī in Gujarāt; this finally edited the canon, and it gave it a form which it is said to possess even now for the most part.

Although Śvetāmbaras have a canon and Digambaras do not have it, and although there are differences in the dogmatism and the cult of the two sects, the dividing line between them, in spite of all antagonism and hatred, had never been so strong. Both the orientations have been constantly aware of their common origin and goal and have never lost spiritual contact with each other. This is most clearly seen in the fact that the members of one group very often use philosophical and scientific works of other and that Śvetāmbaras have written commentaries on the works of Digambaras and *vice versa*.

III

Propagation and Prime

1. JAINISM IN NORTH INDIA

The monuments which were found in Mathurā, a holy city on the banks of Yamunā, and famous today as the centre of Kṛṣṇa-cult, are the oldest authentic records of the propagation of Jaina-faith in the western direction starting from Bihār. They originate from the period of 2nd century B.C. to the 5th century A.D. and show that Mathurā was an important Jaina-centre during this long period. They are a source of information on the history of Jainism in many respects. It is revealed from several inscriptions belonging to the 1st and 2nd century A.D. that the schism of the community in Śvetāmbaras and Digambaras had already taken place at that time and Śvetāmbaras to whom these inscriptions belong, had also disintegrated into a series of sects and schools; the information on individual Gaṇas and their branches, Kulas and Śākhās, the genealogies of the teachers, etc., agree with the information given in Bhadrabāhu's Kalpa-sūtra and thus prove to be a favourable evidence for the tradition in the canon of Śvetāmbaras. The fact that there is a mention of "Vācakas", i.e. of readers in the inscriptions confirms that there were at that time actually written holy texts. These monuments teach further that the idea of the order of a series of Tīrthaṅkaras was common in the 1st century A.D. and that the symbols of the Tīrthaṅkaras were already fixed. There were statues of the prophets; certain deities like Sarasvatī, the goddess of learning, were also worshipped besides the Jinas. The Stūpas had an important position at that time in the places of worship. The layman who provided for the livelihood of the monks and nuns belonged then, as now, to the merchant-class. This and other facts brought to light by G. Bühler[22] show by documentary evidence the very ancient age of the fundamental concepts and institutions of Jainism and confirm the Jaina-tradition in various ways.

Headquarters of Jainism were in the region of Mālvā with its capital Ujjain. Emperor Samprati is supposed to have ruled here. He was a great patron of Jainism. Even afterwards, the reports of Jainas connect this famous city most closely with the legendary history of their faith.

According to a legend,[23] available in several versions, a king called Gardabhilla ruled in Ujjain in the 1st century B.C. He robbed a beautiful Jaina-nun who was the sister of monk Kālaka. When the brother did not succeed in moving the ruler to return the booty, he went to Śāhan Śāhi, the chieftain of Śakas (Scythians), and prompted him to march against Gardabhilla with his army. Gardabhilla was vanquished, dethroned and exiled from the land, but the Śaka-king and his men settled in Ujjain where they enjoyed the fruits of monarchy. They hailed the Jaina-doctrine and "danced around the foot-lotus of the wise Kālaka like bees". But again after a short period, Śaka-rule was brought to an end by King Vikramāditya who was said to have been the son of Gardabhilla according to one tradition. Vikrama has the same position in the Indian legend as King Arthur in the English; Jainas consider him as a follower of their religion and make him a pupil of the great sage Siddhasena. Vikramāditya is supposed to have founded the so-called "Vikrama-era" which begins in the 57th or 58th year B.C. and it is used these days in North India, particularly also by Jainas. But it is doubtful what can be considered as historical of the reports on Gardabhilla, Śakas and Vikramāditya. Much of what is narrated here about Vikramāditya rests apparently upon the confusion of this king with the Gupta-ruler Candragupta II, having the same name Vikramāditya, who conquered Ujjain around 390 A.D. and who was the patron of the great poet Kālidāsa.

According to the tradition, Vikramāditya is said to have been vanquished by Śālivāhaṇa after whom an era is named which began in the year 78 A.D. This Śālivāhana, the ancestor of a famous dynasty in the Deccan, is said to have been a son of a Brāhmaṇa-widow of four years; she was made pregnant by a serpent-king by biting her while she was taking a bath in river Godāvarī. He grew up in Paiṭhaṇ in the house of a potter and Vikrama's protecting spirit had described him as the man who would topple him from his throne. Vikrama attacked him; the young man then formed elephants, horses and soldiers of clay, gave life to them with the help of incantation, conquered Vikrama with their help and became king.[24] Śālivāhana, like Vikrama, is supposed to be a pious-worshipper of the Tīrthaṅkaras.

It is difficult to find out what is really historical from the reports of Jainas on the relationship of the North Indian kings with the Jaina church. Thus the history of Jainism around the turn of our era remains in dark for the time being. The situation for the following period is also not better. We, of course, know that the religion of the Tīrthaṅkaras had spread further and was encouraged by a number of rulers in the different North Indian kingdoms; but the details have to be more accurately researched into. There were setbacks from time to time. Thus Mihirakula, the king of the Huns who brought an end to the glorious rule of the Gupta-emperors around 480 A.D., was considered among Jainas as the main opponent of their doctrine. It is said that once he asked his ministers whether any person was not dependent upon him. When he was told that the Nirgrantha monks were not dependent upon him, he ordered that the first meal that would be given to them by strangers should be taxed. Since now strict ascetics were allowed to take only one meal on a day, at noon, and if they were prohibited from taking this on account of one thing or the other, they had to wait till the next day to get their food; they were thus made to starve by this edict of the tyrant. Fortunately, the villain did not succeed in carrying out his plan. He was finally defeated and killed and he went into hell, where he had to atone for his atrocities.[25]

King Harṣavardhana of Thānesar (606-647 A.D.), who had established a huge empire which included almost the whole of North India and who ruled from Kannauj, emulated the great Aśoka by lending his support to priests and monks of all sects. He pursued in it the tradition of his house in which the greatest tolerance had ruled since time immemorial; his ancestors had been the worshippers of Śiva; his father had worshipped the Sun and his brothers and sisters were the followers of Hīnayāna-Buddhism. He himself practised all cults simultaneously, albeit giving preference in his later period to Mahāyāna Buddhism which was propagated by Chinese pilgrim Hiuen-Tsiang. He organized a big congregation of religions in Prayāg, i.e., Allāhābād of today, every five years; he rewarded in this festival all the holy men belonging to all the faiths, including also Jaina-monks.

A later king of Kannauj, Āma, who resided (8th century) in Gopagiri (Gwalior), is said to have been converted to Jainism by the famous Bappabhaṭṭi, a pupil of Siddhasena. This sage had predicted to young Āma that he would become a king, although he was expelled along with his mother by his father as a result of court-intrigues. He was, therefore, invited to the court and held in high esteem when Āma took over the reign. Āma's adversary was King Dharma of Lakṣaṇāvatī. He proposed to Āma that they should resolve the dispute without shedding any blood with the help of a disputation among the scholars in such a way that the king whose Paṇḍita is defeated in the battle of words should hand over his empire to the other. Dharma's representative was the Buddhist Vardhanakuñjara, and Bappabhaṭṭi appeared for Āma. The disputation of the two men lasted for six months and did not come to any conclusion. Bappa then worshipped Goddess Sarasvatī and knew from her that the Buddhist could not be conquered as long as he had in his mouth the "pill of ceaseless speech" which she herself had given him as a reward for his austerities during his past seven existences. Bappa then prevailed upon his friend; poet Vākpati, who was living in Dharma's court and was in the company of Vardhanakuñjara to arrange that all the participants would have to wash their mouths before the next discussion. Vākpati did what he was told, and the consequence was what Bappa intended: while gargling, the Buddhist lost his pill and he was defeated in the disputation. Dharma handed over his kingdom to Āma, but he returned it generously to him at the request of Bappa.

Subsequently, Bappa exerted a great influence on Āma during his rule. It is also said that he converted his friend Vākpati, who had composed his famous Prākṛta epic Gauḍavaho in the intervening period, to Jainism and prevailed upon him to choose death by starvation by his free volition. Later Bappa prevailed upon Āma to undertake a long pilgrimage during which the most important holy places of Jainas were visited. The king died on completion of this pilgrimage (834 A.D.) and five years later, Bappa followed his master into the eternity.[26]

The real Indian tolerance with respect to the most diverse religious views which was peculiar to Harṣa is also found among later kings, e.g., kings Muñja (974-995) and Bhoja who were highly respected by Jainas. It is related about the latter who ruled during *circa* 1018-1060 in Dhārā that he made scholars from all sects express their opinions and that they then worshipped Sarasvatī, the goddess of learning, for six months, to find out the truth from all these opinions which were contradictory to one another. It is then said that Sarasvatī appeared to them and gave them the following advice for correct behaviour in religious matters:

"Listen to Buddha's speeches on wisdom,
Observe faithfully the laws of Jainas;
Regulate your life according to the Vedas,
Yearn for the highest in meditation."

The teachers then added the following lines:

"Do not harm any one, as the bad people do;
Worship Sarasvatī,
You could attain *mokṣa* through meditation
This is the origin of all teachings."

Thus they could give practical instructions to the king for his action.[27]

The religion of the Tīrthaṅkaras could experience dissemination and reach its bloom in the regime of the tolerant kings; they did not put any hurdles in the way of Jaina-faith, although they themselves did not belong to it. Therefore, the traces of Jaina-settlements are found in almost all the parts of North and Central India, in the present regions of the United Provinces of Āgrā and Audh, in Kaśhmīr and Pañjāb, above all in Rājapūtānā, in the Central Indian Agency and in Central Provinces. The States which existed in these wide landscapes were only seldom Jaina-empires in the sense that their monarchs were Jainas or that the majority of the population embraced Jaina-faith; but Jainas held almost everywhere important positions and exerted, particularly in Rājapūtānā and Central India, quite a considerable influence. They played a great role in the cities and the courtyards of the kings thanks to their education and wealth which they got as businessmen, and they gave to the state excellent officers.

The imposing temple layouts are the testimony to the power and glory which Jainism enjoyed in the past. They could be constructed, thanks to the generosity of pious laymen, at different places like Kampil, Kosam, Lalitpur (11th century) in the United Provinces, in Gohna and Kaṭās in the Pañjāb, near Virāva in Sindh, in Ahār, Jaisalmer, Kāliñjara, Reni (942), and particularly on Mount Ābū in Rājapūtānā; in Ajaigarh (12th-14th century), Baro, Bhojpur (12th-13th century), Kuṇḍalpur, Khaṇḍvā, Osia (783), Un in Central India; the holy places of Khajurāho (10th-11th century) and Gwalior in this region are also particularly a significant symbol of riches and the understanding of art of their creators.

2. JAINISM IN GUJARĀT

Jaina-faith did not get ever in any region of India such a great significance as in Gujarāt. It is said that the 22nd Tīrthaṅkara, Ariṣṭanemi exerted his influence here, that he obtained Nirvāṇa here and that many pious men got their salvation here on the holy mountains of Girnār and Śatruñjaya. The important position which Gujarāt enjoyed even early among Śvetāmbaras could be clearly explained by the fact that the council met there in a place called Valabhī in the year 980 (993) after Mahāvīra's Nirvāṇa. The "white-dressed creed" gave the final form to its holy scriptures in the council.

Rulers and those in power from various aristocratic houses acted in Gujarāt as the patrons of Jainism. King Vanarāja (circa 720-780) from Cāvaḍā-dynasty is said to have been brought up by the Jaina monk Śīlaguṇa Sūri in a forest before he became a king and, therefore, kept up also later his contact with the religion of the Tīrthaṅkaras. When he founded the city of Aṇahilvāḍa Paṭṭana, he got it dedicated according to the Jaina-Mantras and embellished it with a temple in which he was himself represented as a worshipper of Pārśvanātha.[28]

Jainism had great patrons, above all, among a few kings from the Cālukya-dynasty (Soḷaṅkī). Its founder Mūlarāja, although himself a Śivaite built a Jaina temple. The pious layman Vimala built in the year 1032 the famous Jaina temples on the splendid peak of mount Ābū during the reign of King Bhīma (1022-1064). These temples have brought glory to Ābu by their name Vimala-vasahi (Vimala's residence).[29]

Jaina-faith in Gujarāt experienced a boom in the following period, mainly thanks to the activity of the famous Hemacandra, the most significant writer brought to the fore by Śvetāmbaras. Hemacandra or Caṅgadeva, as he was known by his original, worldly name, was born in the year 1088 or 1089 in Ḍhaṇḍhūka in Gujarāt as a son of a Jaina-businessman.[30] Monk Devacandra who took notice of the intelligent boy, requested his parents that he should be allowed to take up his education; he initiated him in holy orders at his age of eight (nine). At this time, he gave him the name Somacandra. Educated in all the branches of Jainism, the youth acquired significant knowledge on account of his extraordinary talent; he even made the Brahmanic learnedness completely his own. At his age of 21, he was ordained under the name Hemacandra as an Ācārya (master) and successor to his teacher. His knowledge and his ready wit in conversation won him the friendship of King Jayasiṁha Siddharāja (1094-1143) from the Cālukya-dynasty.* This prominent ruler who became famous on account of his campaigns and buildings, was an enthusi-

*The name "Siddharāja" means "A king of magicians"; it was given to Jayasiṁha, for he possessed magical powers. He got them by defeating the demon Barbaraka and by subjugating him.

astic friend of literature and philosophy. Although he himself was a believing Śiva-worshipper, he attracted Jaina monks to his palace in Aṇahilvāḍa-Paṭṭana. Hemacandra, at the behest of his royal patron, wrote his famous grammar, the so-called Siddhahemacandra (i.e., the work of Hemacandra which was written for Siddharāja) and a number of other books. The monk knew to exploit cleverly his connections with the king for his religion; although Jayasiṁha did not embrace Jainism, Hemacandra made him build a temple for Mahāvīra in Siddhapura and worship Neminātha on mount Girnār, when he undertook a pilgrimage with him. The fact that a great disputation between Digambara Kumudacandra from Karṇāṭaka and Śvetāmbara Devacandra took place in the palace of the monarch shows that he took a great interest in Jainism; the disputation ends with the victory of Śvetāmbara; of course, the court-intrigues must have played their role in it. But the fact that Jayasiṁha forbade temporarily the hoisting of the flags on Jaina-temples also shows that he was not always well-meaning to Jainas.

When Jayasiṁha died in 1143 without an issue, his grand-nephew Kumārapāla succeeded him to the throne of Gujarāt. Hemacandra got an important position also in his regime. He understood to win over the king gradually to Jainism and finally to convert him completely. Kumārapāla then gave up enjoyment of meat and hunting and forbade in his empire slaughtering of animals, eating of meat and enjoyment of alcoholic drinks and gambling. These measures, transforming Gujarāt into a Jaina-Model-State, were carried out most strictly. The butchers had to give up their occupation for which they were compensated by an amount which was equal to their three year's income; the Brāhmaṇas had to replace the animal sacrifice by offerings of corns. Hemacandra appears to have understood in the most clever manner to keep the ruler true to his vow, even then, when it clashed with the inherited kingly duties.

On this, Rājaśekhara narrates the following anecdote in his Prabandhakoṣa: "The first half of the month Āśvina came shortly after Kumārapāla had ordered that mercy be shown to living beings. The priests of Kaṇṭeśvarī and other goddesses let it be known to the king: 'Master, the king has to sacrifice to the goddesses 700 goats and 7 buffaloes on the 7th day according to the practices of the ancestors, 800 goats and 8 buffaloes on the 8th day, and 900 goats and 9 buffaloes on the 9th day.' When the king heard this, he went to Hemacandra and appraised him of the facts. The great teacher whispered something to the king in his ears, upon which the king got up and promised the priests that he would give them what is due. The animals were driven into the temple of the goddess in the night, the locks of the temple were firmly secured and reliable Rājapūtas were appointed as guards. The king came the next day and got the doors of the temple opened. The animals were seen in its midst ruminating and lying on the ground, invigorated by the place which was protected from wind. The monarch then said: 'Priests, I have given these animals to the goddesses. If they had liked them, they would have consumed them. But they have not been consumed. This means that the goddesses do not like meat. But you like it. That is why, you are quite silent; I shall not allow that living beings are killed.' The priests let their heads hang in shame. The goats were set free. But the king saw to it that food was offered to the goddesses. It was as much valuable as the goats."[31]

Kumārapāla visited many holy places of Jainas and embellished them with buildings; it is said that he got 32 temples erected as an atonement for enjoyment of meat in which his 32 teeth had indulged before he was converted to Jainism.

Hemacandra took up an extensive literary activity under the patronage of his royal master. He wrote the doctrine of salvation of Jainas, the famous *Yogaśāstra*, further an extraordinarily comprehensive universal history, the "History of 36 Great Men" (*Triṣaṣṭiśalākā-puruṣacarita*), a comprehensive historical epic *Kumārapālacarita*, which deals with the history of Cālukya-dynasty of Gujarāt, mainly, however, with the life of Kumārapāla himself, a "brief text on the art of government from the point of view of Jainas" (*Laghvarhannītiśāstra*) and other books. It also appears that the monk had exerted his influence on the administration and the external policy; many legends narrate about the wonderful deeds which he had accomplished with the help of his supernatural magical powers and about his predictions which always came true. When once a hostile king marched against Kumārapāla to conquer his land, Hemacandra predicted to his dismayed master that tutelary goddesses of the Jaina-faith would save his land. It is said that the other ruler really was strangled to death, as he fell asleep on his elephant, because his necklace got entangled in a tree. Hemacandra, who had become 84 years old, ended his life in the year 1172 by fasting. Kumārapāla died also soon thereafter. He also died the wise man's death by starvation. His nephew Ajayapāla who succeeded him to the throne, was a fanatic follower of Śaivism. Jainas were persecuted in his regime. It is thus said that Rāmacandra, a man of letters, was forced to sit on a hot copper-plate at his command.

Jainism experienced a great bloom under the Vāghelās who came to power in the place of the Cālukyas in Gujarāt at the beginning of the 13th century, thanks to the influence of the brothers Vastupāla and Tejaḥpāla who were ministers and who excelled in an outstanding manner.[32] On the advice of Anupamā, Tejaḥpāla's wife, they invested their great wealth in such a way that everyone could see it, but no one could rob it—they built imposing temples on the mountains of Ābū, Śatruñjaya and Girnār. Even today, they are keeping their memory alive.

3. JAINISM IN THE DECCAN

Numerous temples which are now in ruins to a great extent, as also the inscriptions and literary informations prove that Jainism had numerous followers in the past and that it experienced a great boom in Mahārāṣṭra, in the Kannaḍa-language region, i.e., in the southern districts of the Bombay Presidency, in the northern part of the Madrās Presidency and in the princely states of Hyderābād and Mysore. A whole series of rulers from different dynasties ruling in these regions were either themselves Jainas or they supported at least a great number of their subjects in an effective manner by giving them grants or endowments.

The Mahārāṣṭrī-Prākṛta language used by Śvetāmbaras for their literary purposes originated in Mahārāṣṭra, the powerful empire, which was ruled by Āndhra-kings from their capital Pratiṣṭhāna (in the upper Godāvarī-region of present Hyderābād) in the centuries around the birth of Christ. A king of the princedom founded by Śālivāhana (p. 51), Hāla Śātavāhana (Śālivāhana), is considered as an author or a compiler of a famous anthology of Prākṛta-verses, and Jainas rank him among their four learned kings (Vikramāditya, Śālivāhana, Muñja, Bhoja). But it is uncertain, whether Jainas can claim rightfully this Hāla and the other kings from the Āndhra-dynasty having the surname Śālivāhana, because the rulers of this house residing in Dhānyakaṭaka were doubtlessly active Buddhists and they have erected one of the most beautiful monuments to Gautama's religion in the Stūpa of Amarāvatī.

The influence of Jainas extended over the whole continent from the western to the eastern coast. Inscriptions and other documents prove that it was as much dominant in the language-region of "Māhārāṣṭrī" as in the Kannaḍa and Telugu regions till up to Orissā (see p. 44). There is no doubt that the political history of the regions lying at the eastern coast of the present Madrās Presidency needs to be explained in many respects, but the epigraphical findings compiled by B. Sheshagiri Rao in his *Andhra Karnata Jainism* show amply that Jaina-settlements and Jaina-temples certainly existed in the past in the present districts of Vishākāpatnam, Krishna, Nellore, etc.

Jainism, however, played quite a prominent role, above all, in the history of Kannaḍa-regions. These were the main seat of Digambaras in the old period. According to the tradition, Jainism was brought by Bhadrabāhu in these regions, when he emigrated with a group of monks to Mysore during the famine in Bihār. In fact, Bhadrabāhu died in Śravaṇa Beḷgoḷa in a cave as it is told by Digambaras; Emperor Candragupta gave him company in his last days. Candragupta had himself become a monk and had accompanied the wise man as his pupil. It is said that Candragupta, taking example from his master, starved himself voluntarily to death after twelve years. B. Lewis Rice considers that these informations, which are contradictory to those of Śvetāmbaras, are historical. Other researchers think that they are apocryphal and believe that there is a confusion of the name Bhadrabāhu with another teacher of the same name who lived in the first century B.C. and that the story of Candragupta refers to some other personality, if at all a historical fact is at its base.

The masters Samantabhadra (ostensibly 1st century A.D., probably around 600 A.D.), Pūjyapāda and Akalaṅka (around 700 A.D.) promoted to a great extent the spread of Jainism in the Deccan. It is said that Samantabhadra had devoted himself in his youth to such a strict mortification that he got disgusted with his life and wanted to starve himself to death. But his teacher dissuaded him from it and thus saved for Jainism one of their most enthusiastic missionaries. It is said that Samantabhadra visited the whole Indian subcontinent on his lecture tour: in Pāṭilīputra (Bihār), Thakka (in the Pañjāb), in the region of Sindh, in Vidiśā (Bhilsā in Central India), Karhāṭaka (Karhād in Satārā District in Western Ghāṭs), Banāras and Kāñcī (Conjeeveram), achieving great success for the doctrine. He also excelled as a writer, wrote the famous "Āptamīmāṁsā", a depiction of the Jaina logic and metaphysics, and a number of other works. Pūjyapāda also travelled a great deal till he reached Bihār to spread the faith; it is also said that he had miraculous powers. But he carried above all his literary activity in several fields; he not only treated the Jaina-philosophy with great mastery, but he was also an authority in the field of medicine, above all in grammar. Like Samantabhadra, he is considered as one of the earliest writers who used the Kannaḍa language for their literary goals. But no Kannaḍa work either written by him or by his predecessor has been preserved. Akalaṅka wrote a famous commentary on *Āpatamīmāṁsā*; he also wrote many other books.

Jainism experienced the greatest bloom under the dynasties of Gaṅgas and Rāṣṭrakūṭas.[33]

The Gaṅgas ruled over the largest part of Mysore and the surrounding regions from the 2nd to the 11th century A.D. Their inscriptions are found from Coorg in the west to north Arcot and Tanjore in the east, from the extreme south of Mysore to the district and Belgāum of the Bombay Presidency in the north. It is said that the might of the Gaṅgas was founded by a Jaina-ascetic Siṁhanandī. It is said that a king, Padmanābha of the Sun-dynasty was attacked by King Mahīpāla from Ujjain. He wanted to rob him of his five gems which one of his ancestors had obtained from Indra. Padmanābha, therefore, sent both his sons Daḍiga and Mādhava to the south with the precious possession. They met monk Siṁhanandī in Perūr; the ascetic showed sympathy with the boys and created a kingdom for them as a gift of the goddess Padmāvatī. Padmāvatī confirmed the gift by handing over a sword with which Mādhava cut a stone-pillar into two parts—a miracle which was considered as a good omen. Mādhava conquered a big kingdom in a battle against the Bāṇa-princes; Kolār became its capital. He was succeeded by Daḍiga's son Kiriya Mādhava and a number of other rulers, who resided later in Talkāḍ and they all proved to be pious Jainas. The minister of kings Mārasiṁha II and Rācamalla (Rājamalla) IV was the great Cāmuṇḍarāya who patronized the Jaina-faith with special care. He erected an excellent shrine of Ariṣṭanemi in Śravaṇa Beḷgoḷa (around 980 A.D.) as also the famous collosal statue of Gommaṭeśvara; he was also active as a writer. The learned Nemicandra looked after his spiritual welfare. His works dealing with all the aspects of Jaina-philosophy are held by Digambaras in such a high esteem that they have conferred upon him the title *Siddhānta-cakravartī* (Emperor of the Teachings). Cāmuṇḍarāya was also a great patron of the great Kannaḍa Jaina-poet Raṇṇa. The splendour of the Gaṅgas declined when their capital Talakāḍ was conquered by the Cola-king Rājendra in the year 1004; the dynasty did survive, but could not recover itself from this blow which also hit the Jaina-faith quite severely.

The Rāṣṭrakūṭas or Raṭṭas were for some time the mightiest monarchs of the whole western coast. Their capital was in Morkhaṇḍ near Nāsik, but it was shifted to Mālkheḍ in Hyderābād at the beginning of the 9th century. One of the most famous kings of this dynasty, Amoghavarṣa (815-877) was a pupil of the Jaina teacher Jinasena. He wrote *Pārśvābhyudaya*, a poetic biography of Pārśva, as also *Ādipurāṇa* and *Harivaṁśapurāṇa*, two works on the history of the world. These are considered as fundamental by Digambaras. Amoghavarṣa also patronized Jinasena's pupil Guṇabhadra, who completed the *Ādipurāṇa* of his teacher and concluded it by writing an *Uttarapurāṇa*. The king also wrote; he is at least considered by Digambaras as the author of *Praśnottara-*

ratnamālikā, the "Jewel-crown of questions and answers". In this, the riddles of the world are discussed from the point of view of an ascetic. It is said that the work was written by Amoghavarṣa in order to dedicate himself completely to pious meditation, after he had renounced the throne. Kṛṣṇa II, Akālavarṣa the son of the successor of this ruler, encouraged Guṇabhadra's pupil Lokasena. Lokasena completed his master's *Uttarapurāṇa* and consecrated it quite solemnly in the Śaka-year 820. A later king from the same house, Kṛṣṇa III (939-968), was the patron of poet Ponna. He wrote in Sanskrit and Kannaḍa for which the title *Ubhaya-kavicakravartī* (Poet-emperor of two languages) was conferred upon him. The Rāṣṭrakūṭas lost their power in the year 973 when they were defeated by the western Cālukyas. The last Rāṣṭrakūṭa, Indra, tried in vain to get back his empire; when he did not succeed in it, he died in Śravaṇa Belgoḷa in 982, accepting his death by starvation as a pious Jaina.

The Cālukyas whose two branches, one eastern in Bādāmī and one western in Veṅgi, are distinguished and whose secondary branch is represented by the Cālukyas of Gujarāt, we have discussed above, favoured Jainism in several ways by building and renovating their temples, by giving donations to their shrines and attracting poets and writers to their court, like the great Kannḍiga Ādi-Pampa (born 902). The Kalucuryas of Kalyāṇī and a number of princes from smaller kingdoms acted also in similar fashion.

The first kings of the Hoysala-dynasty were also enthusiastic Jainas. They were originally vassals of the Cālukyas, but they founded a mighty empire in Dorasamudra (Haḷebiḍ) after driving the Colas from Mysore in the year 1116. It is said that they owe their name to an incident which is narrated below: Their first ancestor Sala was once worshipping his family-goddess Vāsantikā in a temple in his home-town Sosavūr (Aṅgaḍi in the Western Ghāṭs) and received there instruction from his pastor, the Jaina-monk Sudatta. A mighty tiger came suddenly from the woods and attacked Sala. On seeing this, the ascetic gave his bamboo-stick to him with the words, "Poy Sala" (hit, Sala). Sala killed the tiger and assumed the name Poysala in the memory of the memorable event. This became later Hoysala. The Hoysalas were Jainas up to King Biṭṭideva (1104-1141) who was converted to Viṣṇuism by the Viṣṇuite reformer Rāmānuja, and he assumed the name Viṣṇuvardhana.[34] His first wife, Śāntaledevī, remained faithful to Jainism. When she died childless, simultaneously with her father, her mother Macikabbe became so unconsolable about this stroke of fate and about the desertion by her son-in-law of the paternal religion that she died of starvation after one month's fasting.[35] It appears that a few Hoysala-kings were converted back to Jainism, as its influence must have been generally strong every time in the court, because a number of excellent ministers and generals were worshippers of the Tīrthaṅkaras. Therefore, the decline of the Hoysala-empire at the beginning of the 14th century robbed Jainism of a significant support.

The significance of Jainas for the spiritual life of Kannaḍigas and their neighbours was indeed very great. In ancient period, they were undisputably the most important, why, the only promoters of cultural endeavour. It is, therefore, no wonder that the whole Kannaḍa-literature up to the midst of the 12th century was exclusively Jaina-literature, and Jainism occupies even later a prominent place in Kannaḍa writings. The most ancient and the greatest products of Kannaḍa spirit has, therefore, an unmistakable stamp of Jainism. The same is also true for formative arts. Even in this field, Jainas had an epoch-making influence in these regions, as it is evident from the mighty temples, Bastīs and Beṭṭās, the great statues of Gommaṭa and other monuments.

4. JAINISM IN SOUTH INDIA

The Mahāvaṁśa, Sri Lanka's epical chronicle, composed by poet Mahānāma in the 5th century A.D. reports that there had been temples and habitations of the "Nirgrantha" monks in Anurādhapura, the residence of King Paṇḍukābhaya (around 437 B.C.). If these accounts—one can't really depend upon them—were to be correct, then Jainas must have lived in Sri Lanka in very early times, and then it would have to be presumed that Jainism had found a foothold very early also in the regions lying between its homeland and Sri Lanka.[36] But it is generally presumed that Jainism had spread in the south of the peninsula from Mysore only during the period of Bhadrabāhu. The Brāhmī-inscription found in the districts of Madurai and Rāmnāḍ, which are supposed to belong to the end of the 3rd century and the beginning of the 2nd century B.C., could be deciphered only partially. These are considered as Jaina-documents by few researchers, because the ruins of the Jaina-temples with the statues of the Tīrthaṅkaras were found near the places where the inscriptions were found.[37] If this interpretation were to be correct, then it could be proved that the Jaina-faith can look back to a very ancient age in South India.

Our information on the further course of history of Jainism in Tamil Nādu and the bordering regions is also, for the time being, uncertain and fragmentary. It is only certain that Jainas held an important position in that area and developed a prominent cultural influence. According to Sir Walter Elliot,[38] craftsman's trade, handicraft and industry of the south got a profound encouragement on account of Jainas. But above all, the influence of Jainas on Tamil literature is very strong. Bishop Caldwell is, therefore, right when he says, "The period of the predominance of the Jainas (predominance on account of education and learnedness—very seldom on account of political power) was an Augustan era of the

Tamil literature."[39] It is said that the classical works of Tamil literature originated in the circle of Madurai-Academy, i.e., the school of poets who were mainly Jainas, and that they were submitted to that August body and were approved by it.

The period of Madurai-Academy is not certain. Tamilian writers distinguish its three periods and place, the last, the most important one, in the 2nd century A.D. Others place it to a later period. Reason for Jainas' opposition to Brahmanism must have been partially on account of the fact that they used Tamil, Kannaḍa and other popular languages, whereas Brāhmaṇas favoured the Sanskrit language.

Madurai appears to be generally a prominent place of Jainas through a long period, for the rulers of Pāṇḍya-dynasty supported Jainism. Few of them even belonged to that religion. Even Pallavas who ruled over a mighty empire on the eastern coast in the 4th to 10th century A.D., were well-disposed towards Jainas. Their capital Kāñcī (Conjeeverum) was the focal point of all spiritual endeavours. All religions prospered here next to one another. In the Buddhistic Tamilian epic "Maṇime-khalai", the title-heroine Maṇimekhalai is asked by her grandfather to study, disguised as a monk, from the learned men in Kāñcī the teachings of Vaidikas, Śaivas, Vaiṣṇavas, Ājīvikas, Nirgranthas, Sāṁkhyas, Vaiśeṣikas and Lokāyatas and accept the system which appealed to her the most. The Chinese traveller Hiuen-Tsiang, who visited Kāñcī in the 7th century, saw in this splendid city that the different forms of faith competing with one another were blossoming side by side and mentions the big number of Jainas he found there. Even Jainas themselves mention that Kāñcī was a stronghold of Jainas during that period. It is said that the great Digambara teacher Samantabhadra (around 600 A.D.) had converted King Śivakoṭi from Śaivism to Jainism with the help of a miracle he performed in a temple,[40] and Akalaṅka (around 700 A.D.) had a disputation with the

Buddhists here which ended with the defeat of the latter. It is said that King Hemasītala, on seeing this, was converted to Jainism and he banished the Buddhists to Sri Lanka.[41] The heydays of Jainism in Kāñcī were over when Pallavas accepted Śaivism and above all, when Colas, fanatic Śaivites and unforgiving enemies of Mahāvīra's religion, conquered the city in the 11th century and elevated it to their capital.

IV

Decline

1. RETREAT BEFORE HINDUISM

Jainas had to fight their battle on two fronts since the days of Mahāvīra: against the followers of the Vedic Brahmanic religion and against Buddhists. They fought on the first front for their faith against the Vedic manifestation, its bloody sacrifices and its social order which assured precedence to Brāhmaṇas over all other sections of the society; and on the second, against the Buddhistic denial of the self and its doctrine of salvation which acknowledged asceticism only in a negligible measure and considered the other saints than the Tīrthaṅkaras as those who could guide one's path to salvation. Buddhism had oppressed Jainism for some time quite strongly to such an extent that it had to beat the retreat before Buddhism in many areas: why its home in Magadha had become an exclusive domain of Buddhism, and this region got the name Bihār after its many monasteries (Vihāras). But the might of Buddhism declined completely as the time progressed; it could not resist Jaina-faith in the west and in the south, and the restoration of the orthodox Brahmanism begun by Kumārila (around 700 A.D.) and Śaṅkara (788-820 A.D.) put an end to it in the whole Gaṅgā-peninsula so that it became extinct in the land of its origin.

Kumārila, the restorer of the Vedic sacrificial service, and Śaṅkara, the pioneer of the illusionistic doctrine of non-duality, also proceeded, with all the weapons of their spirit, against the Jaina-doctrine as a heterodoxy which was inimical to the Vedas.[42] The constant progress of the movement coming from the orthodoxy against all heterodox trends increased the pressure, gradually but surely, and it weighed heavily upon the Jaina-church, and although this knew to ward-off the attacks, its position had become much weaker and it was shaken.

The consequence of the awakening of the Brahmanic religiosity was the revival of the Vaiṣṇavite and Śaivite sects. Śaivism and Vaiṣṇavism proved to be particularly dangerous opponents, and they did a severe damage to Jainism, particularly in the Deccan and the south.

The great Tamilian Śaivite singers, Nānasambaṅdhar and Appar (7th century) as also Sundaramūrti (8th or 9th century), Māṇikka-vācakar (around 900) alienated many from Jainism and introduced them to the Śiva-cult. Appar is said to have converted the Pallava-king Mahendravarman to Śaivism in this way; he destroyed Jaina-buildings in Kuḍḍalor and built Śiva-temples.[43] Śaivites were particularly supported by the rulers of the Cola-dynasty in their endeavours. Their influence is supposed to be the reason, why the Pāṇḍya-kings of Madurai who had been so far Jainas embraced Śaivism. The Pāṇḍya-ruler Sundara (11th century?) who was married to a Cola-princess, the sister of King Rājendra, was supposed to have been won over to Śaivism by his wife. Sundara became a fanatic Śaivite and he persecuted the compatriots of his earlier faith, who did not follow his example, with ruthless cruelty. It is said that he sentenced to death by impalement not less than 8000 of his subjects who did not want to be converted: the torturing of these unfortunate people is supposed to have been graphically depicted on many sculptures on the walls of the temple of Tivatūr in North Arcot.[44]

The Śaivite sect of the Liṅgāyats was another mighty enemy of Jainas.[45] This was founded or reorganized by Brāhmaṇa Basava, who was a minister of the Kalacuri-king Bijjala. Bijjala was a ruler in Kalyāṇa in the period 1156-1167, and it is said that he was a follower of Jainism. Basava succeeded with great vigour and, as Jainas maintain, with great unscrupulousness, in attracting numerous followers to his monotheistic doctrine and in propagating his strongly anti-clerical system which was directed against the Brahmanic caste-order. Liṅgāyats proceeded against Jainas extremely fanatically, damaged their properties and life, destroyed their temples or appropriated them for their purpose. It is said that Saint Ekāntada-Rāmayya had particularly excelled in the propagation of the new doctrine. It is narrated about him that he had taken a bet with Jainas. According to this, they were obliged to pull down a Jaina-statue and erect Śiva's image, if he cut his own head and become alive again by Śiva's mercy. When Ekāntada-Rāmayya succeeded in carrying out the miracle, and Jainas did not want to keep the word, he is said to have cut the head of a statue of their Tīrthaṅkara and placed it before the idol of his god as an oblation. When Jainas complained to the king against this act, the saint offered to repeat the miracle and even burn his head to ashes, if Jainas were willing to wage their 700 temples against it. But Jainas did not agree for which Bijjala scolded them and granted a piece of land near Ablūr (in present Dhārwāḍ-district) to the temple of Śiva Vīra-Somanātha which was erected by Ekāntada-Rāmayya.[46]

Liṅgāyats or the "Vīra-Śaivas", as they call themselves, got, as the time passed, more and more ground in the Kannaḍa and Telugu language-regions. Their faith was the state's religion of the Wodeyars of Mysore and Ummatūr from 1399-1610 and of the Nāyaks of Keḷaḍi (Ikkeri or Bednūr) from 1550-1763; even now, a very considerable part of the population of the states of the southern west-coast belongs to them. Their attitude with respect to Jainas is characterized by their great hostility. An inscription reports that a fanatic Liṅgāyat had stamped a Liṅga-symbol on the pillars of the main Basti of the Jainas in Haḷebīḍ in the year 1638. Jainas protested against this, and an agreement had arrived at. But Jainas, however, promised in this that they would always offer first ashes and betel to their temple according to a Śaivite rite and then take up their own ceremonies.[47]

There was also a far-reaching reformation in Viṣṇuism approximately around the same time in which Śaivism got a new significance in South India. Rāmānuja (1050-1137) proclaimed quite successfully, mainly from Śrīraṅgam (near Trichinopally), his "qualified monism" having a Viṣṇuite stamp. The Cola-king desired of him that he should teach that Śiva was greater than Viṣṇu. Rāmānuja had to flee, because he did not want to yield to this order. The Hoysala-king Biṭṭideva gave him protection and became his follower. But it is said that he ordered that Jainas, compatriots in his earlier religion, be thrown in an oil-mill and crushed, if they did not want to get converted.[48]

It is seen from the inscription from the year 1368 that Jainas were oppressed later by the Śrīvaiṣṇavas. Jainas then complained to King Bukkarāya-I of Vijayanagar against the persecutions to which they were subjected on the side of the Vaiṣṇavites. The king then ordered that the members of both the religions should enjoy the same cultural freedom in his land. Further he ordered that 20 guards be appointed near the Gommaṭa-statue in Śravaṇa Beḷgoḷa to protect the shrine from denigration and saw to it that the destroyed temples were repaired.[49]

Another founder of a Vaiṣṇavite sect, Madhva or Ānandatīrtha (1199-1278) was showing his influence in the Kannaḍa region 100 years after Rāmānuja. His doctrine of dualism[50] preached by him got many converts on the west coast and brought a great damage to Jainism. But on the other hand, Brāhmaṇa Nimbārka (13th century?) of Nimba (in Bellary district), the originator of the Vaiṣṇavite *Bhedābheda-vāda* ("Doctrine of dualism and non-dualism"), who taught mainly in the north, in the region surrounding Mathurā, does not appear to have been able to take up the gauntlet against the Jainas; at least, according to a report, his sect is said to have been rooted out by Jainas which was revived by Śrīnivāsa only later.[51] But then Brāhmaṇa Vallabha (1479-1531), the originator of the Kṛṣṇaite *Śuddhādvaita-mata,* who was born in the Telugu-region, proved to be a significant opponent. This system taught by him in Mathurā was propagated in the surrounding region of the holy Kṛṣṇa-city, in Rājapūtānā as also in Gujarāt; particularly many rich businessmen who were earlier Jainas, joined him. Also a saint from Bengāl, Caitanya (1485-1533) whose missionary sermons unleashed storms of enthusiasm in the whole India appears to have alienated many from Jainism and attracted them to Kṛṣṇa's Bhakti-doctrine.

The growing might of Hinduism was not revealed to Jainism only in its losing the followers. It was also expressed in the increasing inclination of its followers towards Hinduistic views and customs. Thus more and more Hindu-deities were mentioned in the Jaina-literature from now on, although they have no place in the Jaina-system. They also used terms which reveal a strong influence of the Vedānta; and in the following period, there was a greater reconciliation even in the religious belief and social life.

2. JAINAS UNDER ISLAMIC RULE

The conquest of India by Mohammedans which began in the year 712 with the foundation of an Islamic State in Sindh and which continued ever since the invasions of Mahmud Gazni (1001) and Mohammad Ghori (1175) subjected Jainas, as also Hindus, to the same persecutions and oppressions at the hands of the new rulers. Thus the armies of Ala-ud-din Muhammed Shah Khilji, while marching through Gujarāt in 1297-98, committed atrocities, and these are remembered even now. Holy idols were desecrated, temples were destroyed or converted into mosques, books were burnt, treasures were looted and many Jainas were killed. Similar atrocities were perpetrated by the fanatic Muslims also in the Deccan and the south when they destroyed the Dravidian states. Jainas had to suffer very much during these difficult times, and their number which had shrunk on account of numerous conversions to Śaivism and Viṣṇuism diminished further. They could save themselves from the fanaticism of the Muslims by going underground. They shifted their libraries to underground vaults. Only the chosen few had an access to them, and the buildings in their holy places, which were similar to the tombs of Muslim saints, could keep the Islamic fanaticism at bay.

The fact that Muslim kings proceeded against Jainas with fire and sword and tried to convert them forcefully to their religion should not mean that the relationship between Muslims and Jainas was always inimical. It appears much more that influencial preachers like the Arabian missionary Pir Mahabir Khamdayat, who came to India in 1304, succeeded in making many Jainas of the Deccan Muslims by his sheer eloquence,[52] and there were often peaceful and friendly contacts between Jainas and Muslims. Ala-ud-din whom Jainas called Khūnī, "the bloody fellow" gave the Jaina poet Rāmacandra Sūri many presents,[53] and Sultan Firoz Shah Tughlaq (1351-1388) honoured Ratnaśekhara, the author of Śrīpālacarita. Particularly a few Moguls distinguished themselves by showing mercy to Jaina teachers. Emperor Akbar (1566-1605) showered kindness on the Śvetāmbara abbot Hīravijaya and took so much active interest in the religious concepts of Jainas that there was even a rumour that he had secretly embraced Jaina-faith. At the behest of Hīravijaya, Akbar issued in the year 1593 an edict by which the five hills of Rājgīr, the mountain Pārasnāth in Bihār and other shrines of Śvetāmbaras were declared as places of cultural interest. The emperor forbade further the killing of animals in the surroundings of the holy districts, returned to Jainas the books which were robbed from them and did them many other good deeds. Akbar had also contacts with Hīravijaya's successor Vijayasena and with Jinacandra, the head of the Kharatara-sect. Emperor Jahangir (1605-1627) attracted similarly Jinacandra and his successor Jinasiṁha, whom he honoured with the title Yugapradhāna, to his court and issued a *Farmān* for the protection of Śatruñjaya. Shahjahan issued a similar *Farmān*, and his sons Murad Baksh (at first governor of Gujarāt, then emperor for a short period till he was murdered by his brother) and Aurangzeb (1659-1707) awarded the district Śatruñjaya with its income of 2 lakhs as *Inām* to the court-jeweller Satīdās, a Jaina. Ahmad Shah (1748-1754) did the same thing with the mountain Pārasnāth. It was awarded to Jagat Seṭh (world-businessman) Mahtāb Rāi and his successors, to secure for Jainas in this way an undisturbed pilgrimage.[54]

3. JAINAS IN HINDU-KINGDOMS

As it is seen, Jainas could follow their religious practices undisturbed even under many Mohammedan rulers. This was naturally to a greater degree the case in the independent or almost independent Hindu-states which were little affected by Islam, albeit the fact that the number and significance of the Tīrthaṅkaras had diminished considerably on account of their fights with the rivalling Śaivite and Viṣṇavite sects. Inscriptions and buildings reveal that the royal patronage of the Jaina faith had not yet become extinct in South-West India. The two Gommaṭa-statues erected by the believing rulers in two places in South Canara in imitation of the colossus of Śravaṇa Beḷgoḷa are a visible sign of the loyalty to the faith of Mahāvīra's religion: the one in Kārkala by the prince Vīrapāṇḍya in the year 1432, and the other in Veṇūr by Timmarāja in 1604. It is interesting to note that Jainism in Mysore had to fight Christianity in the midst of the 16th century. It is reported in an inscription in Humcha written around 1530 that Monk Vidyānanda made the Viceroy of Śrīraṅganagara give up the Franconian faith (Periṅgiyamata) to which he was apparently converted.[55]

Jainas got a great significance in that period, above all, in Central India and Rājapūtānā besides in their old home-state Gujarāt. They had a great influence as businessmen and bankers in different princedoms of these regions, and they gave also excellent officers to the state. Supernatural powers were generally attributed to Jaina monks. Thus it is said that Master Munisundarasūri (who died in 1446), known as an author of Upadeśarat-nākara and other works, could banish famine by reciting a Stotra and prevented in Sirohi the destruction of the harvest by locusts.

Testimony of the glory and riches of Jaina-community are the works of art of this period, above all, the great figures of the Tīrthaṅkaras hewed out from the rock near Gwalior in the Tonvar-dynasty (1440-1473), the temples of Rakhabdev and Rāṇāpur (both from the 15th century), the marvellous victory-towers in Rājapūtānā, etc. Favours shown by the princes of the Śiśodiyā-dynasty are characteristic for the attitude shown by the Rājapūta Hindu-rulers towards them. Since years, Rāṇās of Mevār gave them their patronage and granted them many privileges. Jainas on their part showed that they were always the true servants of their masters. When Pratāp Singh-I (1572-1597) was defeated by emperor Akbar's army and dissolved his fleeing army, a Jaina offered his riches to him to enable him to form a new army. He thus enabled the Rāṇā to continue his march and get final victory. The princes expressed their gratitude by giving Jainas all sorts of freedom. Thus Mahārāṇā Rāj Singh issued an edict in 1693 by which he forbade killing of animals on the pieces of land belonging to Jainas and ordered that every living being entering the district of their holy places be protected, and besides, not only the animals which were taken to slaughter-houses, but also the criminals who had escaped from the arms of the law. Mahārāṇā Jay Singh gave orders in an inscription engraved on one of the pillars in Bakrole that no one should dry out the sea-water in the four months of the rainy season, i.e., from the 11th of the month of Āṣāḍha (June) to the full moon of Āśvina (September), run an oil mill, produce pots, that no one should harm a living being during this season in which life sprouts everywhere.[56]

It is worth noting that Jainism got a foothold even in North India in the 15th century. It is said that King Narendracandra of Kāṅgrā who ruled around 1427 had become a Jaina according to a Vijñapti which is recently published.[57]

4. MOVEMENTS FOR REFORM

A number of reformers appeared among the Hindus influenced by Islamic tendencies which were inimical to idol-worship. They fought very strongly against the use of cult-idols and the worship dedicated to them. The efforts of these men—and we can mention here only the most prominent like Kabīr (around 1470), Nānak (around 1500) and Dādū (around 1575)—found an inspiring response and they prompted the establishment of a number of sects which fought against the superficial rituals.

Even amongst Jainas, there was a movement in the same period which rejected idol-worship.[58] The founder of this movement was an influencial businessman in Ahmedābād. His name was Loṅkā Śā and he was a Śvetāmbara. He visited in the year 1451/52 a temple in which Monk Jñānajī was busy arranging the manuscripts. He offered to contribute to the preservation of these manuscripts which were getting ruined under the influence of time, by taking up the pious work of rewriting them. Jñānajī gave, therefore, some books, and Loṅkā started to copy them. While reading holy books he discovered that there was no mention in them about the idol-worship done in the temples and he also found that many things taught by the qualified representatives during his period did not agree with Jainism. He, therefore, studied further and wrote the Sūtras he got for copying also for his own purpose. Impressed by his discoveries he decided to reform the Jaina-faith, which was according to him corrupted and re-established it in its original purity. Of course, he could not convert Jñānajī, and many others with whom he exchanged his views, but did not also agree with him. But finally, succeeded in winning over a group of pilgrims who were coming from Śatruñjaya and marching through Ahmedābād. But the establishment of the sect was not possible till there was a monk who could be its master (Ācārya). A layman by name Bhāna became ascetic to get over this shortcoming and ordained himself (in 1467). He was the first spiritual head of the community of the Loṅkās (Lūṅkās) or Lumpākas, and his position was inherited by his pupils.

Later there were splits and divisions in the Loṅkā-sect. The reform of Lavajī, Vīra's son, a layman from Sūrat who had become an ascetic, was the most significant among them. He found that the life of the Loṅkās, with respect to the strictness, fell short of the precepts of the holy scriptures. He, therefore, founded a new sect. It was propagated in the course of time to such an extent that it became later the most important custodian of Loṅkā's teachings. This community established in 1653 got the nickname Ḍhūṇḍiyā (seekers) from the population of Gujarāt, and it meant an honour. But the Ḍhūṇḍiyās gave themselves the name Sthānakavāsīs, because all their religious actions took place in the community house (Sthānaka = Upāśraya), and not in the temples. Today, their number is more or less the same as that of Digambaras and of idol-worshipping Śvetāmbaras, and they are to be considered to some extent as the third creed of the Jaina-church. But they count themselves among Śvetāmbaras. The only difference they have, apart from some subordinate points, is that they recognize 32 canonic scriptures (Loṅkā had accepted only 31 scriptures; but the Vyavahāra-Sūtra rejected by him was considered as authoritative by the Sthānakavāsīs). Their main difference from Śvetāmbaras in the cult was that they do not worship any idols, do not possess temples and give no importance to pilgrimages. There were again among them different branches. They led a stricter life of monks.

Reforms introduced by Loṅkā and his successors were not directed against the iconolatry and the form of worship, but they were meant for a general improvement of the discipline and customs. Even though Loṅkā's opponents fought against his reforms in the cult and the ritual, they had to concede that Jainism needed a thorough reformation, because the discipline in monk-orders had become partially slack in the course of time. Lax interpretation of the strict rules of Mahāvīra was made so that they were even partially reversed. The ban (except during the rainy season) from staying for long at one place was disregarded, as also the rule of "Aparigraha", i.e. of not possessing any property. The monks all too often gratified their desires, appropriated the property of the church and neglected their spiritual duties. Heads of many monasteries acted like Śaṅkarācāryas and other heads of Hindu-maṭhas and appeared on elephants and in palanquins followed by their satellites and servants and they utilized the richly flowing charities of their lay-followers in leading a comfortable life. Discerning leaders had again and again tried to fight against these abuses, but without getting a lasting success. It appears that materialism among Śvetām-baras had particularly strongly spread in the 17th century. This can be partially explained by the general feeling of insecurity and the degeneration caused by it. But a number of highly talented men filled with genuine piousness succeeded in forming a very powerful tribe of followers who once more brought respect to the old ascetic ideal. Ānandaghana, Satyavijaya, Vinayavijaya and Yaśovijaya (1624-1688) were the leaders of the movement which was aimed at realizing the old, strict rules meant for monks.[59] The two last named were also fruitful and active writers; we owe to Vinayavijaya the great compendium *Lokaprakāśa* (Torch of the world), an overall depiction of the Jaina-doctrine in its different ramifications, while Yaśovijaya has made a name as a writer of nearly a hundred works in Sanskrit and Gujarātī. The ascetics who are the followers of these masters wear saffron-yellow clothes to distinguish themselves from the others who wear white clothes. Even now, the community of the "Saṁvegīs" exists and it is respected everywhere for its exemplary conduct of life.

There were also significant radical changes among Digambaras. The ancient, strict discipline of nude asceticism had already become slack in the last centuries of the 1st millennium A.D. This can be seen from the moving complaints of the writers of that period. The Muslim rulers made it impossible for the monks to move around in nude, for Muslims persecuted the naked Yatis. It became thus customary that Munis clothed themselves in the public. This practice is said to have found its mouthpiece in Vasantakīrti (around 1200); his Digambara-followers were later called Viśva- (Visa- or Bisa-) Panthīs, the followers of a "universal" path, i.e., an easy path, accessible to all. Friends of older, stricter views opposed this practice. They later found their main representative in Paṇḍita Banārsīdās, who founded in Āgrā the Terāpanthī-sect around the year 1626.[60]

V

The Present Time

Jainas could pursue their religious practices under the British rule, unhindered by political confusion and inimical persecutions; the peace and order and the extraordinary improvement in the system of communications brought by the Pax Britannica promoted trade. The major part of the community lived from it, and thus raised the standard of living of the big Jaina-businessmen. These people had been important since time immemorial. True to the traditions of the past, big bankers and tradesmen never hesitated to show their respect for the Tīrthaṅkaras by giving them large donations and to get for themselves a good Karma by establishing foundations which were useful for all. The great temple of the 15th Tīrthaṅkara Dharmanātha which was got built by Seṭh Hatthisiṁha in white marble in Ahmedābād in the year 1848 and many other expensive buildings completed during the last century are a testimony to the great riches the community enjoys and to the readiness of its members for sacrifice.

However, in spite of its glamour, the numerical strength of these communities has constantly gone down. This is a fact which cannot be denied. Jainas themselves have lamented it, although, according to their view, it was predicted by the all-knowing elders. The reason for the constant decrease among the followers of Mahāvīra's religion is the conversion of a great number of laymen to Hinduism which was constantly growing in strength. The teachings of the Jinas are known to only very few in their real form, and far lesser people read the holy texts or the authentic writings of their faith; for many, belonging to Jainism means almost only that certain ceremonies are carried out and certain conceptions about body and soul, about rebirth and Karma are considered to be correct. And in their vague generality, they are little different from those of Hindus. Adoption of the Hinduistic views and rites, above all, the worship of Hindu gods and participation in Hindu festivals effaced more and more the borders between the religion of the Brāhmaṇas and that of the Munis, so that many Jainas do not feel at all that their faith is different, and they are counted as Hindus and not as Jainas in the census. The numbers given below from the Indian census-reports clearly show how quickly this has happened:

1891 .... 1416638 Jainas
1901 .... 1334148 Jainas
1911 .... 1248182 Jainas
1921 .... 1178596 Jainas[61]

At first the spiritual leaders, and since the last century the laymen, tried to check the decline of Jainism. Master Vijayānanda Sūri was one among the Śvetāmbara-monks, who was particularly active in this respect. He emulated Yaśovijaya whom we have mentioned above. Better known as Ātmārāmjī (1837-1897), he not only re-established an exemplary discipline in his order, but made Jainism known to larger circles by publishing several books (he also wrote many works in popular style). Master Vijaya Dharma Sūri (1868-1922) propagated Jainism in a successful manner in our days. This prominent man, who as a layman was known as Mūlacandra, and who came from Mahuvā in Kāṭhiāvād, was won over by Master Vṛddhicandra for monk's life at his age of 19.

By his sheer industry and intelligence, the young boy, who drove his parents and teachers to despair in the school, left all his companions behind. He marched through Kāṭhiāvād, Gujarāt, Rājapūtānā, bare-footed and bare-headed, preaching in the cities and villages and re-establishing the right faith. He succeeded in overcoming the hatred cherished by Brāhmaṇas against Jainas as heretics, in Banāras, the citadel of orthodox Hinduism, and in founding a Jaina-school and library. After visiting Bihār and Bengāl, he returned to Gujarāt in 1911 and established a school called Yaśovijaya Jaina Gurukula in Pāliṭāṇā. He organized in Jodhpur the first Jaina-Literature-Conference on his another journey which took him to United Provinces and Rājapūtānā. He died in September 1922, untiringly busy in the interest of his endeavours. Vijaya Dharma Sūri's work was not only practical and organizational, but it was also literary. He wrote a great number of works in Sanskrit, Gujarātī and Hindī; they reveal a clear and a distinct presentation of the Jaina philosophy and ethics. Further, he edited a number of texts and inscriptions which are testimony to his significant historical and archaeological knowledge and his critical acumen. Research is greatly indebted to him, also for the publication of a number of Sanskrit and Prākṛta works, which was begun by him and given a direction. These works would have otherwise been forgotten. He published further *Yaśovijaya Jaina Granthamālā* and a collection of historical legends (*Aitihāsika Rāsa Saṅgraha*). He was constantly in touch with almost all the European and Indian Jainologists and assisted their studies by giving them advice and sending them books and manuscripts; even the author of this book is indebted to him for his kindness. The life-work of this excellent man, which came to an early end on account of a disease, is now continued by his pupil and successor, Ācārya Vijaya Indra Sūri.[62]

Monk Ratnacandra (born in 1879 in Bharorā, Kāṭhiāvād) is greatly respected by the Sthānakavāsīs. He renounced the world at the age of 15 when his wife was snatched away from him by death three years after their marriage. He has written a number of works in Sanskrit and Gujarātī, and he is an editor of the important Ardhamāgadhī Dictionary which was promoted by Kesarīcand Bhaṇḍārī.

Even laymen felt more and more strongly in the last decades of the last century that something must happen to make Jainas keep to their religion and to concentrate their strength for a unified action.[63] Rājacandra Rāvjībhāī (1868-1900), a jeweller from Morvi (Kāṭhiāvāḍ) State, one of the Sthānakavāsīs who had made a name as a poet in his mother tongue and who was known as "Kavi" (poet), was one of the first and the most active promoters of the idea that all Jainas should work together for the welfare of all without any consideration for their individual creed or sect.

The idea of consolidating the devotees took a concrete shape among the individual creeds. Digambaras founded the "All India Digambara Jain Conference" (Bhāratavarṣīya Digambara Jaina Mahāsabhā); their main office is in Khurai (Central Provinces). The first conference of Śvetāmbaras was held in Mārvār in 1903 with their permanent office in Bombay. Sthānakavāsīs whose main office is in Ajmer held their first conference in 1906. The aim of all these conferences was the same: they want to bring together the members of the individual creeds and unite them and to defend their faith against the onslaught of Hindus, Muslims and Christian missionaries. The plan is carried out partially in the conference itself and partially by communication with the local groups which are connected with them. Periodicals were published in Indian languages and in English. Books and brochures were published, old texts were reprinted, libraries were built, scholars and students were assisted, speakers for the mission were appointed, temples were renovated and charitable institutions like widow-homes, orphanages, veterinary hospitals, etc. were founded or promoted.

An inter-creed organization trying to comprise Jainas of the whole of India is an association which was founded in the year 1899 as "Jain Young Mens' Association"; it assumed the name "All India Jaina Association" (Bhārata Jaina Mahāmaṇḍala) in 1910. Its main objective is to promote unification of all trends fighting among themselves and carry out reforms in a progressive spirit. Its organ is "Jaina Gazette" which appears in Madrās. The society could do many good things under the single-minded guidance of Jagmandarlal Jaini (at present: Chief Justice of the Indore Princedom). Its grand festival meeting was held on 27th December, 1913 in which the honorary degree "Jaina-darśana-divākara" (Sun of Jainism) was conferred on Professor H. Jacobi who was personally present on the occasion.

While the societies mentioned so far had far-reaching goals embracing all the branches of Jainism, others sought to restrict themselves more or less to limited fields for the benefit of the whole. Thus there is a "Śrī Jīva Dayā Jñāna Prasārak Fund" in Bombay; its aim is to protect animals and promote vegetarianism. The association to which also non-Jainas belong, does this by publishing books and pamphlets in India and also those introduced from England and America. They also make an appeal to the public and Indian princes to do away with animal-sacrifices. The societies like the "Jaina Students' Association" seek to bring together the educated among Jainas, whereas the "Jaina Ladies' Association" gets women interested in Jainism. "Ṛṣabha Brahmacarya Āśrama" serves the cause of educating the ascetics; this was founded in Meerut in the year 1911. The Syādvāda Mahāvidyālaya in Banāras and other such institutions want to keep the interest alive in the knowledge of Sanskrit- and Prākṛta-grammar and in logic and philosophy. The numerous projects supported by wealthy men with the goal of republishing old Jaina-works are also important for European Jaina-research. They are taken up by societies like "Jaina Vidyā Prasāraka Varga" in Pāliṭānā, the "Jaina Vidyā Śālā" in Ahmedābād; the collections "Yaśovijaya Jaina Grantha Mālā", "Rāyacandra Jaina Śāstra Mālā", "Sanātana Jaina Grantha Mālā" instituted by Seṭh Devacand Lālbhāī Javeri, by Seṭh Bhāgubhāī Mansukhbhāī and others and the series published in their names are also to be included in them. Even the publications of reference works on grand scale was possible on account of magnificence of patrons, thus the works like *Jain Religion Cyclopaedia, Illustrated Ardha Magādhī Dictionary* and the Lexicon of *Abhidhāna Rājendra*, etc. The volumes of Bibliotheca Jaiṇica and the proposed publication of English translation of the *Sacred Books of the Jainas* in two series, one for the Śvetāmbaras and the other for the Digambaras are meant for the English-knowing readers. Even the number of books wrịtten by the Jainas in English is not small; they are meant to present Mahāvīra's teachings to those who can understand English and to get followers for them; I am mentioning here only the names of a few authors who have made name by publishing such works: Jagmander Lal Jaini, P.C. Nahar, A.B. Latthe, Rickhab Das Jaini, Hirachand Liladhar Jhaveri, Champat Rai Jain, U.D. Barodia, Kesarichand Bhandari, Manak Chand Jaini, Banarsi Das Jain and the scholar Muni Jinavijaya. The literary life of the Jainas is enriched by the "Jaina Literary Conference" (Jaina Sāhitya Sammelana) which takes places from time to time—we have already mentioned above that its first meeting took place in Jodhpur (1913)—and the "Jain Literature Society" (founded in 1910) having its seat in London and the branches in India; it publishes works in all the fields of Jaina-research in English language.

Thus it can be seen that Jainas of today do not restrict their activity to working in India for their religion but also seek with the help of publications in English language in making persons not coming from

India take interest in Jainism. This is a development which took shape in the last decade of the last century. Jainas at that time were asked by the organizers of the "Parliament of the World-religions" to depute a delegate to America who could represent his paternal religion. The President of the Congress had first turned to the prominent monk Ātmārāmjī we have mentioned above. But he was not able to accept the invitation in view of the rule of not crossing the "black water" (Kālā Pānī, i.e., the ocean) which was observed by pious Hindus and Jaina-ascetics alike. He, therefore, sent the young advocate Vircand R. Gāndhī (b. 1864) who had already made a name as a representative of his fellow-Jainas in many law-cases. After preparing himself for the mission under the guidance of Ātmārāmjī, he went to Chicago where he successfully participated in the meetings of the Congress (1893). After the end of the Congress, Gāndhī visited a number of American cities, gave lectures on Jainism there and founded a "Gāndhī Philosophical Society". Then he went to England, where also he organized meetings and returned to India in 1895. Here he held a series of lectures in the Institute "Hemacandrācārya Class" which was founded by him. He went again to America and England in 1896, devoting himself to law-studies in England. After a short stay in India where he was called by Jainas to look after their interest in an important matter, he again went to England leaving it only in 1901. He died on August 7, 1901, two weeks after his return to Bombay.[64]

Gāndhī's work in England did not only awaken an interest for Jainism among the people there, but it also got followers for it. The Englishman Herbert Warren was won over by Gāndhī for Mahāvīra's religion; he published a booklet *Jainism in the Western Garb as a Solution of the great Riddle of Life* which is mainly based on Gāndhī's lectures. Warren converted few other persons to Jainism so that a "Mahāvīra Brotherhood" could be founded in London on August 24, 1913 with the assistance of the advocate Jagmander Lal Jaini who was in England at that time and who has been often mentioned. This brotherhood was supposed to form the centre of Jainism in the West and promote Mahāvīra's teachings. We have to wait and see whether this having for the time being four European members (Warren, Alexander Gordon, Mrs. Ethel Gordon, Louis D. Sainter) succeeds in getting a home for the ideals of Jainism in the Occident.[65] In any case, it testifies to the astonishing viability of the thousand-year old doctrine of the Tīrthaṅkaras that it is capable of getting believing followers on a foreign soil even today.

REFERENCES

1. "Alberunis India" English translation by Ed. Sachau, London, 1888, II, p. 10.
2. Modern Jaina-writers try to prove the historicity of Ṛṣabha, Ariṣṭanemi and other Tīrthaṅkaras before Pārśva by showing that their names appeared in the Veda and other works of older literature by employing bold interpretative tricks, e.g., Barodia, *History of Jainism*, p. 15; Seeker, *Notes on the Sthānakavāsī Jains*, p. 17; Mehta in his Introduction to Nyāyavijaya's *Adhyātmatattvāloka*, p. IV; particularly Sri Prem Chand (late name Nanak Chand) treats the question in details from the Jaina point of view in the book *Mithyā Khaṇḍana Containing the Origin of Jainism*, Ludhiana 1914.—Even A. Weber found the mention of the Jainas in the Veda itself when he interprets the "bacchants dressed in air" (*munayo vatarashanās*) in Ṛgveda X.136.2 as the Digambaras (in his essay "Zur indischen Religionsgeschichte", *Deutsche Revue*, 1899, page 21 of the special reprint).
3. Compare the last summary in Bimala Charan Law, *Historical Gleanings*, Calcutta, 1922, p. 76 ff.
4. R. Hoernle in *Proceedings of the Asiatic Society of Bengal*, 1898, p. 39 ff.
5. H. Jacobi, *Die Entwicklung der Gottesidee bei den Indern*, Bonn and Leipzig, 1923, p. 25; Th. Stcherbatsky, *The Central Conception of Buddhism*, London; 1923, p. 72.
6. Jacobi, *ibid.*, p. 25; Stcherbatsky, *ibid.*, p. 73; agreeing also Sten Konow in *Chantepie de la Saussaye, Lehrbuch der Religionsgeschichte*,[4]

Tübingen 1924, II; p. 109.

7. Stcherbatsky, *ibid.*, p. 68.
8. The information in Bhadrabāhu's *Kalpa-Sūtra, Jinacarita* § 160 on Pārśva's followers does not agree with other records; comp. M. Bloomfield, *Life and Stories of Pārśvanātha*, p. 18.144; Hoernle, *Ind. Antq.* XIX, 1890, p. 233 f.—5 heads of the sect are nothing for 50 years!
9. The year 527 B.C. is presumed as the year of Mahāvīra's death by the Śvetāmbaras as also by the most of the Digambaras (comp. Nemicandra's *Trilokasāra*, stanza 850; see also Kamaṭā Prasāda Jaina, *Bhagavān Mahāvīra*, p. 211 according to the information given by Prof. Jacobi); other Digambaras fix the date 60 years earlier (J.L. Jaini, "Outlines of Jainism", p. XXVII)—Cf. about the whole question H. Jacobi's introductions to his editions of *Kalpasūtra* and *Pariśiṣṭaparvan*, G. Bühler, *Denkschr, d. Wiener Akademie* 37, p. 248; J. Charpentier, *Ind. Antq.* 43, p. 118 ff., A.F.R. Hoernle *ERE* I, p. 261 (presumes 484 B.C. as the year of Mahāvīra's death), as also V.A. Smith, "Early History of India" 4th ed. Oxford; 1924, p. 49. Venkateshvara's opinion in *JRAS*, 1917, p. 122 ff. that Mahāvīra had died around 437 B.C. and the "Niganthas" of the Piṭakas were Pārśva's followers is less probable. Cf. Sir Charles Eliot, *Hinduism and Buddhism*, London, 1921, I, p. 105—See M. Winternitz, *Geschichte der Indischen Literatur*, II, p. 2.363 and V.A. Smith, *ibid.*, p. 49 f. for the compilation of the most important views on the year of Buddha's death.
10. Ernst Leumann, *Buddha und Mahāvīra, Zeitschrift für Buddhismus*, IV, p. 130 f.
11. *Uttarādhyayana Sūtra*, Chap. 23.
12. Cf. the last discussion by B.C. Law in *Historical Gleanings*, Calcutta, 1922, p. 26 ff.
13. A.F.R. Hoernle, *ERE* I, p. 259 gives the most extensive depiction of the history and the teachings of the Ājīvikas.
14. Cf. H. Jacobi, *ZDMG* 35, 1881, p. 667 on this.
15. See on this L. Rice, *Ind. Antq*, 3, 1874, p. 156 ff.; H. Jacobi, *ZDMG* 38, 1884, p. 9 ff.; J.F. Fleet, *Ind. Antq.* 21, 1892, p. 156 ff. V.A. Smith who with Fleet had rejected the information on Candragupta's abdiction and monkhood as a fantasy; has accepted its historicity in the 4th edition of his *Early History of India*, 1924.
16. The legends narrated about Cāṇakya are found in Hemacandra's *Pariśiṣṭaparvan*, 8 (German in Joh. Hertel's *Ausgewählte Erzählungen aus Hem. Par.*, Leipzig, 1908, p. 186 ff.).
17. Cf. also E. Thomas, "The early Faith of Asoka" (JRAS 9, 1877, p. 155 ff.).

18. With some changes, the translation as rendered by G. Bühler, *Beiträge zur Erklärung der Aśoka-Inschriften*, Leipzig, 1909, p. 278.
19. Beal, *Si-yu-ki, Buddhist Records of the Western World* (2nd ed. London, 1906) II.66, 158, 169, 195.
20. R.D. Banerji and K.P. Jayaswal (*JBORS*, III, Dec. 1917, p. 425 ff.) were the last to write on Khāravela; see V.A. Smith, *Early History of India*, 4th. ed., London, 1924, p. 44—Hiuen Tsiang, see Beal, *ibid.*, II.208.
21. Cf. particularly H. Jacobi, *ZDMG* 38, 1884, p. 1 ff.; 40, 1886, p. 92 ff.—Information on 22 differences in the teachings and the cult of the two creeds is available in W. Miles, *As. Researches* III, p. 368 ff. and on 84 in *Jaina Gazette* IX, No. 6-9 (reprint: XX, p. 93 ff.).
22. Bühler, *WZKM*, 1, p. 165; 2, p. 141; 3, p. 233; 4, p. 169, 313; 5, p. 59, 175; 10, p. 171.
23. See H. Jacobi, *ZDMG*, 34, 1880, p. 247; E. Leumann, *ZDMG*, 37, 1883, p. 493.
24. Śālivāhana's stories are told in Jinaprabhasūri's *Kalpapradīpa* (14th century); see V.N. Mandlik, J. Bombay Branch, *RAS* 10, 1873, p. 131 f. as also *Bombay Gazetteer* I.2, p. 169 f. The legend that Vikrama was dethroned by Śālivāhana would be quite an anachronism. It is, besides, contradictory with respect to other traditions according to which Vikrama's dynasty ruled for 135 years. But the Jainas are absolutely certain that Vikrama belonged to their religion; his name as also the one of Śreṇika is taken in the *Saṁkalpa* before the *Sandhyāvandanā*. On Vikrama comp. finally Harit Krishna Deb, *Zeitschr. für Indologie*, I, p. 250 (1922), R. Shamashastri, *JRAS*, 1925, p. 81.
25. K.B. Pathak, *Ind. Antq.*, 1918, p. 18; see also H.R. Bhide, *ibid.*, 1919, p. 123.
26. The information on Āma is taken from *Bappabhaṭṭisūri-caritra* which was written in the 13th or 14th century; but it is doubtful how far it is historical. Cf. Shankar P. Paṇḍita in the introduction to his edition of "Gauḍavaho" (*Bombay Sanskrit Series*, No. 34), p. CXXXV ff.
27. Merutuṅga's *Prabandhacintāmaṇi* (Tawney's trans. p. 63).
28. *Ibid.*, p. 19.
29. *Bombay Gazetteer* I.1, p. 169.
30. G. Bühler, "Über das Leben des Jaina-Mönches Hemachandra", *Denkschriften der K. Akademie der Wissenschaften*, Vienna, 1889.
31. Cf. also Tank, *Some Distinguished Jains* (2nd ed. Agra, 1918), p. 1 ff. on Kumārapāla.

32. Vastupāla's actions were the subject of Someśvara's art-poem "Kīrtikaumudī" (The Moonlight of Fame). August Haack, Ratibor, 1892 renders it in German (under a wrong title: "Die Lotusblume des Ruhmes"). There is more information on Vastupāla's life in the Introduction. Cf. also U.S. Tank, *Some Distinguished Jains*, p. 47 ff.
33. Cf. for the following particularly B. Lewis Rice, *Mysore and Coorg*, London, 1909.
34. It is said that Biṭṭideva was converted in 1096 when he was not yet crowned, but when he was still an administrator of border provinces. According to R.G. Bhandarkar, *Vaishnavism, Shaivaism* etc., Straβburg, 1913, p. 52, "Biṭṭi" is a currupted form of the name "Viṣṇu". Thus the king was called Viṣṇudeva from the beginning.
35. E.P. Rice, *History of Kanarese Literature*, 2nd ed., Calcutta, 1921, p. 22.
36. M.S. Ramaswami Ayyangar, *South Indian Jainism*, p. 32.
37. *Ibid*., p. 33 f.
38. Sir Walter Elliot, *Coins of Southern India*, London, 1886, p. 38, 40, 126.
39. Caldwell, *Comparative Grammar of the Dravidian or South Indian Family of Languages*, 3rd ed., London, 1913, p. 184.
40. Rice, *Kanarese Literature*, p. 26.
41. *Ind. Antq.* 2, 1873, p. 15; Rice, *Epigraph. Carnatica* II, p. 47.
42. See K.B. Pathak, *Transact. 9. Int. Orient. Congress*, London, 1893, I, p. 186 ff. on Kumārila and the Jainas. Śaṅkara on *Brahma-Sūtra* II.2.33-36.
43. *Ind. Antq.*, 1911, p. 215.
44. Elliot, *Coins of Southern India*, p. 126; V.A. Smith, *Early History of India*[2], p. 475; more literature in it. See also *Ind. Antq.*, 22, p. 63—*Madurā-sthalapurāṇa* relates the legends of the battles between the Jainas and the Śaivites which were fought with the help of magical powers. This work is analysed by William Taylor in the first volume of *Oriental Historical Manuscripts*, Madras, 1835, particularly pages 70 f., 76 f. and 111 f.
45. Cf. Glasenapp's *Hinduismus*, p. 393 f. and missionary Würth in the *Magazin für die neueste Geschichte der evangelischen Missions— und Bibel-Gesellschaften*, Basel, 1853, No.1, p. 86 ff. on the Li. See in it a legend on Basava's conversion by the Jainas, p. 117.
46. *Bombay Gazetteer* I.2, 1896, p. 482 f.
47. Rice, *Mysore and Coorg*, p. 208.
48. It is said in the biography of the Master, "Yatirāja-vaibhava" by

Āndhrapūrṇa, a contemporary of Rāmānuja, in verse 97: "niṣpiṣṭadehā api Jaina-vargāḥ". See the edition and translation of this text by S. Krishnaswami Aiyangar in *Ind. Antq.*, 38, 1909, p. 129 ff., G.A. Natesan tries to show to Krishnaswami Aiyangar in the appendix of his work, *Śrī Rāmānujāchārya. A Sketch of His Life and Times*, Madras that this cruelty ascribed to the "Constantine of Viṣṇuism" does not go together with what we otherwise know about his behaviour in religious questions and is, therefore, banished to the realm of the fable.

49. Rice, *Ind. Antq.* 41, 1912, p. 231; Rice, *Mysore and Coorg*, p. 113, 207.
50. Cf. v. Glasenapp, *Madhvas Philosophie des Vishnu-Glaubens*, Bonn and Leipzig, 1923.
51. Sir G. Grierson, *ERE*, 2, p. 545b (according to Harishcandra's *Vaishnavasarvasva)*.
52. Sir T.W. Arnold, *The Preaching of Islam*, 2nd ed., London, 1913.
53. U.D. Barodia, *History and Literature of Jainism*, p. 75.
54. V.A. Smith, *Jain Teachers of Akbar: R.G. Bhadarkar Commemoration Volume*, Poona, 1917, p. 265 ff. The documents are completely translated in P.C. Nahar and K.C. Ghosh, *Epitome of J.*, Appendix, pp. VI-XXX; see also Guérinot *Epigraphie Jaina*, p. 21 and Nos. 682, 684 and 692.
55. Rice, *Epigr. Carnatica*, VIII, Nagar No. 46.
56. James Tod, *Annals and Antiquities of Rajasthan*, London, 1829, I, p. 519 ff.; 553 f.—The story of the Jaina-minister Bhāma Śā "the saviour of Mevār" is discussed by U.S. Tank in *Some Distinguished Jainas*, p. 45. The same author discusses in details several other Jainas who had excelled themselves in the service of the Rajput-princes.
57. *Ind. Antq.*, 1917, p. 276.
58. Seeker, Notes on the Sthānakavāsī Jains, *ibid.*, 1911.
59. M.D. Desai, *Shrimad Yashovijayaji, a Life of a Great Jain Scholar*, Bombay (undated).
60. I owe this information to my correspondence with Chhotelal Jain and to Śrī Sammeṭa-Śikhara Campāpurādi Digambara-Jaina Tīrthakṣetra Kameṭī in Calcutta.
61. There were 1, 22, 1896 Jainas according to the census of 1881. The increase in the period 1881-1891 must have been on account of the Jaina-propaganda which began at that time (in case, it is not explained by a mistake of the first census). It is unfortunate that the number of Jainas gradually decreased, although there was progress in the endeavours of reviving Mahāvīra's religion and in coming together of its followers.
62. Vijaya Dharma Sūri's life was discussed in several European languages, e.g. A. Guérinit, *Journ. Asiatique*, 18, p. 379 ff., L.P.

Tessitori, *Vijaya Dharma Sūri, A Jain Acharya of the Present Day* (undated and without mention of the place), A.J. Sonavala, *Vijaya Dharma Sūri*, Cambridge, H.S. Bhattacharya in *Modern Review*, Calcutta, 1923, XXXIII, p. 465.

63. Cf. for the following particularly H. Jacobi, *Archiv für Religionswissenschaft*, XIII, 1910, p. 615 f., XVIII, 1915, p. 273 f. and J.N. Farquhar, Modern Religious Movements in India, New York, 1915, p. 324 ff.

64. On Gāndhī, cf. the biographical sketch in *Speeches and Writings*, Virchand R. Gandhi. Vol. I. *The Jain Philosophy*, Collected and edited by Bhagu F. Karbhari, Bombay 1911, p. iv ff. On the Parliament of Religions in Chicago Comp. "The Chicago-Prashnottar or Questions and Answers on Jainism for the Parliament of Religions held at Chicago, U.S.A. in 1893 by Late Mahamuni Shrimat Vijayanand Śuri, translated and published by Shri Atmanand Jain Pustak Pracharak Mandal, Agra, 1918".

65. According to H. Warren's information, even Robert Wightman and J.H. Dunn were converted later.

SECTION III

Literature

PRELIMINARY REMARKS

Jainas have developed a rich literary activity at all the times. The majority of Jaina-writers belong to the spiritual class: they are either monks who take advantage of the four months of monsoon during which they are not allowed to wander and carry on their literary activity, or those who have settled down at a place like Hemacandra and other great personalities of the Jaina history of literature. The character and the content of Jaina-literature shows the predominance of the clerical element among the authors, and this, incidentally, agrees fully with the Indian literatures in general. These works are mainly theological and philosophical treatises, legends of saints, didactic works and laudations of the Tīrthaṅkaras. The basic religious feature also emerges strongly in works having mundane contents, in books of science and in poetry and works of narrative literature. This is also true of dramas and inscriptions.

The Jaina literature is written in many languages and dialects, in Aryan as well as in the non-Aryan Dravidian.

Indo-Aryan languages have, as it is well-known, three stages of development. They are:

1. The old Indian or Sanskrit.
2. The middle Indian or Prākṛta and Apabhraṁśa.
3. The new Indian or Bhāṣā.

Jainas have made use of the languages of all the three stages; however, the oldest Jaina-works are not written in Sanskrit, as one would expect, in the old Indian, Sanskrit, but in Prākṛta. We have, therefore, to say at first a few things about the relationship between Sanskrit and Prākṛta.

The oldest linguistic monument of the Aryan Indians that is preserved for us are the hymns of the Ṛgveda. But the language in which they are composed was doubtlessly not the colloquial language which was generally used in the Pañjāb at the time of its origin, but a poetic language used in priestly circles. It differed by its literary artistic polish from the commonly used dialects of the Aryan tribes, which, albeit closely related, must have been dialectically differentiated. Sanskrit used in the older hymns of the Ṛgveda experienced further development in the songs of the 10th book of this oldest work of the Indian literature, as also in the individual parts of other Vedas and further in the ritualistic works (*Brāhmaṇas*) and theosophical treatises (*Āraṇyakas* and *Upaniṣads*) and further in the theological texts (*Sūtras*). Sanskrit of these groups of prose-works just mentioned was grammatically decided by the famous grammarian Pāṇini (4th century B.C.?). They had, therefore, a definite form which has been preserved even now. Sanskrit of the national epics and the classical literature is mostly according to this standard. It has, therefore, remained pure, but it has distanced itself more and more from the colloquial language and became a standard language which was used and understood only by the educated.

The usual language of communication must have, therefore, been different in the Vedic period itself from the one used in the holy works of the Brāhmaṇas. We have, therefore, to presume a coexistence of an artistic standard language and a colloquial language, "Prākṛta" in the most ancient period. H. Jacobi[1] says about it:

"We have clear indications of the existence of such a dialect, of original Prākṛta which was different from the Vedic Sanskrit. For, many words in the Veda have a Prākṛta phonetic form which is not compatible with the Sanskrit phonetic laws—these are thus paronyms from original Prākṛta which was spoken in the Pañjāb at a time when the hymns of the Ṛgveda were composed. If now this Prākṛta had been developed according to the natural laws of history of the language, then it would be unthinkable, as Walter Petersen[2] has correctly emphasized, that the Vedic poets defied the gradual changes of the language of which a speaker himself was not aware and had adhered to the older stage of the language. But the examination of Prākṛta-languages coming down to us shows that they neither come from the Vedic nor from the classical Sanskrit. J. Wackernagel[3] says on this: 'The heritage of the language preserved in the middle Indian monuments shows with the help of numerous and clear proofs that there were really Indian dialects which represent an Indian development of the Indo-Iranian inheritance, that was independent of the Vedic language.'"

The disparity between the two languages used side by side by the educated and the other groups of the population which could understand Sanskrit but could not speak it, increased in a proportion in which the popular dialects progressing in an active development distanced themselves from Sanskrit which was closely related to them but which was different from them on account of its artificial stabilization. It can, therefore, be understood that religious reformers of the 5th century B.C. who taught, in opposition to the priestly wisdom of the educated, a path of salvation accessible to all people, used the popular language for their preaching and not the standard language of Sanskrit. The dialect spoken in Mahāvīra's homeland Magadha was called Māgadhī. This language is different from Sanskrit mainly in three respects: R becomes L, S, Sh, and the Nom. Sing. ends in "e" (instead of "as"). The language used in the Jaina-canon shows only the last-mentioned characteristic, i.e., only the half of the special characteristics of Māgadhī; it is, therefore, called "Ardha-Māgadhī", i.e., "Half-Māgadhī". All Jaina-texts teach, agreeing with one another, that Mahāvīra preached in this language which is a variation of the real "Māgadhī". Ardha-Māgadhī is supposed to be a mixure of languages. It consists mainly of Māgadhī, but it also borrowed elements of foreign dialects. Mahāvīra is said to havc used this mixed language so that he was understood by all people with whom he had to deal, thus also with the inhabitants of the border areas of his narrow homeland. It is also said that this had no parallel: why, even today, religious teachers preach in the Pañjāb in a mixure of Pañjābī and Hindī.[4] According to the tradition, Śvetāmbara canon is written in a language spoken by Mahāvīra. But this does not appear to be true, because its form before us comes from a period which is many centuries later. In fact, the dialect in which it is written, is closer to Māhārāṣṭrī than to Māgadhī. That is why, the European research has proposed for it the name "Jaina-Prākṛta". Jainas usually call the language of the canon by the name "Ārṣa", i.e., the language of the "Ṛṣis" (holy seers) and consider it as the language of gods and the foundation from which Sanskrit and other languages are said to have emerged.

Jainas have used the "Māhārāṣṭrī" quite extensively. It is a middle Indian dialect which was spoken in Mahārāṣṭra, a land of the Marāṭhās on the Indian west coast. Mahārāṣṭrī has the first place among all the literary Prākṛtas. It was also used by Brāhmaṇa poets in lyrical stanzas. Jainas have used it not only in their poetic works, but also in their prose-literature and in the commentaries on their canonic works.

Digambaras have used a Prākṛta in their metrical works which agrees no doubt with the later parts of Śvetāmbara canon, but it corresponds to Śaurasenī in an important point (the sound-shift from t to d). R. Pischel[5] called this Prākṛta by the name "Jaina-Śaurasenī". According to H. Jacobi[6] the homeland of this language must have been Hindustān and the Pañjāb, an area in which Śaurasenī was also spoken.

Apabhraṁśa is regarded by a few Indian grammarians

as a type of Prākṛta, by others as an independent language equal to Sanskrit and Prākṛta. In fact, it has a median position between Prākṛta and the modern Indian languages. Some of the works written by Jainas are in this language, but our knowledge of the Apabhraṁśa-literature is limited only to the works which come from 10th-12th century A.D.

When Jainas wrote their literary works in the middle Indian popular languages and not in Sanskrit, their intention was to make them accessible to a larger public. In the course of time, Prākṛta-dialects themselves became rigid and became literary languages which were not generally understood any more; but the predominance of Sanskrit was so deeply rooted in the whole of India in its scientific use that Jainas also had to make use of it.

Digambaras used Sanskrit even in early days; Śvetāmbaras used Prākṛta for their exegetic works till the period till Haribhadra (around 750 A.D.) started writing the commentaries in Sanskrit; only a few Sanskrit-works were written by them before him. The Sanskrit of Jaina-writers is distinctly different; while many authors try to use the language correctly and according to the classical norms of grammar, others try to write in such a way that it is understood, as far as possible, by all, and therefore, intersperse their works with expressions which are borrowed from the popular language.

Modern Indian languages in use in modern India are gradually developed from Prākṛta-dialects. They could develop their own literatures since the beginning of the second millennium A.D. They first displaced Prākṛta completely and questioned in ever higher degree the predominance of Sanskrit, so much so that it lost more and more now its character as a common Indian standard language understood by the educated among the upper classes. In fact, there are now only a very few scholars today who can speak Sanskrit, and the number of educated people who can read it without difficulty is becoming smaller and smaller.

Modern Indo-Aryan languages are quite numerous and are quite different from each other in spite of their relationship. The most important of them spoken by about 230 million people are: Pañjābī, Rājasthānī, Hindī, Bihārī, Oriyā, Bengālī, Gujarātī and Marāṭhī. Of these, Rājasthānī, Hindī and Gujarātī are significant for the Jaina literature. All these languages are further divided into vernaculars and dialects; they show besides different stages of development; of them, few older ones are used even now in literature, although they are not any more spoken in daily intercourse.

Of the non-Aryan languages of the Gaṅgā-peninsula, the Draviḍian of the south got their significance for and on account of Jainism. As we have mentioned earlier, Jainas used these languages very early, and they even partially converted them into the languages of literature. The oldest poets who used the Kannaḍa language were Jainas: the predominance of Jainism in Kannaḍa literature remained up to the middle of the 12th century A.D. The cult of Liṅgāyats which emerged during this period began to compete with them in this field, and yet Jainas gave significant authors to the Kannaḍa language even later. Jainas had a similar position also in the history of Tamil literature; thus a few of the great classical works of Tamil literature were written by Jainas. Repression of Jainism by Śaivites and Viṣṇuites reduced also here the literary activity of Jainas.

Iranian and Mongolian languages spoken in the border lands of India had never any significance for Jainism. There are, of course, Jaina works in English in the recent period—a language propagated by the British rule in India—but it is restricted for the time being mainly to the presentations of the doctrine according to the older sources, to polemical treatises and newspaper articles on relevant themes.

Jainas, like Hindus and Buddhists, bequethed their holy texts orally in the earliest periods of their history. The oldest written documents preserved for us are those of the inscriptions of Mathurā we have mentioned above. They trace back to the 2nd century B.C. We do not possess any handwritten manuscripts of that period, because the climatic conditions in India are extremely unfavourable for the preservation of the written palm leaves. Thus all the manuscripts we have of the Jaina-works are of recent period; the handwritten manuscripts of the 14th century are already rare. The oldest manuscripts found in India are from the 11th century A.D.; much older Indian manuscripts were discovered in Nepal, East-Turkey and Japan; they come from the 1st century A.D. These most ancient handwritten manuscripts are of Buddhistic origin; Jaina-manuscripts which could compete with them in terms of age have not been found as yet.

Jainas used for their script the precursors, derivatives and modifications of the Devanāgarī-alphabet as also the different South Indian alphabets. Since the Mohammedan conquest, they used in exceptional cases Hindī interspersed with Persian-Arabic words, the so-called Urdū, for the reproduction of the texts, as also the Arabian alphabet. Since the recent past, they have even been using Latin script.

Stones and metal plates were used as a writing material for the inscriptions and palm leaves and paper beside birch barks, wooden boards and pieces of cloth for the handwritten manuscripts; paper was introduced by the Muslims. The most ancient Jaina-manuscript written on paper is, according to G. Bühler, the one of *Āvaśyaka-sūtra* which is dated 1132 A.D.

Jaina-manuscripts are characterized by clean and correct script, and this gives them advantage over other manuscripts; use of many coloured inks and inclusion of miniatures lends a special charm to many works. Majority of books consists of oblong pages, put over one another, protected up and down by a firm cover and bound together by a string; a hole is found in the midst in the old manuscripts; a thread is pulled over it and the individual pages are threaded to it.

The outer shape of the manuscript is preserved even now in many Jaina-editions which have appeared since the last century. But now even the European form is also introduced in many books.

The number of Jaina-manuscripts which have come down to us is quite significant, because Jainas have been since long great friends of literature. Besides, the copying of holy scriptures was considered as a religiously rewarding work. It must also be noted that the introduction of the printing press has immensely increased the number of Jaina-publications. Monasteries and temples have big libraries (Sarasvatī-Bhāṇḍāgāra, "treasure-house of the Goddess of Speech," today also called in short Bhaṇḍāra). H. Jacobi[7] writes about the arrangement of the monastery library in Anhilvāḍa Paṭṭaṇa:

"The Bhaṇḍāras visited by me were in best condition. The manuscripts were tied in a bundle and they were protected against the insects by the use of suitable means (formerly root of the Ghodavaj-plant was used for it). They were packed in strong wooden cases which were kept in a secure small room which is kept, as far as possible, dry. Particularly, the Saṅghavīyapāda Bhaṇḍāra which is known on account of the 384 old palm-leaf-manuscripts appeared to me to fulfil all the sensible expectations. Also the manuscript-collections I saw elsewhere in Upāśrayas are excellently preserved; the manuscripts are wrapped in packets with long and firm cotton clothes. This, of course, makes its use a little complicated."

If now in the following we have to try to give an idea of the rich literature of Jainas in a narrow space, then we have to restrict ourselves to mentioning what is the most common and the most important. It is not possible to give the history of Jaina literature in view of our present fragmentary knowledge. Such a work, in the absence of preliminary work and a number of problems, would be beyond the strength of an individual as also the framework of this book. For further details, I refer to the chapter *Die heiligen Texte der Jainas* in M. Winternitz's *Geschichte der Indischen Literatur* (Vol. II, pp. 289-356), to the information in Guérinot's "Essai de Bibliographie Jaina" and to the useful chronological compilation in J.N. Farquhar's *Outline of the Religious Literature of India.*

I

The Canonic Literature

1. THE ORIGIN OF THE CANON

According to the Jaina-tradition, the teachings of the holy religion were recorded in the period of the first Tīrthaṅkara Ṛṣabha himself; the holy scriptures always existed in the times in which the churches of the individual Tīrthaṅkaras prospered. It is true that they were forgotten in the intervals (in between the periods of a few Tīrthaṅkaras), during which the doctrine disappeared, but they were proclaimed again anew by every prophet.

According to a tradition of the orthodox people which is propagated today, the holy scriptures from the period of all the Tīrthaṅkaras should essentially agree with one another (as also the life stories of the Tīrthaṅkaras in their important points), and only the names are supposed to vary in them.

Like the teachings of his predecessors, Mahāvīra's teachings also have been recorded in certain works. His disciples, the Gaṇadharas, brought them down to the posterity in 12 Aṅgas (parts) of which the last consists of the so-called 14 "Pūrvas" ("earlier" works). According to one tradition,[8] the apostles are said to have brought the contents of the lectures of the Master at first in the 14 Pūrvas in a text-form and then worked them out into the Aṅgas. The canon consisting of these and other works was faithfully preserved by the leaders of the community among the first followers of Mahāvīra. However, the parts of the canon fell into disarray with the time.

A council was called around 300 B.C. in Pāṭaliputra, according to the tradition of Śvetāmbaras, to put together the canon anew. It was found in it that the last of the great holy scriptures, the so-called 12th Aṅga, which comprised the 14 works called Pūrva, were not any more in an authentic tradition. Since Bhadrabāhu who was absent knew this completely, the community sent to him two monks who should prompt him to appear. Bhadrabāhu who was then in Nepal where he had carried out a twelve-year penitential vow, said that he was not in a position to go over to Pāṭaliputra, but was ready then and there to teach the Pūrvas to the pupils. Sthūlabhadra was, therefore, instructed along with 500 monks to learn Pūrvas from him. While Sthūlabhadra's companions showed that they were not capable, he heard all the 14 Pūrvas from Bhadrabāhu. But he was only partially useful to the community, because the saint desired from him that he should not tell the last four Pūrvas to any one. Thus the canon remained incomplete in spite of the efforts put on it. This lasted in this incomplete form for seven generations of teachers after Sthūlabhadra, but then the knowledge of the 10 Pūrvas was completely lost. But the remaining holy works were preserved and they were finally edited in the Council of Valabhī in the year 980 after Mahāvīra under the leadership of Devarddhi and first time put down in script (till then, all the holy "scriptures" are said to have been committed only orally from teacher to pupil). Mathurā's Council is supposed to have then (993 after Vīra?) taken up the final revision under Skandila.[9] The canon of Śvetāmbaras of today is, according to their opinion, the corpus of work which was fixed at that time.

Digambaras agree with Śvetāmbaras that Bhadrabāhu is considered to be the last teacher of 14 Pūrvas. But according to them, the genuine canon is also forgotten like the 12th Aṅga with its 14 Pūrvas in the future. Eleven generations after Bhadrabāhu knew 11 Aṅgas and 10 Pūrvas, the next five, only 11 Aṅgas and finally four, only 1 Aṅga, the Ācārāṅga. According to another tradition, these four knew still 10, 9, 8, resp. 7 Aṅgas, and five persons who knew only one Aṅga succeeded them. The last two of these, viz., Puṣpadanta and Bhūtavalyācārya are supposed to have committed the canon to writing, but could not stop its disappearance by doing it. According to this tradition, the last knower of all the 11 Aṅgas, Bhūtavalyācārya is said to have died in the year 436, i.e., 683 after Mahāvīra's Nirvāṇa.[10] Since then, all knowledge about the doctrine proclaimed by Mahāvīra could not any more be derived from the Aṅgas or the canonic writings, but only from the works whose contents rest indirectly upon the lost canon.

While thus Śvetāmbaras boast to possess even today the genuine canon, albeit in incomplete form, Digambaras are of the view that the canon is lost once for all and that the holy scriptures of Śvetāmbaras are not genuine; a collection of books written in a later period serve them as a guiding principle of their faith. They can be regarded as a "secondary canon" in view of the authority they enjoy.

2. THE CANON OF ŚVETĀMBARAS

The canon of Śvetāmbaras, as it is before us today, consists of 45 works, partially written in prose and partially in verse. The following survey should give a brief view into the existence and the contents of the canon; a detailed information on the contents of the individual works would be a fingerpost through the Jaina-canon. W. Schubring has promised to give it in his contribution to the *Grundriß der Indo-arischen Philologie und*

Altertumskunde. Valuable details can also be found in Albrecht Weber's comprehensive essays *Über die heiligen Schriften der Jainas* in his *Indian Studies,* Volumes 16 and 17 (1883/85).

The titles given below are in Sanskrit; the Prākṛta-titles are in brackets:

(1) The 11 Aṅgas

1. Ācārāṅga (Prākṛta: Āyāraṅga) deals with the life of the ascetics.

2. Sūtrakṛtāṅga (Sūyagaḍaṅga) also deals with the instructions for the life of the monks and fights against the hostile heretical doctrines.

3. Sthānāṅga (Ṭhānāṅga) gives a category-wise enumeration of the Jaina-doctrine and explanation of its main concepts.

4. Samavāyāṅga (Samavāyaṅga) has similar contents like the preceding work and it is its continuation.

5. Vyākhyāprajñaptyaṅga also Vivāhaprajñapti (Viyāhapaṇ-ṇatti) or Bhagavatī deals with the whole doctrine in dialogues and legends.

6. Jñātādharmakathāṅga or Jñātridharmakathās (Nyāyādh-ammakahāo) illustrates the doctrine with the help of stories and similes.

7. Upāsakādhyayanāṅga or Upāsakadaśās (Uvāsagadasāo) recounts the legends of the pious householders who became followers of Jainism.

8. Antakṛddaśāṅga or Antakṛtadaśās (Antagaḍadasāo) tells of 10 ascetics who ended their Karma.

9. Anuttaraupapātikadaśāṅga or -daśās (Aṇuttarovavāiya-dasāo) gives the legends of the saints who climbed into the highest heavenly worlds.

10. Praśṇavyākaraṇāṅga or Praśṇavyākaraṇāni (Paṇhāvāgara-ṇāim) deals with the precepts and injunctions in a dogmatic form.

11. Vipākasūtrāṅga or Vipākasūtra (Vivāgasuyam) contains legends on retribution of good and evil actions.

(2) The Lost 12th Aṅga and the 14 Pūrvas

There are references to the contents and the structure of the lost 12th Aṅga, the Dṛṣṭipravādāṅga or the Dṛṣṭivāda (Diṭṭhivāya) in some works of the canon of today. Accordingly, it consisted of five groups of works which are given below:

(a) Parikarma

The Parikarma (Parikamma) is divided in 7 groups and gives according to A. Weber "the preparation for the correct understanding of the Sūtra, in accordance with the analogy of 16 arithmetical operations which one must know to be able to calculate independently".[11]

(b) Sūtra

The Sūtras, 88 in number, deal with the correct and the heretical doctrines.

(c) Aṇuyoga

Describes the legends of great men of the holy history.

(d) Pūrvagata

This most important part of the whole Dṛṣṭivāda contains the 14 Pūrvas we have often mentioned before. They are:

1. Utpāda-pūrva (Uppāya-puvva) treats the substances in their origin, existence and decay.
2. Agrāyanīya-pūrva (Aggeanīya-puvva) deals with the basic truths, substances, etc.
3. Vīryapravāda-pūrva (Vīriyappavāya-puvva) describes the powers of the substances, great men, gods, etc.
4. Astināstipravāda-pūrva (Atthinatthippavāya-puvva) discusses the 7 types of expression and the nature of the substances from 7 viewpoints of logic.
5. Jñānapravāda-pūrva (Nānappavāya-puvva) deals

with the types of correct and wrong knowledge.

6. Satyapravāda-pūrva (Saccappavāya-puvva) deals with true and false speech.
7. Ātmapravāda-pūrva (Āyappavāya-puvva) discusses the qualities of the soul.
8. Karmapravāda-pūrva (Kammappavāya-puvva) talks about Karma.
9. Pratyākhyānapravāda-pūrva (Paccakkhānappavāya-pūvva) discusses the renunciation that leads to the nullification of Karma.
10. Vidyānupravāda-pūrva (Vijjānuppavāya-puvva) describes individual sciences and how one acquires them.
11. Kalyāṇavāda-pūrva or Avandhya-pūrva (Avañjha-puvva) describes the main events in the life of 63 great men.
12. Prāṇavāda-pūrva (Pāṇāvāya-puvva) deals with medicine.
13. Kriyāviśāla-pūrva (Kiriyāviśāla-puvva) deals with music and other arts as also with rites.
14. Lokabindusāra-pūrva (Logavindusāra-puvva) discusses the worlds, certain rites and actions, mathematics and salvation.

(e) Cūlikā

The Cūlikās (Cūliyā) are addendas.

(3) The 12 Upāṅgas

The Upāṅgas (subdivisions; in Prākṛta: Uvaṅga) are dogmatic and mythological works. They are 12, for every Aṅga must have one Upāṅga; but there is no inner connection between the individual works of the one or the other group. The Upāṅgas are:

1. Aupapātika (Ovavāiya) describes in introduction the pilgrimage of a king to Mahāvīra and then teaches how an existence in the world of gods can be attained.

2. Rājapraśnīya (Rāyapasenaījja) recounts how King Pardeśī was converted by Keśi, a follower of Pārśva, and later, having become god, made obeisance to Mahāvīra.
3. Jīvābhigama describes the world and the living beings in it.
4. Prajñāpaṇā (Paṇṇavaṇā) discusses different forms and characteristics of living beings.
5. Sūryaprajñapti (Sūriyapaṇṇatti) describes the sun and the other heavenly bodies.
6. Jambūdvīpaprajñapti (Jambūddīvapaṇṇatti) gives a description of the continent Jambūdvīpa and subsequently legends on the earlier rulers of the world, etc.
7. Candraprajñapti (Candapaṇṇatti) describes the moon and the other heavenly bodies (this is partially identical with No. 5).
8. Nirayāvalī narrates about 10 princes who marched along with their half-brother Kūṇika against their grandfather, King Ceṭaka of Vaiśāli and who died in the battle and went to hell.
9. Kalpāvatansikās (Kappāvaḍamsiāo) narrates about the sons of these princes who were converted to asceticism and who went to different worlds of heaven.
10. Puṣpikās (Pupphiāo) describes the earlier births of the deities which paid homage to Mahāvīra.
11. Puṣpacūlikās (Pupphacūliāo) contains stories like No. 10.
12. Vṛṣṇidaśās (Vaṇhidasāo) narrates the story of the conversion of the princes from the Vṛṣṇi-dynasty at the hands of Tīrthaṅkara Ariṣṭanemi.

(4) The 10 Prakīrṇas

The Prakīrṇas (Paiṇṇa), i.e., "scattered pieces" are mainly treatises on different objects; they are composed in verse:

1. Catuḥśaraṇa (Causaraṇa) contains prayers, rules for confessions, etc.
2. Ātura-pratyākhyāna (Āurapaccakhāṇa) deals with the death of the sages.
3. Bhaktaparijñā (Bhattapariṇṇā) gives rules on the same subject.
4. Saṁstāra (Santhāra) tells of the Kuśa-grass-seat upon which sits a sage who voluntarily seeks his death, etc.
5. Taṇḍulavaitālika (Taṇḍulaveyāliya) deals with embryology, anatomy, etc.
6. Candāvīja (Candāvijjhaya) deals with the characteristics of a teacher and a pupil, of life, death, etc.
7. Devendrastava (Devindatthava) gives an enumeration of the kings of gods.
8. Gaṇividyā (Gaṇivijjā) deals with astrology.
9. Mahāpratyākhyāna (Mahāpaccakkhāṇa) is a form of confession.
10. Vīrastava (Vīratthava) enumerates the names of Mahāvīra.

(5) The 6 Chedasūtras

The Chedasūtras or Chedagranthas (Cheaggantha)—the word *cheda* means, in fact, "section"—deal with the discipline of the order:

1. Niśītha (Nisīha) deals with the duties of a monk and atonement in case they are infringed.
2. Mahāniśītha (Mahānisīha) deals with offence, confession and atonement.
3. Vyavahāra (Vavahāra) contains rules of discipline.
4. Ācāradaśās (Āyāradasāo) or Daśaśrutaskandha gives, among others, rules pertaining to life; the 8th Chapter of this work is Kalpa-sūtra which is composed by Bhadrabāhu and which contains the life stories of Tīrthaṅkaras, lists of

schools and rules for the ascetics.

5. Bṛhat-(sādhu-) Kalpa-sūtra gives rules for monks and nuns.
6. Pañcakalpa (Pañcakappa) has similar contents; others say that Jitakalpa is the sixth Chedasūtra.

(6) Two Sūtras

1. Nandī deals with the types of knowledge.
2. Aṇuyogadvāra (Aṇuogadāra) gives an encyclopaedia of various sciences.

(7) The Four Mūlasūtras[12]

1. Uttarādhyayana (Uttarājjhayaṇa) contains legends, parables, dialogues, sayings and sermons on various themes.
2. Āvaśyaka (Āvassaya) deals with daily duties, but subsequently with various other things.
3. Daśavaikālika (Dasaveyāliya) gives rules for ascetic life.
4. Piṇḍaniryukti (Piṇḍaṇjutti) gives rules for receiving alms by the ascetics; others call it Oghaniryukti.

Further 20 Prakīrṇas, 12 Niryuktis and some other books are added to these 45 works; thus the total number of holy works comes to 84.

A series of other holy works which are a sort of a supplement to the canonic works, the "Āgamas", are the "Nigamas" or Upaniṣads. They are 36:[13]

The works of the Śvetāmbara canon listed are not regarded as equally authoritative by all Śvetāmbaras. The Sthānakavāsīs do not acknowledge the 10 Prakīrṇas, the 2nd and the 6th Chedasūtras and the Piṇḍaniryukti. Thus the number of their holy books is only 32.

Our brief remarks about the contents of the canonic works show how extraordinarily many-sided they are. More exact information would further strengthen the impression, because many of these books contain in the form of deviations or interpolations discussions on things of various types which do not really belong to the themes treated in them and which one cannot at all, therefore, presume in them. In spite of the variety that is offered, not all works are interesting for reading. For, many of them end up in very monotonous enumerations and in a dry heaping up of the precepts which are only now and then interrupted by a couple of nice aphorisms or an apt simile. Even the legends contained in the canon are narrated mostly in a very unlively, wordy language. A characteristic peculiarity of many holy works is that there are many repetitions in them and expressions which have ossified into clichés. This goes so far that the authors or the copiers of the texts before us do not consider it to be necessary to reproduce even once what they want to say in its whole content; they are rather satisfied with giving only a couple of key words and leaving it to the reader to insert certain constant sentences and expressions from other works in an analogous manner. There are similarly clichés for the descriptions of the places, persons, etc., which are in a definite place in the canon and to which a reference is made each time, when the relevant place or the relevant person appears. These descriptions are called "Varṇakas" and are written in a broad poetical style. They are clearly distinguished from the basic tone of the text by use of compound words of gigantic size and by heaping up of explanatory attributes, etc. The canonic works cannot claim great appreciation, if they are considered from the literary viewpoint. Not only the didactic, but also the narrative parts often suffer from an "incurable jejuneness", and only seldom does the language rise to a pathos which may be able to carry away today's reader.

According to the information given by Śvetāmbaras themselves, the individual canonic works originate from quite different periods. While the Aṅgas, Upāṅgas and other books trace back to the Gaṇadharas, particularly to Sudharmā, who gave literary form to Mahāvīra's words, other works are attributed to later authors. Thus it is said that the 4th Upāṅga, Prajñāpaṇā, comes from Āryaśāma, who is identified with Kālakācārya (1st century A.D.), Nandīsūtra from Devarddhi (5th century A.D.), Anuyogadvārasūtra from Āryarakṣita (1st century A.D.), Catuḥśaraṇa from Vīrabhadra, Daśavaikālikasūtra from Śayyaṁbhava, the last one with the aim of informing the essence of the doctrine in shortest possible time to a young ascetic who was likely to die in six months. We have already mentioned that Bhadrabāhu authored (300 A.D.) the 4th Chedasūtra; it is said that he also had his share in the other texts of this group.[14] It is also said that Haribhadra (8th century A.D.) reedited Mahāniśītha. Thus the present canon comes from different periods and different persons; it is not a record of the thought of a definite period, but the work of many generations.

The Aṅgas are considered as the oldest parts of the canon; but they are not fully preserved, since the 12th Aṅga containing the 14 Pūrvas was lost very early. There is, of course, no reason to doubt that the 12th Aṅga did exist, because not only all informations hold the same view in this respect, but even quotations from it exist and many works are considered as based upon it.[15] We do not know why Dṛṣṭivāda is lost. It probably contained things which were partially of no interest to later generations, like the controversies with the opposing sects which do not exist any more, etc.; partially they were explained in a better and more lucid way in other works, so that it was not studied any more and was gradually forgotten.

The 11 Aṅgas before us, further 11 of the 12 Upāṅgas and some other works are supposed to have been written, according to the tradition, by Mahāvīra's pupil Sudharmā. They must have been passed on orally and then, after the final editing, committed to writing by Devarddhi, 980 years after Mahāvīra, and propagated in many handwritten manuscripts. If it is presumed that the late recording of the canon is correct, then it would be, in fact, extremely doubtful, whether we have before us in the canonic texts really authentic information on Mahāvīra and his doctrine. "Let us think," says Albrecht Weber,[16] "what would we know of Christ, if the New Testament had not existed in a written form till the year 980 A.D. (resp. approx. 950, since we calculate the years after Christ's birth, and the Jainas, after Vira's death) and if we had restricted ourselves to a codification of the tradition on him which had taken place under Pope Sylvester II and which was based on an oral tradition and not on a written one"! We need not doubt from the outset the genuineness of the tradition of the canon only because it was codified later. For, this information does not need to say that the holy works had never been written till the period of the Council of Valabhī, but only that their text was then finally determined and had been propagated to a greater extent with the help of their copies. This view has a degree of probability, because the art of writing as it is evident from the existence of the Jaina inscriptions from the 2nd century, was in use among Jainas since long time. But this should not be forgotten that many works in India were delivered for centuries from the teacher to the pupil most exactly with the means of a highly developed mnemonics as it was possible only in a period without newspapers and telecommunication.

It is out of question that even the most ancient texts of the canon experienced a later reworking and various interpolations. And yet they may claim a fairly old age. H. Jacobi has convincingly shown[17] that the language of these works, the metres used in them and certain historical facts indicate that the oldest works of the canon trace back to the period of 300 B.C. which speaks for the historicity of the Council of Pāṭaliputra. But it need not be presumed that during the 200 years which come between the period of Mahāvīra's death and the origin of the oldest parts of the canon, there were only vague traditions; it is rather probable that the traditions about the life and the teachings of the prophet had obtained already much earlier a definite form in the circle of his pupils and that they formed the basic stock for the later literary tradition of the community.

If now many parts of the canon trace back to an early period, it is at the same time certain that considerable changes were made in the form of the Aṅgas and other works of Śvetāmbaras we possess now and which apparently trace back to Sudharmā. It is to be presumed that later generations have revised them to make them agree with their modern views. The fact that Digambaras maintain that the whole Śvetāmbara-canon is apocryphal suggests that these changes must have been really quite considerable.

3. THE CANON OF DIGAMBARAS

(a) The Lost Old Canon

As we have often mentioned, Digambaras do not possess any old canon; they believe that the old canon was lost and the canon of Śvetāmbaras is not genuine. On the other hand, there are several references to the compilations and contents of the lost holy scriptures in the works of Digambaras.[18] The titles of the books mentioned in these enumerations agree partially with those of the works of the present Śvetāmbara-canon; also what is said about the contents is partially identical with the actual contents of the Śvetāmbara-works, but there are crass differences in many cases. I am giving here below a brief survey:

The works of the canon are divided in two groups, viz., "Aṅgas" and "Aṅgabāhyas" (those which are outside the Aṅgas).

(i) Aṅgas

The Aṅgas have the same names as those of

Śvetāmbaras. There is a significant difference with respect to the contents of the 12th Aṅga, the Dṛṣṭivāda, insofar as the particulars pertaining to the Parikarmas and Cūlikās differ.

The 5 Parikarmas

1. Candra-prajñapti deals with the moon.
2. Sūrya-prajñapti deals with the sun.
3. Jambūdvīpa-prajñapti deals with the continent Jambūdvīpa.
4. Dvīpa-sāgara-prajñapti deals with the continents and oceans.
5. Vyākhyā-prajñapti deals with the basic truths: soul, non-soul, etc.

The 5 Cūlikās

1. Jalagata-cūlikā teaches how one can stop water with the help of magic-*mantras*, etc., go through water, devour fire and do other things.
2. Sthalagata-cūlikā teaches how one can go to distant lands with the help of magic.
3. Māyāgata-cūlikā teaches how one can accomplish all sorts of miracles.
4. Rūpagata-cūlikā teaches how one can assume the form of a lion, an elephant and other animals and how one can metamorphose plants and metals into other forms.
5. Ākāśagata-cūlikā teaches how one can fly through the space.

As it can be seen, some works of astronomical and geographical nature are listed as belonging to the Parikarmas; Śvetāmbaras include them among the Upāṅgas. Digambaras do not include the Upāṅgas in the list of canonic works.

(ii) The Aṅgabāhyas

The Aṅgabāhyas are divided into the following 14 Prakīrṇakas:

1. Sāmāyika deals with types of devotion.
2. Caturviṁśatistava deals with the life of the Tīrthaṅkaras, their powers, attributes, etc.
3. Vandanā deals with the cult of the temple.
4. Pratikramaṇa deals with confession.
5. Vinaya deals with upbringing.
6. Kṛtikarma deals with the worship to be made to the Jinas, etc.
7. Daśavaikālika gives the rules for the life of an ascetic.
8. Uttarādhyayana deals with troubles and disturbances in the life of an ascetic, etc.
9. Kalpavyavahāra contains precepts for discipline.
10. Kalpākalpa (vidhānaka) deals with what a monk should need, etc.
11. Mahākalpa (saṁjñaka) deals with the rules and practices of Jina-kalpīs and Sthavirakalpis (i.e., of independent monks and members of the order).
12. Puṇḍarīka deals with actions which justify rebirth in the heaven of gods.
13. Mahāpuṇḍarīka deals with actions which cause a rebirth as Indra, etc.
14. Niṣiddhikā deals with the means used for the purification of soul from mistakes, etc. (Others call it Aśītikasama).

Some (7, 8, 9) of the titles mentioned here agree with those of the Śvetāmbara canonic works, others are connected with them (1-4 with the sections of the 2nd Mūlasūtra).

(b) The Modern Secondary Canon

Today a series of works which are regarded as authoritative accounts of the doctrine take among Digambaraṣ the position of the lost old canon. These works are distinguished in four groups, depending upon the subject like history, cosmography, philosophy and ethics they deal with. These four groups are given the name "four Vedas" by Digambaras. The number of works belonging to the individual group does not appear to be exact; in fact, some titles figure constantly in all enumerations; since all these originated before 900 A.D., it could be presumed that the secondary canon was first time proposed around this period. I am giving the list below:[19]

1. Prathamānuyoga (world history): Raviṣeṇa's "Padmapurāṇa" (650 A.D.?); Jinasena's "Harivaṁśapurāṇa" (783); Jinasena's "Ādipurāṇa"; Guṇabhadra's "Uttarapurāṇa" (completed 879).
2. Karaṇāṇuyoga ("cosmography": Sūryaprajñapti, Candraprajñapti, Jayadhavalā).
3. Dravyānuyoga (philosophy): Kundakunda's 1. "Pravacanasāra", 2. "Samayasāra", 3. "Niyamasāra", 4. "Pañcāstikāya".

   Umāsvāmī's "Tattvārthādhigamasūtra" and its commentaries by Samantabhadra (600), Pūjyapāda (700), Akalaṅka (750), Vidyānanda (800), etc.
4. Caraṇānuyoga (ethics and ritual): Vattakera's "Mūlācāra" and "Trivarṇācāra".

   Samantabhadra's "Ratnakaraṇḍaśrāvakācāra" (600).

II

The Non-Canonic Literature

1. THEOLOGICAL AND SCIENTIFIC WORKS

Numerous writers have undertaken to explain and interpret Mahāvīra's teachings and to improve upon them, to give to the ascetics and laymen precepts for their life and to lay down the rules for the cult. One of the most senior amongst them, held in high esteem equally by Śvetāmbaras and Digambaras, was Bhadrabāhu, the last of the Śrutakevalīs. He lived around 300 B.C., and the tradition connects his name with the emigration of a group of monks to Mysore. But different traditions say different things about him. While Śvetāmbaras make him go later to Nepal, Digambaras let him die in Śravaṇa-Beḷgoḷa, looked after by his pupil, the former emperor Candragupta. A crass anachronism makes him a brother of the astronomer Varāhamihira, who died in 587 A.D.

Bhadrabāhu wrote *Niryuktis*, i.e., commentaries on several holy works; his *Kalpasūtra* was considered by Śvetāmbaras as such an authoritative work that they rate as a canon. A *Saṁhitā*, a book dealing, among other things, with legal cases, is also supposed to be written by him; it is also said that he was an astronomer.

Umāsvāti, as far as we know, was the first dogmatist of Jainas who put together the whole system into brief tenets as it was done by Brāhmaṇa philosophers. He wrote the famous *Tattvārthādhigama-sūtra*, a "handbook for understanding the meaning of the basic truths". This work is considered by both the creeds as an authoritative presentation of their faith. Both Śvetāmbaras and Digambaras claim this famous man as their own. But he was probably, as Jacobi has shown, a Śvetāmbara, because only Śvetāmbaras acknowledge the commentary on his work which he himself has written, while Digambaras prefer other commentaries. The fact that both the creeds respect Umāsvāti as their master shows that differences between the two creeds were not so much acute during his period, as it was the case later. But Umāsvāti's period cannot be exactly fixed. Jainas themselves claim that he lived at the beginning of the 1st century A.D. But this period is probably to be fixed in the 4th or 5th century A.D.[20]

Siddhasena Divākara was a significant Śvetāmbara theologian after Umāsvāti. Jainas know to tell many wonderful things about this theologian who must have been a contemporary of the great Vikramāditya, but he must have probably prospered after 650 A.D. According to their report, Divākara was originally a learned Brāhmaṇa, who was conquered in a disputation by a Jaina by name Vṛddhavādī and was converted to Jainism, when he assumed the name Siddhasena. Once he evolved a plan before his teacher to translate all the Jaina-works from Prākṛta into Sanskrit; as a punishment for this sin, the master imposed upon him the penance of visiting all the existing Jaina-temples. When he had done this faithfully for 12 years, he came once to a Liṅga-temple in Ujjain; instead of worshipping the Liṅga, he slept in the temple by leaning his feet against the symbol of Śiva.

When Śiva-devotees saw this, they called for the help of Vikramāditya, who let the sage being beaten up as a punishment for his indecent behaviour. But hardly the first blow was given, there came a cry from the king's harem; it was found, that the saint had arranged with the help of a miraculous power that not he, but the favourite consort of the king would receive the blows. Siddhasena was then set free; when he raised his hand against the Liṅga, it broke into two, a glitter of light came from it in which Pārśva's majestic figure became visible.[21]

Siddhasena was the first Jaina writer who had written an independent work on pure logic, *Nyāyāvatāra*; this work treats the whole subject extensively in 32 stanzas. It is important for the period of this work, that he reveals, according to H. Jacobi,[22] the knowledge of *Nyāyabindu* of the great Buddhistic philosopher Dharmakīrti (7th century).

A rich activity of the commentators came soon after the codification of the holy texts of Śvetāmbaras which was supposed to have been taken up in Valabhī in 980 after Vīra (i.e., 5th century A.D.). Devarddhi, the president of the Council, appears to have taken part in it. Other commentators are: Siddhasena Gaṇi in 7th, Haribhadra in 8th, Śilaṅka in 9th, Śāntisūri, Devendra and Abhayadeva in 11th and Malayagiri in 12th century. Many of these authors do not restrict themselves to explaining the holy works, but wrote also important, independent works. The greatest among them was doubtlessly Haribhadra.

Haribhadra was a Brāhmaṇa who had studied all sciences. He promised to become the pupil of the master who knew what he did not still understand. Once he heard a Jaina-nun recite a text which he did not understand. When he asked her, she referred him to a Jaina-teacher. He converted him to the teachings of Mahāvīra. Haribhadra then studied all the holy scriptures and finally became a Sūri (master) himself. His two nephews, Haṁsa and Paramahaṁsa became his pupils. To hit the Buddhists with their own weapons, they went to a Buddhistic monastery disguised as Buddhistic monks, so that they could study the doctrines of the heretics. But the Buddhists suspected that the two young men did not belong to their order; they, therefore, painted the pictures of the Tīrthaṅkaras on the steps of the entrance gate so that nobody could go in without stepping on the pictures. The two Jainas who were disguised made a small change with a chalk on the pictures (by which these became heretic from the Jaina-idols) and stepped on them without any fear. Caught by a Buddhists, both Haṁsa and Paramahaṁsa had to flee and they were killed by the pursuing army of a Buddhistic king. Angered by the loss of his pupils, Haribhadra decided to kill all the 1444 monks of the Buddhistic monastery by burning them in boiling oil in a couldron. Prevented from this plan by his Guru (or his mother), he repented the great sin he would have committed and wrote, to atone for it, 1444 books dedicated to the fame of Jaina teachings. Besides a few expositions on Jaina dogma and ethics, Haribhadra wrote also books dealing with the different philosophical doctrines of his period and expounded them in an objective way.

But the famous Hemacandra (1088-1172) is considered to be the greatest Śvetāmbara-writer by his coreligionists. He was given the name "the omniscient of the Kali-era" (Kalikāla-Sarvajña) on account of his versatility. His main dogmatic work is *Yogaśāstra* (textbook on Yoga), also *Adhyātma Upaniṣad* (Esoteric doctrine on the Spirit). He gives in it not only a complete exposition of the Jaina-doctrine, particularly its ethical precepts, but deals also with the theory of contemplation in a detailed manner. Hemacandra's minor work, *Vitarāgastuti* gives a brief general idea about the doctrine in the form of a hymn; this work was commented upon in details by Malliṣeṇa in 1292 in his *Syādvādamañjarī* (Bouquet of flowers of Dialectics); it is an independent philosophical treatise of a sizable length.

We may mention in the following only a couple of most important among the great number of Śvetāmbara-theologians: Devendrasūri wrote the *Karmagranthas*; these discuss the Karma-theory in all its details. Guṇaratna (around 1400) gave a commentary on Haribhadra's work on philosophical systems. Dharmasāgara wrote in 1573 his "Sun for the owls of the false doctrine" (*Kupakṣakauśi-kasahasrakiraṇa*) in which he fought against Digambaras. We have already mentioned the two prolific writers Vinayavijaya and Yaśovijaya who lived in the 17th century. The *Lokaprakāśa* of the former is a valuable encyclopaedic work dealing with all the aspects of Jainism. Yaśovijaya's *Pratimāśataka* is a noteworthy work among his writings besides those which are dedicated to logic and metaphysics. He defends in this the worship of idols. The endeavours directed to the expounding of the Jaina-doctrine in Sanskrit and Prākṛta are continuing right up to our times; the most recent dogmatic work I have come to know is Vijaya Dharma Sūri's *Jainatattvajñāna* which was published in 1917.

Like Śvetāmbaras, Digambaras have also worked with great enthusiasm in the field of dogmatism and the related disciplines. One of the oldest writers in this field was Kundakunda. He lived certainly before 600 A.D. Some say that he lived in the 1st century A.D. His works have been included in the so-called "secondary canon" like those of the other great teachers of the sect. Since we have talked about the other great dogmatists Samantabhadra, Pūjyapāda, Akalaṅka, Vidyānanda and Nemicandra, it is sufficient that we only mention them. Of the others, Prabhācandra (around 825), Amitagati (around 1000), Aśādhara (beginning of the 13th century), Sakalakīrti (around 1464) and Śrutasāgara (end of the 15th century) are the most significant.

All the authors we have mentioned above wrote their works in Sanskrit or Prākrta-verses. They themselves wrote the commentaries on them in Sanskrit, or their pupils wrote them. The ever increasing use of modern Indian languages for the literary purpose induced people to translating the works of the famous dogmatists in Bhāṣā. Thus there is the whole collection of translations of theological writings in Gujarātī language and other dialects. Many authors even wrote down very early their works in the dialect of their native place. Thus Śrīvarddhadeva, also called Tumbulūrācārya after the place of his birth, wrote a commentary on *Tattvārthādhīgamasūtra* in 96,000 verses in the Kannaḍa language. This work whose period of origin is not known, but which is praised in inscriptions has unfortunately been lost. The more we move towards the present day, the bigger is the number of scientific works written on Jaina-philosophy in modern Indian languages. In addition, we have enormous literature which is written in various dialects. Its aim is to make the teachings of the dogmatists palatable in larger circles. There are also numerous works meant for the education of laymen.

The erudite activity of Jainas does not restrict itself to the presentation, interpretation and propagation of their doctrine; they have rather done a prolific work in all the fields of India's spiritual life.

Indians regard grammar as a basic science which is to some extent a prerequisite for all other sciences. A verse says on this:

> "It is a gate to salvation,
> (Medicinal) herb for the diseases of the words,
> Reparation power of sciences:
> It is the super science."[23]

Jaina Sanskrit grammarians go closely together with the Brāhmaṇic Grammar of Pāṇini. The most famous are the so-called *Jainendra-vyākaraṇa* of Pūjyapāda Devanandī and *Śākaṭāyana-vyākaraṇa* of Śākaṭāyana who wrote it during Amoghavarṣa's period (9th century). Hemacandra's (12th century) grammar, the so-called

Siddhahemacandra, was based on this work which F. Kielhorn considers as the best grammar of Indian middle ages.[24] The 8th book of *Siddhahemacandra* contains a Prākṛta Grammar. Since Prākṛta is also the language of the Jaina-church, they have worked upon this subject also in other respects. They have also contributed excellently to the field of grammar of modern Indian languages. Jainas have also made name by compiling dictionaries and similar works. Indian grammarians like to explain their works by giving practical examples. Hemacandra's epic *Kumārapālacarita* is a book of this type which thus tries to link the useful with the pleasant like the famous Brāhmaṇic *Bhaṭṭikāvya*.

Jainas have also dealt with the theoretical foundations of poetry; we have among them Ajitasena (10th century), Hemacandra, Vāgbhaṭa (end of the 11th century), Arisiṁha, Amaracandra (13th century) and others.[25] Hemacandra has worked upon the prosody. A great number of Jaina-writers took upon themselves the duty of explaining and interpreting the famous creations of literature. They did not restrict themselves to the works written by Jainas, but they have also commented upon Brāhmaṇical works without projecting their own religious point of view.[26] Jainas were active even in the field of music theory, as it is evident from Pārśvadeva's *Saṅgītasamayasāra* and *Saṅgītaratnākara*[27] (before 1210) and the Kannaḍa work *Ratnākarajaṅgalapadajāti*.[28]

Jaina-scholars have written separate books on politics and law for Jaina-kings, and as we have seen, there was a great number of them in the past. *Saṁhitā*, which is apparently an excerpt from the *Upāsakādhyayana-Aṅga* and which is attributed to the great Bhadrabāhu, contains chapters dealing with these subjects; Somadevasūri's *Nītivākyāmṛta* (around 950 A.D.), Amitagati's *Vardhamānanīti* (around 1011 A.D.) and Hemacandra's *Arhannīti* (12th century) deal particularly with political science and jurisprudence.[29] Hemacandra's book we have before us is in Sanskrit having the title *Laghu Arhannīti*; from the remarks made in the book,[30] it is an extract from a bigger book *Bṛhad-Arhannīti-śāstra* written in Prākṛta by Hemacandra for King Kumārapāla.

The study of natural sciences was developed among Jainas in connection with their dogmatic views on the universe and its inhabitants. The most theological and philosophical contain, therefore, chapters on the object. Besides, there are many works dealing with cosmography, geography and astronomy treating these subjects briefly or extensively.[31] Bhadrabāhu and Kālakācārya, among others, are considered as great authorities in the field of astronomy.[32] Mathematics, knowledge of which must have been important among Jainas in view of the enormous numbers with which they operated in their doctrine, found enthusiastic young followers among them; a text-book on mathematics, Mahāvīra's *Gaṇitasārasaṅgraha* (9th century A.D.) is even translated into English.[33]

The doctrine of atoms and living beings was several times depicted by theologians and philosophers. Thus Ratnasiṁha has summarized the Jaina-theories on objects and Nigoḍas (smallest living beings) in brief tracts.[34] Śāntisūri (11th century) gives a complete biology, botany, zoology and anthropology *en miniature* in his *Jīvavicāra*.[35] The famous Pūjyapāda deals with medicine in his *Kalyāṇa-kāraka*. This work in which mainly the use of medicinal herbs is recommended was rendered into Kannaḍa by Jagaddala Somanātha around 1150. Manarāja's *Khagendra-maṇidarpaṇa* is another work in Kannaḍa which is dedicated to the same subject.[36]

Many Jaina-writers have dealt with magic and divination. Thus the Kannaḍiga Raṭṭa (1300) wrote a *Raṭṭa-sūtra* in which he deals with the subjects rain, earthquake, lightning and portents of all sorts. Harṣakīrti wrote a handbook on astrology with the title *Jyotiṣasāroddhāra,* and many works deal with oneirocritics, magic-*mantras* and other occult things.

There are detailed references on temple-structure and production of cult-images in the textbooks on rituals. It can be presumed that Jainas wrote works on architecture and sculpture, but they have not yet come to light.[37]

This summary general idea given here which does not, of course, either claim to be complete or strive to be complete, shows how Jainas were literarily active in several subjects, and thereby teaches us that there was hardly a field of Indian culture in which they have not done a useful work. In any case, we shall need a long time, in view of the deficiency of our knowledge, till the Jaina-writings are so thoroughly examined that we shall be able to form a conclusive opinion on the scientific achievements of Jainas.

2. NARRATIVE LITERATURE AND POETRY

The canon is extremely rich in stories and legends of various types. The reports on the prophets, apostles and saints it contains offer a welcome material to the later generations for their literary creations. These, as it appears, eternally youthful legends in prose and poetry in simple, easily understandable form, as also in poetic, artistic and highly stylized form, are again and again treated in countless works in the most different languages. There are numerous biographies of Ṛṣabha, Śāntinātha, Ariṣṭanemi, Pārśva, Mahāvīra and other Tīrthaṅkaras which mostly deal with the popular theme in the usual schematic way; and they strive to get for the theme new angles only by addition of new episodes, of stories from the earlier births of the hero and his followers.

But the hagiography of Jainas did not restrict itself from the olden times to describing the life and work of the in founders of religion and those persons who were connected with them, either as devotees or as adversaries, but it included a great number of other legendary personalities in the sphere of their observations. 12 world-rulers and 27 heroes are the main personalities of the traditional world-history besides the 24 Tīrthaṅkaras. Along with these who appear to be particularly special for Jainas, they also consider heroes known to Hindus, like Bharata, Sagara, Rāma, Lakṣmaṇa, Rāvaṇa, as also Balarāma, Kṛṣṇa and Jarāsandha. Jainas have more or less strongly changed the stories of these men and other persons from the great Epics Rāmāyaṇa and Mahābhārata for their purpose; the heroes in these are obviously all pious Jainas and think and act as such. The great number they have come down to us speaks for the strong preference for Jaina reworking and, as we must often say, for distortion of the Brāhmaṇic legends. Thus we have a *Harivaṁsapurāṇa* of Jinasena (8th century), a Kannaḍa *Vikramārjuna-vijaya* (also called *Pampa-Bhārata*) of Ādi-Pampa (10th century), a *Pāṇḍavapurāṇa* of Śubhacandra (16th century) among other works in which Kṛṣṇa and other Mahābhārata-heroes figure, and a number of Rāmāyaṇas, like *Paümacariya* of Śvetāmbara Vimalasūri (3rd or 4th century A.D.) written in Prākṛta, *Padmapurāṇa* of Digambara Raviṣeṇa (around 660), a *Rāmacandra-caritapurāṇa* (called in brief *Pampa-Rāmāyaṇa*) of the Kannaḍa poet Pampa (younger Pampa: 1100) and many other literary works of this type.

There were also many attempts to treat the history of all 63 "Great Men" or "Divine personages" (*Śalākā-puruṣa*), as the Indians say, and arrange them systematically in one work, like in the *Ādipurāṇa* of Jinasena or its continuation, the *Uttarapurāṇa* of Guṇabhadra (both 9th century) and in the *Triṣaṣṭiśalākā-puruṣa-carita* of Hemacandra (12th century) among others.

The mythical prehistory is continued in the history of

the church among the followers of Mahāvīra. Numerous writings deal directly or indirectly with the depiction of the eventful fates of the Jaina-community in the course of the centuries. Although a series of historical facts are told in these works, they are so full of legends and fairy-tales, that they can be only very cautiously regarded as a historical source-material. The boundaries between poetry and truth become blurred in them without the authors becoming conscious of them, and the crass anachronisms are order of the day in them. We have a great number of works of this type. Jainas differentiate between the Caritras and Prabandhas.[38] The Caritras are the biographies of Tīrthaṅkaras, world-rulers and the others of the 63 "great men", but also of the old great teachers of the church like Āryarakṣita who is said to have died in 557 after Vīra. The Prabandhas deal with the biographies of prominent personalities of the later period, saints, as well as the kings, ministers, business-men, etc. "Rāsas" written in verse in old Gujarātī, as also similar writings in modern Indian languages are also connected with historical personalities. All these works do not want to write only history (albeit embellished fabulously), but also want to entertain with the help of anecdotes, etc. At the same time, they follow mostly the goal of educating the people religiously and morally, of propagating Jainism and giving material to monks for their sermons.

Hemacandra's *Pariśiṣṭaparva*, an appendix of his great work on 63 "great men" is a sort of history of the Jaina-church. It deals with the patriarchs of the community. Continuation of this work is *Prabhāvakacarita* written by Prabhācandra and Pradyumnasūri (around 1250 A.D.) in which biographies of 22 Jaina-teachers are given, including that of Hemacandra. Collection of half-historical reports and anecdotes, like *Prabandhacintāmaṇi* by Merutuṅga (around 1300), poetic chronicles like Hemacandra's *Kumārapālacarita* and panegyrics on patrons of art combine similarly poetry and truth. Let us mention only the Kannaḍa compendium of the Jaina-tradition in the south from among the modern works of this type; Digambara Devacandra wrote it in 1838 for a princess in Mysore under the title *Rājāvaḷikathe.* Its accounts tracing back partially to the older sources evoked at that time lively discussions among European scholars concerning their veracity.

It is a remarkable quality of Jaina-historians that they are not satisfied with describing alone something that has become history, but they also undertake to deal with the future which will once become history. As we shall see below while discussing the dogmatic world-history, Jaina-theologians even undertake to describe in details the gloomy conditions of the approaching bad era. They even know to mention now itself the names of the last Jaina laymen and monks. A popular subject of literary creation is also the writing of biographies of future Tīrthaṅkaras who will revive Jainism again after its complete decline.

Jainas have evoked from time immemorial an extremely fruitful activity in the field of fairy-tale novels, nouvellas and fables. They competed with Hindus and Buddhists in inventing new materials and developing the existing ones. Their writings in the field of narrative literature is so vast that it cannot be estimated at the moment. Of all the most significant books on fables and fairy-tales of India, Jainas have their own recensions of almost all of them; they are different from other versions usually on account of the fact that they express in them their own religious views. Thus there are numerous recensions of *Pañcatantra, Vetālapañcaviṁśati, Siṁhāsanadvātriṁśikā, Śukasaptati* among other works. It is quite astonishing how in different forms often the same book has come down to us. Thus we have a number of Jaina-versions of the *Pañcatantra* of the Vaiṣṇavite Brāhmaṇa Viṣṇuśarmā which appears to have been written in 300 A.D. They are, however, completely different from one another in language and contents. "One writer narrates the old stories in comfortable wealth of details, and the other writer notes down their main contents in brief sentences so that nice school pupils can understand them easily. Some one else collects only the narrative stanzas revealing approximately their awefully distorted Sanskrit and narrates the relevant stories in a popular style and in a dialect, the stories which are completely independent of the basic text....We have also scholars who write independently a new Sanskrit text after the example of an old one, and others who come down to the level of the people and translate the Sanskrit text into the mother tongue and narrate it. The Jaina-monk Ratnasundara who was a poet and a chief of a school of poets, clothes the whole work in the stanzas of the bards in order to offer it to the people in a form so that they could sing it. This is just like the bandsmen of European middle ages who popularized their farcical comedies, nouvellas and fableaus. Some one writes instantly a work for his admirers by polishing the verse and the expression and by additing a few stories, and some one else, Vaccharāja, writes also a work in his mother tongue which depends heavily upon his predecessor, but which is richer in stories. The third person renders this work into Sanskrit, and the fourth person, Meghavijaya, renders this Sanskrit-work again into a mixure of prose and poetry in Sanskrit which is similar to the original Sanskrit-text in its form. And not even hundred years have passed between Ratnasundara's work and its reworking by Meghavijaya."[39]

The consequence of this practice prevalent among Jainas since the old period to adapt community materials to the needs of their church, was that old legends and stories have been preserved for us in this way. They would certainly have been lost, if Jainas had not taken hold of them. The traces of reworking of the old models at the hands of the Jaina-writers can often be easily recognized; they often restrict themselves to giving purely superficial introduction of a conclusion or a frame story which has nothing to do with the real story. In many cases, Jainas think that the changes they made for religious reasons are justified. The motif often occurring in Jaina-stories that a prince is misled into a forest on his ride by a horse of "a wrong training", where he meets a princess and has to undergo other adventures, is obviously, as H. Jacobi has shown,[40] a substitute for the motif, otherwise preferred in the fairy-tale, of going astray while hunting. Jainas could not accept it on account of their aversion to the killing of living beings.

Jainas also dedicated themselves to the invention and development of new stories apart from the reworking of the traditional ones. There are numerous *Kathās* or *Kathānakas* of purely Jaina origin. The writers of these narrative works were not motivated to writing them by sheer pleasure of story-telling, but by certain intentions. The great Haribhadra divided the stories into four groups: into Arthakathās, i.e., stories having useful purpose (particularly of cleverness in life, learning of the statecraft, etc.), *Kāmakathās*, those dealing with love, *Dharmakathās* which are dedicated to religion and morals, and *Saṁkīrṇa-kathās* which depict similarly the attainment of the three goals of life. It is clear that the stories giving the reader rules of worldly wisdom in a pleasing form or acquainting him with different forms of enjoyment of sexual pleasure, have often to describe conditions not corresponding to the moral principles of Jaina-teachings; these, after all, proclaim renunciation of worldly things and enjoyments and conduct of a homeless, possessionless ascetic life as their ideal. The authors then did justice to the demands of religion usually in such a way that they let the hero of the story become a monk at the end of his adventure after he had enjoyed all the worldly pleasures and thus make the religious ideal come true. But the stories of Jainas are also infused with their religious views in another respect; namely by the extensive use of metempsychosis as a poetic motif in them. At the end of many stories, a wise man or a Kevalī appears who explains to the hero, why he experienced in his present life just this amount of happiness or unhappiness, and traces back all the enjoyable experiences to rewards earned in an earlier form of existence and all the sufferings to the lapses in an earlier life.

Kathās and Kathānakas exist in every form and in every size. There are, besides the brief animal fables and succintly narrated fools' tales, long stories in prose, verses or a mixture of both or all-too long stories becoming long on account of incapsulation of new stories. The most significant genre is the fairy-tale novel or the romantic epic (if it is in poetic form).

In view of the great wealth of works of this type produced by Jainas, it is impossible to discuss even the most significant of them in the limited framework of this book. I must, therefore, restrict myself to sketching briefly the contents of some of them.

The most popular theme of the epic is the story of Jīvaka (Jīvandhara). This is repeatedly treated in Sanskrit, thus in Guṇabhadra's *Uttarapurāṇa*, which originates from the 9th century A.D. But the most famous is the Tamiḷ version which is ascribed to Tiruttakadevar (Sanskrit: Śrīdakṣadeva) who lived in the 10th or 11th century. The legend knows to narrate the following about the origin of the latter. Tiruttakadevar was a member of the famous academy of Madurai. His colleagues criticized him that he was unfamiliar with Kāmaśāstra. He replied that he had not so far written anything erotic, but was capable of doing it and offered to write a work which would sufficiently depict love and enjoyment of life. He then wrote *Jīvakacintāmaṇi* treating in 18 songs, 8 marriages of Jīvaka, one marriage of Jīvaka's friend as also an allegorical union of the hero with science, earth, happiness and salvation. A blasphemer said after reading the book that Tiruttakadevar must have been a libertine and must have gathered great experience in erotic field, because he knew to describe love so true to life. But the poet who was celibate all his life long-defended himself against this attack and he took a burning iron ball in his hand for the protestation of his innocence and said, "May it burn me, if I am not pure." The ordeal testified to the correctness of his claim: the fire could do nothing to the monk so that he stood there shining, justifying his claim.

The contents of the story of Jīvaka or Jīvandhara which I have summarized from the oldest famous version in Guṇabhadra's *Uttarapurāṇa* are as under:[41]

King Satyandhara of Rājapura was robbed of his throne by his unfaithful minister Kāṣṭhāṅgāraka and he was killed. His consort Vijayā, who was pregnant at that time, succeeded in saving herself. She gave birth to a boy on a graveyard. A merchant Gandhotkara who had lost his children immediately after their birth on account of his sin in his earlier life, also came to the graveyard to bury his newborn son who had died immediately after the birth. He took the child of the queen and brought it up as his own. Since he had got a living son in place of a dead one, in accordance with a prediction once made to him, he gave the name Jīvandhara (of Jīva, life) to the boy. Jīvandhara grew together with Nandādhya, a son of his foster father and other young boys and showed early the evidence of his extraordinary intelligence and power. He then successfully encountered many adventures and married eight virgins who were chosen for him by destiny; he won each one of them on account of his mastery over a different art each time; the one by playing his lute, the other on account of his ability of taming elephants, the third by curing her from the poison of a serpent-bite, etc. A Yakṣa who had been earlier a dog helped him in his deeds. He had freed this dog from a boy who was tormenting him. Finally, he killed the wicked Kāṣṭhāṅgāraka and climbed the paternal throne. After he had ruled laudably for a long time, he renounced the world on account of Mahāvīra's sermon. He handed over his empire to his son, became Kevalī and attained Nirvāṇa.

The destinies of Jīvandhara and the important persons are all interwoven with one another by a tie of Karma and find their explanation in the past existences as consequences of their actions. Jīvandhara was separated from his relatives for 16 years, because he had kept a young swan away from its parents for 16 days. Even otherwise, the idea of reincarnation plays a great role in the story. Thus Princess Śrīcandrā becomes unconscious when she saw a pigeon-pair cooing; she was reminded of her past existence in which she herself was a pigeon and lived happily with a cock pigeon. The parents then make Śrīcandrā narrate to them all the memories of her past forms of existence and make an artist represent them through pictures. Then a dancing couple was asked by them to go to markets with the exhibition of the pictures to find out the former husband of Śrīcandrā and unite him with her. Nandādhya sees the pictures, remembers his early existence and finally marries the beautiful young lady.

Another famous dramatic epic is the *Bhavissatta-Kahā* of a Digambara merchant Dhanavāla who probably lived in the 10th century. The work is divided into 22 songs and it is written in rhymed stanzas in Apabhraṁśa-language. It represents, in fact, its literary monument.[42] The contents in short are as under: A businessman Bhavisatta in the kingdom Kurujāṅgala is abandoned on his business-journey to the golden island on a forsaken island on account of the intrigues of his step-brother Vandhuyatta. He finds there a beautiful princess under peculiar circumstances and he marries her. After the couple had lived happily for 12 years, Vandhuyatta's ships come by chance again on the island. The step-brothers reconcile and Vandhu requests Bhavisatta to return home. All arrangements of the journey are made, when our hero remembers that he had forgotten a gem; he, therefore, again leaves the ship to fetch it. On seeing this, Vandhu orders to weigh anchor and leaves the other in despair. Having reached home, Vandhu is after his sister-in-law to propose to her and lets everything being done for his marriage with her. Bhavisatta reaches his parental town in an air-car with the help of a phantom-prince. He reveals to the king the felony of his step-brother, gets back his wife and also the hand of the princess and is proclaimed crown-prince. The wicked Vandhu, on the other hand, flees to the king of Poyana. This gives an ultimatum to the prince of Kurujāṅgala in which he demands his subjugation and surrender of both the wives of Bhavisatta. The Kuru-king answers this shameless demand with the declaration of war. Bloody wars ensue, finally resulting in the fall of Poyana's ruler. Now Bhavisatta lives long happily with both his wives. Finally he is moved by a saint who tells him the story of his past existence to renounce the worldly life. He becomes monk and obtains salvation after several rebirths.

A wealth of other legends and stories are braided into what we have sketched here in brief. And again there is a partial use of the popular motif of metempsychosis.

We have a great number of fairy-tale-stories in prose and poetry; I shall mention here only Pādalipta's *Taraṅgavatī* which originates from the first century A.D. It is known to us with the name *Taraṅgalolā* which is a reworking of the original done thousand years later. E. Leumann has translated it into German under the title "Die Nonne".[43] Further, Haribhadra's *Samarāiccakahā* is quite well-known. It is a novel written in Prākṛta-prose interspersed with stanzas. W. Kirfel is translating it into German.[44] In this work, the destinies of two persons who were inimical to each other are followed through nine existences; sometimes they are father and son, sometimes husband and wife and sometimes in other relationship to each other. Each time the wicked fellow persecutes the good fellow; he also succeeds in killing him, till he finally asks for the release.

Allegories enjoy a special place among the Kathās. They are supposed to depict the truth of Jaina-faith in a metaphorical form. We come across such attempts even in the canonic literature; we find them later in various narrative works. Siddharṣi's *Upamiti-bhava-prapañca-kathā* is an allegorical novel of great style. It is a story describing human life in an allegory (completed in the year 906 A.D.). All virtues and vices figure here in the form of persons of various types and give through their combination a colourful picture of life, which is seen through the viewpoint of a Jaina-monk. H. Jacobi compares this work with Bunyan's "Pilgrim's Progress" in terms of its literary significance. It shared the great popularity with other much-read works in the circles of pious people.[45]

Jainas have also written artistic novels in Bāṇa's style. These are works in which special emphasis is laid upon the linguistic expression. They can, therefore, be regarded as "poems" (Kāvya) composed in prose or in a mixure of verses and prose in accordance with the rules of poetics. Such works are Somadeva's *Yaśastilaka* and Dhanapāla's *Tilakamañjarī* (both written around 950 A.D.).

The contents form the centre of interest in all the works of narrative literature which we have discussed so far. This is true not only of the stories written in prose, but also of those in verse, indeed even of the artistic novels. It is true that the description in many of them is elevated to poetic vivacity, but it is the thrilling action which prompts the reader to read them, it may be then that often all too many exhaustive details and getting lost in minutest particulars do not appeal to a European reader. But Jainas have also produced a number of works in which the contents completely recede behind the form. Every stanza in them is supposed to depict the whole which is complete in itself; the author tries to express in every verse something that is spiritual and extraordinary.[46] These efforts take them, of course, to all sorts of artificialities. One fact shows us to what extent this intellectual play can be carried out. Two Jaina-poets took upon themselves to carry out *Samasyāpurāṇa* on Kālidāsa's *Meghadūta* by using a line from this work in each one of the stanzas of their epics dealing with the story of Ariṣṭanemi, resp. of Pārśva and by adding the other verses. The Digambara Śrutakīrti accomplished an astonishing work of art (around 1125): every verse in his *Rāghavapāṇḍavīya* has a double meaning and treats, at the same time, the subject-matter of Rāmāyaṇa and Mahābhārata.[47]

In the field of lyrical poetry, it is to the credit of Jainas that two significant anthologies of very valuable single stanzas in Prākṛta were created in their circles, or at least, they have been collected by them in the form that is available to us today—a credit which is problematic, if it is subjected to an objective evaluation, because none of these two lyrical anthologies possess a clearly recognizable Jaina-character. "The seven hundred stanzas" (*Sattasaī*) composed in accordance with the popular pattern going under the name of Hāla Śātavāhana or Sālivāhana, who as one of the Āndhrabhṛtya-princes of the Deccan is considered by Jainas as their compatriot in faith, describe sufferings and pleasures of love in fascinating genre-imageries. According to a legend, Sarasvatī, the goddess of speech, stayed once in Śātavāhana's camp for one and half days and inspired the whole army, down to horsemen and elephantmen, to compose Prākṛta-poems, and the king selected the best 700 of them and collected them. I shall quote a couple of them:[48]

> Head-gear of the night! O Moon! Diadem of the sky!
> You who brighten the night in clear light
> Touch me with your ray-hands,
> With which you touch my lover.

"You will come," I hope, and swiftly
Half the night has elapsed,
Yet you came not, and the remaining hours
Were to me like a long year of suffering.
Hail and hearty goes my beloved from here
All people will tell me in the morning.
So grow then, grow O sweet night,
That the morning wakes us up not again.
My eyes see his shapely body,
His kisses still burning on my lips,
His heart resting in my heart, in the ears
His voice resounding, can destiny part us?

Even though the contents of most of the stanzas are erotic, the whole collection is not tuned exclusively to this tone; some stanzas celebrate Brāhmaṇic deities, others give only general sentences, like, e.g., the following one:

The mind paints on the wall of heart
The pictures of future with the brush of hope,
Yet the fate, smiling like a boy,
Wipes them out with a light hand.
So laugh that nobody ridicules you
Speak that it sounds friendly in the listener's ears,
Live your life that you get fame
And die that you are not born again.

The other collection of the stanzas to be mentioned here is the *Vajjālagga* of the Śvetāmbara Jayavallabha (period not known, in any case before 1336). Vajjālagga is more comprehensive than Hāla's work so far as it does not restrict itself to the description of love, but depicts all the three goals of life, thus also Dharma (duty, religion) and Artha (utility, life's wisdom). The contents are extraordinarily many-sided. "An interesting piece of culture moves past our eyes; first we are acquainted with the moral views of life of the Indians, their ideal of a good man with whom a wicked man is compared as something disdainful. True friendship and good conduct of life get the applause of the poet; he praises steadfastness and hearty determination; inspired verses are dedicated to an energetic man. But the success coming from outside depends upon the destiny. And with that the second goal of life of man, Artha, is introduced. The sufferings of the poor are described in bitter irony; master is the one, servant the other, thus the further verses say, but wonderful is the one, who fights for the things of his master and finds, as a courageous soldier, his death on the battlefield. Two-third of the Vajjālagga deals with Kāma. The love is sung in the verses from its most tender beginnings to the wild passion, the hot bitter sorrow of separation as also the sulking of the lovers. The verses may speak of bees sucking honey from buds of flowers, or of the elephants losing their freedom in captivity away from their herds, or of Haṁsa or blossoming jasmine. These are only imageries; their real concealed meaning is the love of a man to a woman. An Indian who thinks more harmlessly and naive in sexual things than a European, will not be surprized that verses follow which describe the anomalies of love life in a plain and clear language that is horrifying to us. In this context, the practice of courtesan should not naturally be missing. With the descriptions of the charming play of Kṛṣṇa with the cowherdesses, the poet takes us back again into the proper and serene domain and *Vajjālagga* ends with the praise of the seasons."[49]

A great number of Jaina-poets have written artistic stanzas also in Sanskrit and modern Indian languages describing the different phenomena of human life and beauties of nature among other things. We have, e.g., several collections of this type in Kannaḍa. It is also interesting to note that even women participate in this literary production; thus a nun Kaṇṭī (around 1100) is mentioned to us who became prominent on account of her adroitness in composing stanzas on various topics.

Also in the field of contemplative lyrics, the creations of Jaina-poets do not differ much from those of poets of other religions. This explains the peculiar fact that there are a number of poems of this type whose authors are considered as Jainas by Jainas, while the followers of other Indian religions maintain that they belong to their sects. This is, e.g. the case of *Kurral* of the Tamiḷian weaver Tiruvalluvar, which was placed earlier in the 8th century A.D., but now mostly in the 1st or the 2nd century A.D. *Kurral* contains 2,660 short stanzas: those on the three goals of life—virtue, utility and love. Since every reference to a dogma of a definite religion is missing, it can be understood that Vaiṣṇavas, Śaivas and Bauddhas, as also Jainas claim that the work was composed by a follower of their doctrine. B. Seshagiri Sastriar and M.S. Ramaswami Ayyangar think that there are really references in some stanzas of the *Kurral* which suggest that the author was a Jaina, but saying that he was no other than Kundakunda (Jainas call him also Elācārya) is less probable.[50]

As an example of this famous collection of *vacanas*, I am reproducing here six *vacanas* which are translated into German by our great translator Rückert:[51]

She does not bring oblations to gods,
She embraces faithfully only her husband,
She is so much blessed by the gods,
"Rain", she says, and it rains.
One whose wife is not faithful to him
Should not wander about like a lion
In front of the enemies without shame.
Whithersoever your child stretches its hand,
It tastes to you sweet like ambrosia.
One who likes the sound of flute and lute,
Has never heard his child's babble.
More than giving birth to her son,
Mother is happy then,
When she hears his fame
As man.
One who loves not, has everything for himself;
One who loves, has himself his body for others.

Even Tiruvalluvar's sister Avaiyyār is supposed to have composed similar stanzas dealing with morality.

Nāladiyār is another collection of *vacanas* of gnomic contents.[52] The following is narrated about its origin: Once 8000 Jaina-ascetics came to a Pāṇḍya-king to Madurai driven away from their homeland on account of famine and they were hospitably received by him. Once the famine was over, they got ready to return home; but the king did not want that the strangers who had lent glory to his court should go. So the monks had no other way except to leave secretly by night. When they did this, each one of them left a four-lined verse on the place on which they used to sit. The king ordered that all the palm-leaves on which these verses were written be thrown into the river Vaigai. But to the great astonishment of all, 400 of the leaves came up over water and floated towards the bank against the stream. They were collected and published under the name *Nāladiyār.* Few other stanzas are said to have reached the bank at the other places of the river and they were included in other collections.

Jainism is distinctly characterized in propagandistic didactic poems like the "Collection of Beautiful Sayings" (*Subhāṣita-sandoha*) of Digambara-monk Amitagati (written in 994 A.D.). He describes in this work the transitoriness of all sensual pleasures; describes ageing and dying; fights against the passions, anger, pride, deceipt and greed; warns against the enjoyment of alcohol, meat and honey, against gambling and visiting prostitutes; and reminds people that they should fulfil the precepts of Jainism. He enumerates all the earthly pleasures one after the other and shows that they are all worthless. The following example shows how he works here with a strong realism. As a genuine ascetic he warns against any intercourse with women:

"Women's body grows out of the substances of skin, flesh, bones, marrow, blood, chyle, fat and sperms and has nine orifices for the impurities, stools, urine, blood, tears, etc. A thoughtless person who gloats over the body of a woman which affects the three fluids (in the human body), which is comparable with a toilet and which houses worms and which is repulsive to look at, becomes a worm in the jaws of hell."

"How can a wise man serve a woman who is a treasure-house of all sufferings, a house of incivility, a bolt before a heavenly city, a path to the dwelling in the hell, a source of disgrace, an abode of imprudence, an axe for the pleasure-grove of piousness, frost for the lotus of virtues, a root of the tree of sins and ground for the creeper of deception?"[53]

Calmness of mind of peaceful penitents who have controlled their senses and who have given up all their possession is contrasted with restlessness and wretchedness of those who roam about in the world of Saṁsāra that is burnt by the flames of suffering. They climb the steep peaks of mountains not worried by the heat of the sun in summer, carrying only the "sun-umbrella of determination", and untouched by the severe frost of the winter-nights, they stay quietly on the snow-mountain in pious meditation while the avalanches thunder down and the storms uproot the forests.

Hymnody is a much-cultivated field of Jaina-poetry. Laudatory songs are dedicated in the first place to the Tīrthaṅkaras, either individually or collectively. Besides, there are also such which are dedicated to gods and holy men. The songs are extensively used in the cult; even magical influence is attributed to some of them. Almost all great Jaina-writers have composed such "Stotras". One of the most famous "Stotras" is Mānatuṅga's *Bhaktāmara-stotra*. Its date is uncertain. The tradition makes Mānatuṅga a contemporary of King Bhoja and makes him compose his work in competition with the two Brāhmaṇa-poets Mayūra and Bāṇa (both in 7th century). According to a legend, Mayūra wrote a "Century on the Sun" (*Sūrya-śataka*) by which he disposed the Sun-god mercifully towards him so that he cured him of leprosy, against which he had tried till then, but in vain, all the possible remedies. To show Caṇḍī's (Durgā) power, Bāṇa got his limbs cut-off and then wrote a "Cēntury on Caṇḍī" (*Caṇḍīśataka*); its stanzas were so powerful that his cut-off limbs grew again. To show that Jaina-saints can also accomplish such wonders, Mānatuṅga let himself be tied and imprisoned. When he then sang the *Bhaktāmara-stotra*, each one of the 42 fetters surrounding him opened up at the sound of every stanza so that he was finally freed. The commentators know to recount many cases in which individual stanzas of *Bhaktāmara-stotra* showed even later their miraculous power.

A Stotra addressed to the first Tīrthaṅkara, Ṛṣabha, is in Sanskrit, composed in Vasantatilakī-metre. I quote some of its stanzas here in the rendering of my father:

(1) Profoundly I worship Jina's feet. They spread the shine.
Which is brighter than the gem on God's head.
It destroys the night of the sins, and in the beginnings of our times,
It alone was mainstay and protector of men in the ocean of existence.

(2) Hail to the first Jina: songs sing the news of his fame:
They resound through the three worlds, charming all forever,
Songs from the mouth of heavenly rulers, of the highest gods,
The much talked of. They light the way for the others in song and word.

(3) You, whose tabouret, all heavenly gods desire to worship,
Resolutely shall I venture, O Master, although my heart is uneasy,
To praise you, to laud you, embrace you with adoration,
Like a child longing for moon's image in water.

(11) O Sublime one, one who looks at you intently engrossed in you,
His eyes do not desire to look at others.
One who has drunk once a drop shining like the moon from a sea of milk,
How would he desire to drink the bitter water from the ocean?

(22) Countless mothers give birth to countless sons
But not a single one has given to one, who resembles you.
Every heavenly space houses stars, shining and beautiful,
But only one, the Sun, rises shining brightly from the east.

(40) Where subterranean fire burns* in deep worldly ocean,
Where the monsters live and the wild shark lives,
The boatmen, who remember your teachings, travel without fear,
Even if their boat were to sway on the mountains moved by waves.

(42) Even if the head and the limbs of a man are forged in chains,
Even if his feet are squeezed in thousand strong fetters,
He will be free of fetters, the chains will fall,
When he remembers the holy magic word of your lofty name.

3. DRAMA

Indians consider drama as the peak of their literature, because Epic and Lyric are combined in it into an artistic unity with a mimic depiction. Jaina-poets have also been active in this field.[54] Primarily, holy legends were

*According to an Indian concept, Vaḍavā-fire burns on the bottom of the ocean.

used as material. So also, Rāma's legend was treated by Rāmacandra, a pupil of Hemacandra, in his *Raghuvilāsa*, then by Hastimalla in his *Maithilīkalyāṇa*, the story of Jīvaka by Haricandra in *Jīvandharanāṭaka*, etc. Even historical material has found its dramatic form; thus the Śvetāmbara Jayasiṁha treats in his *Hammīra-mada-mardana* ("The destruction of Hammīra's pride") how a Muslim Amīr "Mīlacchīkāra" was driven away by the Cālukya king Vīradhavala of Ḍholkā. The name Mīlacchī-kāra is a distortation of Arabic "mīr-shikār", i.e., hunter. This title was conferred on the later Sultan Shamsuddin Iltutmish (Altamsh) by his predecessor.

Yaśaḥpāla's *Moharāja-parājaya*, i.e., "Defeat of King Delusion" is an allegorical drama from the end of 12th century. It plays in Anhilvāḍa, and its theme is king Kumārapāla's conversion at the hands of the great Hemacandra. This is presented symbolically as a victory against King Delusion (Moha). Kumārapāla marries Kṛpāsundarī (sympathy), the daughter of King Vivekacandra (Moon of discernment). He was driven away on account of Moha from his residence Janamanovṛtti (Human heart), but returns triumphantly to it after Moha's defeat.

Sten Konow[55] mentions few more allegorical dramas of different authors; among them, there is play of contemporary Padmarāja Paṇḍita. This was written on the occasion of the dedication of the painting of the Tīrthaṅkara Śānti in Mysore in 1897.

4. DAILY LITERATURE

Daily literature in the present expansion originated in India as in other countries only after the introduction of printing press and perfection of the means of transport. Beginnings of such might have been there even earlier to a moderate extent, although very little of it has come down to us, because what was done from the time and for the time, particularly, when it was propagated in very few handwritten copies had soon to fall completely into oblivion, only because it was not any more sufficiently interesting to prompt someone to preserve it, not to speak of copying it again.

The precursor of the modern newspaper correspondence can be seen in the so-called Vijñaptis. These are the letters written by Jainas to their spiritual superiors on the last day of the Paryuṣaṇa-week. As it is known, Jainas are not supposed to carry over any dispute beyond this last day of the year and let go any sin of the last year unatoned. They, therefore, send letters outside to persons with whom they have a dispute, to reconcile with them, and they write to their Guru letters in which they confess their sins in order to get pardon. In the past, the Vijñaptis sent to the Guru often became detailed reports on the events of the last period. Occasionally they became small literary works which were composed in artistic Sanskrit. Thus e.g. the poems *Indu-dūta* and *Ceṭo-dūta* composed in the imitation of Kālidāsa's *Meghadūta* had been originally Vijñaptis. The Vijñaptis of the monks were often considerably lengthy; there are thus some which occupy a length of almost 60 feet. They are occasionally embellished by nice imageries which, of course (like in the modern Indian books), often do not have any connection to the contents, like the description of mosques, acrobats, etc. Often the Vijñaptis are of historical interest as authentic documents, and that is why, the Jaina-Ātmānanda-Sabhā has recently got a few of them published in the collection *Itihāsamālā*. Such a Vijñapti describes, e.g. the journey of a monk in the 15th century of Kāṅgrā, a city in the Pañjāb situated quite in the north close to the Himālayas.[56]

The Jaina-literature of the day in this period is very significant, and on account of its size it can hardly be overlooked. A number of newspapers and periodicals in various languages are trying to take notice of its interests. I am mentioning here only the most important. Digambaras are running a number of papers: the monthly *Digambara Jain* appearing in Surat with essays in several languages, the *Hindi Jain Gazette*, the *Jain Mitra* and the women's periodical *Jain Nārī Hitkārī*. The official organ representing the interests of Śvetāmbaras is the *Śrī Jain Śvetāmbara Kānpharans Herald* (Conference Herald) which contains essays mostly in Gujarātī; other papers are *Jain Shāsan* published in Banāras and the *Jain Dharm Prakāsh*. Sthānakavāsīs publish a *Conference Prakāsh* and a monthly *Jain Hitecchi*. The Central Jain Library in Arrah which wishes to be the centre of the endeavours of all the trends, publishes a monthly *Jaina Siddhānta Bhāskara* in the Hindi language in Calcutta. The All India Jaina Association publishes an English monthly *Jaina Gazette* in Madrās, etc.

Besides these writings appearing periodically, a large number of pamphlets, essays and articles are published every year in different parts of India. They give their views on topical problems and elucidate them from the Jaina point of view.

III

Inscriptions

Inscriptions have a special place in Jaina-writings because these monuments of the past inscribed in stone and bronze reflect, at the same time, the total literary creation in a succint form. They report on the persons and events of ephemeral and historical significance in Sanskrit, in Prākṛta and different Aryan and Dravidian local languages; they bequeath to us legends and poems in the most simple, as well as in the artistic style. The fact that even epics and panegyric dramas have been inscribed on stone can give us an idea of the diversity of the contents of the inscriptions!

Most of the inscriptions are found near the cult-idols, temples and shrines. They bequeath to the posterity the dates of presentations, the names of the pious donors, their family-tree and deeds. Others are dedicated to the memories of the deceased princes and great men, distinguished women, saints, ascetics and nuns or they eternalize events which were considered as important enough to be communicated to the future generations.

The form in which the inscriptions speak to us is very different; some of them are composed in a brief and matter-of-fact manner, in others, the language is elevated to a poetic height and flaunts the ornamental means of speech which are taught by the poetics.

Jaina-inscriptions begin mostly with a word of benediction like "Om! Svasti! Śrī!", with a laudation of the Jaina-doctrine or with the words of respect to the Tīrthaṅkaras or one of them. Again similar forms or the pious wish "May the whole world be blessed!" conclude the inscription. Sometimes there is also a curse spoken against the one, who, e.g. would illegally appropriate a land that is donoted to the temple; one such culprit was cursed: "May he be born again as a worm for 60,000 years."

Many inscriptions are characterized by "Praśastis" (eulogies) in which distinguished men or women are glorified in an exuberant manner. These Praśastis are composed in a excessively artistic language and regale in a genuinely oriental manner in imageries and similes. Thus it is said of a king that he was a head-jewel of his dynasty, an earring of the Goddess of Speech, a moon which swells the waters of the ocean of Jaina-doctrine, a wish-cow (of generosity) for the poets, a ravaging fire for his opponents; it is said of a princess that she was a giver of happiness like Lakṣmī, a mine of gem of excellence, a victory-banner of the god of love, a mad elephant for the other wives of her husband, and it is said of an ascetic that his feet were worshipped even by gods, he turned the world into a blessed place of pilgrimage by his saintliness, his speech was pleasant to the ears like fanning with yak-fans and his fame striving heavenwards intermingles with the rays of the moon.

Such Praśastis are often found as epitaphs at the places which enclose the mortal remains of pious laymen or ascetics, particularly of those who voluntarily died from starvation. However, many epitaphs do without the many embellishing attributes and only inform that the monk X or the nun Y exchanged their abode on the earth with the heaven.

Many epitaphs have particularly a nice effect in their dignified simplicity when general thoughts on the ephemerality of all mundanes are expressed in them in a poetic form. As an example, let us conclude with the epitaph of Monk Nandīsena in Śravaṇa Beḷgoḷa:

"Quickly evanescing like a rainbow, like a lightning and like a dew-cloud,
The present of beauty and riches and of the pleasure and might, who is sure of it?
Should I—striving for the highest—adhere to the world? Speaking thus, the penitent Nandīsena became monk
And attained heaven as the highest reward of virtue."

REFERENCES

1. H. Jacobi, "Was it Sanskrit?" in *"Scientia"*, Vol. XIV, 7th year, 1913, p. 272 f.
2. *Journ. of the American Oriental Society*, Vol. XXXII, p. 419.
3. Wackernagel, *Altindische Grammatik*, I, p. XIX.
4. Banarsi Das Jain, *Ardha-Māgadhī Reader*, Lahore, 1923, p. XI.
5. R. Pischel, *Grammatik der Prakṛta-Sprachen*, Strassbourg, 1900, p. 19 f.
6. H. Jacobi, "Bhavisatta Kaha," *Abh. Kgl. Bayer. Akademie Phil. Klasse*, XXIX, 4, Munich, 1918, p. *86.
7. H. Jacobi, *Archiv für Religionswissenschaft*, XVIII, 1915, p. 275.
8. Weber, *Indische Studien*, 16, p. 215 f.
9. According to R.G. Bhandarkar, *Report*, 1883/84, p. 129, the Council of Valabhī met after the one of Maṭhurā; then the dates have to be exchanged.
10. Bhandarkar, *ibid.*, p. 125. According to a Digambara-tradition reported by J.L. Jaini, *Jaina Law*, p. 3, the canon is said to have been written down after 49 Vikrama (8 A.D.).
11. Weber, *Indische Studien*, 16, p. 349.
12. Compare with this Leumann *ZDMG*, 46, 581 ff.; Charpentier in the introduction to his edition in *Archives d'Etudes Orientales*, Vol. 18, 1/2; Schubring, *Orientalische Literaturzeitung*, 1924, column 483 ff.
13. Nahar and Ghosh give a list of 36 Jaina-Upaniṣads in *Epitome of J.*, Ap., p. XXXVIII. The Sanskrit-forms of the Prākṛta-titles of many works of the canon are uncertain; they are partially given by Jainas in a different way. Even the order in which the holy scriptures are listed is at times different; thus Śvetāmbaras let the Mūla-sūtras, Cheda-sūtras, Prakīrṇas, the two

Sūtras come in order after the Aṅgas and Upāṅgas. The following order is common among Sthānakavāsis: 11 Aṅgas, 12 Upāṅgas, 4 Mūla-sūtras (Uttarādhyayana, Daśavaikālīka, Aṇuyogadāra, Nandī), 4 Cheda-sūtras (1, 3, 4, 5) and as an individual work Avaśyaka-sūtra.

14. See the list in H. Jacobi, *The Kalpasūtra of Bhadrabāhu*, p. 12.
15. See Weber, *Indische Studien*, 16, p. 344, 354; V. Glasenapp, *Die Lehre vom Karman*, p. 9 f.
16. Weber, *Indische Studien*, 16, p. 219.
17. Jaina Sūtras, *SBE* I, p. XXXIX.
18. Cf. Sakalakīrti's *Tattvārthasāradīpaka*, 1st Chap. (see R.G. Bhandarkar, *Report of the Search for Sanskrit* Mss. 1883/84, p. 106 ff., 393 ff.); Nemicandra's *Gommaṭasāra*, Jīva-kāṇḍa, 348 ff. (*Jaina Gazette*, 1905, p. 133 f. and J.L. Jaini, *Outlines of J.*, p. 135).
19. J.N. Farquhar, *Outlines of the Religious Literature of India*, p. 219.
20. *ZDMG*, 60, 1906, p. 287 ff. Digambaras call Umāsvāti "Umāsvāmī" and consider that he is a pupil of Kundakunda. According to them, he was born in 714 after Vīra. The Digambara-version of Tattv. is different from the one of Śvetāmbaras in many respects (comp. the summary in the appendix of J.L. Jaini's translation, p. 204 ff.).
21. Peter Peterson, *Report of Operations in Search of Sanskrit Mss. in the Bombay Circle*, Bombay, 1883, p. 67.
22. H. Jacobi in the introduction of his edition of *Samarāiccakahā*.
23. Quoted in Mādhava's '*Sarvadarśana-saṅgraha* (p. 199 of the Pune ed.); translated by Paul Deussen, *Allg. Geschichte der Philosophie*, I-3, p. 399.
24. *WZKM*, 2, 1886, p. 24.
25. Sushil Kumar De, *Studies in the History of Sanskrit Poetics*, London, 1923, Vol. I, p. 123, 170, 202, 205, 208, 210, 284, 297.
26. P.C. Nahar, *A Note on the Jaina Classical Sanskrit Literature* (Second Oriental Conference, Calcutta, 1922), p. 9.
27. R. Simon, *Zeitschr. f. Indologie* 2. 1923, p. 160.
28. B. Seshagiri Rao, *Andhra Karnata J.*, p. 98.
29. The collected work "Jain Law" published in Delhi in 1923 contains excerpts concerning the law of inheritance from these works as also from Indranandi's *Jina-Saṁhitā*, Somasena's *Trivaṇācāra* and Jinasena's *Ādipurāṇa*.
30. P. 151, 174 of the Ahmedābād edition, 1906.
31. W. Kirfel, *Kosmographie der Inder*, p. 208 mentions a number of works of this type.
32. Compare E. Leumann, *Beziehungen der Jaina-Literatur zu anderen Literaturkreisen Indiens,"* III (Actes du VIe Congr. des Orientalistes III, 2, pp. 469-485, Leiden, 1885) on Jaina-Astronomy.

33. Mahāvīrācārya's *Gaṇitasārasaṅgraha*, ed. and translated by M. Rangācārya, Madras, 1912—On Jaina-Mathematics comp. also "Brief statement of 21 kinds of numbers in J.L. Jaini's "*Jaina Gem Dictionary*," 140 ff.
34. *Paramāṇukhaṇḍa-śattriṁśikā, Pudgala-ś°, Nigoḍa-ś°* (appeared as Vol. 13 of the Śrī-Ātmānanda-Grantharatnamālā).
35. Guérinot, "La doctrine des étres vivants ,dans la religion Jaina" (*Rev. de l'histoire des Religions*, 47, Paris, 1903).
36. Rice, *History of Kanarese Literature*, p. 37, 45—The fame of Pūjyapāda is alive even today among Jainas, and the advertisement-section of the Jaina-periodicals have often advertisements of the physicians who treat the patients according to his precepts or produce medicines according to his recipes. Thus it is said in *Jaina-Gazette*, XX, No. 1: "Every medicine is prepared scrupulously in accordance with the instructions laid down by Śrī Pūjya Pāda Swāmi. Our preparations are so clean that they are useful to both laymen and monks."
37. Brief information on architecture in *Ādīpurāṇa* 16, 162 ff.
38. G. Bühler, *Leben Hemacandras*, p. 5.
39. Joh. Hertel, *Das Pañcatantra*, Leipzig 1914, p. VII f.
40. H. Jacobi, Erzählungen in Māhārāṣṭrī, p. XIX.
41. Chap. 75, 183 ff. of "Triṣaṣṭilakṣaṇa-mahāpurāṇa"; English transl. by E. Hultzsch in *Quarterly Journal of the Mythic Society*, XII, 317-438.
42. Textual edition with an introduction by H. Jacobi, *Abh. Bayer. Akademie, Philos. Kl.*, XXIX, 4, Munich, 1918.
43. Leumann's "Nonne" appeared at first in the *Zeitschr. für Buddhismus*, III, 193 ff., Munich, 1921 later also in book-form.
44. Announced since 1913 by Georg Müller Verlag, Munich.
45. *Jaina Gazette*, X, 1914, p. 146. German transl. by W. Kirfel, Leipzig, 1924.
46. Cf. the characteristic of "Geist und Wesen der indischen Kunstdichtung" in my edition of *Indische Liebeslyrik in Ubersetzungen von Fr. Rückert*, Munich, 1921.
47. Cf. Rice, *Epigr. Carnatica*, II, note on page 54 on other works of this type.
48. Edition of Albrecht Weber, *Abhdlg. f. d. Kunde des Morgenlandes*, V, No. 3 and in improved form, *ibid.*, VII, No. 4, Leipzig, 1876 and 1881. The translated stanzas in both the editions have the following numbers: 1. I, II, 16; 2. II, 385; 3. I, II, 46; 4. I, 135, II, 132; 5. II, 658; 6. II, 818. O. v. Glasenapp has poetically rendered the further stanzas of Hāla in *Indische Gedichte aus vier Jahrtausenden*, Berlin, 1925, pp. 71-75.
49. Julius Laber, *Über das Vajjālaggam des Jayavallabha*, Leipzig, 1913.
50. *South Indian J.*, p. 41 f.
51. F. Rückert in *Weihnachtsbaum für arme Kinder. 6. Christbescherung.*

von Friedrich Hofmann. Hildburghausen, 1847, p. 153 f. Reprinted in L. Hirschberg's *Rückert-Nachlese*, Weimar, 1911, II, p. 346 f.

52. *Nāladiyār with Introd., Transl. and Notes by G.U. Pope*, Oxford 1893.
53. Sanskrit and German by Richard Schmidt, *ZDMG*, 59 and 61, 1905 and 1907, stanzas VI, 20, 24.
54. Comp. E. Hultzsch, "Neue Sanskritdramen" in *Nachrichten der K. Ges. d. Wiss. zu Göttingen, Phil. Kl.*, 1921, p. 36 f.
55. Sten Konow, *Das indische Drama*, Berlin, 1920, p. 95 f.
56. *Ind. Antq.*, 1917, p. 276.

SECTION IV

The Doctrine

PRELIMINARY REMARKS

The Jaina-doctrine, as far as it is known to us from its authoritative works, is different from those of the most of other religions in one very important point: it has apparently undergone no real development. The religion of the Vedas and the Upaniṣads got in Hinduism quite a changed form under the influence of the revelations of the Kali-era, of the Purāṇas, Āgamas and Tantras; new Sūtras emerged in Buddhism and proclaimed the doctrine of salvation of the "Great Vehicle" by which the proclamations of Buddha contained in the Tripiṭaka are said to have been supplemented and perfected; the written word of God experienced in the Catholic Christianity its successive adaptation to the needs of the believers by the Church tradition and Church rules of faith,—but the dogma has remained the same in Jainism in all the periods. The concepts which are peculiar to the fully developed system of today are found in all that is essential in them even in the oldest literary documents which give us information on the views of Jainas. This fact which all the researchers in this field have noticed can be explained only with a great difficulty. Jainas themselves see in it, of course, an evidence of the unsurpassability of their doctrine which alone defied the changes of times in contrast to others, and of the accuracy of the tradition which preserved purely and unsullied the heritage that has come down from the tradition.

The solution of the problem is more difficult for us. We can only presume that the growth and development of the dogma was carried out in a period from which we do not possess any documents, that it was essentially concluded already in the oldest writings which have come down to us. Since both the creeds of Śvetāmbaras and Digambaras completely concur with each other in all the major points of the system, it must be considered as certain that the doctrine existed essentially in the form as it is before us today before the great schism which took place at the beginning of the Christian era. But we can go further with H. Jacobi[1] and assert that very little has changed in the doctrine since the period of Bhadrabāhu (around 300 B.C.), because Śvetāmbaras quote him as an author of many authorative works and he is also greatly respected by Digambaras. It cannot be decided whether and how far the doctrine of Bhadrabāhu has developed beyond Mahāvīra; the reason against it cannot be that the main aspects of the dogma were already taught by Mahāvīra in a similar form. I, therefore, feel that there is no reason to believe that drastic changes have taken place in the dogma so that the Jaina-tradition according to which the system was said to have been proclaimed by Mahāvīra, can be acknowledged as rightfully existing. When the tradition further maintains that Mahāvīra has not invented the doctrine and that it was taken over from Pārśva who lived 250 years before him and altered it according to the dictates of the time, it does not have any positive proof, but the probability speaks for the fact that something real is at the base of this view. The structure of the doctrine itself supports in any case this presumption, because the ancient character of its basic thought—that the Karma was caused in the soul by material particles—justifies the hypothesis that it goes back to 8th/9th century B.C. One may, therefore, presume that the doctrine we are discussing in the following pages was put up in its essence already around 800 B.C. and that it existed approximately at the beginning of the Christian era in the present form and that it was developed and formulated anew in details in the almost two millenniums, but did not undergo drastic changes.[2]

The cause of this remarkable phenomenon is to be sought in the structure of the doctrine itself. Thus H. Jacobi writes, "I think, the reason for the conservation of the old doctrine is that its ideas and terms were incommensurable with those of the later philosophy, and thus they could not be influenced by the latter. The doctrine was fossilized to some extent and was handed over unchanged from generation to generation in *the same* condition. Jaina-philosophy is like a dead language: it is learnt and used, but it cannot be developed further."

The inflexible character of the Jaina-doctrine is extremely advantageous for its description. It enables us to make its sketch in its all aspects which applies in the same manner to Jainism of the past as well as of the present in all its salient features, and nothing of its importance is lost by the fact that its individual aspects are written in somewhat different form by the writers of different periods, localities and trends.

The description in the following pages encompassing uniformly all the fields of Jaina-dogmatism claims that it is a reproduction of the main teachings of the Jainas of today which is directly based on their sources. As it can be seen from the bibliography, Śvetāmbara as well as Digambara works of the past and the present are used for this. The fact that a great deal of more sources of Śvetāmbaras were available to me, was the reason that the description is based primarily on the views of Śvetāmbaras, and the differences of those "clothed in air", as far as they are known to me, are secondarily mentioned.

Umāsvāti's *Tattvārthādhigama-sūtra* and its translation by H. Jacobi was prominently useful for my depiction; in the reproduction of the technical terminologies, I have concurred, as far as possible, with Jacobi. The chapters "Metaphysics" and "Ethics" are based partially on the results of my dissertation *Die Lehre vom Karman in der Philosophie der Jainas* which has appeared in 1915; I have included a few chapters of this work which is now out of print for years, partially in a concise form and after reworking on them; the reader may refer to this work for many details which could have been disregarded.[3] The chapter "Cosmology" endorses partially the views expressed by W. Kirfel in his comprehensive book *Die Kosmographie der Inder*, but there was an opportunity to correct a few details and supplement them. The depiction of the world history and hagiography is new; this had never been done so far in a perfect manner; it is particularly based on Vinayavijaya's *Lokaprakāśa* and Hemacandra's *Triṣaṣṭi-śalākā-puruṣa-carita*, as well as a number of other works; these will be mentioned in the references, whenever the occasion demands.

I

Epistemology

1. SOURCES OF KNOWLEDGE

It is the aim and goal of all philosophy, Jaiṇas teach, to impart knowledge which teaches us to know our true position in the midst of the world affairs and thereby enables us to attain what is good for us and to avoid what is bad. The presupposition for attaining this knowledge is an examination of the means which help us in achieving it. Right knowledge can be obtained by direct or by indirect means.[4]

Knowledge can be directly obtained (pratyakṣa) with the help of five senses and the organ of thinking, or without the use of these media with the help of soul itself by virtue of its inherent transcendental powers. The first type of obtaining knowledge is found among all beings in the world, the latter only among the especially chosen ones among them (gods, ascetics), as also among Siddhas, i.e. among the perfect ones who are elevated above all that is mundane.

One gets indirect knowledge (parokṣa), 1. through memory (Smṛti), 2. through cognition (Pratyabhijñāna), 3. through inference (Anumāna) with the help of syllogism of five parts like the following: There is fire on the mountain because the mountain smokes, for where there is smoke, there is fire, as in the kitchen; there is smoke on the mountain, therefore, there is fire,[5] 4. with the help of believable communication (Āgama) of persons or writings.

A perfect and complete knowledge of all things is possible only for the omniscient (Kevalī), i.e. for the one whose soul can comprehend everything directly by completely detaching itself from all the material factors which restrict it and by being free from external aids. The only source of everything for all other beings, what remains hidden from their organs of sense and from their reflective thinking, is what an omniscient has communicated to them. As at present there are no omniscient persons in our part of the world who are able to give a solution to the riddle of the world and life, one has to depend upon what the omniscient have proclaimed in the earlier period. Their teachings are available in the holy scriptures of Jainism which are to be considered as the highest authority in all the questions of the *weltanschauung.* These Āgamas are, thus, not the timeless-eternal revelations of a personal or an impersonal being which creates, rules and destroys the world, but the communications of perfect masters who have removed on this earth all the ignorance which concealed their spirit by the purity of their life. The canonic texts are thus, at the same time, documents of knowledge whose authority is based on the moral perfection of its creators, records whose absolute correctness could be examined and confirmed by every being who is led to an equally high stage of perfection by its spiritual development.

The fact that Jainas consider the views of the omniscient of the earlier periods which have come down to them through centuries as the source of their doctrine, gives their philosophy a dogmatic character. All precepts given in the holy scriptures are regarded as absolute truths which cannot be shaken. Therefore what philosophy can only do is to summarize, explain, and if possible supplement the dictums of the omniscient masters that have come down to us.

After all, since the validity of the whole Jaina-doctrine is based on the presumption that there were omniscient men, this point of their dogmatism has ever been the goal of the violent attacks of the Brāhmaṇic philosophers. Jainas have tried with keen perception to ward them off and to establish their thesis. Starting from the concept that soul can be known as such, they try to show that the capability of knowledge has to be universal as soon as the restrictive hindrances, like material veils, infatuation and passion fall away. For how could the fire stop to burn the fuel, if there were nothing to stop it?

2. ONTOLOGY AND DIALECTICS

Two ontological concepts oppose each other in Indian philosophy, in fact, in philosophy in general: for the one, only the persistent substance is true and all the changes taking place in it are only unimportant phenomena which do not touch the very essence of the substance. The other doctrine says: the qualities we perceive in a thing are the only real ones; there is no substance at their basis which remains unchanged, for nothing is lasting in the world, everything is ephemeral and therefore, unreal.

The first of these two views (reminding us of the one of Parmenides) is that of the Upaniṣads and of the Vedānta, the philosophy of the orthodox Brahmanism based on them. It is most clearly characterized in the famous passage of the *Chāndogya Upaniṣad* VI.1.3, where Āruṇi says to his son Śvetaketu:

"My dear, as by one clod of clay all that is made of clay is known, the difference being only a name, arising from speech, but the truth being that all is clay—thus, my dear, is this doctrine."

Buddha's doctrine (which could be regarded as

parallel to the one of Heraclitus, albeit with some restriction) is exactly contrary. For him, there is no lasting being, but only a becoming, there is no entity, but only elements of existence which have come together at the same time.

The conversation between the nun Vajirā and Māra, the evil, given in *Saṁyutta Nikāya* 5.10 gives a clear depiction of these views. When Māra asks the pious woman, to frighten her, from where the being comes and where it goes, she answers:

"What do you understand by 'being'? Māra, you are mistaken! There is only a bundle of forms, there is no being. For, as one uses the word 'vehicle' where certain parts are bound together to a whole, one uses the word 'being' where the five groups of the elements of corporeal-spiritual being have been combined."

Jainism tries to mediate between the views of Vedānta and Buddhism; it considers that both are to certain extent correct, but too one-sided in their extreme exaggeration, and therefore insufficient. It, therefore, puts up its doctrine of relative pluralism (Anekāntavāda) against the two by teaching that there is something that is lasting and something that is inconstant in every being. Thus, e.g. the material atoms are inperishable in a pot of which it consists; on the other hand, its form, its colour and its other qualities come and go. All utterances made on something have, of course, not an absolute value, but only a relative one and are, therefore, valid only under certain conditions and with certain restrictions in this way of observation which makes the things, which are generally experienced, the object of its consideration.

The number of points of views from which a thing is seen is very high. Jainas distinguish seven main types of these, the so-called "Nayas", i.e. types to observe and illustrate a thing by emphasizing one side of a thing without taking into consideration the others. The first four refer to the ideas, the last three to the words:

1. Naigama-naya observes an object without making any difference between its general and specific qualities; thus in a mango, it is not considered what is characteristic only for it, but also what it has in common with other fruits.
2. Saṅgraha-naya considers only the general qualities of a thing and not the specific ones.
3. Vyavahāra-naya considers only the specific qualities of an object without bothering about its general qualities.
4. Ṛjusūtra-naya looks at a thing as it is in that particular moment without taking into consideration the condition in which it was and the condition it will have in future.
5. Sāmprata-naya regards in a word only its conventional meaning, without considering its derivative (the words jīva, ātmā and prāṇa are used as synonymous although their etymological derivation is different).
6. Samabhirūḍha-naya distinguishes synonymous words exactly according to their etymological derivation.
7. Evambhūta-naya looks at a word by taking into consideration also the qualities demanded by the derivations appearing in an object which the word denotes, e.g. in the god Śakra (Indra), the power (Śakti) from which his name is supposed to have been derived.

One comes to a deceptive conclusion by wrong application of each of these Nayas. According to Jainas, the one-sided emphasis of one of these seven points of view, must have resulted in the establishment of different wrong philosophical systems.* On the other hand,

*Thus Nyāya-Vaiśeṣika system represents a one-sided exposition of the first, Vedānta the one of the second, materialism the one of the third and Buddhism the one of the fourth Naya.

Jainism keeps itself free from all the false unilateralism, combining all seven Nayas correctly with one another and stands before us as the truth which combines in itself everything which the other systems contain as a partial truth.

The doctrine that an object can be observed from different points of view and that man comes to different utterances on it, is characteristically expressed in the so-called "Syādvāda", the real dialectical method of Jainas. They consider it to be so greatly important that they name their whole religious and philosophical system after it.

According to Syādvāda, there are seven types of utterances which can be made:

1. syād asti "something is"—from one point of view; e.g. there is a pot.
2. syād nāsti "something is not"—from the other point of view; e.g. there is no pot.
3. syād asti ca nāsti ca "something is and is not"—from the third point of view.
4. syād avaktavyam "something is indescribable"—from the fourth point of view.
5. syad asti cāvaktavyam "something is and is indescribable"—from the fifth point of view.
6. syād nāsti cāvaktavyam "something is not and is indescribable"—from the sixth point of view.
7. syād asti ca nāsti cāvaktavyam "something is and is not and is indescribable"—from the seventh point of view.

The word syād with which each of these utterances begins means really "it would like to be" and should express the relativity of the judgement. It stands thus for "kiṁcit" as Jainas say; this can be rendered somewhat by "in certain sense". Syādvāda is supposed to show that the contradictory utterances on something can be correct at the same time, that it depends everywhere upon the point of view. Thus it appears, e.g. at the outset to be ruled out that a man can be at the same time father and son. But this is completely in the realm of possibility that he is father in relationship to A and son in relationship to B. Jainas try to show with the help of Syādvāda that no affirmative or negative judgement is absolute and that it is only in a limited sense correct, because it depends upon the connection in which it is used with respect to something different.[6]

3. TRUTH AND TRANSMISSION OF TRUTH

All philosophical systems, according to Jainas, contain a grain of truth; the arbitrary manner in which they treat what is true in them, and the circumstance that they mix this with all sorts of wrong things comes in their way in reaching complete knowledge. This is rather found only in Jainism because this alone:

1. emanated from the omniscient masters,
2. was never refuted in disputations, because it is irrefutable,
3. cannot be changed or attained by any type of knowledge. may it be indirect or direct, by any sort of perception, inference or tradition,
4. explains all things sufficiently according to their true nature,
5. promotes beings of all types, from gods down to plants and elementary beings morally and does good to them,
6. is so powerful that it is able to destroy everything that is false.

Jainism alone, by virtue of its characteristics, is capable of explaining the riddles of the world and life satisfactorily and to redeem the souls roaming about in the cycle of the eternal change of existence. The diligent study of wise doctrines and the strict observance of certain ethical precepts makes the one *siddha* attain finally the possession of the three gems (Triratna); they are the highest which the world has to show, in its possession of the right knowledge, right faith and right conduct of life.

The form in which Jaina-doctrine is propagated by its prophets is different depending upon the type and the occasion, depends also obviously upon the quality of the teacher as also the capacity of understanding of the listeners and readers. While a simple monk who wants to influence laymen who are philosophically less educated, in the streets of a town or in a community house, speaks in a popular tone and interweaves educative legends and absorbing anecdotes, the master experienced in all the branches of logic and dialectics proceeds with the whole outfit of the Indian scholasticism, when he systematically presents the Jaina-dogma in the battle of words which are so popular in India, justifies them philosophically and defends them against the opposite views. Writings devoted to the presentation of Jainism follow this example; even here, we have the whole scale of works of different types, from the popular treatises to the profound, scientific textbooks. But in spite of the great divergence according to form and expression which exists between the individual works, corresponding to their stipulation, most of them follow the same pattern when they deal with the Jaina-dogmas in their context. At first the basic truths are discussed and they are again divided in subclasses. Then the things in narrower or larger connection are taken into consideration for explanation when an occasion demands it. Further, a detailed treatment of every singularity according to definite, schematically determined points of view which explain and define all that is said, facilitates the understanding. Four of these points of view are: name (Nāma), presentation (Sthāpanā), substance (Dravya) and accidence (Bhāva). Thus the soul (Jīva), e.g. is looked at from the following points of view: Nāma-jīva what is called soul, Sthāpanā-jīva what is figuratively presented or reproduced as soul, Dravya-jīva is the soul as such, without its alterable circumstances, Bhāva-jīva is the soul with respect to its relevant condition. Another way of observation has the following six points of view at its basis: concept, dependence, reason of origin, locality, duration and division. H. Jacobi says on this: "This reminds us of 'quis, quid, ubi, quibus, auxiliis, cur, quomodo, quando'. Thus it is asked, e.g., what is right belief, to whom does it apply, how does it originate, where is it localized, how long does it last, what subdivision it has."[7] In the mean time, there is also the mention of eight points of view, which are in any case contained in those which are already mentioned above: existence, number, place, extension, duration, interruption, condition, more or less.

Howsoever appropriate the usual way of presentation among Jaina-philosophers may be for the Indian readers, it causes a number of difficulties for a Westerner who is not at home with the Indian way of thinking. Attempt made in the following to reproduce the important purport of the textbooks of Jaina-dogmatism which are authoritative today does not adhere, for this reason, slavishly to the order of the contents of the curriculam followed by the Indian authors, but endeavours to bring it in a form which would correspond more to the European needs. The principle followed in every presentation of the Jaina-philosophy to introduce the concepts in a row and explain them and then divide them into subclasses is on the other hand to be adhered to, howsoever it may appear to be so dry; for we are not dealing here with an accidental form of thinking, but the very spirit of Jaina-philosophy is clearly explained here, the spirit of all comprehensive taxonomy which tries to understand, divide and analyse conceptually all the phenomena in this world and in the world beyond the scope of human experience.

II

Metaphysics

1. THE BASIC TRUTHS

The complete contents of Jaina-doctrine are summarized by the dogmatists in 7 terms; they are called the basic truths (Tattva or Padārtha). They are:

1. Jīva, the soul
2. Ajīva, the inanimate
3. Āsrava, influx
4. Bandha, bondage
5. Saṁvara, warding off
6. Nirjarā, wearing away or wiping out
7. Mokṣa, salvation

The seven basic truths were enumerated by Digambaras in this way; Śvetāmbaras postulate, on the other hand, 9 basic truths, viz. Puṇya (reward) and Pāpa (sin) besides those which are mentioned above; they have the 3rd and the 4th position among them. Digambaras do not count these two terms as special categories, but consider that they are included in the following:

The nature of the individual basic truths will emerge from the detailed presentation of Jaina-metaphysics and ethics attempted in the following. But for the sake of clarity and to show the connection between the individual basic truths, let us give here first a brief explanation which should give at the same time an insight into the disposition and manner of presentation of the most of Jaina-scriptures.

There are in the world two groups of eternal and imperishable entities: 1. the animate (Jīva), i.e. the endlessly many, immaterial souls gifted with consciousness; and 2. the inanimate (Ajīva), i.e. the substances space, motion and obstruction (i.e. the media of movement and rest), time and material objects.

The souls lose the perfection that is peculiar to them under the influence of the inanimate, viz. material objects and get a number of new qualities which are alien to their true nature; a matter flows into them (Āsrava) for various reasons and is combined with them (Bandha).

The harmful influx of materal objects determining the destiny and the rebirth of a soul can be fought with one's own moral behaviour; entry of new matter into the soul can be obstructed (Saṁvara) and those which are already contained in it can be wiped out (Nirjarā). When the soul is completely liberated from the influx of the matter, then the final goal of all the earthly endeavours, i.e. salvation (Mokṣa) has been reached.

2. SUBSTANCES

Substances (Dravya) are eternal entities which have certain, unalterable qualities and in which the accidental, alterable conditions (Paryāya) of different types can be developed. Substances are divided into two groups: in animate (Jīva) and inanimate (Ajīva).

(1) Jīva, the Soul

Souls are uncreated, imperishable, immaterial, knowing, active and acceptable entities and are present in endlessly great or endless numbers. Every soul is an individual entity, independent of the others, but can get in touch with other souls and substances. Every soul as such is from nature in possession of perfect knowledge, perfect belief and perfect moral behaviour; it has unlimited energy and unending bliss, complete incorporeity and has equality of position with all other souls. Its movement is directed straight upwards.

These inborn qualities of soul appear in it when it is independent of all the alien influx. This is the case only for a very small number of existing souls. Most of the souls cannot develop their natural qualities, because they are made completely or partially ineffective by an alien element which does not belong to them. This alien element is something that is inanimate (Ajīva).

(2) Ajīva, the Inanimate

There are five substances besides the soul, and they are like them eternal and imperishable, the only difference being that they are inanimate. They are: space, the media of movement and rest, time and matter.

(a) Ākāśa, the Space

Space is the receptaculum of all things, but it is not contained in anything. Its only assignment is to offer place. Differing from all other substances, it is not only in the world, but outside of it in the non-world (Aloka). It consists of an unending amount of space points (Pradeśa).

(b) and *(c) Dharma and Adharma, Motion and Rest*

Dharma and Adharma are a sort of ether. They are the media of movement and rest. This is to be understood in the sense that they themselves do not cause motion and obstruction, but create preconditions for them. Dharma is, therefore, compared with water which is a precondition that a fish swims, and Adharma with ground whose existence enables a wanderer to put himself to rest. They occupy the whole world-space and they have endlessly many space points.

The presumption of two special substances Dharma

and Adharma is a characteristic speciality of Jainism. Since these two words do not appear in Sanskrit in this special meaning, the researchers dealing for the first time with Jaina-philosophy did not understand their meaning and explained them as *virtue* and *vice*; this, of course, does not make any sense. Jacobi gave the correct explanation; H.H. Wilson has already pointed this out. Jacobi also gives the reasons why Jainas have proposed these two substances.[8]

(d) Kāla, Time

Time occasions the changes taking place in other substances; it makes new what is old and old what is new. Just like the stone which a potter lays under his disc enables its movement only by its mere presence, without causing it, time also supports by its being there the changes to which the substances are subject. In the highest sense, it is a continuity without any beginning, end or parts. But seen from the point of view of common experience, it consists of endlessly many moments of which one is present, and others belong either to the past or the future. Since it does not possess any space points (Pradeśa) in contrast to all other substances, it is not counted among substances (dravya) by many Jaina-philosophers. Others consider it as a substance, but teach that its countless atoms like the jewels lying on a heap, rest next to one another in each of the single point of the world-space without ever being mixed with one another.[9] In any case it is not an "astikāya", i.e. it does not belong to the class of entities which occupy countable, uncountable or endlessly many space points, like Jīva and the other four inanimate substances.

Jainas divide time in a special way.[10] The smallest unit of time is moment (Samaya), i.e. the period in which an atom can move forward around its own length in the slowest movement. Countless Samayas form an Āvalikā, 1677216 Āvalikās make a Mūhūrta (48 minutes). 30 Muhūrtas make an Ahorātra (day and night), 15 Ahorātras a Pakṣa (half month), 2 Pakṣas a Māsa (month), 2 Māsas a Ṛtu (season), 3 Ṛtus an Ayana (Semester), 2 Ayanas a Saṁvatsara (year). 8400000 years are a Pūrvāṅga, 8400000 Pūrvāṅgas are a Pūrva (i.e. 8400000^2 years). Then a number of large time-measures are taken up till finally a 77 digited number is reached. Beyond that, the period cannot be determined any more; it can be imagined only by comparison. The time that is needed to empty completely a grain-container filled with tender hairs and of a Yojana diameter and height, when only one hair is taken out every hundred years, is called "Palyopama". 10 Koṭikoṭis (1000000 000 000 000) of Palyopamas are a "Sāgaropama", 10 Koṭikoṭis of Sāgaropama are an "Utsarpiṇī" (increasing period of time), or, what remains the same, an "Avasarpiṇī" (decreasing period of time). Endlessly many increasing and decreasing periods of time following one another in a constant change form a Pudgalaparāvarta.

(e) Pudgala, Material Object

The matter consists of an endless variety of quite tiny atoms which cannot be perceived by senses and which cannot be further divided (Paramāṇu). While all other substances are formless, every atom has a definite smell, a definite taste, a definite colour and two definite varieties of touch.

The smell of the atom is either good or bad, the taste bitter, pungent, astringent, sour or sweet (the salty taste is considered as a variety of the sweet). The colour: black, blue (green), red, yellow or white. The touch: heavy, light, soft, rough, cold, warm, sticky or dry.

An atom occupies a space point. But it can be bound with one or several others to an aggregate (Skandha) which occupies then numerous, uncountable or endlessly many space points. But numerous fine atoms can be contained only in one space point because matter appearing only in crude form cannot be pierced.

By uniting the atoms, aggregates of fine and crude types arise. 6 types of matter are distinguished on the basis of their thickness. They are:

1. Fine-fine (Sūkṣma-sūkṣma) and therefore invisible like the atom.
2. Fine (Sūkṣma) and therefore also invisible like the Karma-substances.
3. Fine-coarse (Sūkṣma-sthūla) like all material things which can be smelt, tasted, heard and touched, but cannot be seen.
4. Coarse-fine (Sthūla-sūkṣma), like sunshine, darkness, shadow, thus the things which can be seen, but not touched.
5. Coarse (Sthūla), like butter, water, oil, i.e. like everything that is fluid which, when separated, can be amalgamated again from itself.
6. Coarse-coarse (Sthūla-sthūla), like stone, metal, in short like everything which cannot be joined together without the appearance of the third.

Matter has a definite form; this can be either such that it can be firmly defined (as round, triangular, square) or it cannot be accurately described (like the form of a cloud, etc.).

A number of special conditions can appear in matter, like the warm radiation of light (as it, e.g. emanates from the sun) and cold radiation of light (as it is given by the moon, jewel, glow-worm, etc.), darkness, shadow and sound. Darkness is not considered as a mere negation of light, but as something material.[11] Shadow and every reflection of a body (in mirror, water, etc.) is considered as something material, it is caused by fine matter emanating from a body. Sound is understood by Jainas as a fine matter, not as a quality of ether as it is understood by the other Indian philosophers (or of space, Ākāśa). It is caused by the aggregates of atoms being rubbed against one another. Two types of sound are distinguished: sound which has a linguistic meaning, and sound which does not have such. The first type is further divided into two classes, viz. in sound which can be expressed by letters and sound which cannot be expressed by letters; the latter includes the tones which beings with 2, 3, 4, sense-organs, as also Kevalīs (redeemed saints) give out. Sound having no linguistic significance is produced by human beings with the help of instruments (of which 4 types are distinguished), or it arises in a different way (like, e.g. thunder).[12]

Matter gets an extraordinary significance by its being able to get connected with souls and completely changing them in their nature. The matter penetrating a soul is expressed as Karma. We shall thoroughly discuss in the following this concept which is basic for Jaina-philosophy.

3. KARMA

Like all Indians, Jainas also believe in Karma, the power of sin and merit having an after-effect. There is a saying:

> "The one who has strewn good or bad seeds
> In the earth of destiny,
> Will also reap good or bad fruits
> When they become ripe"[13]

The concept that a man has to reap what he sows, not strange also to other religions, is connected in India since the ancient period with the doctrine of metempsychosis. Every action, every word and every thought influences the destiny of their contriver. Since the present life would not be enough to award to a man rewards and punishments which are due to his good or bad works, the after-effect of an action is stretched beyond the death, in fact, it will be the cause of a new existence and determines its nature and duration in all details. A rebirth in a new form follows every death because in every existence enough actions are done which have to be atoned for in a new life; but because every existence is a consequence of earlier actions, a different life must have preceded it. This means that every existence is only a link in a long chain of existences which precede it and follow it without beginning and (under normal circumstances) without end. To acknowledge the correctness of this doctrine Indians are, on the one hand, pushed into a position to find a plausible explanation in the actions of an earlier existence for the extraordinary difference of the corporeal and psychic nature of beings, for their conditions of life and their destiny; on the other hand, it is doubtlessly effective as a strong motive for leading a moral life and makes a desire be arisen in the minds of the profoundly inclined natures to renounce action and thereby to find a release from the ocean of rebirths.

The philosophical foundation of the Karma-doctrine is different in the metaphysical systems of Indians; most of the Hindus consider Karma as a transcendent, invisible power (Adṛṣṭa) which accompanies to some extent the fine-material body surrounding the soul as an unalterable moral substratum on its wanderings from one existence to the other, without adhering itself to the soul which truly remains untouched by everything that is material. Jainas have an altogether different, independent conception. According to them, Karma is something material (paudgala), it can be determined as a visible effect of fine matter which has penetrated the soul. Just like the medicinal pill taken by a person can produce important changes in his innards, the fine Karma-matter influences also the soul in many ways when it contaminates it.

A connection between a soul and the Karma-matter is without a beginning and never finds an end in the natural course of things. The moment a soul is activated, the corpuscles found within the space occupied by it penetrate it and stick to it like the dust-particles sticking to a body smeared with oil. The penetration of soul by matter is intensive like the combination of milk and water, fire and iron-ball. Jīva is completely changed by it; its knowledge is concealed, its energy checked, bad impulses are awakened in it and it is afflicted with an abundance of qualities which are alien to its true nature.

Jaina-philosophers discuss in detail the effects caused by the matter in the souls contaminated by it. With their urge seen everywhere to systematize and classify everything, they have also analyzed Karma accurately. According to their theory, there are 8 main types (Mūlaprakṛti) of Karma which are again divided into 148 subclasses (Uttara-prakṛti). In view of the significance of the subject, it is necessary to introduce them here in their order: But to avoid repeating what will be discussed extensively later, I shall be content to give here only a brief enumeration and refer to the details to be given later by indicating the reference. To simplify the matter, I have also not always kept to the traditional order of the individual subclasses as it is given in the *Karmagranthas*, but chosen occasionally a more general one.

The 8 main types of Karma are:

1. Jñānāvaraṇa-karma, the Karma which conceals knowledge.
2. Darśanāvaraṇa-karma, the Karma which conceals sight.
3. Vedanīya-karma, the Karma which produces the feeling of pleasure and pain.
4. Mohanīya-karma, the Karma which disturbs belief and conduct of life.
5. Āyus-karma, the Karma which decides the duration of life.
6. Nāma-karma, the Karma which influences the individual things.

7. Gotra-karma, the Karma which determines the position by birth.
8. Antarāya-karma, the Karma which hinders the soul in its capability of enjoyment and decision.

The nature of the 8 Karmas is explained by symbols: The 1st like a piece of cloth concealing the face of god, the 2nd like a door-keeper who does not allow someone to see the king (in public), the 3rd to the pleasure one has while taking in the mouth a sharp blade of sword smeared with honey, the 4th to enjoying brandy intoxicating a man so much that he forgets what is good or bad, the 5th to a chain hindering one from going where one wants to go, the 6th to a painter who lends individual features to a person depicted by him in his picture with the help of different colours, etc., the 7th to a potter who produces heavy and light vessels and the 8th to a treasurer who hinders distribution of fund.[14]

I shall now describe in brief the significance of these 8 basic types and indicate the subclasses in which they are divided:

1. Jñānāvaraṇa-karma conceals from the soul its own natural knowledge, i.e. it hinders it from knowing a thing accurately with its attributes. This Karma is divided into 5 subclasses corresponding to the five types of knowledge which are distinguished (p. 205).
2. Darśanāvaraṇa-karma conceals from the soul its own natural sight, i.e. it hinders it from knowing a thing in its general contours and in its comprehensive generality. As there are 4 types of "seeing", there are four types of Darśanāvaraṇa-karma. 5 more Karmas are added to this. They produce physio-psychological conditions in which the organs of sense are not active and, therefore, rule out every possibility of perceiving something. Nidrā-karma produces a light and Nidrā-nidrā-karma a sound *slumber*,

Pracalā-karma a sound, Pracalā-pracalā-karma a particularly intensive *sleep.* Styān-arddhi-karma causes *somnabulism,* i.e. acting in an unconscious state.

3. Vedanīya-karma conceals from the soul its natural bliss. It is divided into two subclasses; it imparts to the soul worldly pleasure (Sāta) or a feeling of aversion (Asāta).
4. Mohanīya-karma disturbs the true belief and proper life that is peculiar to a soul. It is divided into 28 classes with 28 subclasses. As a Darśana-mohanīya-karma it causes a disturbance in the knowledge of religious truth. Three subclasses are to be divided on the basis whether this disturbance is absolute or relative (see 1, 3, 4, on p. 206 f.). Cāritra-mohanīya-karma hinders the soul from acting in accordance with the religious precepts by producing 16 passions, 6 "Non-passions" and 3 types of sexual drives.

   There are 4 passions (Kaṣāya), viz. anger (Krodha), pride (Māna), illusion (Māyā) and greed (Lobha). Each one of them appears in 4 gradations of strength (see p. 208) so that 16 passions are distinguished.

   "Non-passions" (Nokaṣāya) are the 6 correlatives of passions, viz. frivolity (Hāsya), love (Rati), revulsion (Arati), sadness (Śoka), fear (Bhaya) and nausea (Jugupsā).

   The sexual drives (Vedas) are of three types corresponding to three types of sexes (see p. 199).
5. Āyus-karma lends to a being a certain quantum of life in one of the four stages of existence as god, human being, animal and a being from hell. Accordingly, it is divided into 4 subclasses. It is to be noticed that Āyus-karma

grants a certain span of life, but not a definitely exact number of years of life. For as the quantity of water in a sponge is definite, but not the period in which it drains it, the quantum of life is also definite, but not the period in which it is used up.

6. Nāma-karma causes individual differences between the souls. It is divided into 93 sub-types:

1-4. Gati-nāma-karmas lend the stages of existence of a god, a man, an animal or a being from hell.

5-8. Ānupūrvī-nāma-karmas cause the soul, when an existence has ended, to go from the place of death in the correct direction to a place where it enters life anew as god, man, animal or a being from hell.[15]

9-14. Jāti-nāma-karmas cause the birth in one of the five classes of beings, i.e. as beings with 1, 2, 3, 4, or 5 senses (see p. 198).

15-20. Śarīra-nāma-karmas give one or several of 5 bodies, as there are earthly body, body of metamorphosis, body of tranference, fiery-body and Karma-body (see p. 195).

21-25. Bandhana-nāma-karmas (bond) cause that the matter of a body newly acquired is bound into an organic whole with those which were assimilated earlier. 5 types are distinguished corresponding to the 5 types of the bodies.

26-30. Saṅghāṭana-nāma-karmas (cohesion) cause that the substances of the 5 bodies hold together.

31-33. Aṅgopāṅga-nāma-karmas (main and subordinate-parts-karmas) cause the origin of main parts (limbs) (arms, legs, back, chest, stomach, head) and the subordinate-limbs (fingers, etc.) of the earthly body and the "metamorphic" body and body of transference (projectile body). (The two other bodies have no limbs.)

34-38. Saṁsthāna-nāma-karmas give each one of the 5 statures (see p. 196).

39-43. Saṁhanana-nāma-karmas lend 5 assemblies of

the joints (see p. 197).

44-48. Varṇa-nāma-karmas give the 5 colours (p. 181).

49-50. Gandha-nāma-karmas give the 2 types of odours (see p. 181).

51-55. Rasa-nāma-karmas give the 5 types of tastes (see p. 182).

56-63. Sparśa-nāma-karmas lend the 8 types of touch (p. 182).

64-65. Vihāyogati-nāma-karmas lend a beautiful or ugly manner of movement ("beautiful" is, e.g. the one of bulls, elephants, geese; "ugly" the one of camels and asses).

66. Trasa-nāma-karma gives a body that can be moved arbitrarily.

67. Sthāvara-nāma-karma causes that the body (of the plants and elementary beings) cannot be arbitrarily moved.

68. Bādara-nāma-karma gives a coarse body.

69. Sūkṣma-nāma-karma gives (to the elementary beings) a fine body that cannot be perceived with our senses.

70. Paryāpta-nāma-karma causes the complete development of the organs and capabilities of nourishment, of the body, senses, breathing, speaking and thinking.

71. Aparyāpta-nāma-karma causes that these organs and capabilities do not attain complete development.

72. Pratyeka-nāma-karma causes that a being has an individual body.

73. Sādhāraṇa-nāma-karma gives (to plants, etc.) a body which is common with the other souls of their species.

74. Sthira-nāma-karma causes that teeth, bones, etc. are firm.

75. Asthira-nāma-karma causes that ears, brows, tongue, etc. are pliant.[16]

76. Śubha-nāma-karma causes that the parts of the body lying above the navel are "beautiful" so that

someone whom one touches with the head feels happy.

77. Aśubha-nāma-karma causes that the parts of the body below the navel are considered as "ugly" so that someone who is touched with the foot feels this as unpleasant.

78. Subhaga-nāma-karma causes that someone is congenial even to those who do not owe him anything.

79. Durbhaga-nāma-karma makes a being uncongenial.

80. Susvara-nāma-karma lends a good voice.

81. Duḥsvara-nāma-karma gives a bad voice.

82. Ādeya-nāma-karma causes that someone is suggestive so that his speech finds agreement and belief.

83. Anādeya-nāma-karma makes someone unsuggestive.

84. Yaśaḥkīrti-nāma-karma lends honour and fame.

85. Ayaśaḥkīrti-nāma-karma gives dishonour and disgrace.

86. Parāghāta-nāma-karma gives the capacity to injure and defeat others.

87. Upaghāta-nāma-karma causes that the parts of the body of a being cause its death (it may be that they are not in right position or that they are so much estimated like the navel of a musk deer that one persecutes them because of them).

88. Nirmāṇa-nāma-karma causes the formation of the body, i.e. it causes that the parts of a being are in the right place.

89. Ucchvāsa-nāma-karma lends the capacity to breathe.

90. Ātapa-nāma-karma causes that the body of a being which is itself not hot emits a warm glow.

91. Uddyota-nāma-karma causes that the metamorphic body of gods, ascetics, moon, stars, gems, herbs and glowworms emits a cold ray.

92. Agurulaghu-nāma-karma makes a being "neither heavy, nor light", i.e. it causes that its body has neither an absolute gravity nor an absolute weightlessness.

93. Tīrthaṅkara-nāma-karma lends the position of a

prophet of the Jaina-religion.

7. Gotra-karma determines the position which one takes by one's birth, and besides, Uccair-gotra-karma gives a higher, Nīcair-gotra-karma a lower position of birth.
8. Antarāya-karma hinders the energy of the soul in fivefold manner:

1. Dāna-antarāya-karma hinders donations. When it works, someone who knows the reward of giving and has to present something, is not able to give although there is a person who is worthy of charity.

2. Lābha-antarāya-karma hinders the acceptance (of charity). When it works, one does not get a reward although there is a kind donor and a suitable gift and the request for it was successful.

3. Bhoga-antarāya-karma hinders the enjoyment of something what can be enjoyed only once (like food, drink).

4. Upabhoga-antarāya-karma hinders the enjoyment of something that can be enjoyed repeatedly (like house, clothes, women).

5. Vīrya-antarāya-karma checks will-power; under its influence, e.g. a powerful, full-grown man is incapable of harming even a blade of grass.

The 148 types of Karma are classified by Jainas from different points of view. The most important of these classifications are those into Ghāti-karmas and Aghāti-karmas. All those destroying the natural qualities of the soul belong to the former, e.g. concealment of knowledge, concealment of sight, disturbances and hindrances (I, II, IV and VIII). Aghāti-karmas are those which do not destroy anything that is essential, but those qualities which a soul does not get as such, i.e. the other Karmas (III, V, VI, VII).

Once a soul is activated, it attracts, within its realm, fine matter which can become Karma and assumes it. The matter thus assumed is then transformed into the

8 types of Karma just like the food eaten in a meal turning into the blood. Then the Karma-matter falling in main part is further divided into its sub-types. The amount of matter divided into different Karma-types is very different: Jainas give here exact figures, but it would be going too far, if we are to consider them here. Particularly the question how many space points (Pradeśa) the matter having become Karma takes in the soul is treated in detail. Thus it is taught that greater is the number of Pradeśas falling in a Karma-type, the smaller the number of Karma-types, in which a piece of the matter is to be divided, and higher the soul is organized which assimilates the Karma. A completely developed, thinking being takes in more matter than an incompletely developed creature with only one sense. If this large quantity of matter is only to be divided into quite a few Karma-types, as it is the case with pious men, because most of the Karmas are not at all produced by the concerned person, then there emerges naturally a larger quantity of Pradeśas in each one of these Karma-type than when the same matter were to be divided into a larger number of Karma-types. This shows that the quantity of the matter assimilated by the soul and allotted to the individual karma-types has no influence on the quality of the soul.

Like the effect of a medicinal pill—to stay with the simile used above—can be of different duration, the period during which a Karma exerts its influence is also different. The Karma-granthas give for each of the 148 types maximum and minimum of its duration (Sthiti), the numbers fluctuating between 70 Koṭikoṭis of Sāgaropamas (maximum duration of Karma "misbelief") and 48 minutes (minimum period of the concealment of knowledge and sight and of the hindrances).

Like a pill which has a sweet taste and the other which has a sweeter taste, Karma shows its effect in more or less perceivable manner depending upon the circumstances. This intensity (Rasa or Aṇubhāga) of the Karma-effect is conditioned by the strength of the passions (p. 208) which a being possesses. Corresponding to 4 grades of passions, we have also four grades of the strength of Karmas.

More the sinful an individual, the more is the duration of his Karma, stronger the effect of his bad Karma-types, weaker the effect of his good Karma-types; with the increasing purity, the duration of Karma and the intensity of the bad Karma-types decreases and the strength of the good Karma-types grows.

With respect to the manner in which Karma shows its effect, Hindus distinguish between three categories of Karma:

1. Āgāmī or Vartamāna is a fresh Karma which can be added any moment to the existing treasure by new actions and thus the amount of existing guilt or reward is increased in every moment.

2. Prārabdha is a Karma that has already begun to be effective and that is manifested as the fate of the concerned being.

3. Sañcita is a Karma that has been stored by earlier actions and that will be developed later at an opportune moment.[17]

Jainas have the same tripartition, but the individual categories have other names; they are "Bandha", "Udaya" and "Sattā".

Bandha "bondage" is the assimilation of the matter which has penetrated the soul in the form of certain Karma-types. Thus if it is said of someone that he binds the Karma "hell's stage of existence", then it means: he causes that the matter which has penetrated his soul is turned by his actions to such that it is the cause of his later rebirth in hell.

Udaya, "production" is the perceptibility of the effect of the Karma that enters at an opportune time. The Karma "hell's stage of existence" has an Udaya when the relevant being which had "bound", is really found in hell and suffers pain there.

Sattā is the presence of the Karma "in potentia" from the moment of the assimilation to the one of the production or some other wiping out. Thus the Karma "hell's stage of existence" exists in the condition of Sattā, when it has been "bound", but does not yet express its effect.

The Karma-granthas deal extensively with the question which Karmas can be produced at the same time and which Karmas can be finally present next to one another in Sattā. I shall abstain from going into this "spiritual mathematics" (as it is called by a well-known Jaina writer) and refer the reader for this to my monograph on the Karma-doctrine of Jainas in which I have discussed this in details.

It is possible under special preconditions that a Karma can be prematurely produced (Udīraṇā), i.e. it expresses its effect earlier than is the case under normal circumstances. In a Karma even increasing (Apavartanā) or decreasing (Udvartanā) of its period or intensity can take place, It can indeed produce a Karma-type as a different one under certain circumstances, this may then be bound or not. This transition of Karma into another is called Saṁkrama; this can, however, take place only between the sub-types of a main group and not among different main groups, and there not also among all.

4. THE SOUL UNDER THE INFLUENCE OF KARMA

(1) The Physical Life of the Incarnate Souls

(a) The Bodies and Their Organs

The connection of soul with matter is seen most clearly in the fact that soul is clothed with material bodies. It fills up the body completely, because it can expand and shrink so that it can equally completely penetrate a body of an elephant as well as a body of an ant in two existences following one after the other. There are 5 bodies according to the doctrine of Jainas. They are:

1. Audārika-śarīra, *the earthly body* of crude substance, peculiar to animals and human beings.
2. Vaikriya-śarīra, *the "metamorphic" body* consisting of fine matter. This can change its form and size according to the wish of the owner. It is present among gods, beings from hell and some animals on account of their nature, but even human beings can obtain it on the basis of their higher perfection.
3. Āhāraka-śarīra, *the body of transference* (or "*projectile*" *body*). This consists of a good and pure substance and is without an active or a passive resistance. It is created by an Apramatta-saṁyata-ascetic (see p. 222) for a brief period, and after being equipped with it, he gets information from a teacher on difficult dogmatic questions. His earthly body, however, stays at one place.
4. Taijasa-śarīra, *the fiery body*. This consists of fire-atoms and serves to digest the food that is eaten. It can be used by the ascetics to burn other beings or things.
5. Kārmaṇa-śarīra, the *Karmic body*. This is a recepta-culum of the Karma-matter. It changes every moment, because the soul constantly assimilates a new Karma and exhausts the existing one.

Of these five bodies, every following one is finer than the preceding one, but contains more material points than this; it is thus thicker. Every being wandering in Saṁsāra including also the one which is on its way from one form of existence to a new one, has constantly two bodies: the fiery- and the Karmic body. These two bodies do not feel any pleasure or pain and do not possess any limbs. There is no resistance against them, they pass through everything coming in their way so that they can measure the whole world and must make a halt at its borders. A being can possess at the same time at the most two other bodies besides these two in a form of existence, but the "metamorphic" and "projectile" bodies cannot appear together, and the latter appears only together with an earthly body. Of the five bodies only the earthly can be perceived by eyes by a common man, but all of them have, like all material things, smell, taste, colour and touch.

The earthly body is extremely different among the earthly beings. There are Jīvas which have one individual body for themselves, but there are others which have one body among several; such a common body is possessed by plants (garlic, onion, etc.). The earthly body of many beings is so fine that it can be noticed by us only when they appear in large numbers, as it is the case with many types of animals (elementary beings and plants).

The body of many beings can be moved by their wish and volition; the body of the others cannot be set into motion by them, but they can be moved from one place to the other by alien influences coming from outside.

Depending upon the shape, the body of a being can be symmetrical or asymmetrical. Jainas distinguish 6 different types of statures (Saṁsthāna), from a complete symmetry to its absolute opposite. The human body is at the basis to determine the concept of symmetry; the following explanation is given: one should imagine a man sitting in the Paryaṅka-posture, i.e. he crosses the legs and puts the hands on the navel. If one imagines that the two knees are connected by one line, and each one straight from the right shoulder to the left knee and from the left shoulder to the right knee and one from the forehead to the hands, then one gets four lines. If they are similar to one another, then there is a symmetry; if they are not, then one of the other five statures results.

The six statures are:

1. *Samacaturasra-saṁsthāna*: The body is completely symmetrical.

2. *Nygrodhaparimaṇḍala-saṁsthāna*: The upper part of the body is symmetrical, the lower is not; thus the body is like a fig-tree, which is beautiful and big above, but small and ugly below.

3. *Sādi-saṁsthāna*: The body below the navel is symmetrical, while the upper part is asymmetrical.

4. *Kubja-saṁsthāna*: The body is hunch-backed, i.e. hands, feet, head and neck are symmetrical, but not the breast and the stomach.

5. *Vāmana-saṁsthāna*: The body is dwarf-like, i.e. breast and stomach are symmetrical, but not the hands and feet, etc.

6. *Huṇḍa-saṁsthāna:* The whole body is asymmetrical.

The firmness with which the bones of the earthly body are connected with one another is significant, particularly among the higher organized beings. The strength of the union of the joints (Saṁhanana) is of 6 grades:

1. *Vajra-ṛṣabha-nārāca-saṁhanana*: This is the first-class union of the joints; the two bones are to some extent hooked to one another, a stick (Vajra) is drawn through the place of the joint, and the whole is bound by a tissue.

2. *Ṛṣabha-nārāca-saṁhanana*: This connection is not so firm like the preceding one because the pin is missing.

3. *Nārāca-saṁhanana*: This union is again weaker, because even the tissues are missing.

4. *Ardha-nārāca-saṁhanana*: This union is on the one side like the preceding one, while on the other side, the bones are only virtually pressed against one another and are nailed.

5. *Kīlikā-saṁhanana*: Still weaker union where the bones are only pressed against one another and nailed.

6. *Savārta- (or chedapṛṣṭha-) saṁhanana*: A completely weak union in which the edges of the bones only touch one another.

These Saṁhananas play a great role in the Jaina-dogmatism. Only the first four make a meditation, i.e. affixing and concentration of a thought possible; only the best, i.e. the first union of the joints allows the highest type of concentration which precedes salvation.

(b) The Body Functions

Certain bodily functions are peculiar to the bodies of the Jīvas which are in Saṁsāra. They are called "Prāṇa".* There are on the whole 10 different Prāṇas.[18] They are:

1. Āyus "vitality" (see p. 186).
2-4. The three Balas or powers of the body, language and thought.
5. Ucchvāsa-nīḥśvāsa (Ānapāṇa), inhaling and exhaling.
6-10. The functions of the organs of sense (Indriya) of touch, taste, smell, seeing and hearing.

All the ten Prāṇas are present in the most highly developed beings; in the lower ones, only few of them, but at least four (vitality, power of the body, breathing, feeling).

The possession of more or less organs of sense as a principle for the division of the beings into classes. One thus distinguishes the beings with 1, 2, 3, 4 and 5 organs of sense and divides further those belonging to the class having 5 organs of senses into those who think and those who do not think.

Beings with one sense are those which have elements (earth, water, fire, wind) or plants as body. They are either "fine" (sūkṣma), i.e. not perceivable at all with the help of our senses, or crude (bādara) and therefore, visible.

---

*The word *prāṇa* here has an older meaning which is peculiar to it in the oldest Upaniṣads. They differentiate five Prāṇas, i.e. the factors of psycho-physical life, viz., breath, speech, face, ears and understanding. In the later period, Prāṇa in the Hindu-philosophy means breath, i.e. the most important of these factors, and its subtypes.

Beings with 2 senses (touch and taste) are: worms, shells, leeches, etc.; those with 3 senses (touch, taste, smell): bugs, ants, spider, etc.; those with 4 senses (touch, taste, smell, eyes) are bees, flies, etc.

Beings with five senses are divided into two groups: those who are judicious and those who are not. The former have an inner sense (manas) and they judge after thinking while taking into consideration the condition of a thing in the present, past and future. Those who are not judicious act only from instinct. All the animals not born of a womb belong to these, the "Asaṁjñīs" like toads, fish, etc. Animals born of a womb, like goats, sheep, elephants, lions and tigers belong to the group of "Saṁjñīs. Human beings, gods and beings from the hell belong also to this group.

Beings of all these types can be present in the fully developed condition (paryāpta) or in an undeveloped (aparyāpta) one. Amongst the latter the organs of the body or its capacities are not fully developed.

(c) Sexes

The views of Jainas on the sexual life of the Jīvas are remarkable. According to them there are three sexes and three types of libidos; there is a male-sex (Puruṣa-veda), a female-sex (Strī-veda) and a third sex (Napuṁsaka-veda); all beings not having sex-organs belong to this.

Man's libido produces in him a need for the union with a woman, just like the phlegm (according to the opinion of the Indian medicinal practitioners) which causes desire for something that is sour. It resembles straw-fire; like the fire flaring up when grass is burnt and then becomes extinct; man has at first an excessive desire, but it disappears the moment it is fulfilled.[19]

Woman's libido rouses in woman a wish for the union with a man, like the bile, the desire for something that is sweet. It resembles the fire of the dung; a dung-heap burns little as long as it is covered, but gives out fierce fire, the moment it is stirred; same is the case with a woman. Her desire is only weak as long as she is not touched, but grows into infinite by the enjoyment of love.

The libido of the third sex is directed towards men and women without any distinction, and therefore it is the strongest of all. According to its effect, it corresponds to the one of phlegm and bile together which produces together a desire for sour milk with sugar. It can be compared with the conflagration of a city which lasts long and burns anything and everything non-stop. Jīvas of all classes of beings belong to the third sex, but no gods; there are men and women only among the Jīvas with five senses, but not among the dwellers of the hell and the beings born out of coagulation.

(d) Birth and Death

The birth of beings can take place in three ways:

1. By conception, i.e. the relevant beings arise from the eggs (like birds and serpents) or as living young ones from a foetus with chorian (like human beings and cows) or without chorian (like elephants).

2. By manifestation (Upapāta), gods and beings from hell appear suddenly at a place where they are supposed to be born as a result of their Karma; they also do not die like other beings as a result of a recognizable cause, but their life ceases on its own.

3. By coagulation (Sammūrchana), i.e. by original production from mud, blood, dirt, etc. This holds good for all beings which are not born by conception or manifestation. As Hemacandra teaches us (*Abhidhāna-cintāmaṇi*, 1355 ff.), acetobacters are produced from the fluids, lice from warm moisture, fish from mud and water-wagtails from the earth. Undeveloped human beings born out of intercourse between man and woman to die again immediately belong, according to the Jaina-belief, to this group.[20]

A being dies once it has reached the quantum of life allotted to it by the Karma. The death follows among human beings and animals on account of a definite cause (Upakrama); it comes spontaneously among gods and beings from hell without any cause. Provided with a fiery- and Karma-life, the Jīva then leaves the body which it had in the existence which had just run its course, and sets out under the influence of Anupūrvī-nāma-karma (p. 188) to a place where it should be reborn again. The period between the death and rebirth is called "Vigraha-kāla" and lasts at the most a few minutes.

A soul, under special circumstances, can leave its body partially during its existence in it, act outside of it and return again later to it. This process is called Samudghāta and can be carried out by beings which have higher powers. On the whole, seven types of Samudghāta are presumed.[21] The Samudghāta to be undertaken with the body of transference (Āhāraka-Samudghāta) is already mentioned above on p. 195. Of the others, Tejas-Samudghāṭa is above all worth mentioning; it is carried out with the help of a fiery body. Of these, a "good" one and a "bad" one is distinguished. A wise man who wants to avert some misfortune makes use of the good one. A white figure comes out from his right shoulder; it obviates the misfortune and once more returns to the body of the saint. The bad Tejas-Samudghāta serves an enraged ascetic to get rid of a person or a thing he hates. A red figure comes out then from his left shoulder and it burns to ashes what has caused his anger. In contrast to the types of Samudghāta mentioned above which are carried out by the beings in Saṁsāra the Kevalī-Samudghāta serves the omniscient who are in the 13th Guṇasthāna to even up their different Karmas among themselves to be able to obtain salvation after their complete destruction.

(2) The Psychic Life of the Incarnate Souls

(a) Activity

The soul has from nature Vīrya, i.e. unlimited power. But the Vīrya is developed completely only then when the soul is completely free from all the Karma-mater. As long as it is not the case, Vīrya is extremely limited. It does not appear spontaneously, but it is bound to matter; it needs an organ as an accompanying cause to express itself, it needs a medium of body, organ of speech and thinking to be able to be effective.

This form of the Vīrya bound to matter is called Yoga (activity).* The activity of the soul consists in the vibration of the particles in it. Thereby the matter needed for the body, speech and thinking organs are attracted to it, transformed into the entities of these organs and they are again expelled. Since Yoga carries matter constantly into the soul, it is the main cause for receiving new Karmas.

Soul is activated in three ways; it is expressed in thoughts, words, works and therefore it is conditioned by the thinking organ, speech organ or the body.

Application of the thinking-organ (Mano-yoga) is of 4 types: true (satya), when it is directed to something that is true and false (asatya), when it is directed to something that is false; it is "true and false" (satyamṛṣā) when, what is thought, is both true and false, e.g. in an Aśoka-forest in which there are also other trees besides the Aśoka-trees, and "neither true nor false" (asatyāmṛṣā), when, what is thought, is beyond the sphere of what is true and false (e.g. in the thought: "Devadatta, give me the cow").

The application of the organ of speech (Vāg-yoga) is divided into the same 4 sub-types.

---

*Thus the word is not used here in the technical sense of the Hindu-philosophy as "practice of meditation, controlling the functions of the thinking substance".

Application of the bodies (Kāya-yoga) is of 7 types depending upon whether one has to deal with the one of earthly body, body of metamorphosis, transference or Karma, or the one where two bodies work together. Application of the fiery body is not especially counted, because it is constantly connected with the Karma-body.

The activity is the least among the lowest living beings; it increases with an increasing organization. Also the variety of activity grows with the class of the being; the developed, fine Jīva with only one sense has only the activity of the earthly body, whereas all 15 Yogas can appear among the thinking beings which have five senses.

Application of the body and of the organs of speech and thinking has to be regularized to check the connection with the bad Karma-types. Once the condition of saintliness has been attained by constant self-training, first the cruder and then the finer application of the body, speech and thinking can be eliminated. The saint thus becomes an Ayogi-kevalī and now possesses eternally infinite Vīrya which is bound to no organ and which is completely withdrawn from the influx of matter.

(b) Epistemological Capacity

Once the soul is completely free from the disturbing influx of matter it is able to know everything in the present, past and future. If it is infected by Karma, this absolute knowledge disappears. The matter conceals the omniscience of the soul like a thick veil of cloud concealing the light of the sun. But likewise, although the sun is concealed, its light breaks through the cloud, a portion of the epistemological capacity of the soul is preserved. If it were to lose it, it would no more be soul. This portion of knowledge is of different size among different beings. Among few, it is extremely significant: they are able to know the absent things and even the thoughts of others with the help of transcendental perception; but it is only negligible among the most, because they can perceive only with the help of organs of sense.

Imagining a thing can be of two types; it is either limited to grasping something in its contours, in its comprehensible generality, then it is called Darśana. In the absence of a better expression, I am translating it by the word "seeing".* Or it grasps the things with its individual attributes. Then it is called Jñāna, "knowledge". Thus the former is formally an indefinite imagination (anākāra-upayoga), and the latter formally a definite imagination (sākāra-upayoga).

"Seeing" and "knowing" don't appear at the same time among the souls wandering in Saṁsāra; the former precedes the latter, but among the redeemed, the omniscient, both go together.

"Seeing" occurs in 4 types:

1. Cakṣur-darśana is seeing that is obtained by the eye; this is in accordance with nature for the beings which have an organ of seeing.

2. Acakṣur-darśana is "seeing" that is obtained by one of the remaining four senses or by the organ of thinking. This occurs in this or the other form among all Jīvas.

3. Avadhi-darśana is supersensual "seeing" of material things. This occurs on its own without the mediation of material organs. It is inborn to gods and the beings from hell, but can happen to the developed, rational animals and human beings as a consequence of higher spiritual development.

4. Kevala-darśana is unrestricted, direct and absolute "seeing" of the omniscient (Kevalī); it appears only when

---

*The word "Darśana" has two meanings in the philosophy of Jainas; firstly, it is as in Sanskrit "view, way of looking (at things), philosophical system" and Samyag-darśana means then "the correct view, the true faith". But secondly it denotes formally indefinite knowledge. It is a *terminus technicus* in this second meaning and it is peculiar to Jaina-doctrine.

all Karmas concealing the "seeing" is completely wiped out.

There are five types of Jñāna, knowledge that is formally determined:

(1) Mati-jñāna is the knowledge obtained with the help of five senses and the organ of thinking. It is divided into four processes:

(a) Avagraha "first observation": I see that there is something.

(b) Īhā "wanting to know": I shall ascertain whether this is a man or a stem of a tree.

(c) Apāya "confirmation": I confirm that it is a tree, because it remains unmoved, it has branches, etc.

(d) Dhāraṇā "impression": I connect the seen tree with the reminiscences of the trees seen before, so that I get a definite idea about it.

(2) Śruta-jñāna is the knowledge which is based on the interpretation of signs, i.e. the understanding of words, writings, gestures, etc.

(3) Avadhi-jñāna is the transcendent knowledge of material things without the mediation of the organs of sense. This is inborn to gods and beings from hell; others obtain it (like the corresponding type of "seeing") with the help of higher perfection.

(4) Manaḥ-paryāya-jñāna is the transcendent knowledge of the thoughts of others without the mediation of the corporeal organs. Only human beings possess it, and they obtain it by dint of their higher perfection.

(5) Kevala-jñāna is unrestricted, direct and absolute omniscience. It is peculiar only to the perfect ones.

The last two mentioned types of knowledge are present only among human beings having proper belief. The other three types of knowledge can also occur also among those who do not believe. But since knowledge is bad, as long as it does not come from proper belief, because the unbeliever "understands the *sat* and *asat* without distinction and arbitrarily, his knowledge is called Ajñāna, "bad knowledge, ignorance". Thus three more types are added to the five above, viz. the negative 3 first types of knowledge (Mati-, Śruta- and Avadhi-Ajñāna, the last being usually called as Vibhaṅga-jñāna). Accordingly, all beings have "Ajñāna" as long as they do not have the right belief, but "Jñāna", the moment they get it. Beings whose belief consists of true and false elements have partially Jñāna, and partially Ajñāna.

1 to 3 of the 4 types of "seeing" and 1 to 4 of the 8 types of Jñāna occur among worldly souls. But the perfect ones (Kevalī) have only Kevala-jñāna and Kevala-darśana; this may be so because in both of these all types of seeing and knowledge are implicitly present—just as in the possession of a village, possession of its ground and land is also included—or it may be so because the absolute knowledge outshines all partial knowledges so that the latter are not noticed like the stars at the time of the sunrise.

(c) Faith

Right belief (Samyag-darśana) consists in the unshakable conviction of the absolute truth of Jaina-religion. It is based on the trust in the teachings of the omniscient masters, the holy scriptures and teachers called upon to explain the teachings. It is an essential quality of the soul. It is wholly and completely lost as a result of the assimilation of Karma that disturbs faith; once Karma is hindered to smaller or greater extent in its efficacy it appears correspondingly in smaller or greater measure; right belief appears completely once Karma is completely annihilated.

On the whole 6 types of faith are possible from the complete heterodoxy to perfect right faith:

1. Mithyātva, heterodoxy. Of this five are distinguished:

(a) ābhigrahika, caused by considering that a particular wrong doctrine is true;

(b) anābhigrahika, without acceptance of a particular wrong doctrine, caused by apathy and indifference;

(c) ābhiniveśika, caused by stubborn preference for something that is wrong;

(d) sāṁśayika, caused by doubt; and

(e) anābhoga, caused by deficient insight, i.e. by the inability to accept truth.

2. Sāsvādana-samyaktva, "a taste of the right faith". It is this feeling of right faith which lasts only for few moments; it soon gives way to heterodoxy. The name is explained in the following manner: a man who does not know that he has eaten milk-rice, feels clearly the taste of milk-rice in the moment when he vomits. A man whose confused mind is directed to heterodoxy feels also likewise a momentary taste of the right faith when he expectorates it.

3. Samyag-mithyātva "mixed faith", considering true and false as true without any distinction. The soul oscillates between right and wrong under its influence, it is indifferent to the religion of the Jina, has neither preference for it nor hatred against it.

4. Kṣāyopaśamika- or Vedaka-samyaktva, "lower right faith". This is a preliminary stage of the true faith, it is, at the same time, heterodoxy in which all the poison inherent to this is removed. Like the milk completely covered with clear water becomes quite pure when all water is removed, so also complete right faith is attained when every Karma disturbing the faith is removed.

5. Aupaśamika-samyaktva, the right faith caused by supression of Karma which disturbs it. In this, all the impeding Karma is eliminated; since this is only supressed, but has not disappeared; there is a possibility of a relapse into an earlier stage.

6. Kṣāyika-samyaktva, the complete right faith caused by complete annhilation of Karma which disturbs the faith.

(d) The Conduct of Life

Once the soul is free from Karma which disturbs one's life, it possesses the completely pure life, i.e. the absolute moral good conduct. As long as this is not the case, its conduct is disturbed by the influence of passions (Kaṣāya), "non-passions" (Nokaṣāya) and sexual drive.

I. Passions (Kaṣāya) are: 1. Krodha (anger), 2. Māna (pride), 3. Māyā (illusion) and 4. Lobha (greed).

Each one of these are of four types, corresponding to the intensity of their eruption. This is:

1. Anantānubandhī, "lasting life-long" and connected with heterodoxy. It disturbs the faith and life completely.

2. Apratyākhyānāvaraṇa, "hindering non-renunciation". It makes indeed every (thus also partial) renunciation impossible, but allows the presence of true faith. It lasts for one year.

3. Pratyākhyānāvaraṇa, "hindering renunciation". It disturbs the complete self-training, but permits the presence of true faith and partial self-training. Its effect lasts for four months.

4. Saṁjvalana, "flaring up". It allows complete self-training and works only towards the attainment of the completely right conduct. It lasts for 14 days.

Intensity of passions is explained by examples. The 4 types of anger resemble a line that is drawn in stone, earth, dust and water. The first can be removed only with great exertion, each of the following with a lighter one. Similarly, anger lasting the whole life is excessively strong in its effect and very difficult to combat, whereas the effect of the three remaining is correspondingly weaker, and therefore can be more easily eliminated. The intensity of pride resembles a stone-pillar, a bone, a piece of wood and the liana of *Dalbergia ougeinensis*; the inflexibility decreases correspondingly. The types of illusion are compared with the root of a bamboo, horn of a ram, cow-urine and chip of wood. The crookedness of each of these things can be more easily removed than in the case of the preceding one. And finally the degree of greed corresponds to the scarlet (colour), greater or smaller dirt and a stain of turmeric. All these stick to the clothes, but the scarlet colour can hardly be removed, dirt with more or less trouble and the stain of turmeric can be very easily removed.

II. Nokaṣāya is of 6 types which can hinder the soul in its practice of pure life. They are: 1. Hāsya, laughing, joke, frivolity; 2. Rati, enjoyment, preference to someone or something and the biased preference resulting from it; 3. Arati, displeasure, dislike for something and the biased discrimination resulting from it; 4. Śoka, sadness; 5. Bhaya, fear; 6. Jugupsā, nausea.

III. We have already mentioned the types of libido above on p. 199 f.

The moral conduct of the soul has three main types. They are:

1. Avirati, completely deficient self-discipline: This refers to the objects of 5 senses and thinking, so also to the damage of 4 types of elementary beings, of the plants and of the beings with a movable body, i.e. it is of 12 types.

2. Deśavirati, "partial self-discipline": This is expressed in giving up the killing of movable beings. It appears after the elimination of both the worst types of the four passions.

3. Virati, self-discipline: It comes when all the passions "hindering the renunciation" are made ineffective. We shall discuss their different forms later.

(e) The Types of Soul

Souls can be divided into 6 categories depending upon the moral value of their activity and accordingly, upon the Karma-type binding them; the first of them gets the highest degree of sinfulness, whereas each following one becomes better and better and the last finally possesses relatively the highest attainable purity. Affiliation of the soul to one of these six classes is revealed externally by the fact, that it is free, on account of its nature, from all that determines what is sensually perceivable, gets colour, smell, taste and touch, in short, a firmly prominent type which—in any case in a manner that cannot be known for our senses—distinguishes it from the other souls. This type of soul is called Leśyā.

The individual Leśyās are distinguished as under according to the colours which the souls get: 1. kṛṣṇa, black, 2. nīla, dark-blue, 3. kāpota, grey, 4. tejas, fiery, 5. padma, yellow or rose, 6. śukla, white.

The nature of the Leśyās is explained with the help of two examples:

Six men see a Jambū-tree which is full of ripe fruits. They wish to eat the fruits, but climbing the tree is perilous. They, therefore, think as to how they could come in possession of the Jambūs. The first suggests that the tree should be hacked from the roots. The second advises that they should cut the boughs; the third recommends that one should cut only the branches; the fourth only the bunches; the fifth wants only to pluck the fruits and the sixth finally says that one should pick the fruits fallen on the ground and eat them. Here the first has a black, the second a dark-blue, the third a grey, the fourth a fiery, the fifth a rosy and the sixth a white Leśyā.

The second simile tells a story of six robbers who want to attack a village. The first wants to kill all beings; the second only the human beings; the third only the men; the fourth only those having weapons; the fifth only those who would fight. The sixth advises that they should only rob the treasures and kill no one. The explanation is like in the first example.

The bearers of Leśyās are described in Devendrasūri's *Karmagrantha* (I, 93) as under:

"A hostile, unsympathetic, gruesome, rough, unholy man who has a bad tongue and takes pleasure in tormenting other beings has a black Leśyā; a treacherous, corrupt, fickle-minded, hypocrytical and voluptuous one has a dark Leśyā. An unthinking one, who does not think of the bad in all actions, an angry man, has a grey Leśyā. A clever one who hinders new Karma, the generous, honourable, who is kindly disposed towards religion, has a fiery Leśyā. The sympathetic, a giver of gifts, firm of character, a sensible man has the yellow Leśyā. The one who is pious, accomplishes good deeds, impassionate and impartial, has a white Leśyā."

The emotions mentioned here are only the basic temperaments of the soul. A different degree of intensity is to be distinguished in each Leśyā. It is, therefore, not surprising when we shall see later that the worst Leśyās are present even in high stages of development, when partial or complete self-discipline has already been attained. Leśyās characterize just only the emotional condition of a soul. The qualities which are described need not emerge in it in such a distinctive manner.

It must also be finally mentioned that a being has at its birth at first the Leśyā which it had at the time of death in the preceding existence; the Leśyā can be changed later.

The saints who do not have any emotions or activity (yoga), and Siddhas do not have any Leśyā.

(f) The Conditions of Soul

The totality of all that a soul as such can develop is classified by the Jaina-philosophers into five conditions (Bhāva). They are:

1. Pāriṇāmika Bhāva, the condition in natural disposition. This includes the qualities of the soul in which nothing is changed by Karma, i.e. spiritual nature, capacity for salvation, non-salvation, etc.

2. Audayika Bhāva, the condition based upon the unhindered production of Karma. It includes all the accidental attributes of the soul which appear in it by the production of Karmas, like ignorance, heterodoxy, emotions, colours of the soul, affiliation to one of the stages of existence, etc.

3. Aupaśamika Bhāva, the condition based upon the suppression of Karma. By this we understand the faith and the conduct of life seen in the soul when Mohanīya-

Karmas (p. 187) appear, i.e. particularly when the emotions have been supressed to the extent that they do not appear, although they exist.

4. Kṣāyika Bhāva, the condition based upon the annihilation of Karma. It comprises the true faith, perfect conduct, capacity to know and to see everything, as also the complete energy, in short, everything that is developed in the soul when the Karma has disappeared without any trace.

5. Kṣāyopaśamika or Miśra Bhāva is the condition of the soul in which the Karma has partially disappeared and is partially suppressed. This condition, however, is not, as one would like to suppose from the name, a combination of 3 and 4, but indicates a deeper stage than these two, insofar as there is only a lower degree of faith and the perfect conduct here and the Karmas which restrict the knowledge, seeing and energy are only partially ineffective.

The five conditions which can be schematically and somewhat arbitrarily divided into 53 sub-types, can be developed in the soul simultaneously in smaller or greater number. The proposition of the doctrine of five conditions aims at giving a principle of division which enables one to determine exactly which conditions of a soul follow from its nature, which are added by the production of Karma and which can arise by making it ineffective.

III

Ethics

1. THE THEORETICAL FOUNDATIONS OF ETHICS

(1) Suffering and the Possibility of Salvation

"Asāraḥ Saṁsāraḥ", "vain is the life in the world"—this is the great equation that describes the value of all existence in the corporeal forms of existence according to the doctrine of Jainas. All the Jīvas, whether they live in hells, in the world of animals and human beings or in heavens, are subject to suffering and under the pressure of desires which can never be quenched and they fall a victim to pain and death. Jaina teachers proclaim these truths again and again in their numerous writings and preachings, in stories and epigrams, and they become never tired of inculcating them most emphatically and repeatedly in the minds of the believers. Hemacandra lets systematically and minutely, the Tīrthaṅkara Padmaprabha show in detail, in *Triṣaṣṭi-śalākā-puruṣa-cāritra* (IV, 3, 82 ff.), that all beings, from the lowest to the highest, are subject to suffering.

Jīvas suffer horrible torments. They atone for their misdeeds in the hot and cold hells. Horrible Asuras cut their bodies to pieces and torment them with horrible torturing instruments; they roast them on pikes and pull out their eyes. Itching of the body causes them unbearable pain; they try in vain to quench their thirst in the river in hell in which hot, molten lead flows in place of water. When they look for a shade under the trees, then sharp swords fall which are the leaves of the trees and tear them to thousand pieces. Unmentionable are indeed the pains which the dwellers of hell, consumed by anger and sorrow, give to one another, and the afflictions to which they are liable on account of their own passions and their evil Karma. All the sufferings in hells are the more bad because they never lead to a premature end of existence; the ill-treated and torn bodies are joined together again because they cannot be destroyed, as long as Karma exerts its influence, and they decay when the Karma has used up its power which can claim up to 33 time-oceans.

The sufferings of the animals are negligible in comparison with those of the dwellers of hells, but they are also horrible in their nature. Elementary beings with one sense are without any protection against any attack. Earthly beings are trampled by horses and elephants, torn to pieces by ploughs and drowned by floods; beings in water are scorched by the sun, stiffened by cold and devoured by the thirsty; the fiery beings are sucked up by water. The windy beings are a burden to one another when they belong to storms having different directions; breath coming out from the mouth of others harm them and the movement of things in space and the swinging of fans end their life. The souls of plants are scorched by the sun, drowned by water, injured by wind and trampled, uprooted and consumed by beings of different types. Animals with 2, 3, 4, 5 organs of sense are a victim of all sorts of suffering, hardship; worms are carelessly pounded and crushed; bugs and lice are crushed; bees are killed by those lusting for honey; fish are caught and roasted on pikes; birds are killed by other birds. Among animals with five senses, the stronger kill the weaker; others are forced by human beings to do heavy work and are ill-treated with the help of whip and goads.

Man is luckier than animal because it is possible for him to give a goal to a new Karma and obtain redemption. But how few utilize this endless advantage of human existence. It is indeed very difficult to be obtained only by a good Karma in earlier existences! Instead of doing good works, they are greedy for gain and look for pleasure. Addicted to vain and unworthy deeds, most of the human beings in their childhood are like pigs which wallow in dirt; they are asses of love in youth and old oxen in their ripe years. Poverty, slavery, disease, complaints of old age and torment of death envenom the life of Aryans and non-Aryans which begins with horrible torments when the Jīva has gone into the hell of the womb and seeks to find out its way from its oppressive narrowness.

Suffering prevails also among gods. Of course, heavenly beings are free from the complaints of the earthly beings and spend their days in glory and joy, but they are also never completely happy. When Devas of lower classes look at the splendour and glory of those of the higher classes, they become envious and start thinking why they also do not have it so good like the others. When the signs appear telling them that they have to leave the heavenly places to obtain a new birth on the earth, they are afraid that they will be banished to a womb, and the worry of the unknown future they have to face envenoms all their pleasure which they have to enjoy.

Thus all life is suffering, and each one of the endless souls which move from one existence to the other since the time without any beginning, is certain that it finds everywhere much suffering and little joy. But although the suffering in Saṁsāra is so big like the Meru mountain, and the joy so small like a grain of mustard, and although all happiness rocks like a wave and so quickly disappears like a lightning, each being hangs to life with all the threads of its heart and forgets over the little joy that is granted to it the whole horrible evil which brings to it in eternal change birth, old age, disease and death.

Thus every being resembles the man in the pit of which a well-known parable narrates.[22] A man—so it is said in this story—was threatened by a gigantic elephant in a big forest. He fled to a large fig-tree, but could not climb it and therefore jumped into a pit which was nearby and which was covered with grass. While jumping he caught hold of a reed-bunch which had grown out of the wall of the pit, while an elephant was stretching out its trunk and even touching his head without getting him. When he looked around, he saw on the bottom of the pit a mighty gigantic serpent which was threatening to devour him, and four smaller serpents with their blown up hoods which were moving threateningly towards him. Terribly frightened, he was clutching to the reed-bunch so that he would not fall down. At this moment he looked up to find to his horror that a white mouse and a black mouse with pointed teeth were nagging at the reed and the elephant was shaking the tree with all its might. Many bees flew from its branch, chased by the shaking of the tree, and they stung the man with their sting. Thus tormented from all sides, the unlucky fellow noticed suddenly that a honey-drop was falling from the tree, touching his forehead and trickling down on to his mouth. Greedily he quaffed it, tasted joyfully its sweetness and forgot all the evil that was threatening him.

The soul resembles the man in the pit: forest is Saṁsāra; tree the life; pit is human existence. The elephant threatening him is death; the gigantic serpent is hell; the four other serpents are the four emotions; the two mice, the brighter and the darker halves of the month; the bees are the diseases. But the drop of honey represents the joy the world has to offer.

Thus like the man in the pit, the soul also forgets often over the fleeting enjoyment of the senses the horrible situation in which it is. When it comes to senses, it longs to come out of all suffering and strives for freedom from all suffering and for salvation.

But only a part of the beings in the world is suited to attain salvation, for not for all does the development come which elevates them from the condition of complete indifference; it does not also lead all to the attainment of salvation.

Of the many, quite tiny, fine beings (Nigoḍa) filling the universe, many have "indifferent" heterodoxy in which they are neither inclined towards the good nor towards the bad. Only when they are rattled by some accidental circumstances from their indifference, their heterodoxy assumes a definite form. But this creates a precondition for a spiritual development which can finally lead to redemption, but which does not need to. For there are Jīvas which are not capable of salvation (Abhavya) in all the classes of beings; they never come out of their heterodoxy and they never try at all to attain salvation. Only the beings which are predestined by fate to have the capability of redemption (Bhavyatva) recognize finally the truth of the religion of the Jainas, get tired of erring-around again and again in new forms of existence, practise self-discipline, asceticism and finally attain salvation.

(2) The Causes of Karma

The necessary requirement for coming out of Saṁsāra is the knowledge of the causes which produce constant binding of new Karmas, and elimination of just these causes.

The causes of binding are:

1. Mithyātva, heterodoxy,
2. Avirati, defective self-discipline, i.e. not paying heed to the precepts,

3. Kaṣāya, passions,
4. Yoga, activity.

Each one of these causes is again divided into a large number of sub-parts;* binding of Karma is ascribed to each one of them. Now since each one of these Karmas can naturally be bound only as long as the cause of its binding exists, its binding ceases the moment the cause is removed. But the causes of binding can only be removed just in a certain order and not outside it. On the basis of this theory, the way from complete heterodoxy to redemption is divided* into 14 stages ("Guṇasthānas") of which the higher is constantly different from the preceding one in as much as one of the causes of binding is eliminated in it wholly or partially, and accordingly, one order of the Karmas is not any more bound again. Once the passions and all the preceding causes of binding are eliminated, the Jīva binds only the Karma "feeling of pleasure"—the only one which lets it assimilate the activity (Yoga) for itself alone; once the activity has disappeared, no more Karma is bound at all, and the *mokṣa* is achieved.

(3) The Path to Salvation

The spiritual development of the soul is conditioned by the elimination of the Karmas which disturb faith and conduct. The binding of a new Mohanīya-karma cannot be hindered by a good condition of the mind, for the production of a Mohanīya-karma causes the binding of a new Karma of the same type which, in addition, has a significant duration (Sthiti). The Jīva has rather to go through three processes for this purpose. They last only

---

*Many consider also a fifth cause: Pramāda, i.e. negligence; others consider it as a sub-type of defective self-discipline.

Karmas "Tīrthaṅkara" "Vaikrīya-śarīre", "Āharaka-śarīre" and "Audārike-śarīre" are not affected by any of the causes of binding mentioned here; they are rather bound by the Jīvas which are especially blessed, and besides, the binding of the Karma "Tīrthaṅkara" is caused by the right faith and one of the two other Karma-types mentioned above by self-discipline.

for a portion of a Muhūrta (48 minutes), and their consequence is the reduction of Karma. Only the rational, completely developed beings having five senses and all four stages of existence, which have a control over body, speech, organ of thinking, knowledge which is formally determined and one of the best Leśyās, are qualified for it.

The consequence of the first process "Yathāpravṛtti-karaṇa" is the reduction of the duration and the intensity of Karma. It can often be repeated, but it leads to the goal only if the two other processes follow it.

The second process "Apūrva-karaṇa" works also in the same manner promoting purity of the soul. By carrying it out, the "knot" (Grantha) in our inside, i.e. the disturbance of the faith and conduct rooted in our heart, is split and thereby a door is opened to the spiritual progress.

The third process "Anivṛtti-karaṇa" again reduces duration and intensity of Karma, but besides, a part of the Karma-matter fallen upon heterodoxy is divided into three heaps, one impure for heterodoxy, one half-pure for mixed faith and one pure for lower (Kṣāyopaśamika) faith. After a short period one of them is realized and thereby determines the further fate of the soul which either returns to heterodoxy—so that the whole process was without any lasting influence—or attains finally the lower form of true faith.

The separation of Karmas from the life-long passions takes place also in similar manner; the one attaining the Kṣāyopaśamika-faith can move forward up to the Apramatta-saṁyata-guṇasthāna, i.e. up to the seventh stage of virtue in which he possesses self-discipline without negligence; if he wants to come further, he must go one of the two methodical ways: the Upaśama-śreṇī or the Kṣapaka-śreṇī. They help in the Karma not being produced.

Upaśama means pacification, appeasement; one who

exercises Upaśama of the Karmas can control himself to such an extent that the Karmas cannot produce their effect. The heaped-up potential (Sattā-) Karma is suppressed so that it cannot be manifested, but it cannot be eradicated with the roots, exists, therefore, in a latent condition and can break forth in an opportune moment. If the suppression of Karma is taken up in a systematic way in a definite order, then an "Upaśama-śreṇī" arises, a rung of the ladder which ends up finally with the complete suppression of all "Mohanīya-karmas". This rung of the ladder can be "climbed" by a soul in the fourth to the seventh Guṇasthāna; then in a regular course it passes to the following Guṇasthānas till the eleventh, and thus we have an Upaśānta-moha. The soul stays in this condition only for a short period, i.e. only for 1 Samaya. The moment this duration is over, it falls down from the Guṇasthāna. The fall is due to two causes: either by cessation of existence, by the death of an individual, or the expiry of the period which is possible for this Upaśānta-moha. If a being dies in this condition, then it is born again as Anuttarasura-god, but falls at once from the eleventh to the fifth Guṇasthāna. If the period expires, Jīva falls to the seventh Guṇasthāna, under circumstances also to one of the Guṇasthānas which are still lower.

The Upaśama-śreṇī lasts on the whole for 48 minutes; it can be climbed twice during one existence; if this is the case, redemption during this birth is impossible. But if it is climbed on the other hand only once, then an individual has still a chance to reach after his fall the Kṣapaka-śreṇī which leads to Nirvāṇa.

The Kṣapaka-śreṇī is a stage to wipe out the Karmas. A man who is older than 8 years having the best articulation (of joints) and who is in fourth to seventh Guṇasthāna is capable of beginning to climb on it. This wipes out successively the different types of the potential Karma. Finally he becomes a Sayogi-kevalī, an omniscient saint, who roams about bodily only for a short while on the earth to go then into Nirvāṇa.

(4) The 14 Guṇasthānas

Fourteen stages, i.e. the Guṇasthānas we have mentioned above, from the condition of complete dependence upon the Karma to the complete detachment from it can be distinguished. They are classified in a *logical* manner, according to the principle of decreasing iniquitousness and of increasing purity, and not in chronological order in which they could pass. For relapses are possible in the case of every soul; they can throw it down from the ascended stages and withdraw completely or partially the development made so far. This can be understood better when it is considered that the stay in many Guṇasthānas lasts for only few minutes so that it is quite possible that someone finds himself in the morning on a high stage, but falls down from it during noon and again climbs to it in the evening. But apart from the posssibility of a relapse, it would be impossible to go through all the 14 stages one after the other because a direct transition from the first stage to the second is out of question and the 11th stage is not directly passed before the 12th to the 14th. We have already referred to the different possibilities of the order of the Guṇasthānas in the previous section.

I shall give below the individual Guṇasthānas in the usual order and give a brief description of each of them:

1. *Mithyādṛṣṭi-guṇasthāna.* This stage is characterized by complete heterodoxy. Many souls, i.e. all those which are not capable of redemption, never come out of this stage. This applies also to those which are born as fully developed, irrational animals having 1 to 5 senses, as long as their existence lasts in this class of beings. Others are elevated from here, and mostly directly up to the fourth Guṇasthāna, but they can descend again to this stage and stay here for a while which would be

minimally a fraction of a Muhūrta and maximally somewhat lesser than 1/2 Pudgala-parāvarta.

2. *Sāsvādana-samyagdṛṣṭi-guṇasthāna,* a stage in which there is a "taste of the right faith" (p. 206). Beings who had the "Aupaśamika-faith" for a fraction of a Muhūrta (p. 207), but had lost it as a result of the eruption of life-long passions, are in this stage lasting only for one Samaya and at the most for 6 Āvalikās. Accordingly, it is a condition lasting only for a short period; it lies between the stage in which heterodoxy was suppressed (like the 4th) and on the lowest when it has full force. The soul returns to the first Guṇasthāna after the expiry of this period. All the rational beings with five senses as also undeveloped animals of every type can be Sāsvādanas.

3. *Samyagmithyādṛṣṭi-guṇasthāna,* a stage of "mixed faith". This stage in which the developed rational beings of all types can be found lasts only for a fraction of a Muhūrta; once the period is over, the soul obtains right or false faith as the conditions permit. Jīvas falling from the 4th stage normally pass through this Guṇasthāna.

4. *Avirata-samyagdṛṣṭi-guṇasthāna.* Beings found in this stage i.e. rational beings of all types having five senses, have right faith (namely a form of what is given under 4, 5, 6 on page 207), but having still no self-discipline. Here a methodical suppression or destruction of the Karma can be begun on one of the two Śreṇīs (p. 220). The duration of this Guṇasthāna is a fraction of a Muhūrta, and at least 33 Sāgaropamas and a little more (i.e. the highest period of life of gods and beings in hell which can be found in this stage) at the most.

5. *Deśavirata-samyagdṛṣṭi-guṇasthāna.* In this the right faith and partially the self-discipline is present (p. 207). This stage, which in contrast to the preceding one is not open to gods and beings from hell, but only to the fully developed rational animals and human beings, lasts

at the most somewhat lesser than a Pūrvakoṭi, and at least a fraction of a Muhūrta. The beings in this stage are either without a Śreṇī or they begin one of the Śreṇīs, respectively are in one of them (see p. 220).

6. *Pramatta-saṁyata-guṇasthāna.* A complete self-discipline is achieved in this stage which is, like the following, accessible only to human beings. But if it has arisen out of flared-up passions, sleep, etc., it is disturbed by negligence (Pramāda). A transcendent knowledge of the thoughts of others can appear from this Guṇasthāna onwards. The duration of the stay in this stage is minimally 1 Samaya, maximally 1 Muhūrta. If someone dies after 1 Samaya, he becomes Avirata (4th stage); if someone dies after a Muhūrta is almost over, he becomes Deśavirata (5th stage). If the Muhūrta is over without any incident, the soul comes into the following, 7th stage in which it stays through a fraction of a Muhūrta to return again to the Pramatta-guṇasthāna, after which the process begins anew. This oscillation between the 6th and the 7th Guṇasthāna lasts at the most somewhat less than a Pūrvakoṭi. This concerns ascetics who have not ascended any Śreṇī; if such is ascended or carried further, this sort of oscillation does not take place. It is characteristic of this stage that the body of transference (p. 195) is developed only in it.

7. *Apramatta-saṁyata-guṇasthāna.* Complete self-discipline without negligence is available in this stage. It lasts for 1 Samaya to 1 Muhūrta. The souls in this Guṇasthāna do not have any of the 6 Leśyās, like those of the preceding one, but only one of the three highest.

8. *Apūrva-karaṇa-guṇasthāna.* This stage, like the following one, is accessible only to a soul which is in a Śreṇī; only the white Leśyā occurs now onwards. The process (see p. 219) called Apūrva-karaṇa is carried out in it; the thoughts to which the one who is accomplishing it abandons himself in his meditation, fill him with joys which he had never known before. One who is in

an Upaśama-śreṇī stays in this stage at least 1 Samaya and at the most 1 Muhūrta, and the one in the Kṣapaka-śreṇī the whole period of a Muhūrta.

9. *Anivṛtti-bādara-samparāya-guṇasthāna.* Here the soul in the Upaśama- or Kṣapaka-śreṇī accomplishes a process called "Anivṛtti-karaṇa". The former stays here at least for 1 Samaya, and at the most the duration of a Muhūrta, the latter for a period of the duration of a Muhūrta. It is characteristic of this stage that the so-called 6 "non-passions" do not appear any more in this stage, but the 4 flaring-up passions do occur.

10. *Sūkṣma-samparāya-guṇasthāna.* The three passions: anger, pride, deceit do not appear in this stage as also libido, but the flaring-up greed appears to a negligible extent. The stay in this Guṇasthāna is 1 Samaya to 1 Muhūrta in Upaśama and the duration of a Muhūrta in Kṣapaka.

11. *Upaśānta-kaṣāya-vītarāga-chadmastha-guṇasthāna.* This is the highest stage that can be reached in the Upaśama-śreṇī. Here all the passions are suppressed. This lasts at least for 1 Samaya and at the most for the duration of a Muhūrta. The soul falls down from the Upaśama-śreṇī after this and comes to one of the lower Guṇasthānas (comp. p. 220).

12. *Kṣīṇa-kaṣāya-vītarāga-chadmastha-guṇasthāna.* This stage like all the following ones is attained by only the souls which have destroyed all the passions in the Kṣapaka-śreṇī. When in the last Samaya whatever greed that is left over has been destroyed, the Kṣapaka (who thus jumps the 11th Guṇasthāna!) is in this stage where he remains for the duration of a Muhūrta. He remains bound now an only the momentary Karma. In the last Samaya of his stay all the Karmas which restricted his knowledge, his seeing and his energy, disappear.

13. *Sayogi-kevalī-guṇasthāna.* The saint is a Kevalī, an omniscient one, in this stage. If there is an unusual case that he had got the "Tīrthaṅkara-karma" in the earlier

existences, then this is realized here; he then becomes a Tīrthaṅkara, a founder or a restorer of the Jaina-church. The Sayogi-kevalī knows everything, sees everything, is capable of everything, yet he has a body and a certain activity which is conditioned by matter, and a number of Karmas obtained earlier are produced in him; but as soon as the Karmas determining the quantum of life (Āyus) are exhausted, he annihilates all these. Accordingly, the Sayogi-condition lasts minimum for a duration of a Muhūrta and maximum somewhat less than a Pūrvakoṭi. The moment the period given to it ends, the saint sinks into deep meditation and then ceases the cruder and finer activity of the mind, speech and body.

14. *Ayogi-kevalī-guṇasthāna.* The saint has no activity (Yoga) and Leśyā in this transitory stage comprising only a period of a Muhūrta.

Then he enters the Śaileśi-condition as long as one needs to express 5 short syllables (a, i, u, ri, li). Gone into meditation he destroys then the rest of the Karmas which still exist. He has thus become free from everything that is material—he is redeemed.

2. THE PRACTICAL ETHICS

(1) Reward and Sin

The doctrine of Karma, as the preceding sections show, is the basis of the theoretical dispensation of Jainas; in the same way, it controls also its whole system of practical ethics. All precepts on action are based on the concept of the influx of the Karma-matter(s) into the soul and on the assumption that one could stop this influx of harmful matter by one's own behaviour.

Like water flowing constantly into a lake through a canals Karma flows constantly into the soul by the activity of body, speech and mind. A good activity is the "inflow", the influx (Āsrava) of reward (Puṇya), bad activity is the influx of the sin (Pāpa).

The influx takes place in 42 ways. The 17 most important of these are: 5 senses, 4 passions, 3 types of activity (application) (p. 202), infringement of the precepts (p. 228). To this 25 actions of different types are added.[23]

The following enumeration gives an idea of the activities which afflict the soul with definite Karmas:

Hostility to knowledge and seeing, to the knowers and the aids of knowing, their rejection, destruction and obstruction, not paying heed to the teachers and their rules, destruction of books, tearing of the eyes, etc., such actions produce a Karma which conceals knowledge and seeing.

Piousness and piety with respect to parents and teachers, gentleness, sympathy, keeping the oath, respectful behaviour, vanquishing passions, giving of alms, fidelity to faith—they cause "the feeling of pleasure", its opposite being "feeling of displeasure".

Teaching of false and obstruction of the true religion, slandering Jinas, saints, idols of gods, of the community and the canon, theft of consecrated objects—all this causes "disturbance of faith". The outbursts of passions and "non-passions" produce the corresponding "disturbance of the life-conduct".

Negligible passionateness, marital fidelity, disposition to a right conduct give a male sex envy, meanness, mendacity, great sensuousness give a female, violent longing for enjoyment and strong passions directed towards sexual intercourse between men and women bestow the third sex.

One who torments other beings and kills them, strives excessively for possession and is controlled by life-long passions obtains the rebirth in hell and a corresponding quantum of life (Āyus). A cheat, crafty fellow who follows heterodoxy, gives himself up to the pleasure of senses, and does not atone for his sins, is reborn as an animal, and an humble upright one and who strives for possession in a negligible measure and harms little other animals, is born as human being. One who has the right faith, but practises only partial or no self-discipline, one whose passions are small, a heretic who practises foolish asceticism and one who annihilates his Karma involuntarily, while he endures without volution hunger and thirst, practises celibacy, withstands difficulties, falls down from mountains, dies in fire and water—he obtains a quantum of life which is proper for gods.

Honesty, gentleness, desirelessness and purity give a good Nāma-karma; its opposite is bad Nāma-karma.

Just acknowledgement of the advantages of others, modesty, reverence for teachers and masters, urge to learn and to ṭeach produces high rank of birth; its opposite is low rank.

Karma "hindrance" is caused by obstruction of the worship of Jainas, withholding of food, drink, shelter, clothing and making other person powerless with the help of magic-*mantras.*

In accordance with such enumerations, Jainas differentiate between good Karmas which have arisen from Puṇya and bad Karmas which are a consequence of Pāpa. On the whole 42 good and 42 bad Karmas are counted.[24]

The need to describe, as far as possible, accurately the nature of Puṇya and Pāpa, has driven Jainas to classify the contents of the two categories. Thus 9 types of Puṇya and 18 types of Pāpa are distinguished.

The 9 types of Pūṇya consist in donating food, drink, clothing, shelter and bed; in doing good by thoughts, words and works, as also by reverence that is shown to elders.

The 18 types of Pāpa are: killing of living beings, untruthfulness, theft, unchastity, excessive attachment to possession, anger, pride, deceit, greed, inclination, hatred, pugnacity, slander, passing on information secretly, captiousness, pleasure, or displeasure, hypocrasy and heterodoxy.

(2) The Moral Precepts

(a) Duties of a Layman

A layman who has the knowledge of the true doctrine, of the true god (Deva/Jina) and the right master (Guru) and who is free from 5 offences: doubt about the faith, desire for other mundane and supermundane teachings and things, indecisiveness in acknowledging the truths of Jainism, admiration and recognition of other believers—such a layman can take upon himself to fulfil the 5 "small vows" (Anuvratas):

1. Ahiṁsā, not to kill or injure a living being intentionally. This precept does not apply to human beings alone, but also to animals which are not allowed to be slaughtered for the purpose of eating meat or for the performance of sacrifices. Even immobile beings, like plants, should not, as far as possible, be harmed. Observance of this precept restricts the number of eatables and drinks which can be enjoyed; it forbids further a number of other activities.

2. Satya, to say the truth, i.e. not to lie.

3. Asteya, not to steal, i.e. not to take what is not given.

4. Brahmacarya, to live in chastity.

5. Parigraha-tyāga, not to desire new things greedily, but be satisfied with possession whose limit that is set by oneself is not crossed.

Observing the Auvratas mentioned above is supported by the observance of the following 3 Guṇa-vratas.

1. *Dig-vrata.* The layman takes upon himself to extend his journeys in each direction only up to a definite point (e.g. Himālayas in the north).

2. *Upabhogaparibhoga-vrata.* He vows to make use of only a definite number of things necessary for life, and to avoid the others. This vow also includes observance of the injunctions about food according to which nothing should be enjoyed that is obtained by harming living beings, and a number of activities are disallowed which could harm the beings by practising them.

3. *Anarthadaṇḍa-vrata.* He vows to keep himself away from all that is harmful, neither to wish bad to someone, nor to cause others to do bad, neither to use weapons or other things causing injuries, nor to commit reckless acts.

Besides these there are 4 Śikṣā-vratas:

1. *Sāmayika-vrata.* A layman vows to meditate daily in imperturbable peace for one or several Muhūrtas (i.e. 48, 96, 144 minutes). This happens in the morning, at the noon time and in the evening.

2. *Deśāvakāśika-vrata.* He vows not to leave certain boundaries (house, village, etc.) for a definite period, not to use certain things, eatables, etc.

3. *Poṣadha-vrata.* He vows to fast through 24 hours on certain days (usually four times in a moon-month) and live as a monk.

4. *Atithisaṁvibhāga-vrata.* He vows to offer to guests, particularly monks, what they need by right.

One more vow is taken by many pious people: they vow to accept death by starvation by voluntarily renouncing all foods. This vow is carried out mostly by old people who feel that their end has come, but also by persons who are completely healthy because they hope to attain supermundane salvation by this act of highest renunciation.

For the sake of complete perfection, a layman is not satisfied by observing these vows; he also observes 11 Pratimās which bring him closer to asceticism. They are:

1. *Darśana.* Belief in the Tīrthaṅkaras, right teacher and the Jaina-faith.

2. *Vrata.* Accurate observance of the 12 vows.

3. *Sāmāyika.* Daily three meditations.

4. *Poṣadhopavāsa.* Fasting on full-moon and new-moon days and on the 8th and the 14th of every half of a lunar month.

5. *Sacitta-tyāga.* Abstinence from eating of living beings, i.e. not only animals, but also fresh vegetables.

6. *Rātri-bhukta-tyāga.* Avoiding eating between sunset and sunrise.

7. *Brahmacarya.* Avoidance of sexual intercourse, also with one's wife.

8. *Ārambha-tyāga.* Giving up all worldly activities, involving injury to living beings (like building a house, etc.).

9. *Parigraha-tyāga.* Giving up possession (by distributing it to children and others, renouncing the service of house-servants, etc.).

10. *Anumati-tyāga (Anumodana).* Renunciation by a pious man of the proper food that is prepared for him and eating only that what others give or what has been left over.

11. *Udiṣṭa-tyāga.* Acceptance of monk's dress and looking for a temple or solitude to meditate there without being disturbed.

These 11 Pratimās are the stages of perfection. A layman obtains them one after the other, and while doing so, maintain the vow of the each preceding stage. The last stage corresponds practically to monkhood, only that the consecration of the order is missing. The significance of the persons who observe the precepts of the last Pratimās is especially great among Digambaras. They consider that those who have given up wearing of clothes are perfect ascetics. They are approximately equally respected like the ascetics among Śvetāmbaras.

(b) Duties of an Ascetic

An ascetic has to keep the same vows as a layman, but their scope is quite far-reaching. Therefore, the duties of an ascetic are called Mahāvrata (great vows), unlike those of a layman which are called Anuvrata (small vows):

1. *Ahiṁsā.* An ascetic must most anxiously try not to kill or to injure any living being even *unintentionally.*

2. *Asatya-tyāga.* He has to examine all his words most accurately so that he does not say anything false even *unintentionally* or in joke.

3. *Asteya.* He should not only take anything that is not given to him, but he must ask for permission to take it, when something is offered to him.

4. *Brahmacarya.* He should not only observe complete celibacy, but he should also avoid all thoughts and conversations on sexual things and avoid everything that could lead him into temptation.

5. *Aparigraha.* He should give up all possessions and be indifferent to everything that is worldly, both persons and things.

Each one of these vows is supported by each of the five others. Constantly remembering them and heeding them enables an ascetic to observe the "Mahāvratas".[25]

(3) Means of Averting Karma

The aim of the path of salvation taught by the Tīrthaṅkaras is to free the soul from the pernicious influx of the Karma-mater. This goal is reached in the life as a monk by strict observance of certain rules. This averts the influx of a new Karma into the soul (Āsrava, p. 226) and thereby causing the stoppage (Saṁvara) of the Karma.

The following help in waiting of (Saṁvara) Karma:

1. Gupti, "discipline", i.e. the correct regulation of the activity of the body, speech and mind.

2. Samiti "caution" while going, speaking, collecting alms, by lifting and putting down a thing and while emptying the body. While doing these things great precaution is necessary, because otherwise there could be

infringement against the precepts (e.g. while talking and collecting alms) or, living beings could be killed (while walking, lifting or keeping something, evaluating or emptying the bladder), if the place where something is to be put down is not carefully examined and living beings are not removed from it.

3. Observance of 10 duties (Dharma) of a monk consists in: consideration for the mistakes of the others, humility in behaviour with all, purity in thinking that is unequivocs, desirelessness, truthfulness, self-control, asceticism (particularly fasting), renunciation of all worldly enjoyments, renunciation of all possession of persons and things, and celibacy.

4. Devotion to the following 12 reflections (Anuprekṣā):

(a) Everything is *ephemeral*, a body is dissolved like a cloud chased by storm, all happiness vanishes like a dream, etc.

(b) Every being right up to gods is *helplessly* a victim of death.

(c) Saṁsāra is like a rented house in which beings go in and go out all the time.

(d) Every being is fully responsible for its action.

(e) Body and all that is material is *different* from soul.

(f) Body is impure, consisting of humours, blood, flesh, fats and bones, marrow and semen and full of dirt which flows out of it through the orifices.

(g) Karma constantly *flows* into the soul as a consequence of earlier actions.

(h) This influx of Karma into the soul can be *hindered* by one's own behaviour.

(i) Mortifications can *destroy* Karma and make the soul pure like gold that is purified in fire.

(j) The world is eternal and indestructible.

(k) *Enlightenment* is the most precious and the most rare possession and it is difficult to be obtained in the world.

(1) The *law* (Dharma) proclaimed by the sublime Jinas is well-proclaimed, is it the only friend of those Jinas is well-proclaimed, it is the only friend of those who are without a friend, the only protection from hell and bad rebirth.

5. Patient endurance of 22 difficulties (Parīsahas) which either directly trouble a monk or threaten to waylay him from the path to salvation. The difficulties are: hunger, thirst, cold, heat, stinging flies (which disturb him in meditation), nakedness, bad clothing, uncomfortable surrounding, women, unpleasant wandering life, inconvenience of the places of meditation, hard bed, abusive language (used against the monk, doctrine, etc.), ill-treatment, lack of dignity of begging (which is particularly felt by people who were rich earlier), failure while begging, disease, pricking of the blades of grass (on which the naked ascetic stands or lies), dirt on the body (a monk is not allowed to wash his clothes in flowing water; at the most he can do it in the water that is given to him), show of reverence (he has to be indifferent to them), conceit of knowledge, dejection on account of one's own ignorance, religious doubts.

6. Cāritra, the five degrees of good conduct:

(a) Sāmayika, relinquishing everything that is bad and dedicating oneself to meditation.

(b) Chedopasthāpanā, repenting all the mistakes committed and reporting them to the spiritual teacher and subjecting oneself to the atonement that is imposed by him.

(c) Parihāra-viśuddhi, purity of mind which is attained by painful care of all the living beings, by the service dedicated to saints and by special exercise of penance.

(d) Sūkṣma-samparāya, general detachment from everything that is worldly. In this passions are expressed only in a subtle form.

(e) Yathā-khyāta, the highest stage of moral self-determination in which there is complete liberation from the worldly passions and in which all the precepts are heeded completely and without any inhibitions.

(4) Means of Destroying all Karmas

Salvation, i.e. complete purification of the soul from all Karma-matter requires that the one striving for Nirvāṇa hinders not only the influx of new Karma by his behaviour, but also sheds off the Karma which still remains. This intentional shedding off of Karma which is bound earlier is called Sakāma-nirjarā. But it is necessary to say a few words on the nature of the shedding off of Karma so that this concept which is so important for the Jaina-doctrine of salvation could be understood.

Each Karma is produced once, i.e. it attains the condition of "Vipāka" (maturity) like a fruit coming out once from a grain of a seed. Once the Karma has shown its effect, it disappears, and it does not exist any more like a fruit that is eaten. Thus a condition should finally appear in the natural course of things for a man who makes it impossible for new Karma to flow into his soul. In this condition, all the Karma that is stored by him is used up, and his soul becomes free from all Karma. But this condition cannot appear in reality because a man has within his soul so much Karma from his numerous existences that it would be exhausted only after a long time, particularly because many Karmas preserve their power for a very long time. It is, therefore, necessary that the annihilation of Karma is accelerated in an artificial way. Just like the mangoes or the fruits of the bread-fruit tree are ripened prematurely by applying artificial means, it can also be tried in the case of Karma that it is produced and consumed in a definite manner. Asceticism—besides the observance of precepts which serve to avert Karma—causes quick annihilation of Karma. Asceticism (Tapas) burns, according to the general Indian view, the seeds of work; thus taking it up, i.e. doing mortification and meditation, causes annihilation of Karma. But if this annihilation should really lead to salvation, then it is necessary that it is done in the right manner. For, there is also "foolish asceticism", as it is practised by heretics and people who are not properly advised. This so-called "Bāla-tapas", which may also include religious suicide committed in a false manner (by jumping from a hill or by drowning oneself), can help in getting salvation, like meditation done in a wrong manner (this is discussed below on p. 236); it has, however, certain beneficial effects inasmuch as it causes a rebirth in the heaven of gods.[26]

Asceticism is twofold: outer and inner.

A. Outer asceticism (Bāhya-tapas) is of the following six types:

1. Fasting (Anaśana).

2. Reduction in food (Avamaudarya) in which only a part of the meal is taken instead of full meal.

3. Restriction of food (Vṛtti-saṅkṣepa) not only according to the number of meals, but according to the place from where they are received, and according to the time when they are taken and according to the circumstances in which they were taken, etc.

4. Renunciation of tasty food (rasa-parityāga) like milk, sugar and other things which taste particularly well.

5. Avoidance of everything that could lead the senses into temptation (Samalīnatā), above all by precaution that persons from the other sex are not in the proximity of the bed.

6. Mortification of flesh (Kāya-kleśa) by meditating in great heat or cold, etc., by renouncing every care of the body, avoiding scratching oneself when one gets an itching sensation, of spitting out, etc.

It can be said from the preceding that the external asceticism of Jainas consists in enduring the difficulties of all sorts. A Jaina-ascetic takes all sorts of pains and discomforts upon himself without balking at them. Jainas have rejected the practice of the Brahmanic penitents of giving oneself artificial pains, like lying on a bed of thorns, etc.

B. Internal asceticism (Ābhyantara-tapas) is also of 6 types:

1. Confession (Prāyaścitta) made before a Guru or Sādhu.

2. Reverence (Vinaya) which is shown to the servants of the religion.

3. Zeal (Vaiyāvṛttya) which is shown to masters and teachers, to monks, to the community, laymen and the sick, etc.

4. Study (Svādhyāya).

5. Indifference (Utsarga) with respect to the body and its passions and temptations coming from outside. This complete disrespect of everything that does not belong to the soul is expressed most excellently in the complete negligence of everything that is corporeal, which leads to voluntary death by starvation.

6. Meditation (Dhyāna), i.e. "fixation and concentration of thought for a Muhūrta", i.e. at the most for 48 minutes. These 48 minutes represent the maximum of what can be achieved. Meditation can be taken up only by the one who has the best dispensation of articulation (of joints) (see p. 197). On the whole, four types of meditation are distinguished. However, only the last two of these are suitable to lead one to salvation:

(1) Ārta-dhyāna, melancholy meditation, consists in constant ruminating about something that is unpleasant that one has experienced. Of this 4 types are distinguished:

(a) Iṣṭa-viyoga, thinking of something pleasant one has lost.

(b) Aniṣṭa-saṁyoga, thinking of something unpleasant one has experienced.

(c) Roga-cintā, thinking of illness.

(d) Nidānārtha, thinking of the future, particularly of

the wishes which should be realized in a later existence. (An ascetic thinks, e.g., "May I be successful in my mortifications that I am born again as a world-ruler and enjoy beautiful women." Such Nidānas which are then realized play a great role in the Jaina-literature.

These types of meditation are found among beings which are on the 1st to the 6th stage of virtue.

(2) Raudra-dhyāna, bad meditation, is directed towards four worldly goals, viz. murder, lie, theft and preserving goods.

These types of meditation are found among beings up to the 5th Guṇasthāna.

Both the following meditations promote salvation in contrast to the first two.

(3) Dharma-dhyāna, meditation consisting in thinking of religion. It is directed towards:

(a) Ajnā-vicaya, the holy doctrine.

(b) Apāya-vicaya, the fact that the soul is obstructed in the development of its true nature by something that does not belong to it.

(c) Vipāka-vicaya, consequences of the Karma that have befallen the soul.

(d) Saṁsthāna-vicaya is focussed on the structure and the nature of universe. This meditation is found in the Guṇasthānas 7 to 12.

(4) Śukla-dhyāna, pure meditation. Of this, 4 stages are distinguished:

(a) Pṛthaktva-vitarka is directed towards the conduct and the contradictions in the process of the world (growth and decay, soul and matter, substances and conditions, etc.).

(b) Ekatva-vitarka is directed towards the soul as the one which sustains all changes.

(c) Sūkṣma-kriyā-pratipāti is directed towards suppressing the activity which still exists in minimal degree.

(d) Uparata-kriyānivṛtti is focussed on complete liberation from all Karmas.

The four stages of "pure meditation" follow one after the other; the first falls in the Guṇasthānas 8 to 11, the second in 12, the third in 13, the last comes in the 14th directly before redemption.

3. SALVATION

When Karma has been wiped out in the last Guṇasthāna (p. 225), then the redeemed one climbs to the peak of the world. This happens on account of the straight movement (p. 179) which is peculiar to the soul from its nature and which can only be now developed because the matter does not exist any more which checked and deviated sidewards the natural upward movement of the soul by their gravity. Just like a gourd cleaned by removing the dirt does not sink to the bottom but hastens to the surface of water, the redeemed also elevates himself in a Samaya up to the top of the universe. He remains here because it is not possible to reach beyond the world the non-world surrounding it, for the medium of movement, Dharma (p. 180) is absent in the non-world.

The accomplished ones (Siddhas) stay in the topmost part of the holy region Īśatprāgbhāra (see p. 270) for all eternity untouched by the change of the world. It is neither light, nor heavy, itself without any visible form, incorporeal and therefore penetrable, but with a spatial (immaterial) extension of 2/3 of the one which it had had in its last existence. All the individual differences which the Karmas had attached to the souls do not exist any more; but on the other hand, they have all the four "infinities": infinite knowledge, infinite seeing, infinite power and infinite joy.

Siddhas are similar to one another, except for the way in which they attain salvation; these ways are divided into 15 groups, but they exclude one another only partially.

Tīrthaṅkara-siddhas are those who were Tīrthaṅkaras before salvation.

Atīrthaṅkara-siddhas are those who were not Tīrthaṅkaras.

Tīrtha-siddhas attained salvation at a time when Jaina-church existed.

Atīrtha-siddhas got salvation at a time when there was no Jaina-church (like Marudevī, mother of the first Tīrthaṅkara who got Nirvāṇa before Ṛṣabha founded a Tīrtha).

Gṛha-liṅga-siddhas were never ascetics, but attained salvation as householders like Marudevi who is mentioned above.

Anya-liṅga-siddhas attained salvation without belonging to the Jaina-faith.

Sva-liṅga-siddhas got salvation as Jaina-ascetics.

Puruṣa-liṅga-siddhas were men before their transfiguration.

Strī-liṅga-siddhas were women before.

Napuṁsaka-liṅga-siddhas belonged earlier to the third sex.

Buddha-bodhita-siddhas were led to salvation by conversion by their Gurus.

Pratyeka-buddha-siddhas were liberated on account of a single experience which showed them that the world was ephemeral.

Svayam-siddhas found their way to salvation on their own.

Eka-siddhas get their salvation alone.

Aneka-siddhas do this together with numerous others.

It is said in *Uttarādhyayana-sūtra* 36, 51 ff. that that salvation was got at the same time by 10 hermaphrodites, 20 women, 108 men, 4 householders, 10 heterodox people and 108 Jaina-monks, 2 persons of the biggest, 4 of the smallest and 108 of average body-size. At the same time, 4 individuals got salvation on mountain, 2 in ocean, 3 in water, 20 below the earth and 108 on the surface of the earth.

This data corresponds only to the views of Śvetāmbaras; according to the belief of Digambaras only men can get salvation, this is not possible to the other sexes. Both hold the view that only human beings can get salvation; gods and other beings which are capable of getting salvation according to other Indian systems, do not have it according to Jaina-teachings. They have rather to be born again as human beings when they become mature for this highest spiritual development to be able to accomplish complete absolution from all earthly passions.

IV

Cosmology

1. EVIDENCES AGAINST THE EXISTENCE OF GOD

According to the Jaina-doctrine the world is eternal and ephemeral. It listens only to its own laws and remains unchanged in its basic nature although its parts change. No god has created it, rules it and can destroy it. In contrast to most other religions, from Jainas deny most definitely the existence of an imperishable, all-mighty highest "Lord"(Īśvara) who creates the universe, rules it, and when he likes, destroys it. The acceptance of a creator and destroyer (Kartā-Hartā) appears to them to be unjustified and self-contradictory and has to be rejected both from the point of view of logic and morality.

The views on the nature of god are very different among the individual Indian and non-Indian systems which Jainas have disputed and do so even now. Above all, Hinduism has produced an abundance of various doctrines on god and his relationship with the world, doctrines which appear to have exhausted all the possibilities of thinking, started with the extreme monotheism which makes the sharpest distinction between god, matter and souls, up to the most perfect theophany for which the world is an empty appearance and god is everything. Three types of belief in god can be mainly distinguished. The first view: God is an absolutely perfect, omniscient, all-powerful, omnipresent, kind and blessed entity which creates and destroys the world which is *toto genere* different from it and controls autonomously the souls and substances in it. This view which is indeed close to the one of Christianity and of Islam, has been advocated particularly by the Nyāya-Vaiśeṣika-philosophers and the theologians of different Vaiṣṇavite and Śaivite sects.

A second group of systems teaches: matter and souls are no doubt different from god at the time of the origin of the world and are ruled by him. But they have emerged originally from god; god has developed himself into them and takes them back again into himself. These theories have been proposed by the Vaiṣṇavite and Śaivite schools in the most different ways.

The third view finally looks at god, Brahma, as the only true *sat*, the absolute. The plurality of the phenommena in the world is only a Māyā, an illusion, which is "built up" from the Supreme Being by the ignorant; in reality, every soul is identical with god, and all difference is only an illusionary appearance, as unreal as a dream or a Fata Morgana. An acosmic theophany of this sort experienced its consequential development in Śaṅkara's Advaita-philosophy; but it is also found among Vaiṣṇavas, Śaivas, Śāktas and in other Indian systems.

Jaina-philosophers considered in depth all these doctrines and tried to refute them in the most acuminous manner. Let us give briefly in the following their most important arguments.[27]

The assumption that the world must have a *creator* originates from the conception that it is a product, like a pot; and exactly so, like the products having a cause, the world as a whole must also have one. As an evidence for this that the world is to be equated with earthly products, it is said that it is subject to change like those.

If this were to be correct, then god must also be a product, because certain changes must also take place in him on account of the activity of creating, destroying, etc. practised by him. Thus we are forced on our part to look again for the cause of god, which leads to *regressus ad-infinitum.*

If it is supposed that the world had a cause, then it would not mean that this cause has to be a thinking being. If we concede this and apply to it the analogy of the potter and the pot, then we do not get a perfect being, for the producer of a product in the world is nowhere perfect in any respect. Then one would have further to presume that god has a body, because it is never observed on the earth that a material thing is created without a body existing as a material basis of the activity of its thinking and volition for its mind and will which it wants to produce. Thus if it is presumed that there is a world-creator, then it has also to be pre-supposed that this creator has a, whatever may be its nature, material body. But everything which consists of matter is alterable and therefore must suffer. Thus god could be neither unalterable nor blissful. But if one believes, on the other hand, that god has created the world without the assistance of a body, to some extent merely by his abstract existence, then one cannot rely at all on the analogies from the world of experience, for no one has ever seen that a potter has produced a pot without body and organs.

A further question is: from what has god produced the world? If he has produced it from nothing, then it would be contredicted by the saying nihil fit. If the world has arisen suddenly out of nothing and has again sunken into nothing, then god must have also emerged from nothing and would perish again later. If *sat* and *asat* are absolute opposites, then the one cannot emerge from the other; if they are not this, then virtue and vice, truth and lie, etc. also do not exist; then all philosophy is vain and the question remains unresolved.

If it is presumed that matter and soul are eternal entities which get certain qualities from their nature, and god's creative activity is limited to classifying and guarding the substances and intelligences which are effective on their own and which condition the happening in the world, then one cannot understand why one should take the assistance of god to explain the world; souls and matter could create the whole world-process themselves with the help of the powers that are inherent in them.

If one justifies the theory that the souls are completely heteronom and need efficacy of god to pursue their activity, then it becomes unclear how god could be the last, autonomous entity responsible for this. Then by the same logic one could presume that he is also kept at his activity again by a superior master standing behind him and above him and so in *infinitum*.

Supposing that god is the only autonomous doer in the world, then he must be the cause behind all evils, because much evil happens doubtlessly in the world. If this is the case, then god is not good. But if god were to be good, but lets the evil rule freely then he is not all-powerful. If it is said that god has created the souls, then one must ask oneself: Why did he not make them good, because he punishes them afterwards for the sins they commit! But if god had called the souls into the world and left it to himself to see whether they act well or otherwise, then he is not omniscient, for if he had been this, he should have foreseen it.

If one opines (like Madhva and other followers of the theory of pre-destination) that god works as a doer of everything without enjoying the fruits of his doing, lets, on the other hand, reward and punishment be given to the beings who act under his will, then it appears to be contradictory that god acts and the beings which are dependent upon him and not having their own will, have to bear the consequences. But above all, it is not worthy of a noble and kind Lord to let the beings fall into hell and suffer there horrible punishments for actions in which they have only an indirect part.

If god has created the world, then one would have to ask for his motive. If he has done it as a result of his desire, then it follows that he was in the state of dissatisfaction before the creation of the world, then he cannot be regarded as eternally blissful and perfect. If god created the world on account of his whim, then one cannot understand how everything happens in it according to law. If he created it to let the souls partake of the reward or punishment for their deeds in a past world-period, then he acted under compulsion, and i.e. he is not all-powerful. If it is presumed that he created the world out of *love,* i.e. on account of the sympathy with the eternal, unredeemed souls to lead them to salvation, then it is not understood why only so few souls reach salvation and why did god conjure up the whole torments of the Saṁsāra, for he could have reached his goal he strived for in a different way because he is all-powerful. If it is believed on the other hand that god let the world be created to let the souls chosen by him partake of the rewards, and others, rejected by him, be condemned, then one would have to charge him of partiality and question his sense of justice. If creation, governance and destruction of the world is a play for god, which he does for his entertainment without any purpose and goal, then he must be a horrible master who finds pleasure in the sufferings of the innumerable living beings.

Even the different attributes which the theists have ascribed to god cannot withstand any criticism. If god were to be omnipresent, then he must be present in the hells and the other places of suffering. If he were to be omniscient, then he would not have produced evil beings, and above all the people, like Jainas, who deny him his existence.

God's existence cannot be proved by usual means of

knowledge, perception and inference. But even the revelation does not prove his existence. "Revelation is done either by him or by someone else. If he has done it, then it proves his omniscience; then his majesty ends up in smoke, because it is not proper for majesties to proclaim their own advantages. Further he could not have made a textbook (Śāstra, i.e. the holy scripture). For, a textbook consists of the sounds which could be articulated with the help of the palate, etc. Articulation is possible, only if a body exists. The reasons against the assumption of the body of god have already been mentioned (p. 242). But if the revelation comes from someone else, then it is to be asked whether he is omniscient or not omniscient. If he is omniscient, then they have to be two, and this would, therefore, exclude his uniqueness which was claimed before; then also a *regressus ad infinitum* follows, when one ponders over the evidence of his omniscience. But if he is not omniscient, who would trust his words?"[28]

The doctrine that matter and souls emerge from god, that they are to some extent a transformation (Pariṇāma) of god, is not better substantiated than the one of the pure theists. Not only much of the criticism made against the theists given above is valid, but it must also be asked: how is it possible that the accomplished god provided with all advantages could be developed into this world which is so defective? And it must remain completely incomprehensible how the spiritual god could be transformed into unspiritual matter.

It is not different with Śaṅkara's theory according to which god is the absolute and the plurality is only "Māyā". Is Māyā something real—what one has to presume from the effects emanating from it—then it would be something that exists beyond and beside god; thus god would not be the only true reality. If Māyā, on the other hand, is something unreal—what the followers of Śaṅkara say—then it can impossibly work. What does not exist can as little produce something like the "sky-flower" or other things which do not exist. To claim of Māyā that it could let something be produced, although it is unreal, is as absurd as speaking of an infecund woman that she is mother. How otherwise can one imagine the relationship between god and Māyā? Is Māyā something that is inherent in god, or something different from him which produces the world after uniting with him? If god were to be inherent in Māyā, then ignorance, unblessedness, etc., in short everything Māyā produces, would belong to the nature of god. If, on the other hand, Māyā is something different, which is united with god, then one has to ask for the reason and the cause of this union. Did it take place with or against the will of god? If it has happened with the will of god, then god could have acted only under the influence of blind desire, thus he would not be pure and without any desire. If this has, on the other hand, happened without or against the will of god, then god is not omnipotent. Thus in whatever way the theory is postulated, it is always unsatisfactory and full of contradictions.

The believers of god of all shades refer to the holy scriptures as an authority for their belief. These are said to have come down from god himself. But these scriptures contradict one another in many nuances. What is then right, what is wrong? The decision on this is quite subjective. If god is to be the creator of the universe, then he must have also created all textbooks, for otherwise he could not have created everything, but there would be things which have originated without his action. But if everything traces back to god, then the false textbooks also have to owe him their origin. How can then someone who shows the right as well as the wrong way, could be considered as a great authority and a great teacher from whom all wisdom emanates?

The order and harmony in the external world and the moral law ruling in it need not in any way force one to accept *one* highest being guiding all happening and distributing reward and punishment. With the same right, one can also look at the plurality of gods as the cause of the world and morality. The objection that several gods cannot work together in the right manner does not hold water; if ants, as it is seen, can bring forth something that is well-organized by their planned cooperation, how should not the beings which are better equipped than the human beings?

There is no reason whatsoever at all to presume the existence of one or several eternal beings to which the order of the world traces back. The unshakable law of Karma is sufficient to explain the difference among the living beings, the multiplicity of their destinies and the harmony ruling over the whole cosmos. The believers of god themselves acknowledge that there is retribution of Karma and say that god acts in agreement with them. If thus god himself cannot change the eternal law and when it rules without any limitation, what is then the use of proposing the hypothesis of the existence of god, when, afterall, everything can also be equally nicely explained without this hypothesis?

As it is seen, Jainas attack with sharp weapons the belief in god who is ruling over the world; they are quite sure that god has no place in their *weltanschauung*. To that extent they are 'atheists'. But this does not mean that they are atheists in the sense we understand this word in the West. In the West—compared to India—there is no great diversity of views pertaining to religion. In the West acknowledgement of god is prerequisite of every religion, so that every "atheist" was considered from the start as an irreligious man and atheism and animosity have become synonyms for many. From ancient times, the situation in India was different. Belief in one or several world-ruling gods was never regarded as a precondition of a religion. Since the old times, we often come across a great number of teachers who negate the existence of a world-ruler (Īśvara) and have completely a religious character in as much as religious concepts like those of moral sin and moral reward, of the transcendent rewards and punishments and of rebirth and salvation are alive in them and religious rites and ceremonies are prescribed by them. The orthodox Hindu systems of Mīmāṁsā and Sāṁkhya are also to be considered in this sense as atheistic, as also the original Buddhism. Like them, Jainism also teaches an atheism having a religious colouring.

It will be shown in the Section on Cult that the worship of eternally blissful supermundane beings can still be linked with its "god-free" system; we shall then also know, how Jainas are right from their point of view, when they don't want to be labelled as "atheists" in spite of their rejection of a god who has created the world and who rules over it.

2. SHAPE AND SIZE OF THE UNIVERSE

The universe has a firm, unalterable shape and a limited size, albeit going much beyond human faculty of imagination. Its dimensions can be accurately measured, and the so-called "Rajju" serves as the measure. This is, according to Colebrooke, a stretch which god traverses in 6 months when he covers 20, 57, 152 Yojanas in a moment.

According to the view of Digambaras the universe is 14 Rajjus high and from north to south 7 Rajjus broad. The breadth from west to east is, at the lowest position, also 7 Rajjus, but it decreases gradually till it measures 1 Rajju in the height of 7 Rajjus, i.e. in the centre of the world. The breadth increases from this point and reaches on expension of 5 Rajjus in the middle of the remaining part (i.e. at the end of the heaven Brahmaloka), and then decreases again till it is 1 Rajju at the highest position. The abode of the blessed ones who are detached from the world is above it, on the peak of the world, 1 Rajju broad, 1 Rajju long and 8 Rajjus high. The total space of the world is 343 cubic-Rajjus.

The view of Śvetāmbaras differs from the one of Digambaras to the extent that, according to them, the breadth from the north to the south does not remain always the same and the breadth from the east to the west *constantly* decreases and increases, but that in both cases the decrease and increase is gradual. Then the total space of the world comes to 239 cubic-Rajjus.

The lowest part of the universe is occupied by the under-world's in which there are hells; the centre is formed by the middle world (Madhyaloka); human beings live here. The world of the heaven is above, like storeys, and at the top finally is the world of the redeemed.

The whole world is surrounded by three atmospheres; they are called dense water, dense wind and thin wind taking into consideration their density. The non-world (Aloka), i.e. the absolutely empty space is beyond them.

The form of the universe is explicated by a series of similes. Thus it is said that it resembles a half drum upon which a whole drum is placed, but the drums are to be thought of as square and not round. It is said further that the individual parts correspond to spindles, dishes, etc. lying over one another. But above all, the form of the universe is compared with a man or a woman who is symmetrically built and who is standing with stretched-out legs. Then the lower worlds are imagined as lying in the lower extremities, the human world lying in the region of the hips and the upper body forming the heaven of gods.

3. THE INHABITANTS OF THE UNIVERSE

The whole world is filled up by living beings; not even a space of a breadth of a hair is free. But the different types and classes of the Jivas are not evenly distributed over the universe. They are distributed in a quick definite manner.

Everywhere there are Nigoḍas. They are quite tiny, fine beings, not perceivable by our senses, having one sense. They do not also possess a body which can be voluntarily moved (like plants and elementary being). The Nigoḍas are divided into 2 classes, in 1. Nitya-nigoḍas, i.e. those which never leave this lowest state of the life and 2. Itara-nigoḍas, i.e. those which had reached a higher stage of existence, but demoted again into this state on account of their Karma.[29]

Beings with their own, voluntary movement are found only in a definite part of the universe, viz. in the so-called "region of the mobile" (Trasanāḍī).[30] It traverses the world in the centre, from top to bottom, and is 14 Rajjus high, 1 Rajju broad and 1 Rajju long.

The Jīvas are distributed within the Trasa-nāḍī, corresponding to their stages of existence, as under:

Animals (plants and elementary beings are also included in them) are found everywhere.

Human beings live only in the middle world, and besides, only on 2½ of its continents.

Beings in hells are persent only in the hells of the under world.

Gods live in the heaven, in the middle world and in the three upper worlds of the nether world.

The total living beings of the world are divided into 14 classes (Jīva-sthāna). The number of the organs of senses and other characteristics serve in this as a principle of classification (cf. p. 198). The classes are: 1. fine with one sense, 2. crude with one sense, 3. those having two senses, 4. those having three senses, 5. those having four senses, 6. those who are insensible and having five senses, 7. sensible animals with five senses, as also human beings, beings from the hell and gods having five senses. Since all these beings occur in developed and undeveloped state, the number of the classes is to be doubled, and we get thus 7 x 2 = 14 Jīva-sthānas.

Like other Indian religions,[31] Jaina-religion also teaches that there are 84 lakhs of life-forms in which a soul can be incarnated. There are each 7,00,000 Nitya- and Itara-Nigoḍas, beings on earth, in water, fire and air, each 10,00,000 of plants, each 2,00,000 of beings with two, three and four senses, each 4,00,000 of animals with five senses, beings in the hell, gods and 1,400,000 of human beings.[32]

Jaina-philosophers indicate exactly what characteristics each class of the beings have, what types of knowledge, activity, colour of the soul, of the faith and conduct they show, which stage of virtue they reach and which Karma can be present in them when they bind it, produce it or could have it potentially. Some of it will be discussed below. More information is available in my book "Die Lehre vom Karma," pp. 63-74. Let us discuss here only briefly the different possibilities of rebirth of the beings of various classes to show how a soul can undergo different forms of life one after the other.

Animals with one, two, three or four senses are reborn only as animals and human beings; fire- and wind-beings only as animals. Animals with five senses can obtain a new life in all the stages of existence. Beings from the hell only as developed animals and human beings having five senses. Gods become human beings or developed crude beings from the earth and water or animals having five senses. Human beings get any form of existence; they are the only ones among the beings who can attain salvation.

4. DESCRIPTION OF THE WORLD

(1) The Middle World

The middle world (Madhyaloka) or the animal world (Tiryagloka) lying on the circular upper surface of the earth, lies, as its name suggests, in the centre of the universe. It is 1 Rajju broad and long. The nether worlds with their hells lie below it and the heavenly worlds, at a height of 1,00,000 Yojanas above it.[33]

Mountain Meru is at the centre of the middle world. The continent Jambūdvīpa surrounds it in the form of a circle; its diameter is 1,00,000 Yojanas. A ring-formed ocean surrounds the Jambūdvīpa, the ocean of salt (Lavaṇoda), its diameter being 2,00,000 Yojanas. The continent Dhātakī-khaṇḍa joins them, again in the form of a ring; its diameter is 4,00,000 Yojanas. Dhātakī-khaṇḍa is again bordered by a circular ocean, this again by a circular continent, and thus follow countless continents and oceans one after the other, finally up to Svayambhūramaṇa-continent and Svayambhūramaṇa-ocean which washes around the whole middle world.

The names of the first 8 continents and oceans are:

	Continent	Ocean
1.	Jambūdvīpa (Rose-apple tree island)	Lavaṇoda (Salt-ocean)
2.	Dhātakī khaṇḍa (Grisleā tomentotosa part of the earth)	Kāloda (Black Sea)
3.	Puṣkaravaradvīpa (Lotus-island)	Puṣkaroda (Lotus-ocean)
4.	Varuṇavaradvīpa (Island where the deities Varuṇa and Varuṇaprabha rule)	Varuṇoda (Varuṇa-ocean)
5.	Kṣīravaradvīpa (Milk-island)	Kṣīroda (Ocean of milk)
6.	Ghṛtavaradvīpa (Buttermilk island)	Ghṛtoda (Buttermilk ocean)
7.	Ikṣuvaradvīpa (Sugarcane-island)	Ikṣuvaroda (Sugar-ocean)
8.	Nandīśvaradvīpa	Nandīśvaroda

The continents have their names from their characteristic marks which are peculiar to them, like the trees which grow on them, etc. The oceans are named after the liquids which their water resembles, although it surpasses them by its outstanding quality.

Of all the continents, Jambūdvīpa is the most significant and it is described in detail by Jainas, first because it is in the centre of the whole world, and secondly, because it is believed that India and our whole earth exists on it.

Jambūdvīpa is surrounded by a very high and broad wall which consists of diamonds. A large lotus-terrace with splendid pleasure woods and ponds built from precious stones rises above it. A big grill-work produced from gold and jewels with four mighty gates protected by deities fences this wall.

The Jambū-continent in its whole length and breadth from east to west; has 6 mighty mountains; they divide it into 7 zones (Varṣa or Kṣetra) of unequal size. The names of the zones and the mountain ranges separating them (from the south to the north) are:

1. Bharata-kṣetra	1. Himavān-mountains
2. Haimavata-kṣetra	2. Mahāhimavān-mountains
3. Hari-kṣetra	3. Niṣadha-mountains
4. Videha-kṣetra	4. Nīla-mountains
5. Ramyaka-kṣetra	5. Rukmī-mountains
6. Hairaṇyavata-kṣetra	6. Śikharī-mountains
7. Airāvata-kṣetra	

The breadth and the height of the mountains and the range of the zones increases in geometric progression from the south to the north up to the centre and then again decreases from the centre in a corresponding manner.

The mountains consist of gold, silver and beryl. They all have several peaks of the form of a truncated cone. On the eastern summit of every mountain there is a Jina-temple embellished with jewels; in the centre of every mountain there is a large lake, with a golden bottom, silvery banks and diamond bathing steps. A gigantic lotus of splendid gems, surrounded by numerous small lotus-flowers, blooms in its centre. The lotus-flowers are inhabitated all by deities of different sorts, and the lakes inhabited by water-birds and fishes.

In all 14 rivers have their source in the 6 mountains. They flow into the salt-ocean after arising from them and flowing through the zones.

The southern-most zone of Jambūdvīpa, bordered by Himavān-mountain in the north and on all other sides by the salt-ocean, is Bhārata-varṣa, the part of the world in which we live. Vaitādhya- (or Vijayārdha-) mountain running parallel to Himavān divides it into the northern and the southern half which are each $238^{3}/_{19}$ Yojanas in breadth. The rivers "Mahā-Sindhu" (great Indus) and "Mahā-Gaṅgā" flowing down from Himavān into the west and the east respectively divide each one of these halves into three parts (Khaṇḍa) so that the whole Bhārata-varṣa consists of 6 parts. While the three northern parts as well as the eastern and the western part of the southern Bhārata-varṣa are inhabited by barbarians (Mleccha), the central-most part of the south, the so-called Ārya-khaṇḍa, is inhabited by the Aryans. Aryans were the Indians belonging to four castes; Ayodhyā, which was supposed to lie in the centre, was considered as the capital of Ārya-khaṇḍa. Modern Jainas believe, on the other hand, that our whole earth, including Europe, Asia, Africa, America and Australia, belongs to Ārya-khaṇḍa.

Bhārata-varṣa is a Karmabhūmi, i.e. a land in which human beings have to work and in which all sorts of Karmas can be bound. The periodical change of six eras takes place in it. We shall talk about this below while discussing the world-history of Jainas.

The zone Haimavata-varṣa lies to the north of Himavān mountain; it is four times bigger than Bhārata-varṣa. The mountain Śabdāpāti lies in its centre. The rivers Rohita and Rohitāṁśā flow through this zone and they flow into the salt-ocean in the east and the west respectively. Haimavata-varṣa is a Bhogabhūmi, i.e. a land in which human beings live only the life of pleasure and live on the fruits of the wonderful "wishing tree", because the Suṣama-duḥṣamā era prevails here for ever.

Hari-varṣa lies on the northern side of Haimavata-varṣa; it is separated by Mahāhimavān-mountain. It is four times broader than the former. The mountain Vikaṭāpāti rises in its centre, its big rivers are Harita (in the east) and Harikāntā (in the west). The conditions of life here are better than in Haimavata, because Suṣamā era prevails here for ever.

The Niṣadha mountain separates Hari-varṣa from Videha-varṣa (Mahā-videha), the largest of all zones. Meru (Mandara) lies in the centre of Videha, and to some extent, it is the centre and the navel of the whole Jambūdvīpa. The mountain has a shape of a truncated cone which is ascending in three ledges; the first ledge consisting of stones, the second of silver and crystals and the third of gold. A layer of beryl crowns the summit which also has the form of a truncated cone. The grove Bhadraśāla lies at the foot of the mountain. On the first ledge there is the grove Nandana, on the second the grove Saumanasa, on the surface of the summit the grove Paṇḍaka, all embellished by lotus-ponds, palaces and temples and inhabited by gods and genii. There is also a temple on the surface of the ledge (platform, terrace). The two main rivers Śītā and Śītodā flow at the foot of Meru.

4 Vakṣāra-mountain ranges start from Meru:

1. Saumanasa-mountain consisting of silver towards south-east.
2. Vidyutprabha-mountain consisting of gold towards south-west.
3. Gandhamādana-mountain consisting of gold towards north-west.
4. Mālyavān-mountain consisting of beryl towards north-east.

The land of Devakurus lies in the south of Meru, between the mountains Saumanasa and Vidyutprabha; the land of Uttarakurus to the north of Meru between the mountains Gandhamādana and Mālyavān. These two regions are the most fortunate on the whole Jambūdvipa, because the conditions of suṣama-suṣamā-period are permanent there. A big ceiba-tree blossoms in the centre of the western half of the Devakurus-land; a big Jambū-tree in the eastern half of Uttarakuru; the two are surrounded by numerous smaller trees of their type and by ponds and temples.

The land Pūrva-videha lies to the east of Meru, and Apara-videha to the west. Each one of these is divided into several provinces and is rich in mountains, rivers and cities whose names are given by Jainas in all details. The general conditions in both the Videhas resemble those in the human world inasmuch as both are Karmabhūmis; there rules the era Duḥṣama-suṣamā.

The zone Ramyaka-varṣa, bordered by Nīla-mountain, comes after Videha-varṣa. It is an exact counterpart of Hari-varṣa. Its middle-mountain is called Gandhāpāti; its main rivers are Narakāntā and Nārī.

Hairaṇyavata-varṣa which is separated by Rukmī-mountain from Ramyaka-varṣa, is exactly like Haimavata. The name of its mountain is Mālyavān; its rivers are called Svarṇakūlā and Rūpyakūlā.

Finally Airāvata-varṣa, the northern-most zone of Jambūdvīpa, separated from Hairaṇyavata by Śikharī-mountain, is completely like Bhārata-varṣa. Its mountain is Vijayārdha; its rivers Raktā and Raktodā.

The whole Jambū-continent having a circular form is encompassed by the Salt-ocean (Lavaṇoda), ring-like from all sides. In its centre, there is a gigantic barrel-like container (Pātāla), surrounded by smaller ones. Gods have their abode in Pātālas. The waters are carried by thousands of Nāgas (serpent-spirits). They live with their kings in their dwelling in the ocean.

There are a series of islands in Lavaṇoda: Gautamadvīpa, the most lovely island of Susthita, who is the ruler of the Salt-ocean, further two islands of the two moons and two islands of the two suns of the Jambū-continent. Finally we have to mention the so-called median islands (Antaradvīpa); they are 56 according to Śvetāmbaras and 48 according to Digambaras. Human beings live here in a fabulous manner: those with animal-heads, with horns and tails, with only one leg, etc. Here rules the era Duḥṣama-suṣamā.

The Dhātakī-continent washed by Lavaṇoda from the other side is described in the same manner as Jambūdvīpa. So also Kāloda-ocean with its black and tasty water like the Salt-ocean. Only its dimensions are double. Thus Dhātakī-khaṇḍa has 12 big mountains, 14 zones (thus each 2 Bharatas, Airāvatas, etc.), etc.

Puṣkara-continent surrounded by black ocean is divided into two equal rings by Mānuṣottara-mountain which spreads across its whole centre. The geographical conditions correspond, only in the inner part which is turned to Kāloda, to those of the two continents we have discussed so far; only here we have 12 mountains, 14 zones, etc. Human beings live nowhere beyond Mānuṣottara only the goddesses' live there. The heavenly bodies do not move here, but remain always at the same place. There is, therefore, no concept of time beyond Mānuṣottara; there rules constant peace. The other characteristic is that there are no water animals in the oceans which come after the Kāloda; they appear again only in Svayambhūramaṇa-ocean which forms the extreme border of the middle world.

2. The Nether World

Seven subterranean regions lie storey-like thousand Yojanas deep under the earth of the middle world. Of these, the uppermost ones serve as an abode for certain divine beings, while the others shelter the hells where the souls have to atone for their bad action by undergoing horrible tortures.

The uppermost subterranean region Ratnaprabhā is divided, according to one tradition, into three storeys lying under one another, viz. (from up to down): Kharabhāga, Paṅkabhāga, Abbahulabhāga (Āpabahula). Gods of the classes Bhavanavāsī and Vyantara live in the two topmost; we shall talk about these when we shall discuss the world of gods. The third part of Ratna-prabhā serves, on the other hand, like all other regions below it, as a place of punishment for those who are condemned.

Each region of the hells has several storeys. Their number is the highest in the uppermost, and it decreases as one comes down. There is a central hell in the centre of every storey. Numerous "row-hells" spread from here into four directions; there are again hells in the spaces in between, the so-called "filling hells". The number of hells of every storey decreases likewise when one moves downwards.

The following are the name of the seven regions, the number of storeys they contain and the number of hells belonging to every region:

1. Ratna-prabhā, "shine of jewels": 13 storeys together with 30,00,000 hells.
2. Śarkarā-prabhā, "shine of pebbles": 11 storeys together with 25,00,000 hells.
3. Vālukā-prabhā, "shine of sand": 9 storeys together with 15,00,000 hells.
4. Paṅka-prabhā, "shine of mud": 7 storeys together with 10,00,000 hells.
5. Dhūma-prabhā, "shine of smoke": 5 storeys together with 3,00,000 hells.
6. Tamaḥ-prabhā, "shine of darkness": 3 storeys together with 99,995 hells.
7. Mahātamaḥ-prabhā, "shine of great darkness": 1 storey together with 5 hells.

Total 49 storeys together with 84,00,000 hells

The inhabitants of the hells (Narakas) are not born like the inhabitants of the earth, but are born in a supernatural manner, by "manifestation" (Upapāta, cf.

p.. 200), by suddenly coming out of the holes in the walls and falling down there. Their complete evolution takes one Muhūrta (48 minutes). Besides the fiery- and Karma-body, which is a characteristic of all beings, they have a "metamorphic" body (p. 195) with a grey appearance; their structure is completely unsymmetrical, and all are hermaphrodites. They have the first three types of knowledge and seeing (p. 204), thus also the transcendent knowledge of material things, but this capability serves only to increase their sufferings. There are unbelievers among them and those who have the three lowest forms of faith (p. 182, Nos. 1-4); self-discipline is not possible among them, and therefore they cannot rise ever beyond the 4th stage of virtue. The unbelievers think of giving sufferings to the others, but thereby suffer themselves the most; those who have the right faith do not do this, but are tortured by the qualms of conscience for what they had done in earlier existences.

The deeper the hells, worse are their inhabitants, and greater are their pains they have to suffer. The hells of the first 4 regions are hot, those of the 5th region partially hot, partially cold, the lowest two are cold. The type (character) of souls (Leśyā, p. 210) is grey in the first and the second, grey or dark in the third, dark in the fourth, dark or black in the fifth and black in the sixth and seventh. The body-size of those who are condemned is, in the individual storeys, very different. Whereas it is only 3 Hastas (ells), e.g. in the topmost storey of Ratna-prabhā, it increases with each lower one, and it reaches a height of 500 Dhanuṣas (bows) in Mahātamaḥ-prabhā. Even the life span in the lowest storeys is longer: in the topmost Ratna-prabhā it is at least 10,000 years and at the most 90,000 years, it is minimum 22 and maximum 33 Sāgaropamas in Mahātamaḥ-prabhā.

The horrible conditions in the hells are described in glowing terms. The stay is equally unpleasant for all senses. A pestilent smell fills all the rooms, as if of decayed cadavers of animals; the air is sharp and pungent, and there is a constant awful darkness. Walls and floors are covered with repulsive dirt; it is on account of it so slippery everywhere that the Nārakas slip whenever they move and collide with the others causing sufferings to one another. The hells resound constantly from plaintive sounds of those who are tormented. Heat and cold, fever and body-itching constantly torture the condemned ones and they cannot be removed. In addition, there are sufferings which the Nārakas cause to one another by falling upon one another and injuring one another in most horrible manner and by persecuting one another with fearful hatred and assuming various forms with the help of their Vaikriya-śarire ("metamorphic" body. Besides, the beings in the hell in the three topmost storeys are subjected to various ill-treatments by the evil Asuras. Special frivolous actions find their special atonement: Thus adulterers have to embrace statues of women of glowing bronze. Meat-eaters have to eat flesh cut from their own body and drunkards have to drink boiling lead. Other sinners are hacked to pieces, broken on a wheel, roasted, skewered, impaled, whipped, cut with knives, drowned in water, boiled in cauldrons, gnawed by worms, devoured by rapacious animals or dealt with different instruments of torture.

All the wounds got by a being in hell, howsoever painful they may be, are never deadly. They are healed soon, pieces of the body cut in thousand pieces are joined again, for a new torture, a new pain. A Nāraka dies only when he has gone through the whole series of punishments prescribed for him by his Karma. Death follows without any known cause. The soul leaves then the decayed body and assumes a new existence as animal or human being, because the hells of Jainas are purgatories. They serve as a temporary stay for sinners and not as abodes of eternal condemnation.

While many put the lowest hell Mahātamaḥ-prabhā directly near the lower end of the world, others presume that there is still a zone without any ground below it which is inhabited by Nigoḍas and other lowly-organized beings which cannot more on their own.[34] The idea that the souls which became Nigoḍas of this type on account of their misdeeds are eternally condemned appears to be common among many Jainas.[35]

(3) The World of Gods

Gods (Deva) are beings with a fine "metamorphic" body who, in terms of mundane concepts, lead their life in great happiness. They are not born, but originate by manifestation (Upapāta, p. 200) where their Karma directs them. The existence of gods is dedicated to pleasure alone; it to full of fun and frolic, and in full draughts they enjoy the pleasures of love in their magnificent palaces. Three first types of knowledge and seeing are inherent to them, they have thus all the transcendent knowledge of material things. They can be unbelievers or they can have the first three types of faith. Their conduct of life could be good or bad, but practice of self-discipline is impossible for them, because every wish of theirs is fulfilled the moment it is expressed. Once their Karma is exhausted, their souls leave the divine bodies without any known cause of death to enter a new existence in the middle world in animal or human bodies.

The gods are divided into four main types; they are:

1. Bhavanavāsīs who live in the palaces (bhavana) of the uppermost region of the nether world.

2. Vyantaras, subterranean demons who live in the nether world and the space between this and the middle world.

3. Jyotiṣkas, the genii of the heavenly bodies who live in the air-space between the middle and the upper-world.

4. Vaimānikas who live in the mobile palaces (*vimāna*) of the upper world.

These four main types are further divided into a great number of subclasses; they are enlisted below. Each of these subclasses show again several ranks, because gods are mostly not like one another, but form a hierarchy which is given in great details. The number of ranks is different in the individual sections. It is the largest among the Bhavanavāsīs and a part of Vaimānikas. This hierarchy is as under:

1. Indras, kings
2. Sāmānikas, princes
3. Trāyastriṁśas, dignitaries of the state
4. Pāriṣadyas, treasurers
5. Ātmarakṣas, bodyguards
6. Lokapālas, policemen
7. Anīkas, warriors
8. Prakīrṇakas, citizens
9. Ābhiyogyas, servants (respectively beings in the form of horses, lions, birds, etc. which have the function of riding animals)
10. Kilbiṣikas, common people.

The 3rd and the 6th stage is absent among Vyantaras and Jyotiṣkas; all differences of rank are altogether absent among the highest subclasses of Vaimānikas.

The members of different sections and classes are very different in their appearance, size of the body, clothing, etc.

The minimum life span of gods is 10,000 years, the maximum 33 Sāgaropamas. The Leśyā of the gods of the first three sections is black, dark, grey or fiery, of the others, it is fiery, yellow or white.

Bhavanavāsīs live in magnificent palaces in cities in the upper part of Ratna-prabhā (p. 259), respectively in the area between the nether and middle world. They look like beautiful young people; the second part of the name of individual classes ("Kumāra") points out to it. The classes are:

1. Asura-kumāra (demon-princes)
2. Nāga-kumāra (serpent-princes)
3. Suparṇa-kumāra (eagle-princes)

4. Vāyu-kumāra (wind-princes)
5. Dvīpa-kumāra (island-princes)
6. Udadhi-kumāra (ocean-princes)
7. Dik-kumāra (princes of directions)
8. Vidyut-kumāra (lightning-princes)
9. Stanita-kumāra (thunder-princes)
10. Agni-kumāra (fire-princes)

There are 2 Indras at the top of each class, the one ruling over the north, the other over the south. Every Indra has several main wives and numerous subordinate wives. Seven armies consisting of 7 divisions under the command of seven commanders are at the disposal of every Indra; the armies consist of infantries, horses, elephants, buffaloes (bulls), chariots, musicians and actors (danseuses). The Leśyā here is black, dark, grey or fiery.

Vyantaras are demons and demi-gods of different types. They are divided into seven classes:

1. Kinnaras (spirits)
2. Kiṁpuruṣas (goblins)
3. Mahoragas (large serpents)
4. Gandharvas (genii playing music)
5. Yakṣas (spirits of treasures)
6. Rākṣasas (monsters)
7. Bhūtas (ghosts)
8. Piśācas (demons)

They live in the cities full of palaces, in the sections Kharabhāga (Bhūtas) and Paṅkabhāga (Rākṣasas) of the netherworldly region Ratnaprabhā, in the space between lower and middle world and in the different part of the latter. There are two Indras at the top of each class. Each one of them has a large royal household and 7 armies. The Leśyā is black, dark, grey or fiery.

Jyotiṣkas are the genii of the heavenly bodies. They encircle clockwise the Meru-mountain at a height of 790 to 900 Yojanas over the plains of Jambūdvīpa, Dhātakīkhaṇḍa and half of Puṣkaradvīpa. They travel in powerful chariots which are drawn by lions, elephants, bulls and horses. Their Leśyā is fiery. They are of 5 types, viz. suns, moons, planets, Nakṣatras and fixed stars. For every sun, there are 1 moon, 88 planets, 28 Nakṣatras and 6697 500 000 000 000 000 stars. The concept of Jainas that there are several suns, moons and a number of stars is unique. Their number in the individual continents is different. Jambūdvīpa has 2 suns, Salt-ocean has 4, Dhātakīkhaṇḍa 12, Black ocean 42, 1/2 Puṣkaradvīpa 72, so that there are in all 132 suns in the human world. The number of moons, planets, Nakṣatras and stars is calculated accordingly.

Jainas have put up this theory—they are the only ones representating it in the Indian systems—on the basis of their doctrine of the structure of the middle world. "They start, from the view that in the course of 24 hours, the moon—as also the other heavenly bodies—can cover only half the circle around Meru; that thus, when the night ends in Bhārata-varṣa, the sun whose light had given the preceding day, has come only to the northwest of Meru. The sun which rises at the same time really in the east of Bhārata-varṣa, cannot therefore, be the same sun which sets in the previous evening, but is a different one which the eye cannot distinguish from the first. Then the first sun appears again on the morning of the third day which has reached around this time the southeast corner of Meru, etc. For the same reason, Jainas assume 2 moons, two series of Nakṣatras, etc. Thus all the heavenly bodies are doubled; but since only one part of each pair is seen in Bhārata-varṣa and since both the parts appear completely alike, the whole phenomena remain unchanged."[36]

The number of heavenly bodies over the other ring-continents and over the oceans of the middle world is obviously greater than the one of Jambūdvīpa, because they are further away from Meru.

Celestial bodies do not move in the part beyond the Mānuṣottara-mountain which Puṣkaradvīpa divides into two halfs, i.e. beyond the middle world, where human beings live. They remain constantly steady in their places, and they are besides united in great numbers into rings which are each at a distance of 100 000 Yojanas from one another.

Vaimānikas live in the heavenly regions of the upper world which begin directly over the crown of Meru mountain and which lie over one another like storeys.

I am giving below an overview of the individual heavenly regions (from bottom to top) with the indication of the number of storeys they contain). There are two heavens for the regions I to VIII, a southern one and a northern one; this is indicated with S and N. Since the views of Śvetāmbaras differ from those of the Digambaras, both are shown next to one another:

No.		*Śvetāmbaras*	*Storeys*	*Digambaras*	*Storeys*
I.	S	Saudharma	13	Saudharma	31
	N	Aiśāna		Īśāna	
II.	S	Sanatkumāra	12	Sanatkumāra	7
	N	Māhendra		Māhendra	
III.	S	Brahmaloka	6	Brahma	4
	N			Brahmottara	
IV.	S	Lāntaka	5	Lāntava	2
	N			Kāpiṣṭha	
V.	S	Śukra	4	Śukra	1
	N			Mahāśukra	
VI.	S	Sahasrāra	4	Śatāra	1
	N			Sahasrāra	
VII.	S	Ānata	4	Ānata	3
	N	Prāṇata		Prāṇata	
VIII.	S	Āraṇa	4	Āraṇa	3
	N	Acyuta		Acyuta	
IX.	Adho- Madhya- Ūrdhva- } Graiveyaka		9	Adho- Madhya- Ūrdhva- } Graiveyaka	9

No.	Śvetāmbaras	Storeys	Digambaras	Storeys
X.	—	—	9 Anudiśa	1
XI.	5 Anuttara	1	5 Anuttara	1

As it can be seen from the Table that the region of Anudiśas is accepted only by Digambaras. The Lokāntika-gods who live around Brahmaloka are outside the hierarchy. According to Digambaras, they are divided into 24 classes: Sārasvata, Āditya, Vahni, Aruṇa, Gardatoya, Tuṣita, Avyābādha and Ariṣṭa, as also 16 others which are the intermediate stages between those we have mentioned. They are without any desire and are, therefore, called "Devarṣis" (god-saints); they serve Tīrthaṅkaras when these appear on the earth, and are finally born as human beings and get salvation.

The divine heavens of the regions I to VIII are called *Kalpas*, their inhabitants *Kalpopannas*, i.e. provided with Kalpas; the higher regions are *Kalpātītas*, lying over the Kalpas. The same word is also used for the gods living there.

Vaimānikas have their name from their palaces, magnificent and mobile houses, which are built of precious stones; they often have the size of individual cities. They are also, like the hells, arranged in storeys, and besides in such a way that a series of Vimānas move out into the four directions from a central Vimāna; the space between these Vimānas is filled with feeder-Vimānas.

The inhabitants of heaven of gods are all marvellous in their appearance, are of radiant youthful beauty, have no shadow, do not twinkle with their eyes, and their hair and nails do not grow. Their mind is always refreshed; pleasant tunes, fragrances, tastes change constantly, and the eyes always see only what is joyful. The magnificent Suṣamā-suṣamā period rules constantly among them, the difference between day and night is unknown there, and everything is illuminated there with the glitter of precious stones.

The higher the region in which a god lives, the greater is his life span, his Avadhi-knowledge, his power and joy, but the smaller is the size of his body, his self-awareness and possession; the smaller is also the extent of the area he covers in the world (i.e. the *wanderlust* of the gods decreases in the higher regions). The Leśyā is fiery in the first region, yellow in the second and the third, and from then on white. Disposition and nature of gods is most sharply characterized by the manner in which they satisfy their sexual desire. Corporeal mating takes place in the heaven of the first region as it is the case with all gods of a lower order. In the second region it is sufficient for the gods to embrace their consorts, kiss them and stroke them to satisfy their sexual desire. The heavenly ones are happy in the third and fourth regions just to look at the beauty of the goddesses, in the fifth and sixth, to listen to their sweet voices, and in the seventh and the eighth to imagine themselves to be in their pleader. Thus the love-life assumes an increasingly finer form in each higher region. The gods are without any erotic desires in the highest, Kalpa-less regions. There are no women here.

There are ten hierarchies in the Kalpa-heavens (I-VIII). One Indra rules over the north and one over the south in the regions I, II and VII, VIII and only Indra each in the regions III to VI. There is no hierarchy in the Kalpa-less regions IX-XI; the gods there are similar to one another, and all have the title *Ahamindra* (I am Indra).

The Jaina-legend deals most extensively with Indra of Saudharma giving him preference over all the Indras of different classes of Vaimānika-gods. It is said there that he has a special name "Śakra", whereas the others are called after their Kalpas. Śakra appears on all occasions which affect the world; he has above all a role in the history of the Tīrthaṅkaras. Whenever a Saviour is to be born, his throne is shaken. He immediately finds out what the matter is with the help of his transcendent knowledge. He orders Hariṇaigamaiṣī, the commander of his infantry, to ring the bell Sughoṣā measuring a mile in circumference in the hall Sudharmā. Once the thundering sound of the loudly ringing bell has resounded, the bells in the 3199999 other palaces of Saudharma-heaven also begins to ring. The gods are thus alerted, know from Śakra, what great event is to take place, assemble according to rule, some on account of their love for the Tīrthaṅkara, some out of curiosity, and some obeying the command of Śakra. Śakra then climbs a mobile palace, surrounded by his retinue, comes down on Ratikara mountain of Nandīśvara continent of the middle world and proceeds to the house of the birth of the Tīrthaṅkara to pay his reverence. Also the Indras of other Kalpas appear on the earth in the same way, extol him and then return again to their palaces. Śakra and other gods also act similarly when a Tīrthaṅkara renounces the world, obtains omniscience and he attains Nirvāṇa.

Believers and unbelievers can be born in all Kalpa-heavens as a result of their good Karma, above all, as a result of reward got through (right or wrong) asceticism; the same thing holds good also for the Graiveyaka-regions* to which even those who are not capable of salvation (*abhavya,* p. 217) can reach, if they have led a good life on the earth.[37] But there are only those who have the right faith in the higher heavens. The gods of the first region can get every Karma which makes them in their next birth developed earth-beings or plant-beings, animals with five senses or human beings; in the regions III-VI only the Karma suitable to become animals with five senses or human beings, from the VIIth only the Karma which makes them human beings.

---

*The Graiveyaka-regions have their name from their being in the neck-region (*griva*) of the universe imagined in terms of the image of a human being.

All gods in the five Anuttara heavens Vijaya, Vaijayanta, Jayanta, Aparājita and Sarvārthasiddha have the right faith and they are in the 4th stage of virtue.

(4) The Abode of the Blissful Ones

The magnificent region Iṣṭaprāgbhāra lies 12 Yojanas over the Sarvārthasiddha-heaven, in its form similar to an opened sun-umbrella, 8 Yojanas high in its highest position. This is whiter than the pearls and milk, more glittering than gold and purer than the crystal. There is a circular rock Śītā (according to the Digambaras: Śilā). It is at a distance of one Yojana from the border of the world and non-world. The redeemed, the Siddhas, live in the uppermost part of this Yojana for eternity and enjoy endless, uncomparable, lasting supernatural happiness of liberation from the bonds of Saṁsāra.

V

World-history and Hagiography

1. THE BASIC CONCEPTS

(1) The World-periods and Eras

The world is eternal, and it is unalterable as a whole. But while in the largest part of cosmos the general conditions remain constantly the same, in spite of individual changes, there is an incessant and regular sequence of ascending and descending world-periods in some parts of the human world. In this, climate and vegetation of the land, size of the body, life span and the virtues of the inhabitants are subject to a better or to a worse change.

Jainas assume two world-periods which succeed each other taking turns since eternity and in eternity: the "ascending world-period" (Utsarpiṇī) at the start of which the condition in the human world is the worst, but becomes gradually better till finally the climax of the best-possible of the condition is reached, and the "descending period" (Avasarpiṇī), which begins with this best-possible condition which successively becomes worse till finally the nadir is reached. The duration of each of these two periods is 10 Koṭikoṭis of Sāgaropamas.

Each world-period is divided into 6 eras; their duration is unalterably fixed. Their names signify the quality of conditions prevalent in them: the good average condition is called Suṣamā, the bad average condition is "Duḥṣamā". The four others are indicated by the names which are combined from these two words. The following makes the whole thing more clear:

	Era	Period
1.	Suṣama-suṣamā, "best" era, lasts for 4 Koṭikoṭis of Sāgaropamas.	Avasarpiṇī
2.	Suṣamā, "good" era, lasts for 3 Koṭikoṭis of Sāgaropamas.	
3.	Suṣama-duḥṣamā, "good-bad" era, lasts for 2 Koṭikoṭis of Sāgaropamas.	
4.	Duḥṣam-suṣamā, "bad-good" era, lasts for 1 Koṭikoṭi of Sāgaropamas less 42,000 years.	
5.	"Duḥṣama", "bad" era, lasts for 21,000 years.	
6.	Duḥṣama-duḥṣamā, "the worst" era, lasts for 21,000 years.	
1.	Duḥṣama-duḥṣamā, "the worst" era, lasts for 21,000 years.	Utsarpiṇī
2.	Duḥṣamā, "bad" era, lasts for 21,000 years.	
3.	Duḥṣama-suṣamā, "bad-good" era, lasts for 1 Koṭikoṭi of Sāgaropamas less 42,000 years.	
4.	Suṣama-duḥṣamā, "good-bad" era, lasts for 2 Koṭikoṭis of Sāgaropamas.	
5.	Suṣamā, "good" era, lasts for 3 Koṭikoṭis of Sāgaropamas.	
6.	Suṣama-suṣamā, "best" era, lasts for 4 Koṭikoṭis of Sāgaropamas.	

One ascending and one descending world-period form together one turning of the wheel of time (Kāla-cakra). 6 eras of every period are called spokes (Ara) of the wheel of time.[38] The wheel of time turns in unchanged regularity, without beginning, without end so that

Avasarpiṇīs and Utsarpiṇīs succeed one another without break.

The history of the human world is the history of the periodical turning of the wheel of time.* Jaina-philosophers report how the things appeared on the earth in the different eras and what happened before. On account of the information given by their omniscient masters they also know what shall happen in future, when the wheel of time would roll further, how the era Duḥṣamā in which we are living would give place to a worse one, till finally the conditions would become better again with the beginning of a new Utsarpiṇī.

While the description of the most of the eras occupies only a small place in Jaina-works, because only the general conditions in which human beings live are described, the Suṣama-duḥṣamā and Duḥṣama-suṣamā eras are dealt with in detail. The sixty-three "great men" (Śalākā-puruṣa) who are in the limelight of the Jaina-world-history appear here regularly in these two eras. They are: 24 Tīrthaṅkaras (prophets), 12 Cakravartīs (world-rulers) and 27 heroes, viz., 9 Baladevas, 9 Vāsudevas, and 9 Prativāsudevas; each one of the Tīrthaṅkaras and one Cakravartī appear in Suṣama-duḥṣamā and all the rest of the prophets, world-rulers and heroes in Duḥṣama-suṣamā, irrespective of the fact whether one is concerned with descending or ascending world-period.**

The biographies of the "great men" of each one of

---

*As already remarked, the periodical change of the eras takes place only in the parts of the human world which are inhabited. The same condition exists constantly in other parts of the world. "It is eternally Suṣama-suṣamā among the Kurus; it is Suṣamā in Harivāsa and Ramyakavāsa, Suṣama-duḥṣamā in Haimavata and Hairaṇyavata and Duḥṣama-suṣamā in Videha and the islands lying inbetween."[39]

**The number of important persons of the hagiography is still more, if others are counted, viz. the 9 Nāradas, 11 Rudras and 24 Kāmadevas; let us not go into information on them, because their significance is less than the one of the 63 Śalākā-puruṣas, and therefore, only briefly considered by Jaina-writers.[40] Even the 24 fathers these five classes are quite similar. Their characteristics are the same, and even the destinies of their lives are similar in essential points. Therefore, before we describe the Jaina-world-history, let us, to save space, characterize briefly the recurrent components of the history of Śalākā-puruṣas.

(2) The 63 Great Men

(a) The 24 Tīrthaṅkaras

Tīrthaṅkaras are the religious prophets of Jainas, who proclaim the ancient holy doctrine and lead the men who follow them to redemption by their preaching and their example. The word "Tīrthaṅkara" (or Tīrthakara) is generally explained in the Occident as a "maker of ford, pioneer", i.e. as a designation for the one, who makes (paves) a ford, way, through the ocean of Saṁsāra, upon which a believer goes with his help without any danger and can attain the place of Nirvāṇa which is removed from all sorrows. But Jainas themselves define the term, differently, they understand by him a man who has created the four orders (Tīrtha) or the Jaina-community: monks, nuns, laymen and laywomen. A number of other expressions are also used in place of Tīrthaṅkara. The most well-known are: Jina and Arhat. He is called Jina "conqueror", because he has liberated himself from Karma by overcoming love and hatred;* Arhat "venerable", because he is worshipped by Indras and gods at the time of the five great events of his life (conception, birth, renunciation of the world, attainment of omniscience and going into Nirvāṇa).

---

and 24 mothers of the Tīrthaṅkaras as also the 7 (14) Kulakaras are counted among the great persons in the mean while; brief reference would be made to them at appropriate place.

*The expression "Jina" is applied not only to Tīrthaṅkaras, but also to all saints who have attained omniscience. Thus, e.g. Bāhubali is always called Jina in the inscriptions of Śravaṇabeḷgola. Even Gandharvas are called Jinas. To distinguish Tīrthaṅkaras from these, they are often called Jineśvaras, "Masters among the Jinas."

A soul attains the position of a Tīrthaṅkara, when it binds the "Tīrthaṅkara-nāma-karma" (p. 190) after doing good actions and having become ripe for it. The prerequisites for the Tīrthaṅkara-karma are: "Perfection of faith, possession of reverence, no offence against the vow and precepts, constant efforts made to acquire knowledge, *weltschmerz*,* charity according to one's capacity and asceticism, succour and readiness to help with respect to the community and the monks, love for the Arhats, masters, wise men and the teachings, observance of Āvaśyakas (of the six necessary daily duties), the glorification of the way to salvation; as also affection for the followers of the true religion."[41]

Every Tīrthaṅkara, before he brought enlightenment to the world, had to go through numerous existences in different forms, before he attained his lofty rank. The history of these different prior births is a popular subject of the didactic writings.** Once a person becomes capable of being a Tīrthaṅkara, he is first reborn in one of the heavens of gods from where he returns to the earth after a long period of supermundane enjoyment and enters a queen's womb which resembles a golden house embellished with pearls.

All Tīrthaṅkaras are born in a royal family: of those of the present world-period, two are born (the 20th and the 22nd) in the Hari-family and all others in the Ikṣvāku-family.

The future birth of the prophet is proclaimed to the mother by 14 (16***) dreams. The images in the dreams are: 1. a white elephant having a sound like a thunder, 2. a white bull, 3. a white lion, 4. the goddess of beauty resting on a lotus on Himavān, 5. a wreath (2 wreaths)

---

*Sadness over the evils of the world.

**Only the legends of the prior births of the two most famous Tīrthaṅkaras Pārśva and Mahāvīra are narrated in the text. Similar stories are told about the other Tīrthaṅkaras.

***Śvetāmbaras talk about 14, Digambaras 16 dreams. The dreams mentioned in the brackets in the following are those in which Digambaras differ from the view of Śvetāmbaras.

of beautifully fragrant flowers, 6. the moon shining white, 7. the sun shining red, 8. a banner (two fishes) fixed to a golden staff decorated with the feathers of a peacock, 9. one (two) golden container with pure water, 10. a lotus-pond inhabited by ducks, fish and other water-animals, 11. Ocean of Milk with its waves crowned by foam, (12. a throne embellished by gems,) 12. (13) a Vimāna, i.e. one of the mobile heavenly palaces in which heavenly spirits are making excellent music, (14. a palace of Asuras,) 13. (15) a heap of jewels, as big as the Meru mountain, 14. (16) fire shining white.

The queen informs her consort immediately what she has seen; he immediately knows the meaning of the dreams; they spend the rest of the night without sleep, occupying their mind with religious thoughts so that the effect of the propitious dreams are not lost on account of other dreams. Oneirocritics who are called the next morning explain that these dreams are from the 30 great dreams which prophesize the birth of a Tīrthaṅkara, and prophesize to the king the birth of a son who would attain this position.

The pregnancy of the queen passes without any incidents in between. The Tīrthaṅkara does wonderful things already in the body of his mother. Events taking place during this period (viz. the desires of the pregnant lady) prompt the parents later to decide the name to be given to the newborn.

Then the expected prince is born after about 9 months under favourable astrological sign. The event draws attention of the whole world. Gods fall from their seats and hasten to honour the child. Heavenly beings offer him laudations; they make the air fragrant and serve the boy in many ways: Some put the mother and child on the resting bed; others cut the umbilical chord, throw it in a ditch embellished by jewels and plant flowers over it, and others give bath to the Tīrthaṅkara. The king organizes a great festival of joy in which the whole population participates and in which rich alms are given and the prisoners are set free. But not only the gods and men, nay, all the beings are delighted and happy on account of the birth of the Jina, even the dark hell becomes bright for a short while, and the sorrows of the condemned are mitigated a little.

The boy then grows in all pomp and glory, which a prince deserves. Five nurses are at his disposal; one to suckle him, one to wash him, one to dress him, one to play with him and one to carry him. When he is hungry, he licks the nectar which Indra has put into his thumb. The older the child becomes, more handsome and wiser does he become. Even very early there are evidences of his extraordinary power and talent shown by his wonderful deeds.

Taught most excellently in all the arts and sciences, the prince grows into a stately young man and enjoys all earthly pleasures in a virtuous manner. Finally he marries with great pomp a beautiful princess and becomes father. Some future Tīrthaṅkaras wield royal power after their fathers have accepted the holy order.

But all the pomp and glory cannot mislead the young man. He knows that earthly pleasures are worthless and worldly endeavours even futile. Gradually a wish grows in his mind to renounce the world. An external event (in the case of Pārśva, e.g. the observation of the picture of his predecessor) converts the wish into a decision. Gods strengthen him in his desire and respect him as a future saviour of the world. For a year, he presents all his treasures and gives great alms. Once the day of the great renunciation has arrived, he is festively decorated by Śakra and gods and accompanied in a sedan to a forest, encouraged and hailed by the people. He puts down all ornaments here and tears his hair in five strands. Indra collects the falling hair in a dish of gems and throws it into the ocean of milk.

Fully devoted to the pious conduct of life, the saint now neglects his body; he spends his days in meditation; he fasts and practises asceticism. He makes a pilgrimage from place to place and does not stay anywhere for a long period. The purity of his nature is elucidated in 21 similes: as no water adheres to a copper pot, no collyrium to the mother of pearls, so no sin adheres to a saint; his course is unchecked like that of life; like the sky, he does not need support; he does not know any obstruction like the wind; his heart is pure like water in autumn; nothing can make him dirty like a lotus-leaf; he has withdrawn his senses from the world like a turtle its limbs; he wanders alone like a rhinoceros; he is free like a bird; he is always awake like a griffin (Bhāruṇḍa); he is brave like an elephant, strong like a bull, unconquerable like a lion, unshakeable like the Mandara-mountain, profound like the ocean, mildly pure like the moon, of shining power like the sun, as pure as gold, he endures everything like the earth and gives dazzling shine like fire.[42]

Indifferent to the world and its joys, singularly striving to purify his soul from all Karmas, he obtains first the fourth stage of knowledge, the transcendent knowledge of the thoughts of the others (Manaḥparyāya-jñāna) in addition to the three which he possesses from his birth. Finally he gets omniscience. This makes him Kevalī. Then gods hasten to revere him, and he preaches at first the holy doctrine to them. Then he sets out to proclaim the true faith to all the beings.

A Tīrthaṅkara normally preaches in a precious festive hall (Samavasaraṇa), erected solemnly for him by gods. For this purpose, Vāyukumāras clean at first the surface of the earth in a circumference of one Yojana, Meghakumāras sprinkle fragrant water and Vyantaras spread flowers and gems. Then gods build the hall; it is either round or square. It has three walls: Vaimānikas build the first, the inner one from precious stones; the second, central one is built by Jyotiṣkas from gold; and Bhavanapatis build the third, outer one from silver. Vyantaras put up in the centre a Caitya-tree, and an estrade of jewels under it. Four lion-thrones are erected in the centre of this, one on each side. Three sun-umbrellas are held over each throne; two Yakṣas carrying fans stand on its sides and a crystal wheel of Dharma stands in front of it resting on a lotus of gold. Then the Tīrthaṅkara enters the hall from the east and sits down on the eastern lion-throne with his face turned towards the east. The reflections of the Tīrthaṅkara are simultaneously seen on the three other chairs of the throne so that he appears to be looking at all the directions at the same time. The saint then proclaims the doctrine to the 12 assemblies which stand and sit around the hall on the places which are determined by tradition. Nuns and the wives of the Bhavanapatis, Vyantaras, Jyotiṣkas and Vaimānikas stand and the male gods of the four classes mentioned above, ascetics and laymen, men and women sit. Animals stand within the second enceinte; escorts within the third enceinte. The gates are guarded by the gods of four classes.[43]

A Tīrthaṅkara roams about in the land to propagate the true religion. Wherever he is seen, beings come in his joyous proximity to listen to him, because his words are understood by all beings, whatever then their local language.

According to a later speculation, a Tīrthaṅkara does not speak in the style of earthly beings, but in supermundane manner, in a language which is "syllableless" (Anakṣarī). He conveys his thoughts to some extent in a telepathic manner and thereby influences his listeners most convincingly; one main pupil (Gaṇadhara) translates his lectures then into the local language; they are then written in this form.

A Tīrthaṅkara preaches everywhere with great success and wins over thousands for his doctrine. Numerous men and women follow his precepts as his disciples and many leave the house to become homeless to dedicate their life to a saintly conduct as monks and nuns.

All Tīrthaṅkaras possess 34 virtues. The Jaina-theologians have systematized them into the minutest details.[44]

They are born with four of them: their body is wonderfully beautiful; it has wonderful fragrances; it is not subject to diseases and it is free from sweat and impurity. Their breath has the fragrance of a lotus; their blood is as white as the gushing milk of a cow; the flesh is without the smell of the flesh. It is not seen (by normal eyes) when they take their food and when they evacuate.*

11 insignias arise in them by the annihilation of the Ghāti-karma: One Koṭikoṭi of gods, human beings and animals stand (on account of their power) on a place which measures only one mile; their speech is heard simultaneously in the worlds of gods, human beings and animals and is audible in the area of one mile. There is an aura (Bhā-maṇḍala) around their head which shines like the sun; there is no disease around them in the vicinity of 200 Gavyūtis and 1 Agra, no enmity, no want of land, no epidemic, no floods and no want of rain, no famine and no danger either from alien or their own rulers.

19 insignias are divine: a holy wheel (Dharma-cakra) hovers in the air in front of a Tīrthaṅkara, 2 fly whisks, 1 lion-throne with a stool for the feet, 3 sun-umbrellas and a banner embellished with precious stones surround him; golden lotus-flowers are placed under his feet by the genii; 3 precious walls surround him; he appears to be looking at everyone in all the four directions; there is an Aśoka-tree near him, the thorns pointing downwards so that they don't harm him; the trees are

---

*This is the view of Śvetāmbaras. According to Digambaras, Kevalī does not eat at all, for if he eats, he would be hungry, but hunger pre-supposes an unfulfilled need and thus the presence of infatuation, of Karma. Śvetāmbaras teach, on the other hand, that food for the Kevalīs serves only for the preservation of the body and it is different from the food of the other beings.[45]

inclined towards him; heavenly drums resound; cooling airs move around him; birds fly on his rights (a favourable omen); fragrant water and colourful flowers fall down from the sky; his hair, his beard and his nails do not grow at all any more; a Koṭi of gods belonging to all the four classes listen to him; the seasons delight him by giving blossoming flowers; and everything he perceives with senses, is pleasant.*

Tīrthaṅkaras' speech has the following 35 insignias purity, loftiness, affability, thunderous sound, echo, honesty, harmony, momentousness, consistency, erudition, unequivocalness, irrefutability, power of conviction, logical connection, ability to act according to circumstances, fidelity to truth, absence of confusion and verbosity, of self-praise and captiousness, propriety, extraordinary mildness and charm, excellence, leniency, sublimity, persistence with what is right and useful, grammatical correctness, freedom from intrigue, etc., causing amazement, esquisiteness, absence of excessive slowness, variety of figures of speech, use of attributes, energy, clear pronunciation of sounds, words and sentences, uninterrupted flow and ease.

Tīrthaṅkaras are free from 18 deficiencies, viz. from the obstruction in giving and taking, in vigour, in enjoyment and profiteering (p. 191), from laughing, preference, dislike, sadness, fear and naucea, from greed, heterodoxy, ignorance, sleep and deficient conceit, from love and hatred.

They have, on the other hand, four infinities: infinite perception, infinite knowledge, infinite power and infinite bliss.

A male and a female spirit (Yakṣa and Yakṣiṇī) each attends upon every Tīrthaṅkara, and a main-pupil (Gaṇadhara) and his counterpart a female main-pupil (Āryā) are at his beck and call.

---

*Aśoka-tree, rain of flowers, divine music, fly whisks, throne, halo, heavenly kettle-drums, sun-umbrellas: all these appearing with a Tīrthaṅkara are called 8 Prātihāryas (marvels).[46]

Once a Tīrthaṅkara has converted many to the holy doctrine and a pious conduct of life and has shaken his Karma, he decides to obtain Nirvāṇa. After not taking any food and drink, he leaves after the annihilation of all Karmas the mortal frame of the body and climbs to the top of the world. The corpse of the redeemed one is bathed by Indra in the water of the milk-ocean and embellished. Gods then place him on a pyre of sandal and aloe which the heavenly genii set on fire. Gods erect a Stūpa of precious stones over the mortal remains of the saint.

The life of all Tīrthaṅkaras is spent in more or less this form, and their biographies show some deviations only in details. Therefore, many Jaina-works are satisfied with enlisting the deviations in tabular form. The following information is given on each Tīrthaṅkara: history of the earlier births and specification of the heaven of gods from which the future Tīrthaṅkara descends to the earth; the name of the parents and the place of birth; the constellation under which he is born; the place where he took the ordination and attained omniscience; the tree under which he got knowledge; the place where he went into Nirvāṇa; particulars about his blazon; the colour of his body; the size of his body; number and names of his Gaṇadharas (chiefs); monks, nuns, laymen and women, Yakṣas and Yakṣiṇīs who serve him; particulars about the period that passed from the Nirvāṇa of his predecessor to his birth; the period during which he covered the individual stages to perfection till he attained Nirvāṇa.

(b) The 12 Cakravartīs

Cakravartīs are emperors who rule over a part of the world (e.g. Bhārata-land having six parts). Their life is embellished with similar features like those of the Tīrthaṅkaras. Every Cakarvartī obtains his high rank on account of good actions done in earlier existences and on account of a Nidāna, i.e. a wish which is passionately cherished in an earlier life. He is born in the royal family of Ikṣvāku, grows in pomp and glory and is experienced in all arts and sciences. Having beauty and power, being brave and clever, he is embellished with 36 insignias[47] of mind and body. After vanquishing all the opponents in battle, he conquers the world; served and praised by gods and genii, he is anointed emperor. He rules for a long period and powerfully, enjoying all the pleasures with his many wives and treasures which the earth can offer. The end of the life of Cakravartīs is very different. Whereas some renounce the world or even become Tīrthaṅkaras (like the 16th, 17th and 18th Cakravartīs of this world-period) and get redemption, others come to the heaven of gods after their death, and some others fall into hell on account of their bad actions.

Cakravartīs owe their success not only to their capability and power and the support they get from their supermundane beings, but also, above all, to the wonderful "gems" (Ratnas) and precious "treasures" (Nidhi) which are in their possession.

The 14 gems are the living beings of different types which serve the Cakravartīs. They are divided into those which are provided only with one sense (Ekendriyaratna) and those which have five senses (Pañcendriyaratna).[48]

The seven gems with one sense are:

1. Cakra, a discus embellished with jewels; the Cakravartī hurls it in the battle against his opponent. Provided with unfailing power, it returns into the hand of the one who has thrown it, after it has smashed the head of the enemy. If it does not immediately kill the opponent for some reason, then it follows him, like a falcon its booty where it can destroy him.

2. Daṇḍa, a splendid staff with which the earth can be bored into its depths, but which also alliviates the pain and misery by its touch.

3. Khaḍga, a sharp sword which breaks all resistance.

4. Chatra, a glittering white sun-umbrella. It is for the Cakravartī not only as a symbol of his dignity as a ruler, but it also cripples his enemy by its look. It protects against rain and sun, against wind and weather and gives cool shade in hot season and a warm shade in cold season.

5. Carma, a wonderful hide which cannot be pierced by cut and thrust. It can, at the same time, be used as a raft while crossing rivers and oceans and also serves occasionally as a field on which the grains sown in the morning carry fruits in the evening.

6. Maṇi, a gem of uncomparable dazzle belonging to a particular type of cat-eyes (Vaidūrya). It lends victory, cures wounds and illuminates darkness as bright as the sun.

7. Kākiṇī, a sort of a very hollow mass in the form of a dice of a shining luminosity. This is used by a Cakravartī also to get light while entering a dark cave by grazing its walls and to remove the effect of poison, etc.

The seven gems with five senses are:

1. Senāpati, the commander of a Cakravartī. He is a reliable and an uncorruptible servant of his master, alert and far-sighted, commanding the language of the Yavanas (Greeks) and the Mlecchas (barbarians) in word and script, well-versed in politics and art of life, a powerful fighter and a clever strategist.

2. Gṛhapati, chamberlain who looks after the kitchen and storeroom and has the wardrobe and provisions under his command.

3. Vārddhaka, architect who is entrusted with the building of houses, palaces and cities.

4. Purohita, house-priest who conducts the religious ceremonies, conversant with magic *mantras* and is an artistic poet.

5. Gaja, elephant of unsurpassable power.

6. Aśva, beautiful horse which is endowed with auspicious signs.

7. Strī, a most beautiful woman, eternally young, warm at touch in cold season and cool in hot season, energising the husband constantly to new pleasure by her look and driving away disease by her touch.

The nine "treasures" (Nidhis) with which a Cakravartī is endowed, are, according to one view, collection of books in which there is literature on 9 different branches of science, according to another, containers or treasure-houses in which there are things whose application is taught in those books. Names and contents of the 9 Nidhis are: 1. Naisarpa: houses, 2. Pāṇḍuka: rice and corns, 3. Piṅgalaka: ornament, 4. Sarvaratnaka: 14 gems, 5. Mahāpadma: clothing, 6. Kāla: determination of time for astrological predictions, 7. Mahākāla: mines of metals and precious stones, 8. Mānavaka: weapons, warcraft, 9. Śaṅkha: poetry, dramaturgy, music.

(c) 9 Baladevas, 9 Vāsudevas and 9 Prativāsudevas

Baladevas, Vāsudevas and the Prativāsudevas are three heroes who appear always simultaneously, and that too on the whole nine times in a world-period. Baladeva and Vāsudeva are half-brothers, sons of a king from different wives; the Prativāsudeva is their antagonist.

Baladeva (also called Balabhadra) has a bright, white body-colour, always wears a blue-black robe and toddy palm is his banner. His four insignias are: bow, two different clubs (Gadā and Musala) and ploughshare; according to Digambaras: chain of precious stones, two clubs and ploughshare. His appearance in the world is announced by his mother by telling that she has seen four of the famous dreams.

Vāsudeva (also called Nārāyaṇa or Viṣṇu) is a younger brother of Baladeva, but emerges more strongly mostly in the legend than Baladeva, for he is a powerful fighter, whereas Baladeva is of a gentler mind. His privileged position is seen from the fact that his mother sees seven (five)—explanation is given earlier that bracket indicates the view of Digambaras—of the famous dreams. His body has a dark-blue shine; his robe is of yellow silk. Śrīvatsa-mark on the chest, a white sun-umbrella, fly whisk and Garuḍa-banner are his insignias. He has seven insignias: the conch, Pañcajanya, which only he can blow, discus Sudarśana, club Kaumodakī, bow Śārṅga, sword Nandaka, Vanamālā, a wreath of flowers of the season and the precious stone Kaustuba. (Insignias according to Digambaras are: bow, conch, discus, sword, scepter, Śakti and club.)

Prativāsudeva is a powerful evil ruler; his birth is announced through a dream.

Baladeva and Vāsudeva are closely linked through a series of existences and hostile to the Prativāsudeva. The battle is caused by Prativāsudeva subjugating a large part of the Bharata-land and demanding as a ruler of the half of the world obedience from Vāsudeva. Irritated by this or by other challenges of Prativāsudeva, Vāsudeva attacks him and kills him finally so that he comes to hell to atone for his evil deeds. Then Vāsudeva rules happily for a long period as a "half-emperor" (Ardha-Cakravartī) and enjoys all the pleasures of the world with his numerous wives. Finally he dies and goes into hell on account of his bad Karma got through the wars. His faithful brother, Baladeva, is so much sad on account of his death that he does not find any more happiness in the world, takes up ordination and finally gets redemption.

2. HISTORY OF BHARATA-LAND AND ITS GREAT MEN

(1) Preliminary Remarks

The wheel of time rotates in the whole human world. Since the 63 famous men appear everywhere, where the eras Suṣama-duḥṣamā and Duḥṣama-suṣamā prevail, the series of these important heroes of the hagiography appear in the most different parts of the world. Jainas, therefore, give the lists of the Tīrthaṅkaras, etc. of Bharata, Airāvata,[49] Mahāvideha, of the 2½ continents

Jambūdvīpa, Dhātakikhaṇḍa and Puṣkara-dvīpa, and they inform not only the names of those of them who lived in the present world-period, but also know to name partially those who existed in the earlier Avasarpiṇīs or Utsarpiṇīs[50] and those who will appear in the future epochs. There are even speculations given on the simultaneousness of "famous men" in different parts of the world. It is particularly taught that in the same period of time at the most 170 and at the least 20 Tīrthaṅkaras can appear in the 2½ continents which are inhabited by human beings. The maximum number is explained as under: in each of 5 Bharatas (1 in Jambūdvīpa, 2 in Dhātakīkhaṇḍa, 2 in the half of the Puṣkaradvīpa inhabited by human beings), each one, i.e. together 5; in each of the 5 Airāvatas (which are also divided into the continents like the Bharatas) each one, i.e. together 5; in each one of the 32 provinces (Vijaya) of the 5 Mahāvidehas (which are also similarly divided into continents) each one, i.e. together 32 x 5 = 160, total 5+5+160 = 170. The minimum number thus: in one Mahāvideha of Jambūdvīpa 4 and in 2 Mahāvidehas of Dhātakīkhaṇḍa and in the 2 Mahāvidehas of Puṣkaradvīpa each 8: 4+8+8= 20. The other great men also appear in the other parts of the world in corresponding number. It emerges from the information in the *Jñātadharmakathā* that the Śalākāpuruṣas living in the same period know each other. According to this work, Kṛṣṇa, the Vāsudeva of Jambūdvīpa and Kapila, the Vāsudeva of Dhātakīkhaṇḍa, let their shanks blow together across the salt-ocean.[51]

The Jaina-theologians have dealt in detail only with the 63 famous men of the Bharata-land in the present world-period. In spite of the volume of the literature dedicated to the history of Bharata, the most important contents of the world-history of Jainas can be described in a few pages. The destinies of most of the Tīrthaṅkaras as also of other heroes are, as we have already mentioned, so similar that they have been sufficiently repro-

General idea about the eras of the present world-period (Avasarpiṇī) of Bharata-kṣetra and its 24 Tīrthaṅkaras (T), 12 Cakravartīs (C), 9 Baladevas (B), 9 Vāsudevas (V), and 9 Prativāsudevas (P)

	I. Suṣama-suṣamā			
	II. Suṣamā			
	III. Suṣama-duḥṣamā			
1. T.: Ṛṣabha (Ādinātha)	1. C.: Bharata			
	IV. Duḥṣama-suṣamā			
2. T.: Ajita	2. C.: Sagara			
3. " Saṁbhava				
4. " Abhinandana				
5. " Sumati				
6. " Padmaprabha				
7. " Supārśva				
8. " Candraprabha				
9. " Suvidhi				
10. " Śītala				
11. " Śreyāṁsa		1. B.: Acala	1. V.: Tripṛṣṭa	1. P.: Aśvagrīva
12. " Vāsupūjya		2. " Vijaya	2. " Dvipṛṣṭa	2. " Tāraka
13. " Vimala		3. " Bhadra	3. " Svayaṁbhū	3. " Meraka
14. " Ananta		4. " Suprabha	4. " Puruṣottama	4. " Madhu
15. " Dharma	3. " Maghava	5. " Sudarśana	5. " Puruṣasiṁha	5. " Niśumbha
	4. " Sanatkumāra			
16. " Śānti	5. " Śānti			
17. " Kunthu	6. " Kunthu			
18. " Ara	7. " Ara	6. " Ānanda	6. " Puruṣapuṇḍarīka	6. " Bali
19. " Malli	8. " Subhūma	7. " Nandana		
20. " Munisuvrata		8. " Padma (Rāma)	7. " Datta	7. " Prahlāda
21. " Nami			8. " Lakṣmaṇa	8. " Rāvaṇa
22. " Ariṣṭanemi	9. " Mahāpadma	9. " Balarāma	9. " Kṛṣṇa	9. " Jarāsandha
23. " Pārśva	Rāvaṇa			
24. " Mahāvīra	10." Hariṣeṇa			
	11." Jayasena			
	12." Brahmadatta			
	V. Duḥṣamā			
	VI. Duḥṣama-duḥṣamā			

duced mainly in the remarks made above on p. 276 ff. and what remains to be done is to add some details. Besides, the interest of Jainas in individual persons is different for different persons. Thus while the edition of Hemacandra's "Triṣaṣṭiśalākāpuruṣacarita" published in Bombay devotes in all 360 pages to the life of the first Tīrthaṅkara and the first Cakravartī, the biography of the fourth Tīrthaṅkara is given in 12 and the one of the third Cakravartī in 3 pages; the story of the eighth Baladeva, Vāsudeva and Prativāsudeva is given in 162 pages, and the one of the seventh group of heroes of this type only in 3 pages.[52] In view of the numerous repetitions and interpolations, the essential contents even of the extensive sections devoted to the Śalākā-puruṣas are not so substantial as one would expect them to be from their size.

Let a short resumé be given to make the orientation a little easy. It will be known from this in which order the 63 great men of our Avasarpiṇī have lived and which of them were contemporaries. (The Tīrthaṅkaras 5-7 figure twice in the table, because they were, at the same time, Cakravartīs. Thus the actual number of the Śalākā-puruṣas of our world-period is only 60 and not 63.)

This Table is valid in this form only for Śvetāmbaras. The hagiography of Digambaras shows some differences. Thus Vijaya is considered by them as the first, Acala as the second Baladeva, and the order of the Prativāsudevas 4-7 among them is usually: Niśumbha, Madhukaiṭabha, Bali and Praharaṇa,[53] but the others follow in the order: 4. Madhusūdana, 5. Madhukaiṭabha, 6. Niśumbha, 7. Balīndra.[54] We cannot consider all these details in the following. My presentation reproduces mainly the views of Śvetāṃbaras and mentions only in special cases more important points in which Digambaras have a different opinion.

(2) The Eras, Saints and Heroes of the Present World-period

(a) Suṣama-suṣamā

In Suṣama-suṣamā, the best of all eras, the earth was full of beautiful trees and plants and shone in the decoration of five-coloured precious stones. The airs were filled with precious fragrances and luck and happiness prevailed everywhere. The human beings were as white as snow, having an excellent form and embellished with 32 marks of beauty. There were no diseases and dissatisfaction among them, nor were there any kings and castes; all were equal in their rank and lived contentedly and happily. They spent their days in play and enjoyment. They did not have to run after any trade and business because they got everything without any efforts. For, when the people had a wish, they went to one of the 10 wish-trees; then they got everything they wanted.

The 10 wish-trees (Kalpadruma) beautifying the earth then were: 1. Mattāṅga which spread health and cheerfulness, 2. Bhṛtāṅga which granted beauty. 3. Turyāṅga. whose leaves gave out fine music, 4. Dīpaśikhā which illuminated darkness by its shine, 5. Jyotiraṅga (Jyotiṣikā) which shone like the sun, meteors, lightning or fire, 6. Citrāṅga which gave out wonderful wreaths, 7. Citrarasa which gave fragrant food, 8. Maṇyaṅga which gave precious stones and jewels, 9. Gehākāra which gave house and shelter, 10. Anaṅga which lent fine clothes.[55]

The people lived only on fruits, took them only in a negligible quantity once in three days. Their life span at the beginning of this era was 3 Palyopamas, but decreased gradually; the size of their body at the beginning of Suṣama-suṣamā was 3 Gavyūtis (Krośa). Children could grow only in 49 days so that they did not need the care of their parents. Their development was very fast: they licked the thumb in the first week; in the second they could crawl; in the third they began to speak; they attempted to walk in the fourth; they were on their legs in the fifth; they knew all arts in the sixth; they were capable of enjoying love in the seventh. All children were born as twins, and that too, a boy with a girl, but these brothers and sisters were united for a lasting companionship of life. The people were born shortly before the life of their parents came to an end so that there was never overpopulation on the earth. As soon as they were born, father died by yawning, mother by sneezing.

When the people died then, their corpses were not cremated, because the use of fire was not yet known, but they were embedded in the forest, and birds lifted them and carried them into the ocean or Gaṅgā. The souls of the deceased obtained all their new existences in the world of gods.

The Suṣama-suṣamā era lasted for 4 Koṭikoṭis of Sāgaropamas.

(b) Suṣamā

The conditions in Suṣamā were the same as those in Suṣama-suṣamā, but there was a considerable decline in happiness and virtue. The people were at the beginning only 2 Gavyūtis tall and their life span was at the most 2 Palyopamas. They took the fruits of the Kalpa-trees once in two days; the growth of the children took 64 days.

The Suṣamā-era lasted for 3 Koṭikoṭis of Sāgaropamas losing every moment a little of its shine.

(c) Suṣama-duḥṣamā

The people reached a height of 1 Gavyūti and a life span of 1 Palyopama at the beginning of the "good-bad" era (Suṣama-duḥṣamā); it lasted for 2 Koṭikoṭis of Sāgaropamas. They enjoyed day after day the fruits of Kalpa-trees, and the children took 79 days to grow. In the first period, the souls of the deceased were reborn in the heaven of gods like the two previous eras; later they were born in all the four stages of existence. The wishing trees began to disappear, they did not give any more their fruits as abundantly. Even the virtues of people decreased and greed and passion began to be aroused. The general deterioration of morals required the establishment of laws. Seven patriarchs (Kulakaras) appeared one after the other when only 1/8th Palyopama of the era still remained, and they gave the humanity rules about their action. The Kulakaras were: Vimala-vāhana, Cakṣuṣmān, Yaśasvī, Abhicandra, Prasenajit, Marudeva and Nābhi.

Digambaras presume 14 Kulakaras and they also call them "Manus" and describe in detail how the deterioration of the conditions in the world came about under each one of them.

The dazzle of the Kalpa-tree Jyotiraṅga decreased under the first Kulakara, Pratiśruti, to such a degree that sun and moon were seen by the people for the first time; till then their light was so much eclipsed by the tree that people did not notice the two at all. Stars became visible during the period of the second Manu, Sanmati; men were attacked by animals during the period of the third, Kṣemaṅkara; Manu ordered them to keep aloof from them. The animals became still more savage during the period of the fourth, Kṣemandhara, so that people had to keep them away with the help of sticks and stones. The productivity of the wishing trees was reduced under the following Kulakaras so that people started fighting with one another for fruits. The fifth Manu, Sīmaṅkara, distributed certain landstrips among the individuals to let them enjoy their benefits; his successor Sīmaṅdhara was compelled to make the boundaries of the individual areas by distinctive marks. The seventh Manu, Vimala-vāhana, taught the use of elephants and horses as riding animals. Parents under the eighth, Cakṣuṣmān, did not die when children were born, and the time the parents spent together with their children increased constantly under the ninth, Yaśasvān, tenth, Abhicandra and eleventh, Candraprabha; the Kulakaras had, therefore, to explain this unusual event to the people. Hills and rivers were formed under the 12th Kulakara, Marudeva; the patriarch showed to the people how a road is made over the mountains and ships built to cross the rivers. People were born with an embryonic egg-skin under the 13th Manu, Prasenajit; he showed them how it was removed. The 14th Kulakara, Nābhi, gets his name from the fact that the children during his period were born with a navel, and he taught them at first how it is to be cut. It rained for the first time under his regime, and the plants and bushes grew on their own. Nābhi taught the people, who could not live any more on the fruits of the wishing trees, how one could make use of them as food and for other purposes.[56]

Nābhi and his wife Marudevī had a son Ṛṣabha (Vṛṣabha). He became the first *Tīrthaṅkara.*[57] His birth was proclaimed by the famous dreams; but a bull (vṛṣabha or ṛṣabha) appeared—against the rule—as the first dream; the boy was named after it, when he was born. Ṛṣabha grew into a handsome youth in the place of his birth Ayodhyā or Vinītā in the shortest period and married two women; gods participated in the marriage which was celebrated with great pomp. According to Digambaras, the names of the two wives of Ṛṣabha were Yaśasvatī and Sunandā and they were sisters of two men called Kaccha and Mahākaccha. Ṛṣabha's wives, according to Śvetāmbaras, were Sumaṅgalā and Sunandā; Sumaṅgalā was Ṛṣabha's twin-sister and Sunandā a girl whose twin-brother (who should have been her husband according to the tradition) had died when a fruit of a toddy tree had fallen on his head (this is the first violent death that took place in this world-period!). Ṛṣabha had a son Bharata from Sumaṅgalā, a daughter Brahmī and 98 twins, a son Bāhubali and a daughter Sundarī from Sunandā, i.e. on the whole 100 sons and two daughters. Since he had eaten sugarcane (*ikṣu*)—something that did not exist so far in the world—offered to him by Śakra (Indra)—his progeny got the name Ikṣvāku.

Ṛṣabha was, at the advice of Nābhi, made king by the people when he had become 20,00,000 Pūrva years old—he was the first who was decorated with this title. He laid the foundations of all later civilization during the long period of his rule. He arranged marriages between Bharata and Sundarī and Bāhubali and Brahmī, and thus broke the tradition which made marriages between twins. Thus marriage and family-life was introduced; this gave rise to inequality among men and to caste-practices, as also to property, but also, at the same time, to the greed for possession and to the necessity of administration and judicature.

With the foresight that soon the Kalpadrumas would be completely gone and people would have to fight for their food, he taught his subjects the 5 basic handiworks of potter, tailor, painter, weaver and barber, occupations which were not necessary so far because the Kalpa-trees had satisfied all the needs of life, and hair and nails never grew on people during the good world-eras. He taught them farming, trade, the art of cooking which was used for the first time when it was seen that two dry wood pieces catch fire when they are rubbed against one another. He showed to Brahmī how to write 18 characters of the script and to Sundarī how to calculate. He taught on the whole 72 arts to men and 64 to women.

After Ṛṣabha had ruled powerfully for 63,00,000 Pūrva years, he became aware that all that is mundane is transitory and decided to renounce the world. He made his sons the heirs to his kingdom, gave many donations and became ascetic in the park Siddhārtha near Vinītā. He was thus the first beggar of the whole world-period. After devoting thousand Pūrva years to pious contemplation, he obtained omniscience in a grove in the proximity of the city Purimatāla. Thus he had attained the position of a Tīrthaṅkara as the first in the Avasarpiṇī, and he is, therefore, called Ādinātha, "the first master". He roamed about preaching and converted many thousands to the true faith. After working for 99,000 Pūrva years he retired, 84,00,000 years old, to the peak of the mountain Aṣṭāpada along with 10,000 monks. He went into Nirvāṇa after fasting for 6½ days and sitting in the Samparyaṅka position. The gods cremated his mortal remains with festive pomp and thus introduced to the world this new way of disposing the dead.

Ṛṣabha's son Bharata was the first Cakravartī of the Bharata-land. It has its name from him. He did wonderful things on his war expeditions. When once the Nāgas who were allied with the barbarians living on the north border of his kingdom let a rain of missiles fall on his army for seven days one after the other, he hid his warriors in the hyde-jewel and put his sun-umbrella upon this, so that all were secure against every harm, as if in a hemisphere-like can. One could easily take care of subsistence, as we have already mentioned on p. 284, by sowing corns which could easily grow. After subjugating the whole Bharata-land Bharata returned to his residence. He now asked his 98 brothers to obey him. They were undecided, whether they should follow his order or not, because Ṛṣabha had given each one of them a kingdom. They, therefore, went to their father and asked him, whether Bharata be allowed to rob their land, whether they should fight or obey him. Ṛṣabha then preached them the holy doctrine. When they listened to him, they knew that the mundane joys are futile, and they all renounced the world. Thus Bharata could also annex their kingdoms, and Bāhubalī was now the only one who had still not taken shelter under his dominion. Bharata, therefore, sent his messengers to him and demanded of him that he should acknowledge his superiority. But Bāhubalī decided to defend his rights with the help of sword. When the armies of the two brothers confronted one another, it was agreed on Bāhubalī's suggestion that only the two brothers should fight against each other. Bāhubali defeated Bharata one after the other in eye to eye battle, wordy duel and fist fight. Even Bharata's discus could do nothing against Bāhubalī. Although Bāhubalī won the battle, he suddenly had a desire of becoming ascetic like his other brothers. He gave his kingdom to Bharata and stood at one spot without moving for one year so that plants entwined his limbs and serpents clasped his feet which were protruding from the anthills. Bāhubalī then attained omniscience by the power of asceticism.[58]

Bharata enjoyed the pleasures of his world-dominion in wisdom. One of his most important governmental actions was the composition of the four "genuine Vedas" (Ārya Vedas); the worship of the Tīrthaṅkaras, of the true faith and proper life-conduct was proclaimed in them.[59] Excellent men were entrusted with their studies; they were called Brāhmaṇas or "twice-born" because a holy thread was worn by them and thereby, they had experienced a second, spiritual birth.[60]

Bharata got a temple of Ṛṣabha erected on the Aṣṭāpada and also one in Śatruñjaya. But finally he felt lonely because his father and most of his relatives, who had also found salvation, had died, and became weary of the worldly life. When once a ring fell from his finger as he was sitting on his throne splendidly ornamented, and when he saw how unattractive it looked without an ornament, he recognized the ugliness and worthlessness of the body and became aware of the complete difference between soul and body. He therefore, renounced power and devoted himself to pious meditation. Nobody ordained him, but Indra let him himself tear off five strands of hair and provided him with a penitential robe. Bharata, after destroying all Karmas, obtained omniscience and salvation on the Aṣṭāpada-mountain; he was then over 84,00,000 Pūrva years old.

Bharata's one son, Marīci, had become monk and heard, how his grandfather had told Bharata that he as

Mahāvīra would be once the last Tīrthaṅkara. This made him so conceited that he bound the Karma "lower position" (p. 191) which made him enter later the womb of a Brāhmaṇa-mother. Marīci found that the precept for the Jaina-monks of possessing threefold control (*daṇḍa*) over thoughts, words and works cannot be easily carried out. He proposed, therefore, the wrong doctrine that each one who carries the three staffs (*daṇḍa*) which are bound together, is sure of salvation. Many were converted to this belief. The doctrine was further developed by his pupil Kapila, and it is prevalent even today among the Brāhmaṇas whose penitents, as it is well-known, carry a triple staff (*tridaṇḍa*).

The era Suṣama-duḥṣamā ends three years and eight and half months after Ṛṣabha's Nirvāṇa after it had lasted for 2 Koṭikoṭis of Sāgaropamas.

(d) Duḥṣama-suṣamā

There were no more Kalpa-trees in the Duḥṣama-suṣamā era and the human beings who were now taking food daily had to sustain themselves by the work of their hands. All conditions became increasingly worse. The body size at the beginning was 500 Dhanuṣas, the life span 10 million Pūrva years. Misfortune and illness afflicted humanity in increasing degree, and heterodoxy gained more and more ground. All the rest of the great men of the world-history appeared in this era which lasted for 1 Koṭikoṭi of Sāgaropamas less 42,000 years.

The second Tīrthaṅkara, *Ajita*, was born in Ayodhyā in the Kosala-land as a son of the king Jitaśatru and his wife Vijayā when almost half of the "bad-good" era had passed, 50 lakhs of Koṭis of Sāgaropamas less 72,00,000 Pūrva years after Ṛṣabha's Nirvāṇa. He got his name from the fact that he was not vanquished (*ajita*) by passions or that his father could not defeat his mother in game when she was pregnant with him. Brought up in a way that is proper for a prince, he was made ruler by the king who now accepted ordainment; but then he renounced the world, became omniscient, proclaimed the doctrine and attained salvation on the Sameṭa mountain at the age of 72,00,000 Pūrva years.

Ajita's nephew, son of Jitaśatru's brother Sumitravijaya and his wife Yaśomatī, was *Sagara,* the second Cakravartī.[61] When Ajita became monk, he took the reigns, ruled over the empire successfully, subjugated the whole Bharata and was anointed world-ruler. Sagara had 60,000 sons. They once marched through the whole land and reached the temple embellished with precious stones and which was erected by Bharata on the Aṣṭāpada-mountain. When Jahnu, the eldest of the brothers, saw the treasures of the shrine he thought anxiously that bad people could rob later the precious things on account of the progressive worsening of morals. He, therefore, decided to make a big trench around this with the help of his brothers to protect the Caitya. The earth was dug to the lowest depth with the help of a bar-diamond. But this disturbed the houses of the serpent-spirits which were living under the earth. The serpent-king asked Jahnu to stop his operation, but pardoned the brothers when he heard of their good intention. But when Jahnu got the trench filled by the Gaṅgā-water and caused floods in the serpent-city, the serpent-king became angry and sent out his whole army; this burnt the 60,000 young men to ashes with their poisonous look.

Sagara's men returned horror-stricken to the king and thought how they should communicate the horrible happening to the king. They met a Brāhmaṇa on the way who offered to do this for them. He took a dead boy to Sagara and asked him to bring him back to life. The king referred him to a physician; but the physician said that he needed ash from a house in which nobody had ever died. When it was found that it was not possible to get it, Sagara consoled the Brāhmaṇa by saying that one cannot escape death. Then the Brāhmaṇa told him about the death of his 60,000 sons. Sagara fell down from the throne and became unconscious, but finally composed himself and let the funeral-ceremonies be completed.

The next day he sent his grandson Bhagīratha to Aṣṭāpada. He brought back Gaṅgā which was threatening to flood the whole surrounding to her bed with the help of the bar-diamond and finally into the ocean. Gaṅgā now flows through this bed. Since Gaṅgā was brought by Jahnu, she is even now called *Jāhnavī*, and because Bhagīratha brought her further, she is called *Bhāgīrathī*, and the ocean is called *Sāgara* because the ocean accepted her on the command of Sagara.

After Bhagīratha had completed his task, Sagara appointed him his successor, renounced the world and attained Nirvāṇa along with Ajita.

Saṁbhava, the 3rd Tīrthaṅkara, was a son of King Jitāri of Śrāvastī and Queen Senā. His name is supposed to indicate that the rise (*sambhava*) of the abundance of happiness was associated with his birth. After enjoying mundane pleasures, he became a monk, proclaimed the doctrine and when went into Nirvāṇa on the Sameṭa mountain, he was 60,00,000 Pūrva years old. 30 lakhs of Koṭis of Sāgaropamas after Ajīta.

Abhinandana, the 4th Tīrthaṅkara, was born in Ayodhyā as a son of King Saṁvara and Queen Siddhārthā. His name was given to him as a reminiscence of the joyful welcome (*abhinandana*) that was given to him in the world by gods and human beings. He attained salvation in the Sameṭa mountain, 50,00,000 Pūrva years old, 10 lakhs of Koṭis of Sāgaropamas after his predecessor.

Sumati, the 5th Tīrthaṅkara, was also born in Ayodhyā (Sāketa). His parents were King Megha and Queen Maṅgalā. His name owes its origin to an event which took place before his birth and in which his mother showed that he had an extraordinarily keen power of understanding (*sumati*). A wealthy man had died and had left behind two wives and one son. Each one of them claimed that the son was their own. Since they could not agree they took their legal quarrel before the king. The king was not able to solve the difficult case and asked the queen for her advice. She proposed that the son should also be cut into two parts like all other property and divide them among the two wives. The real mother said that she would prefer to give up her right on the son and the property rather than seeing her son being killed; the other wife, on the other hand, behaved as if it was not her concern. So the son was given to the first.[62] Sumati lived the typical life of a Tīrthaṅkara and died finally redeemed on the Sameṭa mountain, 40,00,000 Pūrva years old, 9 Koṭis of lakhs of Sāgaropamas after his predecessor.

Padmaprabha, the 6th Tīrthaṅkara, came from Kauśāmbī (Sukośā), where his father Dhara (Śrīdhara), husband of Susimā, was the king. Since his mother desired to have lotuses (*padma*) during her preganancy and wished to rest on a bed of lotuses, he was named Padmaprabha (shine of lotus). After going through the usual stages of a Tīrthaṅkara, he attained salvation on the Sameṭa mountain, in the 30,00,000th Pūrva year of his last existence, 90,000 Koṭis of Sāgaropamas after Sumati's Nirvāṇa.

Supārśva, the 7th Tīrthaṅkara, was a son of King Pratiṣṭha and Queen Pṛthivī of Banāras. He was named Supārśva because his mother had a beautiful side (*supārśva*) when she was pregnant with him. Since she saw that she was resting on a bed of serpents in her dream and since the Tīrthaṅkara was surrounded by serpents since his birth, he is shown under a baldachin formed by serpents. He attained Nirvāṇa when he was 20,00,000 Pūrva years old, 9,000 Koṭis of Sāgaropamas after the Nirvāṇa of his predecessor.

Candraprabha, the 8th Tīrthaṅkara, was born as a son of King Mahāsena and his wife Lakṣmaṇā in Candrapurī. He got the name "Moon-shine" because his Leśyā was snowwhite, like the light of the full moon, or because his mother, when she was expecting him, wished to drink the moon—a desire fulfilled by a person giving her water to drink from a silver-cup in which the moonlight had fallen. After becoming omniscient, he died on the Sameṭa mountain, 10,00,000 Pūrva years old, 900 Koṭis of Sāgaropamas after Supārśva.

Suvidhi or *Puṣpadanta*, the 9th Tīrthaṅkara, experienced his last earthly existence as a son of King Sugrīva of Kākaṇḍī and his wife Rāmā. He was named Suvidhi because the pregnant Rāmā had practised many holy customs (*su-vidhi*); Puṣpadanta, because his teeth resembled flowers. He attained salvation on the Sameṭa mountain, where he died 2,00,000 Pūrva years old, 90 Koṭis of Sāgaropamas after Candraprabha.

Although the Jaina-doctrine was propagated, in spite of the spreading heterodoxy, throughout the millenniums from Ṛṣabha's period, it got lost regularly after Suvidhi's death and the following Tīrthaṅkaras up to Śāntinātha, and it had to be revived through the emergence of new prophets. The extinction of Jainism (Tīrtha-vyavaccheda) in the period between the 9th and the 10th Tīrthaṅkara lasted for a period of 1/4 Palyopama.

Sītala, the 10th Tīrthaṅkara, was born in Bhadilapur (Bhadrikā-purī). He was named the cooling-one (*śitala*) because his mother, when she was pregnant, cured her husband Dṛḍharatha from high fever by her cooling touch. He attained salvation on the Sameṭa mountain 1,00,000 Pūrva years old, 9 Koṭis of Sāgaropamas after Suvidhi. The period between him and his successor, during which the real faith disappeared, lasted 1/4 Palyopama.

Sreyāṁsa, the 11th Tīrthaṅkara, came from Siṁhapura where his father was a king. His mother Viṣṇā (Viṣṇudrī) desired to sit on a bed possessed by a demon, when she was pregnant by the force of the influence coming from the unborn child; the prince got the name Śreyāṁsa on account of the overall good (*śreyāṁsa*) which he accomplished even before his birth. He died on the Sameṭa mountanin, 84,00,000 ordinary years old, 1 Koṭi less, 100 Sāgaropamas and 66,26,000 years after Śītala.

King Ripupratiśatru lived in Poṭaṇapura during the period of Śreyāṁsa. His wife dreamt once, when she was pregnant, four of the famous dreams and then gave later birth to a son *Acala*, the first Baladeva. Later she gave birth also to a daughter Mṛgavatī. Blossomed into a young woman, she was so much beautiful that her father mortally fell in love with her and decided to marry her. To give a legal basis for the intended marriage, he called a great assembly and put the following question to those who were present: "To whom does a precious stone belong which is found in my land?" He was told that he was the master of the land and therefore owner of everything which it produced. When he repeated the question two more times and got the same answer, he married Mṛgavatī according to Gandharva rite (i.e. without further ceremony) to the horror of his subjects who then named him Prajāpati*). His wife Bhadrā was so much shocked by the action of her husband that she emigrated to the Deccan, accompanied by Acala; he built there the city of Māheśvarī where his mother stayed, but he returned to Poṭaṇapura.

Ripupratiśatru had a son from Mṛgavatī. He got the name *Tripṛṣṭa* who proved to be the first Vāsudeva on account of seven dreams [He was a rebirth of Marīci (p. 296) and prebirth of the 24th Tīrthaṅkara Mahāvīra]. In spite of the difference in age, there was a friendship between Acala and Tripṛṣṭa and both were inseparable from each other.

The first Prativāsudeva, King Aśvagrīva (Hayagrīva), a son of King Mayūragrīva of Alakā and Queen Nīlāñjanā lived in Ratnapura during this period. When he had

*The word Prajāpati has a double meaning. It means firstly the master (*pati*) of the subjects (*prajā*), i.e. thus the king and secondly the god Brahmā as the Lord of the creatures (*prajā*). Brahmā was married to his daughter Sarasvatī according to the mythology of the Hindus.

conquered a great part of the world, he once asked an astrologer whether he would be vanquished and killed by someone. The astrologer replied that he would lose his life through a man who would ill treat his envoy Caṇḍavega and kill his lion. Aśvagrīva was very much depressed by this answer and thought day and night how he could escape his fate. When he later sent his mission to Prajāpati, Caṇḍavega was really offended by Tripṛṣṭa and his lion killed. So a horrible hatred against Tripṛṣṭa seized him; his anger grew when the prince married Svayaṁprabhā, the daughter of Vidyādhara-king Jvalanajatī; he was hoping to get her hand. He, therefore, sent his envoy to Jvalanajatī immediately after the marriage and demanded that his daughter be delivered to him. After long battles he was finally defeated and killed and went into hell.

Tripṛṣṭa undertook thereupon a big expedition of conquest through half the world and returned to Poṭaṇa where he was solemnly made Ardhacakravartī. Deriving pleasure from his rule and in possession of 32,000 women, he sank into an ocean of sensual pleasures. He was constantly surrounded by musicians who delighted his heart with the help of their songs. He had asked his treasurer that he should send out the singers when he fell asleep. Carried away by the beauty of their lovely melodies, he missed once to send the singers out of king's room at the right time. Tripṛṣṭa got up again and got so much angry on account of the disobedience of his servant that he got glowing tin and copper poured into his ears. The servant died immediately as a consequence of this gruesome punishment. Tripṛṣṭa got a new existence in the hell as an atonement for his crime when he died. Acala grieved so much at the death of his brother that he became monk and finally attained redemption.

The true faith disappeared between the 11th and the 12th Tīrthaṅkara for a period of 3/4 Palyopama.

Vāsupūjya, the 12th Tīrthaṅkara, was born as son of King Vāsūpūjya and his wife Jayā in Campā. He derives his name from his father; another explanation suggests that the prince was worshipped by gods (Vasu). Vāsupūjya attained Nirvāṇa in his home-town Campā in the 72,00,000 th year of his life, 54 Sāgaropamas after Śreyāṁsa.[63]

Vijaya, the 2nd Baladeva, a son of King Brahmā of Dvārakā and Queen Subhadrā and *Dviprṣṭa*, the 2nd Vāsudeva, a son of Brahmā and Umā, were Vāsupūjya's contemporaries. Dviprṣṭa fought against the 2nd Prativāsudeva, *Tāraka*, and defeated him. He was a son of Vijayapura and his wife Śrīmatī. He conquered then a part of the world and ruled in Dvārakā. Vāsupūjya converted him to the right faith, but he could not save him from the hell to which he had to go on account of his bad actions. Vijaya renounced the world and was redeemed.

The Jaina-faith disappeared for a period of 1/4 Palyopama after Vāsupūjya's death.

Vimala, the 13th Tīrthaṅkara, came from Kāmpilya where his father Kṛtavarmā and his queen Śyāmā (Dig.: Suramyā) were ruling. The purity (*vimalatā)* of his mother gave him the name. According to others it was his clear power of understanding which he had developed at the following occasion even before he was born. A man was sleeping with his wife in a temple in which a female demon was living. The witch fell in love with the man and assumed the form of his wife. The husband could not distinguish between the real wife and the false one and requested the king to decide. The king made the man step back quite a distance and asked the two women to touch him. The true wife could not do it because the husband was too far, the witch could, however, do it without any difficulty because the witches are capable of expanding themselves. Thus it was known who was the true wife and could refute the claim of the witch.[64] Vimala died, 60,00,000 years old, on the Sameṭa mountain, 30 Sāgaropamas after Vāsupūjya.

The 3rd Baladeva, *Bhadra* (Dig.: Dharma) and the 3rd Vāsudeva, *Svayambhū*, both, sons of King Rudra of Dvārakā, the former one from Queen Suprabhā, the latter from Pṛthivī, lived during the period of Vimala. Svayambhū killed the 3rd Prativāsudeva *Meraka*, the son of King Samarakesarī of Nandanapura and his wife Sundarī. After a life filled with great deal of activity, Svayambhū came into hell, and Bhadra got salvation as a monk.

Jaina-faith disappeared again for a period of 3/4 Palyopama between the 13th and the 14th Tīrthaṅkara.

Ananta, the 14th Tīrthaṅkara, was born in Ayodhyā as a son of King Siṁhasena and his wife Suyaśā (Dig.: Sarvayaśā). Since he possessed infinite (*ananta*) knowledge and his mother had seen infinite number of strings of precious stones he was called Ananta. Warned of the ephemerality of the mundane by a falling meteor, he renounced the world and was finally redeemed on the Sameṭa mountain. His life lasted for 30,00,000 years and his death followed 9 Sāgaropamas after Vimala's salvation.

A king Soma lived in Dvārakā during his period. He had two famous sons: the brightly-shining *Suprabha*, the 4th Baladeva from his wife Sudarśanā and the dark-blue *Puruṣottama*, the 4th Vāsudeva, from his wife Sītā. After conquering the 4th Prativāsudeva, King *Madhu* of Pṛthvīpura, son of Vilāsa and Guṇavatī, ruler of half the world, Puruṣottama went into hell, while Suprabha achieved salvation.[65]

A "Tīrthavyavaccheda" of 1/4 Palyopama falls in the period between the 14th and the 15th Tīrthaṅkara.

Dharma, the 15th Tīrthaṅkara, was born in Ratnapura. His parents were King Bhānu and Queen Suvratā. Since the latter had most painfully fulfilled all the precepts of the religion (*dharma*) during her pregnancy, he got the name Dharma. He died on the Sameṭa mountain,

10,00,000 years old, 4 Sāgaropamas after his predecessor.

Fifth Baladeva, Sudarśana and the fifth Vāsudeva, Puruṣasinha, sons of King Śiva of Aśvapura and respectively of Vijayā and Ammakā lived during his period. Niśumbha, king of Haripura was the fifth Prativāsudeva. Puruṣasinha killed him, became Ardha-cakravartī and went into hell. His half-brother Sudarśana achieved salvation.

The 3rd Cakravartī *Maghavā* (Maghavan) ruled after Dharma. He was born in Śrāvastī where his father Samudra-vijaya ruled with his wife Bhadrā. Embellished with all the jewels of a world-ruler he subjugated the whole Bharata-land with its six parts, but finally recognized in his old age the ephemerality of Saṁsāra, practised holy conduct of life and was reborn in a heaven of gods.

The 4th Cakravartī, *Sanatkumāra*, who lived after him, was born in Hastināpura as a son of King Aśvasena and Queen Sahadevī. Educated in all sciences and arts, he grew together with his friend, Prince Mahendrasiṁha. When he was riding out on the most beautiful spring-day on a horse "ocean-wave" that was only recently presented to him and which was, what he did not know, wrongly trained, the horse went in such a way that he was separated from his companions and was brought in the neighbourhood of the Mānasa-lake. He experienced here several adventures, had to succeed in many battles, married a large number of beautiful women and was made the emperor of Vidyādharas. Finally he was found again by Mahendrasiṁha and returned home with him. After his father had become monk, he ruled there as Cakravartī and rejoiced the possession of the earth with its six parts, bathed in the nectar of incomparable happiness. When he became old, two gods once came to him dressed as Brāhmaṇas to admire the famous beauty of his body, but noticed that his body had become flaccid. When he also noticed this, he became weary of worldly life and took ordination. As an ascetic he endured patiently all the diseases which broke out as a consequence of his unusual lifestyle although he could have cured them. Finally, he starved himself to death on the Sameṭa mountain, 3,00,000 years old and was reborn in the Sanatkumāra-heaven from where he will once come down to attain salvation as a king of Videha.[66]

The Jaina-faith became extinct for a period of 1/4 Palyopama between the 15th and the 16th Tīrthaṅkara. This Tīrthavyavaccheda was the last of those which took place in the period of the "middle" Tīrthaṅkaras and it covered in all a period of 2¾ Palyopamas. The Jaina-religion did not disappear any more from Śānti's period.

Śānti, the 5th Cakravartī and the 16th Tīrthaṅkara was a son of King Viśvasena of Hastināpura and Queen Acirā. Since he had freed the people from all evils while in the womb of his mother itself, he was given the name Śānti (rest, peace). He grew up in royal splendour and married the beautiful Yaśomatī. She saw once in a dream how a Cakra (disc) entered her mouth. He explained to her that it was Dhṛḍharatha, his brother in an earlier birth, who has come down from the Sarvārthasiddha heaven to be born again as his son. At that time he himself as Megharatha offered his flesh to a hungry falcon thus to free a dove and attained his present position by this religious action. The heralded son was then born after some time and he was given the name Cakrāyudha. Śānti ruled over his kingdom with full power and conquered the whole world subjugating the Aryans and the barbarians in the same manner. He was made the 5th Cakravartī in a solemn manner in his capital. After ruling for 25,000 years he renounced the world and handed over the reign to Cakrāyudha. Having become Tīrthaṅkara, he made Cakrāyudha his main pupil after he had installed his son Kavacahari as his successor. He was redeemed on the Sameṭa mountain at the age of 1,00,000 years, 3 Sāgaropamas less ¾ Palyopama after

Dharma.

Kunthu, the 6th Cakravartī and the 17th Tīrthaṅkara came also from Hastināpura; his parents were Sūra and Śrīdevī. The name Kunthu came from a heap of jewels which his mother had seen in her dream. After victorious campaigns, he became Bharata-land's emperor, but then dedicated himself to asceticism and propagation of the pure doctrine and attained Nirvāṇa on the Sameṭa mountain, 95,000 years old, ½ Palyopama after Śānti.

Ara, the 7th Cakravartī and the 18th Tīrthaṅkara came also from Hastināpura where his father Sudarśana and his mother Devī (Mitrā) were the rulers. He got the name from a wheel (*ara*) which his mother saw in a dream. After a glorious emperorship he attained salvation at the age of 84,000 years on the Sameṭa mountain, ¼ Palyopama less 1,000 Koṭis of years after Kunthu.

Two sons were born to King Mahāśiva (Mahāśiras) in Cakrapura during the period in which Ara was the Tīrthaṅkara. The 6th Baladeva. Ānanda, was from his first wife Vaijayantī. The 6th Vāsudeva, Puruṣapuṇḍarīka was from his second wife Lakṣmīvatī. The 6th Prativāsudeva, King Bali, who wanted to rob Puruṣa's wife was vanquished and killed by him; Puruṣa then ruled for a long time, finally came into hell, whereas his half-brother was redeemed.

The 8th Cakravartī, Subhūma (Subhauma) who lived after them was a son of King Kṛtavīrya and his wife Tārā. His lifestory is closely connected with the Paraśurāma-legend of Jainas which again spreads to the other series of legends. Two gods were disputing whether the Jaina or the Śiva-faith was the correct one; they decided to test two penitents of these two religions to find out who among them was right. After the Jaina had passed the test with flying colours, they went to a Brāhmaṇa Jamadagni and sat in his beard, metamorphosing themselves into sparrows. They spoke in their conversation that Jamadagni is a great sinner because he was practising asceticism without producing a son. Jamadagni was so much infatuated by these words that he desired to woo a woman—by which the spiritual uncertainty of a Brāhmaṇa ascetic and the superiority of the Jaina-Sādhus was cogently shown. Under the influence of his desire Jamadagni went to King Jitaśatru and asked for the hand of his hundred daughters. When the girls saw the lean receiver of alms approaching them, 99 of them spat before him and refused to marry the penitent. Jamadagni angered by this cursed them so that all of them became hunchbacked. But the hundredth daughter, Reṇukā, agreed to marry the ugly old man. Jamadagni married her after he had made the other girls healthy again, moved her into the woods, enjoyed the pleasures of love with her with his decayed body, but full of unsatiated desire. When now her period approached, the penitent prepared a pot of sacrificial mush and asked his wife to enjoy the contents because she would then give birth to a son who would possess all the virtues of a Brāhmaṇa. At Reṇukā's request, he prepared one more mush for her sister, the wife of King Anantavīrya of Hastināpura, so that she would give birth to an excellent Kṣatriya-boy. But Reṇukā thought that it would be better to have a strong Kṣatriya-son than to have a penitent who would live in the wilderness like animals of forest. She, therefore, exchanged the pots. Then after some time, Rāma was born as Reṇukā's and Kṛtavīrya as her sister's son. Rāma became a strong war-hero and got a magical axe (*paraśu*) from one Vidyādhara; he was, thus, called Paraśurāma.

Reṇukā once went to Hastināpura to visit her sister. Her brother-in-law, Anantavīrya, had an affair with the wife of the penitent; as a result a son was born to her. When Reṇukā returned with the offspring to her husband in the forest, Rāma killed both. To avenge their death, Anantavīrya forced his way into the hermitage and destroyed it completely in the absence of Rāma. Rāma then killed Anantavīrya. Kṛtavīrya, who had become king in his place, killed Jamadagni, but himself became the victim of Rāma's axe. Rāma then usurped power in Hastināpura and got all Kṣatriyas exterminated. But Kṛtavīrya's widows Tārā who was then pregnant was saved by the penitents; she gave birth to a son Subhūma whom 14 dreams proclaimed as the future ruler of the world.

Subhūma, supported by Vidyādhara, who had given his daughter in marriage to him, marched towards Hastināpura and killed Paraśurāma. He then conquered the whole Bharata-land with its six parts and started a great persecution of the Brāhmaṇas to avenge the killing of the Kṣatriyas done by Paraśurāma. Finally he wanted to conquer even the Dhātaki-khaṇḍa and got ready, without paying any attention to the warning of his ministers, to cross the ocean on the "hyde-jewel" with the help of ships. But the gods who were carrying this conveyance left it because they were tired and they wanted to rest. So Subhūma was drowned in the ocean and was born again in hell on account of his greed.

The 7th Baladeva, Nandana, and the 7th Vāsudeva Datta, both sons of King Agnisiṁha of Banāras, the former from Jayantī, the latter from Śeṣavatī, lived in the succeeding period. The 7th Prativāsudeva, Prahlāda, king of Vidyādhara-city Siṁhapura in the Vaitādhya mountains, was vanquished by Datta, after which Datta, on becoming the ruler of half the world, came into hell; Nandana, however, attained redemption as a monk.

Malli, the 19th Tīrthaṅkara, came from Mithilā (Mathurā) where King Kumbha was ruling with his wife Rakṣitā (Prabhāvatī). Malli, according to the view of Digambaras, was a man like all other Tīrthaṅkaras, and his life was spent in the same way like the others. Śvetāmbaras, on the other hand, who think that it is possible that even women can be redeemed, worship in Malli the only *female* Tīrthaṅkara. The cause of the peculiar circumstances that Malli was born as a woman is, according to them, the following. Malli was King Mahābala (Vaiśramaṇa) in an earlier existence. He had renounced the world with his several friends and become an ascetic. They had—to be reborn together in a later life—agreed to do penance in exactly the same measure. But contrary to the agreement, Mahābala fasted somewhat longer than his companions and got the dignity of a Karma that is given to a Tīrthaṅkara in contrast to them. The Māyā he practised against his friends had naturally to show its effect; it made him bind the Karma "Strī-veda" which causes rebirth as a woman. Thus he became a woman on the earth after enjoying heavenly pleasures with his companions in Vaijayantī, the heaven of gods. Since Queen Prabhāvatī liked very much to rest on wreaths of flowers (*mālya*), a wish which was fulfilled by gods, the newborn daughter was named Malli.

Malli grew into a very beautiful young woman. The friends from her existence as Mahābala, who were reborn as sons of kings were prompted to woo for her hand on account of her charm and on account of love they cherished from their earlier existence. But her father refused to give his daughter to any of them. So the angry wooers came together and declared war against Mithilā. When the city was besieged by them and the king did not know to help himself, Malli advised him to call them—with a promise that he would give them his daughter—into an "illusory bower" developed by her, from which one could see a bench through a netted wall. A doll resembling Malli was made to sit on the bench. The kings saw the figure and thought that it was Malli herself; but the princess appeared and opened an entrance which was concealed by flowers. This caused the doll to give out an unbearable stench. Malli who had foreseen with the help of her transcendent knowledge that the princes would woo for her hand had got a doll made long time ago and threw daily remains of food into it through an opening so that it gave out an unbearable stench. Malli then explained to the astonished princes how the earthly beauty is ephemeral, reminded them of their joint Tapas in their earlier existence and induced them to renounce the world. All then took ordination, and Malli attained Nirvāṇa on the Sameṭa mountain, 55,000 years old, 1,000 Koṭis years after Ara.[67]

Munisuvrata, the 20th Tīrthaṅkara, was a son of King Sumitra of Rājagṛha and his queen Padmāvatī. His name was given to him because his mother had fulfilled all the good vows (*su-vrata*) of the Jainas when she was expecting. After renouncing the world and attaining omniscience, he got Nirvāṇa on the Sameṭa mountain at the age of 30,000 years, 54,00,000 years after Malli.

The 9th Cakravartī, *Mahāpadma*, lived during Munisuvrata's period. He was born either in Banāras or Hastināpura; his parents were King Padmottara and Jvālā; the name of his elder brother was Viṣṇukumāra. A Brāhmaṇa Namuci was living as a minister in the king's court. He was earlier a house-priest of King Śrīvarma of Ujjayinī. When a pupil of Tīrthaṅkara Munisuvrata conquered him in a wordy duel, he wanted to kill him on account of his thirst for revenge. He could not fulfil his plan because his deity made his limbs immovable. Unable to stay in Ujjayinī on account of this, he left the city and came to Hastināpura where he wooed for the favour of Padmottara so that he made him his councillor. Once he earned the gratitude of the crown-prince Mahāpadma by freeing him from the neigh-bouring prince Siṁhabala who had attacked him. Mahāpadma asked him to express any wish which he could fulfil; but Namuci kept it for a later period.

Now once Jvālā wanted to be driven in a chariot used for the Jaina-procession during a festival, and Lakṣmī, the subordinate wife of her husband, a Brahma-chariot. Since both the wives insisted that their chariot should have a preference, the king had no other choice—to be impartial—than to forbid the running of the chariots. Saddened by the insult caused to his mother, Mahāpadma left the king's court and went into the forest. He experienced many adventures, conquered the whole Bharata-land and finally returned home. Converted by Munisuvrata's pupil Suvrata, Padmottara and Viṣṇu accepted initiation; the former attained redemption, the latter got supernatural powers.

Having become Cakravartī, Mahāpadma became a great patron of Jainism and arranged a great Jaina-chariot-procession in the honour of his mother. Once Suvrata brought rainy season into his empire. The wicked Namuci then reminded the king of his wish he was free to express and demanded a great sacrifice from him in which he desired the transfer of the dominion of the kingdom in his name. When Mahāpadma conceded this, Namuci began to persecute the Jaina-monks and threatened them with death. The ascetics were helplessly at the mercy of Namuci since they could not roam about in the rainy season because they would then be exposed to the danger of killing so many creatures. They, therefore, magically invoked the ascetic Viṣṇu who was engrossed in contemplation and who was powerful in magic so that he could pacify Namuci and make him permit them to stay. Namuci finally permitted the penitents to occupy as much land as one could traverse in three steps; but if they were to step on a place beyond these three steps, they would have to die. Viṣṇu then traversed the whole world from east to west in two steps with the help of his body of transference (p. 195) and knocked down Namuci with the third. The wicked Brāhmaṇa could not now do anything against the hated Jainas and was afterwards banished by Mahāpadma from his empire. Viṣṇu thus became well-known to the whole world as "Trivikrama";* he continued to practice penance and attained Nirvāṇa. Even Mahāpadma finally renounced the world and got salvation.

The 8th pair of heroes, the 8th Baladeva, Rāma or Padma and the 8th Vāsudeva, Lakṣamaṇa or Nārāyaṇa,

---

*Trivikrama, "the one who has done the three steps" is a nickname of god Viṣṇu; he had wrested the dominion of the demon-king Bali over the three worlds with the help of his three steps in his capacity as a dwarf (comp. "Hinduismus", p. 121 ff.). The story of Viṣṇu and Namuci represents the Jaina-version of the said legend.

lived during the same period. Both were the sons of King Daśaratha of Ayodhyā and of his queens Aparājitā and Sumitrā, and half-brothers of Prince Bharata, Kaikeyī's son, and Śatrughna, who was Suprabhā's son. Rāma married Sītā, daughter of Janaka* who was the king of Mithilā. Daśaratha wanted him to take up the reign and himself to become a monk. He was, however, compelled to make Bharata the ruler and banish Rāma at the instigation of Kaikeyī whom he had promised a fulfilment of a wish. But although Bharata did not accept the position offered to him, Rāma went into the forest accompanied by Sītā and Lakṣmaṇa.

The mighty Vidyādhara king Rāvaṇa, the 8th Prativāsudeva, was ruling over one part of the world during this period. He was also called a ten-headed one since he was always carrying a chain around his neck with nine head-sized pearls. His people were called "Rākṣasas", as they were the progeny of their first ancestor Mahārākṣasa or they had a Rākṣasa in their banner.

This Rāvaṇa kidnapped Sītā for whose hand he had tried to woo from Janaka in vain. Rāma marched against him to win her back with an army of Vidyādharas who were called "Vānaras" (monkeys) on account of their monkey-banner. Rāma, supported by their princes Hanumān and Sugrīva conquered Laṅkā; Rāvaṇa was killed by Lakṣmaṇa and fell into hell. Rāma returned to Ayodhyā with Sītā who was now freed and his entourage after making Rāvaṇa's brother Vibhīṣaṇa king who was devoted to him. He ruled here with glory with Sītā, the joyous moonshine of his eyes. Sītā once drew a picture of Rāvaṇa's feet at the request of her co-wives. This was secretly informed to Rāma with the remarks that Sītā still thought of beautiful hours she spent with Rāvaṇa. On account of this and other harmless incidents, backbiters started bad rumours concerning Sītā. This forced

*Sītā, according to some versions, is a daughter of Rāvaṇa and Mandodarī, but was brought up by Janaka.

Rāma, to his sorrow, to banish Sītā although she was pregnant. Sītā went into the solitude of the woods and gave birth to two sons, Aṅgalavaṇa and Madanāṅkuśa. Taught by a pious Jaina in arts and sciences, they grew into powerful heroes and traversed the whole world fighting. They finally turned also against Rāma. When father and sons recognized one another, Sītā was taken home in an air-chariot Puṣpaka. She convinced the whole people of her purity by undergoing an ordeal by fire and then became nun. Lakṣmaṇa died soon after and went into hell. Saddened by the loss of his brother, Rāma renounced the world and attained Nirvāṇa along with Śatrughna, Sugrīva, Vibhīṣaṇa and others.[68]

Nami, the 21st Tīrthaṅkara, was a son of King Vijaya of Mithilā and Queen Vaprā. When he was in his mother's womb, the enemies threatening his hometown yielded (*nam*) to the power emanating from him. After having spent the normal life of a Tīrthaṅkara, he died liberated from the Saṁsāra on the Sameṭa mountain, 10,000 years old, 6,00,000 years after Munisuvrata.

The 10th Cakravartī, *Hariṣeṇa*, a son of King Mahāhari of Kāmpilya and his wife Merā, lived during Nami's period. He conquered the whole Bharata-land, but then gave up pleasures, became monk and attained Nirvāṇa.

The 11th Cakravartī, *Jayasena* lived after him in Rājagṛha. He was a son of King Vijaya (or Aśvasena) and his wife Vaprā. After conquering the whole world, he renounced it and went into Nirvāṇa.

Many chiliads later, there lived a king Yadu from the famous Hari-dynasty (Hari-vaṁśa). His son Śūra had two sons Śauri and Suvīra. Śauri's son Andhakavṛṣṇi had 10 sons, the Daśārhas. One of them, Vasudeva, produced Balarāma, the 9th Baladeva and Kṛṣṇa, the 9th Vāsudeva; another son Samudravijaya became the father of Ariṣṭanemi, the 22nd Tīrthaṅkara. Suvīra had a son Bhojavṛṣṇi. He had two sons Ugrasena and Devaka. Ugrasena was the father of Kaṁsa and Rājīmatī. Devaka was the father of Devakī who was Kṛṣṇa's mother.

Let us turn, after these introductory remarks on the relationship between Kṛṣṇa and Ariṣṭanemi, to their story. We shall consider them individually for the sake of clarity, although their legends are closely connected with one another.[69]

King Vasudeva of Sauryapura was married to the beautiful Rohiṇī. The 9th Baladeva, Rāma, was their son. Later the king married also Devakī, Devaka's daughter. Jīvayaśā, Kaṁsa's wife who had drunk too much of wine made fun of Saint Atimukta at the time of the marriage-celebration. The saint prophesied that Devakī's seventh child would kill her husband Kaṁsa. He got frightened and took promise from Vasudeva that he would hand over to him Devakī's first seven children as soon as they were born. There lived at the same time in the city of Bhaddilapura a master of guild, Nāga and his wife Sulasā; it was prophesied to them that they would give birth to still-born children. A god brought Devakī's six newborn children to this virtuous woman (who then brought them up) who used to deliver at the same time as Devakī and brought her still-born children to Devakī; they were handed over to Kaṁsa. But Devakī's seventh son, whom the famous dreams proclaimed as the 9th Vāsudeva, Kṛṣṇa, was handed over by the gods to the cowherd Nanda and his wife Yaśodā after they had put the guards installed by Kaṁsa to sleep. Yasodā's daughter was brought to Kaṁsa who cut her nose. Kṛṣṇa grew up in Gokula among the cowherds and accomplished there many heroic deeds with his half-brother (Bala-) Rāma. Finally he marched to Mathurā, killed Kaṁsa and put his father Ugrasena on the throne. Kaṁsa had appropriated the reign from him.

Jarāsandha, Kālayavana's king, the 9th Prativāsudeva, declared war against Kṛṣṇa at the call of his daughter Jīvayaśā to avenge the death of his son-in-law Kaṁsa. He defeated Rāma and Kṛṣṇa and compelled them to leave Mathurā. Kṛṣṇa then built the city of Dvārakā in Gujarāt and enjoyed there all the pleasures of the reign in the company of many beautiful women. He then took part on the side of the Pāṇḍavas in their war against the Kauravas and won a series of battles in which finally even Jarāsandha was defeated and killed.

It so happened in Dvārakā that the seer Dvaipāyana was offended by Kṛṣṇa's son Sāmba under the influence of intoxication. Angered by this, Dvaipāyana practised strict asceticism and burnt, as he had become an Agnikumāra-god on account of this, Dvārakā with the help of the fire spread by him in which Kṛṣṇa's 16,000 wives and all Yādavas died. Rāma and Kṛṣṇa turned again towards Mathurā. Kṛṣṇa was seriously wounded here by Jarākumāra as he was resting under a tree. Jarākumāra thinking that he was a deer shot him with an arrow. He died of this injury and went into the 3rd hell although he had the right faith, because he had nourished hatred against Dvaipāyana in the last moments of his life. His brother renounced the world and was reborn in the 6th heaven as a god after he had done penance for hundred years. When he saw that Kṛṣṇa was suffering in hell he wanted to save him. But when he tried to lift him up, Kṛṣṇa was in a danger of being melted like butter in the sun and suffered severe pains so that the attempt had to be given up again.

Kṛṣṇa's cousin Ariṣṭanemi (Nemi), the 22nd Tīrthaṅkara, was a son of King Samudravijaya of Sauripura and his wive Śivā. Since she had seen in her dream a broken (*riṣṭa*) wheel-rim (*nemi*), he was called (by adding "A" to remove the bad omen) Ariṣṭanemi. Even in his early days he made a mark by his excellent body-strength. Thus he once entered Kṛṣṇa's chamber where he kept arms and began to blow Kṛṣṇa's Śaṅkha which no one else besides Kṛṣṇa could blow. When Kṛṣṇa heard this he was frightened that his cousin could deprive him of his reign. Thinking that Ariṣṭanemi could lose his strength by indulging in love-making, he arranged his marriage with Ugrasena's daughter Rājīmatī.

When finally Ariṣṭanemi decided to marry, it was arranged with great pomp. The bridegroom had already completed the preliminary rituals and he was riding on an elephant embellished with precious ornaments to the place where the holy rite was to take place, when he saw on the way anxiously crying animals which were kept ready for the festive meal and for the sacrifice. This view filled his heart so strongly with sympathy that he renounced the world. He went to the mountain Raivataka (Mount Girnār in Kāthiāvāḍ), practised there asceticism and attained the highest stage of saintliness. He then preached for all the true doctrines and prompted the Pāṇḍavas to give up worldly life so that they got Nirvāṇa. When he had become thousand years old, he attained salvation on the Raivataka mountain, 5,00,000 years after his predecessor Nami.

Rājīmatī followed in the footsteps of her bridegroom and became nun; even Rathanemi, Ariṣṭanemi's brother, became monk. But since he had not overcome his libido, he burnt in sinful passion for Rājīmatī and proposed to her. Rebuffed by her, he went into himself and attained perfection also like her.

The last, 12th Cakravartī, Brahmadatta, lived after Ariṣṭanemi.[70] He was a son of King Brahmā of Kāmpilya and his wife Culaṇī. When he was a boy, his father fell sick and assigned the care of the son to his neighbouring princes who were closely befriended with him because he saw his end coming. They assigned the guardianship to one among them, King Dīrgha of Kośala. Dīrgha was not only satisfied by ruling over Brahma-datta's kingdom, but began an affair with the king's widow. When Brahmadatta was informed about this by his minister Dhanu, he rebuked the infidel lovers in the language of imaging; Dīrgha and Culaṇī decided to kill him. They arranged a marriage celebration for Brahmadatta and led him and his young wife into a lacquer-house which was specially built for the purpose; it was then put on fire on the marriage night. But the devilish plan misfired; Brahmadatta ran away from the burning house through an underground passage which the prudent Dhanu had got made. Then Brahmadatta marched through the land in disguise accompanied by the son of the minister, won many battles and married many beautiful women. He came finally to Dvārakā, gathered an army with the help of the local king Kaṭaka and other friends of his father and marched against Dīrgha. He defeated and killed him, was made king and got the position of a world-ruler by conquering the six parts of Bhārata-varṣa.

When Brahmadatta was once seeing a play, flowers in it reminded him of his earlier existence in the Saudharma-heaven and of his companion who had accompanied him through his six existences. He, therefore, spoke a verse referring to this and promised a high reward for the one who could say its remaining half. A merchant's son who had become an ascetic knew to complete the stanza. It was found on account of this that he was Brahmadatta's brother Citra in an earlier existence when he himself was called Sambhūta.[71] Brahmadatta had renounced the world along with him and had become a monk, but could not kill all the passions within himself. So it happened that he cherished a desire to possess beautiful women as a Cakravartī in his future existence, when a lock of hair of the principal wife of the Cakravartī Sanatkumāra fell near his feet. This desire was fulfilled. Now Citra tried in vain to make him renounce the world. While he himself soon attained Nirvāṇa by asceticism, Brahmadatta continued to enjoy the pleasures of the earth.

Once a Brāhmaṇa came to him and requested him to permit him to eat from his royal meal. Although Brahmadatta warned him not to enjoy the food of a Cakravartī, because it could be enjoyed only by a Cakravartī, the fool begged him so much that he gave him and his family some of his food. Under the influence of the strong food there awakened in the

Brāhmaṇa such an uncontrollable sexual desire that he engaged himself in sexual pleasure with his mother, daughter-in-law and his sister. Ashamed of his misdemeanour, the Brāhmaṇa decided to take revenge against the Cakravartī as the cause of his sins and prompted a cowherd to shoot his two eyes. Brahmadatta got the priest and all his relatives killed and ordered his minister to tear their eyes and to leave them in a pot so that he could himself take the pleasure in gouging them out. The minister noticed that the king was under the influence of a bad Karma and therefore kept flowers in the pot instead of eyes; but Brahmadatta spent the rest of his days in evil meditation thinking that he had gouged out the eyes. He died finally, 716 years old, came into the 7th hell in which he had to atone for 33 Sāgaropamas for his vindictiveness.

Pārśva, the 23rd Tīrthaṅkara, is considered by most of the researchers as a historical personality in contrast to all the preceding heroes of the Jaina world-history as they have a completely legendary character. His life falls, according to tradition, in a historical period, around 800 B.C. while his predecessor Neminātha is said to have lived 84,000 years before him. The great significance of Pārśva justifies that we consider his life as also the life of his successor Mahāvīra somewhat in detail. The biographies of these two men are surrounded by a plethora of legends. The stories of their earlier births are particularly interesting, and we shall consider them here as examples of practical application of the Karma-doctrine.

Nine rebirths of Pārśva[72] are mentioned before he got salvation; in each one of them, he has to fight an adversary who accompanied him through all his existences:

(1) Pārśva lived once in the city of Poṭaṇa as a Brāhmaṇa Marubhūti together with his brother Kamaṭha. He became an ascetic under the influence of Saint Hariścandra, whereas Kamaṭha continued to give himself up to sensuous pleasures. Vasundharā, Marubhūti's

wife, could not stand abstinence forced upon her by her husband who had renounced the world. She had an illicit affair with Kamaṭha. When Marubhūti noticed it, he informed King Arvinda who made Kamaṭha ride an ass through the town as a punishment and then banished him. Kamaṭha then went into the forest and practised asceticism. Marubhūti, fearing that his brother would do him harm on account of his anger, went to him and asked for his pardon, but Kamaṭha shattered his skull with a stone.

(2) Marubhūti was engrossed in sad thoughts in his last moments. He was, therefore, reborn as a wild elephant. As such he was converted to the right faith by King Arvinda who had become in the mean time a Jaina-ascetic. Since then he lived on dry leaves and the water made warm only through the sun. Kamaṭha was reborn in the mean time as a poisonous serpent and had killed many living beings; finally it bit the pious elephant so that it also died.

(3) The elephant then became a god in the Sahasrāra-heaven, but the serpent came into the 5th hell.

(4) The god then obtained a new existence as a prince of elves *Kiraṇavega,* in the city of Tilaka. As such he renounced the position as a king which he had taken over from his father and practised asceticism. The inhabitant of the hell who was again reborn as a serpent, bit him and he died.

(5) He then went into the 12th Kalpa of the heaven of gods; the serpent died in a forest-fire and came into the hell Dhūmaprabhā.

(6) The god was reborn as Vajranābha, son of King Vajravīrya of Śubhaṁkara; later he took initiation and was killed by the arrow of a Bhil Kuraṅgaka when he had dedicated himself to a pious contemplation on Mountain Jvalana; his murderer was no one else but his enemy who had constantly persecuted him in his last existences.

(7) Vajranābha became then Graiveyaka-god, but Kuraṅgaka had to suffer pains in the 7th hell.

(8) Graiveyaka then came into the womb of Sudarśanā, wife of the king Kuliśabāhu (Vajrābāhu) of Surapura. Called Suvarṇabāhu, he became Cakravartī. Tīrthaṅkara Jagannātha prompted him to renounce the world. Devoted completely to religious practices, he bound the Tīrthaṅkara-karma. Finally he was torn to pieces by a lion, namely the villain who had climbed up from the 7th hell to an earthly life.

(9) Suvarṇabāhu then became god in the 10th Kalpa, but Prāṇata, the lion came into the 4th hell.

Owing to the Tīrthaṅkara-karma, Marubhūti's soul obtained the last of its existences. The Prāṇata-god entered the body of Queen Vāmādevī, wife of Aśvasena who was the ruler of Banāras. His mother had seen a serpent creeping by her side (*pārśva*) on a dark night when she was pregnant. He was, therefore, called Pārśva. He became a great war-hero, defeated King Yavana of Kaliṅga and married the beautiful princess Prabhāvatī. As he was looking outside the palace, he saw a big crowd of people gathered around the penitent Kaṭha who was practising asceticism of five fires by sitting in the midst of four burning fires and allowed himself to be singed by the sun as the fifth fire. There was a serpent in one of the fires which an uncanny man allowed to be quietly burnt. This man was no other but Kamaṭha who was reborn. Pārśva rebuked the villain for his wicked deed and saved the serpent. This was reborn as the Nāga-king Dharaṇa, while Kamaṭha entered his new (11th) existence as the Asura Meghamālī.

Once Pārśva saw the image of his predecessor Ariṣṭanemi in his garden. Impressed by the image he decided to become ascetic. He took the initiation and roamed about as a homeless beggar. Meghamālī tried to kill him in a forest by releasing a horrible storm, but the serpent-king Dharaṇa spread his hood like an umbrella over his head so that nothing could happen. Dharaṇa then explained to Meghamālī that he should not hate the Tīrthaṅkara, but rather thank him because he had saved him in his existence as Kamaṭha from killing a living being. Meghamālī then understood that he was unjust and was converted to the right faith. After some days, Pārśva returned to his hometown Banāras and obtained there omniscience after mortifying. himself for 84 days. Then he went preaching. through the lands and attracted many followers for the Jaina-faith. Finally he died, redeemed on the Sameṭa-mountain at the age of 100 (the mountain is also called after him Pārśvanātha-mountain), 83,750 years after Nemi.

Vardhamāna (Mahāvīra), the 24th Tīrthaṅkara, i.e. the last one, lived 250 years after Pārśva. Jainas also report about his earlier existences, and besides details are given on not less than 26 of the earlier incarnations.

The birth in which he obtained the right faith is reckoned as the first among the numerous births of the later prophet. He was then called Nayasāra and lived in the Western Videha-land. When once he had gone to forest to fetch wood, he met holy men who had lost their way and were roaming about aimlessly hungry and thirsty. He looked after them with sympathy, refreshed them and got instruction on true faith from them. As a reward for his good deed he came (2) into the Saudharma-heaven. Coming out from there he was reborn (3) as Marīci, the grandson of the first Tīrthaṅkara Ṛṣabha. We have already discussed him on p. 296. He was alternately God and Brāhmaṇa in his next 10 existences (4th to 14th). Then after (15th) living in Brahmaloka-heaven, he was (16th) reborn as Prince Viśvabhūti in Rājagṛha. He was initiated into asceticism by a pious man. As once he was going on his way after fasting for a longer period, he was hit by a cow and thrown to the ground. His relative Viśākhānandī who was not well-disposed towards him, ridiculed him. So Viśvabhūti became angry, held the cow by the horns and threw it into the air. But then he desired, while doing penance, to be reborn as an extremely strong man in his next existence. This Nidāna was also fulfilled, for after enjoying (17th) pleasures of the Mahāśukra-heaven, he was (18th) reborn as the first Vāsudeva Tripṛṣṭa (p. 302). On account of bad actions he committed as this, he went (19th) into the 7th hell. He then (20th) became a horrible lion and again went (21st) into the hell, but this time in the fourth. He climbed up from it (22nd) into a human existence and achieved a good Karma. On account of this (23rd) he became world-ruler Priyamitra. After living a saintly life he came (24th) into the Mahāśukra-heaven and then became (25th) Prince Poṭṭila who renounced the world and became monk. He then enjoyed (26th) the pleasures of the heavenly world and then got his last (27th) existence as the Tīrthaṅkara Mahāvīra.

The new prophet should have been born as a Brāhmaṇa as a consequence of the Karma that was attached to him (p. 296) on account of his arrogance as Marīci. He, therefore, went into the womb of a Brāhmaṇa-woman Devānandā, wife of the Brāhmaṇa Ṛṣabhadatta of Koḍāla-gotra who lived in the Brāhmaṇa-area of the city Kuṇḍagrāma, and Devānandā had the famous dreams which prophesied the birth of a future saviour of the world. When the king of gods Indra saw this and considered that all the Tīrthaṅkaras, Cakravartīs, Baladevas and Vāsudevas have had their origin in noble families in the past, present and will have in future and that it would be improper that the venerable Mahāvīra be born in a low family, i.e. in a Brāhmaṇa-family. He, therefore, ordered Hariṇaigamaiṣī, the general of his infantry, to transfer the embryo of the Brāhmaṇa-woman Devānandā into the womb of a Kṣatriya-woman

Triśalā. So Hariṇaigamaiṣī went to Devānandā, put her in deep sleep, took the embryo of Mahāvīra from her body and carried it with folded hands into the Kṣatriya-area of Kuṇḍagrāma which was also known as Vaiśālī. There he put Triśalā, the wife of the Kṣatriya Siddhārtha, into deep sleep and put Mahāvīra's embryo in her womb; then he returned to the heaven. That a child was taken away from Devānandā and given to Triśalā happened according to a legend as an influence of the Karma that was attached to Devānandā; she had got it by stealing a precious gem from her sister-in-law in her earlier existence; this sister-in-law became later Triśalā.

Once Mahāvīra's embryo entered Triśalā's womb, she had these famous dreams and she gave birth to a male child under an auspicious constellation after nine months and 7½ days. He got the name "Vardhamāna" because during the period Triśalā carried him under her heart, the treasures and the fame of the parents had constantly increased.

The prince got an excellent education and shone on account of his power and intellect. Even as a boy he defeated a god from Indra's heaven who had come down to wrestle with him, and therefore, got the name Mahāvīra (great hero). When he was still small, Indra appeared in disguise as a Brāhmaṇa and asked him difficult things. To the great astonishment of all, he knew to answer all questions, although he had not heard of these questions in the school. Although he knew of his ordainment in his early youth itself, he decided not to renounce the world as long as his parents were alive so that he could spare them from their pains. He enjoyed, therefore, all admissible pleasures of the five senses, married and became father (see p. 29 f.)

When Siddhārtha and his wife Triśalā accepted voluntary death by starvation on a bed of Kuśa-grass as pious devotees of the doctrine of Tīrthaṅkara Pārśva and were reborn as gods in the Adbhutakalpa-heaven,

Mahāvīra could not tolerate the world any more and he decided to become a monk. His brother Nandivardhana did not want to concede this, but finally he succeeded in getting his permission and then he left, after giving away all his treasures, with a great pomp in a palanquin carried by gods and spirits and came to a park in the surroundings of Kuṇḍapura which was called Śandavana. Here he renounced the world in the usual way. Soon thereupon he acquired the supernatural knowledge of the thoughts of others (Manaḥparyāyajñāna). He then decided to roam about for 12 years without having any home; he wore clothes for one year and one month, then he gave them up and started roaming about in nude, collecting alms in the hollow hand and defying the vagaries of weather. He wandered eight months in a year, never spent more than one night in a village and more than five days in a city; only during the four months of the monsoons, he used to stay at one place.

The lifestory of Mahāvīra we have narrated here in its essential moments is reported in this form by the holy scriptures of Śvetāmbaras. Accounts given by Digambaras differ from these in important points. According to them, Mahāvīra was born as a son of Triśalā without going before into the womb of a Brāhmaṇa-woman; thus the whole legend of the transfer of the embryo is altogether missing. Mahāvīra, according to Digambaras, was not married at all (like the 12th, 19th, 22nd and the 23rd Tīrthaṅkaras). Rather he had taken the vow of a Jaina-layman at the age of 8 itself and lived a life of abstinence. He decided to renounce the world at the age of 30. He also carried this out although his mother (who was thus still alive according to this report) tried to stop him from doing it. As soon as he became an ascetic, he gave up 24 Parigrahas and with that also all clothes. The supernatural knowledge of the thoughts of others was not obtained by him for a long time; it came only after hard penance. After renouncing the world he meditated at first for six months, staying at one place without moving. Then he went to Kulapura where he was honourably received by the king of that place, and took his first meal after fasting for six months. He visited after this several places and possessed eight magical powers with the help of strict asceticism. He came finally to Ujjain on his further wanderings. When he was meditating on a graveyard in the vicinity of this city, he was disturbed in his contemplation by a certain Rudra and his wife Pārvatī; but he was so much deeply engrossed that he was not disturbed at all so that Rudra and his wife admired him and worshipped him. He came to Kauśāmbī from Ujjain. Then he returned to the solitude of the forest, obtained the supernatural knowledge of the thoughts of the others and made a vow of silence which he kept for 12 years.

Howsoever different may be the reports of Śvetāmbaras and Digambaras about the individual incidents which happened during the period after Mahāvīra renounced the world, they agree on one point that he got omniscience in the 43rd year of his life on the bank of river Rijupālika (today Barakar) not far from the place Jrimbhikagrāma on a field in the vicinity of an old temple under a Śāla-tree. He then roamed about for a period of an average man's life, preached everywhere the holy doctrine quite successfully winning over many men and women, among them also great kings like Śreṇika of Magadha, Kuṇika of Aṅga, Ceṭaka of Videha for his faith.

According to *Kalpa-Sūtra* (§122) Mahāvīra spent the 42 monsoons of his ascetic life at the following places: 1 in Aṣṭikagrāma, 3 in Campā and Pṛṣṭicampā, 12 in Vaiśālī and Vāṇijagrāma, 14 in Vaiśālī and Nālandā, 6 in Mithilā, 2 in Bhadrikā, 1 in Ālabhikā, 1 in Panītabhūmi, 1 in Śrāvastī and 1 in Pāvā. The later tradition lets him extend his journeys to Himālayas, right up to Prayāga, etc. Finally he got Nirvāṇa in the 72nd year of his life. This happened, 250 years after the salvation of Pārśva, at Pāvāpurī at dawn, after he had recited the Uttarādhyayana-Sūtra. The description of the salvation of the Tīrthaṅkara differs in different sources. Whereas some let him depart without any pomp in the chancellory of King Hastipāla, others let him leave this world with great pomp. Hastipāla had organized accordingly a great festival where the neighbouring princes had appeared. Mahāvīra preached untiringly for six days before a great crowd of people, sitting on a throne shining with diamonds in the midst of a magnificent hall which had been erected for him in a forest which was not quite far from a lake. On the 4th night-watch (vigil) of the 7th day, all the listeners had fallen asleep. The prophet knew that the moment of his parting had come. He sat down in the Samparyaṅka-position and thus attained his Nirvāṇa. When the listeners woke up, they noticed that the Tīrthaṅkara had left them. His body was cremated with a great display of splendour; according to a legend, the body of the saint had completely disappeared except for his hair and nails so that his worshippers could only burn these. When the saint had attained salvation, a great comet had appeared in the sky, the night was lit by the gods climbing down to the earth from heaven, and the kings of the neighbouring kingdoms organized grandiose illuminations to honour the dead.[73]

The Duḥṣama-susamā-period ended 3 years and 8½ months after Mahāvīra's Nirvāṇa; it had lasted for 1 Koṭikoṭi of Sāgaropamas less 42,000 years.

(e) Duḥṣamā

The Duḥṣamā-era (in which we are now living) which is going to last for 21,000 years is characterized by the things which are becoming worse and worse. The climatic conditions are becoming worse, famines and floods are devastating wide stretches of land, and there are horrible deaths by starvation. Human beings live at the most for 100 years and their height does not go beyond 7 Hastas; virtue and morality are being seen less and less. There is a "fish-order" on the earth, i.e. the strong eat the weak. Right and law are disappearing. Lie and deceit spread their wings, fornication and incest have become a common practice; infatuated by greed and thirst for the blood, the rulers torment their subjects and bring their lands to the edge of the abyss through wars so that villages and cities resemble graveyards. Bad kings, the so-called "Kalkis" appear every 100 years; they persecute the saints; and every 500 years the "Upakalkis".[74] Wrong faith and heterodoxy are becoming stronger and stronger till finally the holy faith becomes extinct.

The whole evilness of the Duḥṣamā-era is gradually becoming evident. At the beginning there were tolerable conditions and when the community of the last Tīrthaṅkara existed, and now, that we are in the seventh part of this period, the horrors cannot be anticipated to which humanity is being exposed. But the general decay cannot be stopped, for no more Tīrthaṅkaras will appear in the world who would show the way to salvation, and no Cakravartīs, Baladevas and Vāsudevas would appear who would create order with their strong hand.

There were still pious men only at the beginning of this era. They were the pupils of Mahāvīra who survived him and who could obtain omniscience and attain Nirvāṇa.

The most important disciple of the master was Gautama Indrabhūti. He was a learned Brāhmaṇa who was converted by the Tīrthaṅkara. This happened, according to one tradition, when he wanted to make a great animal sacrifice; according to another tradition, when he could not explain a verse told to an old man by the prophet and therefore, had to ask Mahāvīra for explanation. Gautama was taught the doctrine most thoroughly by Mahāvīra; in fact, many of the preachings contained in the scriptures are addressed to him. In contrast to the other disciples of the prophet who attained omniscience and salvation during his lifetime, Gautama became Kevalī only at the moment of the prophet's death because till then he could not prevent a complete indifference to love and hatred from arising in him—and which was the prerequisite for all knowledge—on account of the excessive love and respect he cherished for his teacher. He lived further for 12 years as Kevalī and attained Nirvāṇa in Rājagṛha at his age of 92.

Sudharmā, Mahāvīra's other disciple who survived him, was also a Brāhmaṇa. He took up the organization of the community after Mahāvīra's death. He attained omniscience after 12 years and put down his office. He lived then for 8 years more and got salvation when he was 100 years old.

Sudharmā's successor was his pupil Jambūsvāmī.[75] He was a son of a big businessman who was childless for a long time. When he was once listening with his wife to Sudharmā's preaching on the Jambū-tree, the saint prophesied to him the birth of a boy who would get the name Jambū. The prophesy was fulfilled, and Jambū grew up to the joys of his parents. When he came of age, he was supposed to marry 8 girls, daughters of 8 rich merchants in Rājagṛha. Influenced by Sudharmā's sermons, he wanted, to the horror of his relatives, to renounce the world, and he vowed to remain celibate. But he married the 8 girls to satisfy his parents. A chieftain of robbers, Prabhava, a prince, came in the night of the marriage which was celebrated with great pomp; he came with his gang with the hope that he would make a rich booty there. Prabhava was in possession of magic by which he could make all doors open and put the people to sleep. When he entered Jambū's house with its help, he found that he was alone awake among his sleeping wives. Jambū told him that no magic had effect on him because he was an ascetic and he was going to accept the initiation the very next day. Prabhava then tried to make him give up his vow and to enjoy his life with his wives. But Jambū explained to him and to his wives who had by then got up the unsteadiness and worthlessness of the worldly life with the help of the story of the man in the pit (above p. 216). The wives then decided to accept the initiation and even the robber repented, went to his parents and requested them to allow him to become a monk. Jambū was initiated on the next day by Sudharmā, and even his wives and relatives entered a spiritual position. Prabhava became also an ascetic shortly after and an inseparable pupil and companion of Jambū.

Once Sudharmā obtained omniscience, Jambūsvāmī became his successor. He became Kevalī one year after Sudharmā's Nirvāṇa and then himself attained Nirvāṇa (in the year 64 after Mahāvīra's death). Afterwards, nobody obtained any more the transcendent knowledge of physical things (p. 207); nobody the transcendent knowledge of the thoughts of the others; no one the omniscience and no one the salvation which is preceded by omniscience. Nobody attained Kṣapaka-śreṇī (p. 207) which is also a prerequisite for omniscience. Besides, few of the supernatural powers cannot be obtained from that time.[76] According to Śvetāmbaras, the practice of roaming about in naked practised by Mahāvīra was not any more in vogue since the death of the last Kevalī.

Series of men who had a complete insight into the nature of the world on account of their suprasensuous knowledge ends in our period with the death of Jambū. All knowledge about existence and life was now obtained only with the help of the study of traditions which go back to the omniscient of the past. But the mass of the tradition which has come down to us is decreasing again and again in the course of time; the further the Avasarpiṇī went, the more negligible it became. The first followers of Jambūsvāmī had still the knowledge of all the 12 Aṅgas; they were followed by those who knew only 11 Aṅgas and only the 10 Pūrvas of the 14 of the 12th Aṅga. The patriarchs after them knew only 11 Aṅgas, a condition which, according to Śvetāmbaras, had remained even now, whereas Digambaras believe that later even the other Aṅgas were also forgotten. The names of the patriarchs who possessed more or less knowledge of the holy scripture vary among the two sects. I shall mention them here:[77]

Śvetāmbaras	*Digambaras*
Śrutakevalīs (Possession: 12 Aṅgas)	
Prabhava	Viṣṇu
Śayyambhava	Nandimitra
Yaśobhadra	Aparājita
Śambhūtavijaya	Govardhana
Bhadrabāhu	Bhadrabāhu
Sthūlabhadra	
Daśapūrvis (11 Aṅgas, 10 Pūrvas)	
Mahāgiri	Viśākha
Suhastī	Proṣṭila
Susthita	Kṣatriya
Indradiṇṇa	Jayasena
Diṇṇa	Nāgasena
Siṁhagiri	Siddhārtha
Vajra	Vijaya
	Buḍḍhila (Buddhiliṅga)
	Raṅgadeva (Gaṇadeva)
	Dharmasena (Sudharmā)

Digambaras teach further that Dharmasena as the last knew 10 Pūrvas. A number of teachers ("Sūri") after him still knew the Aṅgas, but the texts were gradually forgotten in the course of time. According to the tradition,[78] Nakṣatra, Jayapāla, Pāṇḍu, Dhruvasena, Kaṅsa knew: 11 Aṅgas; Subhadra: 10 Aṅgas; Yaśobhadra: 9 Aṅgas; Bhadrabāhu II: 8 Aṅgas; Loha: 7(?) Aṅgas; Ahivallyācārya, Māghanandī, Dharasena, Puṣpadanta,

Bhūtavalyācārya (died 683 after Vīra): 1 Aṅga. According to another tradition all the teachers from Subhadra onwards knew only *one* Aṅga.[79]

The biographical data of the most of the patriarchs are given with legendary embellishments. It would be too much to go into their details.[80] We can also desist from mentioning here numerous masters and the heads of the sects who were not any more distinguished by the knowledge of the texts which were lost later and who played some role in the history of the church.

Although Jainism had at the beginning of the Duḥṣamā-period many enthusiastic followers and even got in the following period many numerous worshippers, it will be exposed to a gradual decrease in the numbers of its devotees as the bad world-period progresses and it will finally completely disappear. A king Vimalavāhana and his minister Sumukha will erect the last Caitya. The last members of the Jaina-community will be: the monk Duḥprasaha Sūri, the nun Phalguśrī, the layman Nāgila and the lay-sister Satyaśrī. (According to Digambaras the last monk will be Vīraṅgaja, the last nun Sarvaśrī, the last layman Agnila and the last lay-sister Phālgusenā.) They will live in Ayodhyā, die 3 years and 8½ months before the end of the Duḥṣamā-period and will be reborn in the 1st heaven.

There will be only heterodoxical doctrines once the Jaina-religion becomes extinct in the world. Marriage and pious conduct of life will be completely out of practice, and the fire and the custom of cooking the food will be lost.

(f) Duḥṣama-duḥṣamā

The worse period Duḥṣama-duḥṣamā comes after the bad Duḥṣamā-period. It will also last for 21,000 years like this, and conditions would be still more horrible. The whole world is filled with sorrow and echos the lamentations of its inhabitants. The sun gives out unbearable heat, the moon unbearable cold so that the days are horribly hot and the nights extremely cold. Deadly winds rage across the surface of the earth and raise horrible black dust which fills all the directions of the sky. People attain an age of 20 at the beginning; it decreases gradually so that at the end of era they will only be 16 years old. The size of the body at the beginning will be 2 Hasta and at the end only 1 Hasta. People will live only in the caves because they will be troubled by vermins; they can come out of the caves only at dawn and in the dusk because the heat of the day and the cold of the night would make their stay in the open difficult at other times. They will catch fish and tortoise with great difficulty which would be their only food. As they will have no fire they will not be able to cook their food. They will, therefore, consume their fish raw after leaving them untouched for sometime, because fresh fish would be too difficult for digestion. After dying, people will be reborn in hell or as animals.

There will be, according to some, a great catastrophe at the end of the Avasarpiṇī; it would rain acidic substances for 49 days which would devastate everything till a new, ascending world-period begins in which all conditions would start becoming gradually better.

(3) The Future World-periods and Their Holy Men[81]

(a) Duḥṣama-duḥṣamā

The first era of the future world-period will follow soon after the preceding one. The general conditions would be different to the extent that it would become slowly better. Thus the size of the body would increase from 1 Hasta to 2 Hastas and the span of life from 16 years to 20 years. Once 21,000 years have passed during which it would last it will be followed by:

(b) Duḥṣamā

At the beginning of the Duḥṣamā-period 5 clouds would appear one after the other and it would rain for

7 days and 7 nights from them. A Puṣkarāvartta-cloud would refresh the dried out earth with the nectar and make it fertile again, then a Kṣīra-cloud would let milklike beautiful water arise. Upon this a Ghṛta-cloud would give the earth stickiness and an Amṛta-cloud would let the seeds of all sorts of plants and trees grow. Finally a Rasa-cloud would give the plants five types of taste.

The plant-world will blossom on the earth on account of the influence of the beneficial rain. Human beings will come out of their caves and would decorate themselves with the fresh green plants and rejoice. They will give up the eating of fish and tortoise and will be henceforward satisfied with eating plants. With the time, they will learn, as a consequence of earlier existences or at the instruction of the deities, the art of ploughing and cooking, wearing clothes, building of houses and villages, the administration of the state, upholding of law, etc.—in short, everything will come in usage what was lost in the evil Duḥṣama-duḥṣamā periods. Everything will improve day by day. The life span will increase from 20 to 100, the size of the body from 2 to 7 Hastas.

(c) Duḥṣama-suṣamā

Once 21,000 years of Duḥṣamā have passed, Duḥṣama-suṣamā will begin in which the life span would be 1 Pūrvakoṭi and the body size 500 Dhanuṣa. 23 Tīrthaṅkaras, 11 Cakravartīs, 9 Baladevas, 9 Vāsudevas and 9 Prativāsudevas would appear in this era. It would last in all 1 Koṭikoṭi of Sāgaropamas less 42,000 years.

(d) Suṣama-duḥṣamā

The human beings who will be born again as twins would finally reach a life span of 1 Palyopama and a height of 1 Gavyūti in the "good-bad" era which would last for 2 Koṭikoṭis of Sāgaropamas and they would enjoy the fruits of Kalpa-trees which would now be growing. Two "great men" will appear in Suṣama-duḥṣamā, the 24th Tīrthaṅkara and the 12th Cakravartī. Kulakaras or patriarchs (p. 289) would appear after their deaths. Law and piousness would be then so great, the passions so little and the virtues so common that the men would not require any teacher.

(e) Suṣamā

Suṣamā would last for 3 Koṭikoṭis of Sāgaropamas. People would become up to 2 Palyopamas years old and attain a height of up to 2 Gavyūtis, live in idle pleasure and happiness.

(f) Suṣama-suṣamā

The most happy condition that can be attained on the earth will be realized in this last era of the coming world-period which would last for 4 Koṭikoṭis of Sāgaropamas. Human beings will live then for 3 Palyopamas and their height will be 3 Gavyūtis. The Utsarpiṇī would end once the proper duration of the period would be over. Then the new "descending world-period" would begin; it will begin with Suṣama-suṣamā which will be followed by the other fixed eras till finally the worst condition is reached and the end of Avasarpiṇī has come. Then it goes again upwards to become later worse—and so on and so forth, without end.

63 famous men will appear in the Utsarpiṇī that would succeed our present world-period. Their lives would resemble those of ours in their general basic features (see p. 274 ff.). Jainas know to name these holy men and heroes and they also give information as to the souls of which men of our world-period will be reborn as such.

I shall restrict myself to mentioning the names of the 24 Tīrthaṅkaras of the future among Śvetāmbaras and Digambaras (the latter in the brackets).[82] They are: 1. Padmanābha (Mahāpadma), 2. Śūradeva (Suradeva),

3. Supārśva, 4. Svayamprabha, 5. Sarvānubhūti (Sarvātmabhūta), 6. Devaśruti (Devaputra), 7. Udaya (Kulaputra), 8. Peḍhāla (Udaṅka), 9. Poṭṭila (Proṣṭhila), 10. Śatakīrti (Jayakīrti), 11. Suvrata (Munisuvrata), 12. Amama (Aranātha), Niṣkaṣāya (Niṣpāpa), 14. Niṣpulāla (Niṣkaṣāya), 15. Nirmama (Vipula), 16. Citragupta (Nirmala), 17. Samādhi (Citragupta), 18. Saṁvara (Samādhigupta), 19. Yaśodhara (Svayambhara), 20. Vijaya (Anivartī), 21. Malli (Vimala), 22. Deva (Vijaya), 23. Anantavīrya (Devapāla) and Bhadrakṛit (Anantavīrya).

While the names of the Tīrthaṅkaras of the future are fixed among the two sects, there is a difference of opinion among the authors about what these future prophets had been in our world-period. According to the prevalent view, Padmanābha is supposed to be a rebirth of King Śreṇika of Magadha who lived in Mahāvīra's period, Sūradeva a rebirth of Mahāvīra's uncle Supārśva, and Kṛṣṇa, Balarāma, Devakī, Rohiṇī and other persons of the holy legend would be reborn in the others.

CONCLUDING REMARKS

For Jainas, their doctrine is infallible, the most sublime and the most profound what the human wisdom has created. All other metaphysical systems are not by far anywhere near them; what is common in them with the Jaina-doctrine is only a borrowed reflection of it, and what is different in them is only an error that is caused by ignorance. The "Bhavyas" (those who are capable of getting salvation, as Jainas call themselves as those having the right faith) see, therefore, in the followers of other religions heretics from whom a pious man keeps himself at the best far in order not to be misled to idolatry and sin through him. This point of view emerges blatantly in the works of fanatical believers who think that their faith is the right one, as in "Ṣaṣṭi-śataka" of Nemicandra in which it is said:[83]

"Avoid a teacher of heterodoxy,
Albeit rich in mind and virtue,
For he is like a gem on the hood
Of a poisonous serpent."

But not all Jainas are so crass in their judgement. Many even justify the views of the other systems and are of the opinion that one should accept the good wherever it is found. Thus Haribhadra wrote the verse which has become famous:[84]

"I did not choose Mahāvīra as my friend
And Kapila my enemy and others like him;
Listen to him only and follow him,
Whose teachings reveal the genuine truth."

The Jaina-doctrine as such, as we have discussed it in the preceding chapters, is virtually a compromise between these two extremes. On the one hand, the Jainas adhere with dogged conservatism to the theories proclaimed by the ancestors, although they appear to be outdated in many points on account of the results of the progressive scientific and philosophical research, like the astronomical hypotheses of two suns, etc. On the other hand, they have enriched and expanded their system by adding a number of things to them which must have grown on the other ground, like the legends of Rāma and Kṛṣṇa, etc.

It is also now, as it was in the past. Jainas of today take care with pious enthusiasm that their doctrine is preserved in its purity; they, however, try to do justice to the demands of the modern *weltanschauung* by making sensible additions or reinterpretations. The Jaina-writers of today have made it their task to prove that the philosophy of as-if was already anticipated in the theory of relativity of Syādvāda, the modern atom theory in the theories of the nature of matter, psychoanalysis in the doctrine of suppressed passions, among other things.

The religious and philosophical value of Jainism is

viewed quite differently in India and Europe since time immemorial. The opinion of Jainas that their religion is the most perfect is conceded by the Europeans like H. Warren[85] and O. Pertold.[86] The latter considers that Jainism is the highest form of religion one can ever think of, because three elements of true religiousness—the emotional, intellectual and practical—keep an equilibrium, because its concept of the highest being represents like Nietzsche's superman a more perfect conception of a spirit which is superior to the world, than an idea of creator-god because its Ahiṁsā ethics is more far-reaching and in its practical application more effective than all the ethical principles of other religions, etc. As against this, the others did their best to disparge the Jaina-doctrine. Śaṅkara compared it with the gabble of a drunkard and a fool. Kabīr branded it as heterodoxy; Dayānand Sarasvatī considers it as ridiculous and its followers as dreamers and madcaps.[87] Even western scholars have equally sharply criticized, where one of them had gone even to the extent of saying: "A religion in which it is taught as a major point to refute god, to worship man and to feed the vermins; it has no right to exist."[88]

An objective judgement would indeed keep itself free from the exaggerations on both the sides. It would know to value, according to its worth, what is sublime in Jainism, without being blind to its weakness. A historian who knows to observe the things coolly will confirm that Jainism is inferior to the other forms of religion in the depth and the power of formation of the religious experience, but he will also acknowledge the imposing compactness of its *weltanschauung* and admire the incomparable life-force of this doctrine which knows to bind pious followers who are willing to do sacrifice, today as in the distant past, and thus has preserved again and again its right to exist.

REFERENCES

1. *ZDMG* 38, 1884, p. 18.
2. W. Schubring, *ZDMG* 75, 1921, p. 254 ff. deals with the individual changes of cosmography.
3. Since I have given extensive information on the sources of every single point in the doctrine in the work-mentioned, I have included here only those which concern new material.
4. The Jaina-philosophers understand the concept "pratyakṣa" differently. Whereas some—like the *Sthānāṅga-sūtra* and Umāsvāti (*Tatt.* I.11 f.)—consider the knowledge (Avadhi, Manaḥparyāya, Kevala) attained through the soul itself as "direct" and the one got by activising the senses and the organ of thinking as "indirect", the later thinkers like Siddhasena Divākara, Māṇikya Nandi and Devasūri are of the view that even, sensual perception is to be understood as "direct" knowledge. In this, they agree completely with the language-usage of the philosophers of the most of the other Indian schools (Comp. S.C. Vidyabhusana, *History of the Mediaeval School of Indian Logic,* particularly p. 9, 28 and 38).
5. Many distinguish even knowledge which is got by argumentation (Tarka) from the one which comes from inference. Example for the first is the sentence: "Smoke arises only, where there is fire, but it does not arise, where there is none" and the example for the latter is "Here is fire, for here is smoke."
6. Cf. for individual points Satis Chandra Vidyabusana, *History of the Mediaeval School of Logic,* Calcutta, 1909 and *A History of Indian Logic,* Calcutta, 1921; S.N. Dasgupta, *History of Indian Philosophy,* Cambridge, 1922, I, p. 173 ff.; S. Radhakrishnan, *Indian Philosophy,* London and New York, 1923, I, p. 302; Nahar and Ghosh, *Epitome of J.*, p. 103 ff.; Jacobi on *Tattv.* I.35.
7. H. Jacobi on *Tattv.* I.7.
8. H. Jacobi on *Tattv.* V.17.
9. *Dravyasaṅgraha* 22.
10. More in Jacobi on *Tattv.* IV.15; Kirfel, *Kosmographie,* p. 337; Jaini, *Outlines,* p. 15; *Gem Dictionary,* p. 153.
11. This doctrine has provoked numerous discussions in the Indian philosophy; it is most violently fought by the followers of Vaiśeṣika philosophy; comp. Hultzsch, "Aṇṇambhaṭṭa's Tarkasaṅgraha" (Abh. Göttinger *Ges. d. Wiss.*, 1907), p. 8.
12. *Dravyasaṅgraha* 16 and Comm.
13. *Vetālapañcaviṁśati,* ed. Uhle, 1881, XI, 2.
14. *Gommaṭasāra, Karmakāṇḍa,* Verse 21.
15. This means that, e.g. a being which has attached itself an

Ānupūrvī of hell when it has ended its existence in the hell, goes to its new place of birth on its own from the hell by the force of its Ānupūrvi-karma and keeps to its form in the hell during the "Vigraha-gati", i.e. during its wandering from one existence to the other.

16. According to Digambaras, Sthira-karma is responsible for the transformation of the 7 basic components of the body (Dhātu), viz., humours, blood, flesh, fats, bones, marrow, semen as also the 7 subordinate parts (Upadhātu), viz., wind, bile, phlegm, arteries, muscles, skin digestive fire taking place on its own (as in the male) and the Asthira-karma causes the opposite (as in the female), J.L. Jaini on *Tattv.* VIII.11.
17. Glasenapp, *Hinduismus,* p. 240.
18. *Gommaṭasāra, Jīvakāṇḍa,* Verse 130.
19. Six stages of sexual feeling in man are listed as possible, W. Schubring, *Mahānisīha-sutta,* p. 66.
20. V.R. Gāndhī, *Karma Philosophy,* p. 145; W. Schubring, *ibid.,* pp. 70, 73.
21. *Dravyasaṅgraha* 10. Comm.
22. Jaina-versions of the story which has become widely known through Rückert's poem "Es ging ein Mann durchs Syrerland führt' ein Kamel am Halfterband" are found in Haribhadra's *Samarāiccakahā,* ed. Jacobi, p. 110 ff.; Pradyumna, *Samarādityasaṁkṣepa,* ed. Jacobi, II, 320 ff., p. 58 (German by Joh. Hertel, *Ausgewählte Erzählungen aus H's P.,* Leipzig, 1908, p. 64 ff.); Amitgati, *Dharmaparīkṣā,* Par. II.5-21 (contents in N. Mironow, *Die Dh. des A,* p. 39). Comp. E. Kuhn, "Der Mann im Brunnen" in: *Festgruß* an O. v. Böhtlingk, Stuttgart, 1888, p. 68-76 on different versions of the legend which is widely known in the world; see also Chauvin, *Bibliographie des overages arabes* II, p. 85, No. 113; 17; III, p. 100.
23. These are enumerated in J.L. Jaini on *Tattv.* VI.5; Stevenson, *Heart of J.,* p. 141 and 305; Nahar and Ghosh, *Epitome of J.,* p. 532 ff.
24. v. Glasenapp, *Lehre vom Karman,* p. 35; Stevenson, *ibid.,* 113 f.; 132 f., 301 f.; Nahar and Ghosh, *ibid.,* 493 f., 514 f.
25. These 25 Bhāvās are listed in *Ācārāṅga-sūtra* II.15 (Jacobi, *Jaina Sūtras,* I, p. 202 ff.).
26. Torments suffered unwillingly are often rewarded in the other world, even for the culprits who are sentenced to death. Cf. *Aupapātika-Sūtra,* §§ 69-70; J.J. Meyer, *Indian Tales,* p. 9.
27. The question whether there is a creator is discussed in detail in Jinasena's *Ādipurāṇa,* 4, 16 ff.; Guṇaratna's Comm. on Haribhadra's *Ṣaḍdarśana-samuccaya,* 45 f. Malliṣeṇa's *Syādvādamañjarī* (Chowkhamba-Series, Ed., particularly

p. 23 ff.), German by H. Jacobi in *Die Entwicklung der Gottesidee bei den Indern*, p. 102 ff. Comp. also: F.O. Schrader, *Über den Stand der indischen Philosopbie zur Zeit Mahāvīras und Buddhas*, p. 62 ff.; S.N. Dasgupta, *History of Indian Philosophy*, I, 203 ff. H. Jacobi, "Atheism (Jain)", *ERE* 2, p. 186 f.; Rickhab Dass Jaini, *An Insight into Jainism*, p. 59 ff.

28. Malliṣeṇa, *Syādvādamañjarī*, VI, 69ff. (Translation by H. Jacobi, *Die Entwicklung der Gottesidee bei den Indern*, p. 209 f.
29. *Gommaṭasāra*, *Jīvakāṇḍa*, 197.
30. Nemicandra, *Trilokasāra* I.143; Comp. Kesarichand Bhandari's *Ardha-Magadhi Dictionary*, I, p. 410.
31. Cf. *Hinduismus*, p. 229; Schomerus, *Çaiva-Siddhānta*, p. 223 f.; F.S. Growse, *The Rāmāyaṇa of Tulsī Dās*, translated (6th edition, Allahabad, 1922), p. 8 note.
32. J.L. Jaini, *Jaina Gem Dictionary*, p. 157. Others do not include the two groups of the Nigoḍas at the beginning, but count 14,00,000 (plants with a common body) which are distinguished from the other groups of plants i.e. the "plants with a single body".
33. The following description of the world is restricted to giving only what is the most important without going into all details and individualities or emphasizing the differences in the teachings of the different schools because the whole field of Jaina-cosmography is extensively treated by W. Kirfel in his work, *Die Kosmographie der Inder*, pp. 208-331. Comp. further the review of this book by W. Schubring (*ZDMG* 75, 1921, pp. 254-275) which brings in a great deal of material, besides Umāsvāti, *Tattv.* III-IV, Brahmadeva in comm. on Nemicandra's *Dravyasaṅgraha* 35 (text pp. 47-62).
34. Brahmadeva, *Comm. on Dravyasaṅgraha* 35 (p. 48).
35. Stevenson, *Heart of J.*, p. 271.
36. G. Thibaut, Astronomie, Astrologie und Mathematik in *Grundriβ der Indo-arischen Philogie u. Altertumskunde* III.9, Straβurg, 1899, p. 21.
37. Hemacandra, *Triṣaṣṭi-śalākāpuruṣa-carita* IV.3.211; Amṛatacandra *Tattvārthasāra* II.167.
38. Cf. F.O. Schrader, *Über den Stand der indischen Philosophie zur Zeit Mahāvīras und Buddhas*, p. 58 ff.
39. *Tattv.* IV.15, comm. These references are of great importance for the Jainas. During the Duḥṣmā-era which is now running in Bharata, salvation cannot be attained, but in other parts of the world, like Videha, this is possible. Thus, a Jaina who is mature for salvation can be reborn in Videha and can attain perfection there.
40. Jaini gives the enumeration in *Outlines of J.*, p. 127.

41. *Tattv* VI.23 (Jacobi).
42. Bhadrabāhu, *Kalpa-sūtra*, § 118.
43. D.R. Bhandarkar treats Samavasaraṇa in detail in "Jaina Iconography" *Ind. Antq.* 40, 1911, p. 125 ff.; 153 ff.
44. Hemacandra, *Abhidhāna-cintāmaṇi*, 57 ff. Translation (with few changes) in accordance with O. Böhtlingk and C. Rieu. Cf. *Lokaprakāśa* 30, 984 ff., *Pravacana-sāroddhāra* I, Sūtra 450.
45. Cf. Jacobi, *ZDMG* 38, 1884, p. 13.
46. *Pravacana-sāroddhāra* I, 440 ff.
47. These advantages are mentioned in *Lokaprakāśa* 31, 23 ff.
48. Hemcandra, *63-śalākā-p-c* 7, 13, 11 f.
49. Cf. *Pravacana-sāroddhāra* I, 298 ff.
50. *Ibid.* 288, Hemcandra, *Abhidhāna-cintāmaṇi*, 50 ff. The names of the 24 Tīrthaṅkaras of our part of the world Bhạrata in past Utsarpiṇī are: Kevalajñānī, Nirvāṇī, Sāgara, Mahāyaśas, Vimala, Sarvānubhūti, Śrīdhara, Datta, Dāmodara. Sutejas, Svāmī, Śivāśī (or Munisuvrata), Sumati, Śivagati, Astāga (Abādha), Numīśvara, Anila, Yaśodhara, Kṛtārdha, Dharmīśvara (Jineśvara), Śuddhamati, Śivakara, Syandana, Samparti.
51. E. Leumann, Actes du 6ième Congrès des Orientalistes III, Leiden, 1885, p. 548.
52. See v. Glasenapp in the Jacobi-Festschrift on the uneveness in the treatment in *63-lakṣaṇamahāpurāṇa.*
53. Nemicandra, *Trilokasāra* 828, It is again different in J.L. Jaini, *Outlines*, p. 126.
54. It is so in Guṇabhadra's Uttarpurāṇa.
55. The wish-trees have different names among Digambaras. I am giving here the names mentioning what these give. 1. Madyāṅga: wine; 2. Tūryāṅga: music; 3. Vibhūṣāṅga: ornaments; 4. Sragaṅga: wreaths; 5. Jyotiraṅga: light; (It shine constantly so that there was no difference between day and night); 6. Dipāṅga: also light; 7. Gṛhāṅga: houses; 8. Bhojanāṅga: food; 9. Pātrāṅga: pots; 10. Vastrāṅga: clothes (*Ādipurāṇa* 3.39).
56. Cf. *Ādipurāṇa*, Chap. 3.—We find individual references, but now needing partial corrections in A. Weber's treatise, Über das *Çatruñjaya Māhātmya*, Leipzig, 1858, p. 26 ff. on the patriarchs, on Ṛṣabha, Bharata and their progeny.
57. L. Suali narrates about Ṛṣabha's earlier births in the incompleted treatise "Analisi dell' Ādiçvaracarita di Hemacandra" *(Studie Italiani di Filologia Indo-Iranica*, 1909); see also H.H. Wilson's brief enumeration of it in accordance with the *Ādipurāṇa* in *Descriptive Catalogue of the Oriental Mss.*

Collected by the Late Colin Mackenzie, 2nd ed., Calcutta, 1828, p. 192 f.

58. Bāhubalī's legend is narrated in *Kathākośa* (C.H. Tawney's transl. p. 192 ff.).

59. Cf. *Ācāradinakara,* p. 8a. The names of the 4 "Genuine Vedas" are supposed to be: Saṁskāradarśana, Saṁsthāna-parāmarśaṇa, Tattvāvabodha, Vidyāprabodha. The Sanskrit-mantras used in the holy ceremonies are said to have come from the Jainaveda.

60. I have narrated the legend of the establishment of the Brāhmaṇa-caste in the "Jacobi-Festscrhift".

61. Sagara's legend is narrated in detail in Devendra Gaṇi's Commentary on Uttarādhyayana-Sūtra. The text is published with its German translation by Richard Fick in his dissertation "Eine Jainische Bearbeitung der Sagara-Sage".—The common, Brahmanic version of the Sagara-myth is reproduced in v. Glasenapp's *Hinduismus,* p. 94 f.

62. According to the version given by Hemacandra *(63-Śalākāpuruṣa-carita* III.3. 169 ff.) the answer of the queen, obviously in accordance with the precept of Ahiṁsā, gets weakened to the extent that she said that the women should wait till a Tīrthaṅkara is born who will give the judgement. The false mother was satisfied with this while the right one broke into tears and insisted that justice be done to her.—The whole legend in one of the numerous parallels to the judgement of Solomon (1. King 3, 16-28). Compare on this Hertel in *Geist des Ostens,* I, 1913, p. 192; L.P. Tessitori, *Ind. Antq.*, 1913, p. 148 f. More literature on the question of origin in R. Garbe, *Indien und das Christentum,* Tübingen, 1914, p. 25 f.

63. A. Ballini gives an extensive account of the life-story of Vāsupūjya and the other three "great men" of his period as also the legends connected with them in *Rivista degli Studi Orientali,* I, Rome 1907/08, pp. 41 ff., 169 ff.; 439 ff.; II, 39 ff.; 239 f. (based on Vardhamānasūri's *Vāsupūjya-carita* (around 1243 A.D.).

64. Mrs. Stevenson narrates the legend in *Heart of J.*, p. 54.

65. H.H. Wilson narrates the story of Ananta and the 4th pair of heroes—which is based on *Cāmuṇḍarāya-purāṇa*—in *Descriptive Catalogue of the Mss. Collected by Col. Mechenzie,* p. 179.

66. The legend of Sanatakumāra which is embellished with episodes is a very popular narrative material among the Jainas. Of the adaptations let us mention the one written in Prākṛta in Devendra Gaṇi's Commentary on Uttarādhyayanasūtra (English in J.J. Meyer, *Indian Tales,* French by G. de Blonay, *Revue de l'Histoire des Religions* 31, Paris, 1895, pp. 29-41 and the one written in Apabhraṁśa in Haribhadra's

Neminātihacarila (German by Jacobi in *Abhdlg. der Bayerischen Akademie der Wiss., Kl.* XXXI, 2 Munich, 1921).

67. Cf. W. Hüttemann, *Die Jñāla-Erzählungen im 6. Aṅga des Kanons der Jinislen* (Dissertation, Straβburg, 1907), p. 29 ff.

68. The Jaina-version of the Rāma-legend is different from the Brahmanic version in many respects. It exists besides in a series of adaptations which also show a great difference among themselves. For details cf. N. Mironow, *Die Dharmaparīkṣā des Amilgali*, p. 28, 49 ff.; Rājendralāla Mitra, *Notices of Sanskrit Mss.* 6, 1882, p. 70 ff. *(Pūrṇacandrodaya Purāṇa);* Willem Stutterheim, Rāma-legenden und *Rāma-Reliefs in Indonesien,* Munich, 1925, p. 93; D.C. Sen, *The Bengālī Rāmāyaṇs,* p. 35, note and p. 206.

69. Cf. on this A. Weber, *Uber das Çatruñaya Māhālmya*, p. 35 ff. and the English transl. in *Ind. Anlq.* 30, 1901, p. 139 ff.; *Anlagada-dasāo* (transl. by L.D. Barnett, London, 1907, pp. 13-15, 67-82); *Ullarādhyayana-sūlra* 22 (translated by H. Jacobi, *SBE* 45, p. 112 ff.); further the legends on the fall of Dvāravatī and the death of Kṛṣṇa in Devendra's commentary on *Ullarādhyayana-sūlra* (German by H. Jacobi, *ZDMG* 42, 1888, pp. 493-529) as also the account of Ariṣṭanemi-legend from the same source (German by Jarl Charpentier, *ZDMG* 64, 1910, pp. 408-429).

70. Brahmadatta's legend based on Devendra's commentary on *Ullarādhyayana-sūlra* has been translated into Italian by P.E. Pavolini, *G.S.A.I.* 6, 1892, pp. 111-148; into English by J.J. Meyer, Hindu Tales; P.E. Pavolini deals with the commentary on Hemacandra's *Yoga-śāstra,* etc. in *G.S.A.I.* 7, 1893, pp. 339-342.

71. The story of the brothers Citra and Sambhūta is available in a Brahmanic commentary (*Harivaṁśa* I.18-24), in a Buddhistic one (*Jālaka,* No. 498) and in several others; comp. E. Leumann, *WZKM* 5, pp. 111-146; 6, pp. 1-46 (Vienna 1891/92). See also *Ullarādhyayana-sūlra* 23 (English by H. Jacobi, *SBE* 45, p. 56 ff.; German also by him in Edv. Bloomfield, Textbuch zur Religionsgeschinchte, Leipzig, 1912, p. 207 ff.).

72. Major Delamaine gave the first account of Pārśva-legend in *Transactions of the RAS* I, 1827, p. 428 ff. Jarl Charpentier translated the version in Devendra's commentary on *Ullarādhyayana-sūlra* in *ZDMG* 69, 1915, pp. 321-359. Maurice Bloomfield gave in his book *The Life and Stories of the Jaina Savior Parçvanālha,* Baltimore, 1919 a detailed analysis based on Bhāvadevasūri's *Pārśvanālha-carila.*

73. Mahāvīra's life is described by the Jainas exceptionally too often. Compare on the following among others Bhadrabāhu's

Kalpa-sūtra (transl. by Jacobi, *SBE* 22, p. 217 ff.), Manak Chand Jaini, *Life of Mahāvīra*, Allahabad.

74. Cf. H.B. Bhide, *Ind. Antq.* 48, 1919, p. 123 ff. on the Kalkis.
75. Jambūsvāmī's legend are narrated in Hemacandra's *Pariśiṣṭaparva*, Chap. 2 f.; Analysis of H. Jacobi in his edition, p. 20 ff.; German transl. in J. Hertal, *Ausgewählte Erzählungen aus Hemacandras Pariśiṣṭaparvan*, p. 44 ff.
76. Cf. note 39, p. 341.
77. The names differ in their details in different traditions (Gaṅgādeva instead of Raṅgadeva, etc.). According to Bhandarkar, Report 1883/84, the Yugapradhānas who knew the 10 Pūrvas were: Mahāgiri, Suhastī, Guṇasundara, Śyāma, Skandila, Revatīmitra, Dharma, Bhadragupta, Gupta and Vajrasvāmī.
78. Bhandakar, *ibid.*, 125.
79. Guérinot, *Epigraphie Jaina*, p. 36, Jinasena, *Ādipurāṇa* 2, 141 ff.
80. Numerous legends like this are found in Bhandarkar's analysis of Dharmaghoṣa's *Ṛṣimaṇḍala-prakaraṇa* (Report 1883/84, p. 130 ff.), in Jacobi's analysis of Hemacandra's *Pariśiṣṭaparvan*, etc.
81. There are differences among the individual writers with respect to the period of events in the future world-periods. Many let the bountiful clouds appear in the Duḥṣama-duḥṣmā period itself and the Kulakaras in the Duḥṣamā-period, etc. (comp. *Uttarapurāṇa* 76. 477 ff.).
82. Hemacandra's *Abhidhāna-cintāmaṇi*, 53-56; *Lokaprakāśa* 34. 297 ff.; *Pravacanasāroddhāra* I, Sūtra 457 ff, ; *Uttarapurāṇa* 76. 477 ff.).
83. *Prakaraṇa-ratnākara*, Vol. II, No. 61, verse 18. A number of other stanzas having the same contents.
84. Haribhadra, *Lokatattvanirṇaya* I. 38 (Suali, *GSAI* 18, 1905, p. 278).
85. Herbert Warren, *Jainism in Western Garb, as a Solution to Life's Great Problems*, Madras, 1912.
86. O. Pertold, *the Place and Importance of Jainism in the Comparative Science of Religions*, Bhavanagar, year not mentioned, particularly p. 14 f.
87. Śaṅkara in his commentary on *Brahma-sūtra* II.2.33; Kabīr, Bījak, *Ramaṇiṇī* 30 (ed. of Ahmed Shah, Cawnpore, 1911); Dayānand Sarasvatī, particularly in the 12th Chap. on his *Satyārtha-prakāśa.*
88. E. Washburn Hopkins, The religions of India, Boston and London, 1895, p. 296.

SECTION V

SOCIETY

I

The Foundations of the Society

1. JAINISM AS THE "RELIGION OF THE WORLD"

Jainism is universal; it is, according to its own theory, a world-religion that tries to include all the beings. Not only human beings, but also animals, gods, inhabitants of hell, can absorb its teachings. Gods of all classes may have the Jaina-faith; it is always their own for those who are above the classes beyond the Graiveyakas. It is already mentioned above on p. 260 that the beings in hell could be Jainas. All the fully developed animals with 1 to 4 senses are heterodoxical, also those senseless ones with 5 senses; the undeveloped among them may, on the other hand, possess "Sāsvādana-samyaktva" (see p. 207) for a short period. Sensible animals with 5 senses may be partially or fully in possession of the right faith, could even practise self-discipline to some extent. We have already mentioned a pious elephant above on p. 321; a well-known story of an animal having the right faith is the legend of the frog which, when Mahāvīra was preaching in Rājagṛha, could remember its earlier births and got even ready to worship the feet of the saint by offering flowers. But before it could do it, it was trampled by an elephant; but it was reborn at once as god due to its piousness.[1]

If the gates of the Jaina-faith remain open even for animals, it is just but natural that it turns to all men without any distinction of race and caste. It is always emphasized in the stereotype introductions to Mahāvīra's sermons that he proclaimed the law to the Aryans and non-Aryans. Thus, as G. Bühler[2] remarks, "conversions of the people coming from lower classes like gardeners, painters, etc. are not uncommon even today". It is not only very often emphasized in the canon, but it is also seen from the reports of Jaina-historians that the Jain-mission did not only comprise the nations belonging to Hindu-culture, but also tried to win over the uncivilized non-Aryan tribes. Thus Hemacandra tells of King Samprati (see p. 44) that he has constructed the colonies of monks in the uncivilized areas to propagate Jainism among savages. He even took recourse to guile to see that Sādhus got everything from the people that they needed for their survival. He sent officials in the disguise of monks to the areas where missionary work was to be done before the ascetics began their expedition. These then ordered the savages to give as taxes certain food articles and other things which the monks needed to the tax-collectors whenever they would appear from time to time. Samprati then sent the monks as the alleged tax-officials to the lands of the Āndhras and Dramilas, and they found there everything they needed for their life.[3]

It is seen from the legend of Kālkācārya, the apostle of Indo-Scythians (see p. 50) as also from the report on the alleged conversion of the great Mogul emperor Akbar (see p. 75) that Jainas extended their propaganda also to the Mlecchas (barbarians) who had immigrated to India. G. Bühler proves that the Muslims find acceptance even today in the Jaina-community. He informs that a few cases of this type were communicated to him in the year 1876 by the Jainas in Ahmedābād as a great triumph of their faith.[4]

Jaina-missionaries have tried to propagate their religion even outside the boundaries of India. This is seen from the report of the Chinese pilgrim Hiuen Tsiang (629-645) about the presence of Digambaras in Kiapishi (Kapisha)[5] and from the legend according to which Haribhadra's (8th century) disciples Haṁsa and Paramahaṁsa were murdered by the Buddhists in Tibet (Bhota),[6] as also from the Tibetan reports on Kucā translated by A. Grünwedel.[7] Even the ocean put no limits to the enthusiasm of the messengers of Mahāvīra's religion to propagate their faith. It is quite often narrated in fairy-tales that the inhabitants of distant islands were converted to Jainism, and Digambaras claim that there is a fabulous island, 1,500 km. from Jaipur, on the other side of Rāmeśvara, called Jainabhadrī, and that it is the main seat of Jaina-scholarship.[8] A legend even claims that there were Jainas in Arabia before Mohammed.[9] It is of course not improbable that in view of the size of the trade of Jaina-businessmen that Jaina thoughts were brought into foreign lands by the seafarers in the past; we shall have to discuss later the Arabian philosopher Abu-l-'Ala al ma'arri. Jainas have tried even in this century to work for their ideas in the Western countries and converted people even in England and America as we have already mentioned on p. 89 f.

It is thus seen from what is said that Jainism knows no national borders like, say, Hinduism. It turns to people of every folks and positions who are capable of absorbing their doctrine.

2. THE CASTE SYSTEM

All sorts of beings belong to Jainism, but it does not

mean that they are equal in their status. All Jīvas are divided into four levels of existence; gods, human beings, animals and beings in hell. Each one of them has a number of classes which are precisely distinguished from one another, and the individual classes are further divided into subclasses. Even human beings have different groups. Jainism, like Hinduism, divides mankind into a number of castes (Varṇas) which are further divided into numerous sub-castes (Jātis). The uppermost three castes are called "twice-born" because their males experience a second, spiritual birth by a special consecration in which they are encircled by a holy thread (or at least are supposed to be encircled). The castes of Brāhmaṇas or the priests, Kṣatriyas or the warriors and Vaiśyas or the businessmen are the "twice-born". The castes coming after these privileged ones and which are behind them in ritual purity are those which cannot share the sacrament of being clothed with the thread, the fourth (*caturtha*) caste of the Śūdras, the fifth (*pañcama*) caste of the so-called "Pañcamas" and the great number of barbarians (Mlecchas), i.e. the people who are outside, and therefore, below the Indian caste-system, like Muslims, Christians, etc.

The present grouping of humanity in castes and subcastes was not, according to the Jaina-theologians, always prevalent. In the first, lucky eras of our world-period all men were equal. The division into castes came only during Ṛṣabha's period, and besides, there were only three castes at the beginning: Kṣatriyas who were supposed to protect humanity with the help of the weapons, Vaiśyas who were to look after trade, agriculture and cattle-breeding and Śūdras whose duty it was to do all sorts of works. Śūdras were divided into two groups: workmen and others. The former were either "touchables", i.e. ritually pure (like barbers) or impure (like those who have to live segregated from others). Caste-system experienced further development under Bharata. Bharata founded the Brāhmaṇa-class; he instructed pious men to dedicate themselves to the study of holy tradition and to the organization of the religious ceremonies.[10]

The children of those men who were entrusted by Ṛṣabha and Bharata with clearly defined duties are the members of the present castes, whether they still belong today to the Jaina-faith or they have lost it, as it is particularly the case with Brāhmaṇas who, in the course of time, did not believe in it any more and disowned the teachings of the Tīrthaṅkaras. The four castes of Brāhmaṇas, Kṣatriyas, Vaiśyas and Śūdras were further divided in the following period into a number of subcastes and further castes arose by forbidden combination of different castes which were considered below the caste of Śūdras.

In any case, so much is correct in this account of Jainas that the caste-system prevalent in India today is a result of a long development. It cannot be estimated yet for the time being how it was developed to the present form, in what way and under which influences. It is certain that in the older historical periods of Jainism there was no such division of the society, as it is now, into a countless number of "Jātis" which cannot eat with one another nor marry among one another. The four Varṇas appear to be originally ranks and belonging to them was conditioned more by profession than by birth. According to the law-books, marriage among the member of the different castes was not rare. Thus the *Bhadrabāhu-saṁhitā* contains in Verse 31 ff. rules of inheritance among the sons of a man who was married to women of different castes. Even the social respect given to the different castes was a different one among the Jainas in the old period from the one of the Hindus of today. In accordance with the anti-Brahmanic character of their religion, they conceded the first position in the society to Kṣatriayas, and Brāhmaṇas were much below them. This fact is clearly expressed in the Śvetāmbara-legend of Mahāvīra's birth. He was first supposed to have been born as a son of a Brāhmaṇa, but his foetus was transferred to the womb of a queen because Indra thought that Tīrthaṅakaras are not born in "small families, in low families, in poor families, in beggar's families and in Brāhmaṇa's families", but only in high families, noble families and in royal families.[11]

There are today a great number of castes (Jātis) among Jainas, i.e. endogamous groups of persons who are characterized by common names; they practise the same traditional occupation, trace back their origin to a definite human or divine personality and are connected with one another by fixed, inherited rights, duties and views. These Jātis in their nature have only very little common with the "Varṇas" of the old period; theoretically they are connected in such a way that the present Jātis are classified under the individual "Varṇas" and are considered as their subdivisions. The castes of today form fixed organized bodies which regulate the private life of their members by their precepts on marriage, food and avoidance of ritual impurity and this is done to the smallest detail. A special body (Pañcāyat) watches over the strict implementation of the caste-laws; offences against the caste-order are punished by it. Such punishments consist in performing certain ceremonies of atonement, organization of a festive meal for the members of the caste, payment of cash to an animal asylum or to another charitable institute among other things. In grave cases a person can be expelled from the caste; today not paying attention to food regulations, a forbidden marriage and a journey across the ocean besides gross offence against the interests of the caste are a sufficient reason for excommunication. The loss of caste-membership calls for social boycott and professional ruin. Thus one Visāśrīmālī in Ahmedābād who had married a widow was expelled from the caste. The cloth-traders' guild (Mahājana) of Ahmedābād consisting of members of different castes and both Jainas and Vaiṣṇavas excluded him immediately from business and the unfortunate fellow was, thus, compelled to close his shop and to leave the town.[12] Many misdemeanours can be made good again by corresponding atonements; it is also often possible to avoid the strict precepts of the castes in a clever way. The journey across the "black water", i.e. the sea, is considered by Jainas, as well as Hindus, as an offence against the caste-laws—in contrast to their ancestors who made journeys across the ocean in connection with their business. Jainas who want to visit Europe or other distant lands, proceed in such a way that they are making a pilgrimage to Śatruñjaya or some other place of pilgrimage. Thus one travels to a place across the sea from a harbour and in a ship. Once the longer halt in a foreign country has ended, a Jaina returns home via the place of pilgrimage and is assured, because he had officially made a pilgrimage, although everyone knows where he had been for so long.

Efforts are being made presently by the enlightened Jainas to break the rigid barriers of the caste system. Thus it is reported that hundred people from the castes of the Caturthas and Pañcamas pledged in writing not to acknowledge any difference between the two castes in future. This agreement got a practical significance when a Pañcama A.B. Laṭṭhe married his niece Śermatibāi to a Caturtha boy.[13] Very often the reformers tried to establish a social unification among the different castes by organizing meals in which people from different Jātis participated and thus openly declared their intention of bridging the segregating laws. All these efforts, howsoever they may be laudable, had so far only a negligible success, for most of Jainas hang to the old traditions because Jainas "are more than Hindus in the strictness of their caste exclusiveness".[14]

Let us examine in brief the most important castes into which Jainas of today are divided; in no way, however, does it mean that it is complete in all respects to depict the complicated conditions exhaustively.

The number of Jaina-Brāhmaṇas is today quite negligible. They are still there in South India;[15] some persons have got their name as such included in the census.[16] The Pāṇḍes in Barodā must have been originally Śrīmālī-Brāhmaṇas; they had immigrated from Mārvār and were later converted to Jainism by Kumārapāla.[17] The Bhojaks and Sevaks in Rājapūtānā consider that they are Brāhmaṇas, but they are not fully accepted by these because they observe the cult in Jaina-temples. The servers in the temples of Śvetāmbaras are, of course, in part Brāhmaṇas, but they are not Jainas, although they are appointed to execute the prescribed Jaina-rites.[18] We often come across a peculiar phenomenon that persons are professionally active in the cult of a certain religion without belonging to it, thus, e.g. the Rabābīs who are musicians in the temple of Amritsar are not Sikhs, but belong to a Mohammedan guild of street singers. Jainas who perform, partially by inheritance, sacral functions on the West-coast and who are "Upādhyāyas", are mostly not Brāhmaṇas.[19]

Kṣatriyas from whose circles Jainism has emerged are represented even now among Jainas. Thus Buchanan found around 1801 a few princes who were Jainas.[20] Even now, there are a few (e.g. the mediatized Cautar in Mudabidire) of them. A few merchant-castes claim that they are Rājapūtas.[21]

Quite a majority of Jainas belong today, as since centuries, to the rank of businessmen, Baniyās. There are castes of businessmen in great numbers. They have come out of their hometowns and many of them have spread across a great part of India in pursuit of their business activity. Śrīmālīs,[22] Porvāls[23] and Osvāls belong to the most distinguished castes among the businessmen. They claim that they originate from the Soḷankī-clan of the Agnikula-Rājapūtas, and they have, therefore, a strong mixing of Indo-Scythian blood.[24] Śrīmālīs and Porvāls appear to have formed originally a community, and according to a legend of their caste, they come from the city of Śrīmāl or Bhīnmāl in Mārvār which is now in ruins. It is said that they created a goddess from their toe or a garland of flowers.[25] They worship this goddess even now as their family-goddess. The Osvāls have sprung from the Śrīmālīs as it is narrated in the following legend. The Śrīmāl-king Desal allowed only millionaires to live within the walls of his city. Some of them who were unhappy on account of this left the city-area under the leadership of Desal's son Jayacandra and settled down in a place which they name Osa. The inhabitants, mostly the Rājapūtas, were worshippers of Śiva. The Jaina-monk Ratnasūri converted Jayacandra and his subjects to Jainism; this happened apparently in August 166 A.D. Other legends put the origin of Śrīmālīs and Osvāls in the period of Saint Prabhava (who died approximately in 397 B.C.).[26]

Another caste of the businessmen is the one of the Agarvāls. They come either from Agar near Ujjain or they are the descendants of King Agrasena who was ruling in Sirhind and whose capital was Agraha (in Fatehbād Tahsīl, Dist. Hissār, Pañjāb).[27]

Other castes of this type are the Khaṇḍarvāls and Bahirvāls, the Ummads whose head-quarters are in Sāgvāḍa near Duṅgarpur (Rājapūtānā). These castes are mostly further divided into sub-castes, thus in "Visās" and "Dasās"; the origin of these two sub-castes is explained in different ways;[28] according to Sir A. Baines[29] the latter had shown a higher percentage of lower blood than the former. The division goes further among some of these castes; thus among Śrīmālīs in Gujarāt Lādvās are distinguished besides Visās and Dasās; this is considered as the lowest group. The Visā Śrīmāls are then further divided into 7 subgroups and the Dasā-Śrīmāls into 3. Visās and Dasās can eat together, but cannot marry among themselves.

The circumstance that all members of the castes of the Śrīmāls, etc. are not Jainas is quite remarkable. Among the Śrīmāls in Gujarāt, e.g. all Visās are Jainas, of the Dasās, a part are Jainas and the others are Vaiṣṇavas.[30] The fact that Dasā Śrīmāl Śrāvakas (Jainas) enter in marriage bond with the Dasā Śrīmāl Meśaris (Vaiṣṇavas) and the other way round, but that a marriage between Dasā Śrīmāl Śrāvakas and Visā Śrīmāl Śrāvakas is out of question is a characteristic proof for the phenomenon one comes across in India that the caste-barriers are stronger than the religious ones.

Other castes of businessmen are: Svahitvāls in Mahārāṣṭra, Nevaḍs (Hyderābād), Kambojās (in Telaṅgaṇā right northwards up to Banāras and Nāgpur).[31]

The Jaina-Baniyās have occupied such a significant position in the business-world, particularly of Gujarāt, as big businessmen and bankers that they are given preference in the commercial corporations by the businessmen of other religions. The Vaiṣṇava-businessmen of Ahmedābād made early payments in favour of the Pāñjrāpols (p. 371) of Jainas and closed their shops on Jaina-holidays—a custom which is less and less practised in the recent times. The great respect shown to the owners of Jaina-firms is clearly revealed from the fact that the hereditary chairmen of the council of the trade-guild were chosen from amongst them.

Thus a" Nagar Seṭha" (the businessman of the city) is a Jaina in Ahmedābād for many generations. The privileges and duties of a "Nagar Seṭha" are many. Thus if there is famine in the town, he has to atone solemnly for the town by going round the place and sprinkling milk to appease Indra. Many Nagar Seṭhas have done a great service to their towns. Thus Kuśālcand Lakṣmīcand saved Ahmedābād in 1725 from the plundering done by the Marāṭhās. The guilds, to thank him, permitted him to take ¼th value of all the goods which were weighed in the city trading centre. Indian princes decorated him and his descendants with a number of honours, thus the right to sit on the State-chair, to use baldachin and to carry torches, among other things.[32]

The members of the castes we have discussed above and which can be considered as aristocracy among Jainas, are not busy only as businessmen, but are also jurists and administrators. On the other hand, commerce is also a profession of Jainas who belong to the ranks of those who are not "twice-born", thus Caturthas (Śūdras) and Pañcamas.

Most of Jainas take to a commercial profession because here they come least in conflict with their principle of "Ahiṁsā". But there are also Jainas who earn their livelihood by other means where they cannot prevent killing of all sorts of animals, as this, e.g. happens unintentionally in ploughing. There are numerous Jaina-farmers in Satārā district in Bombay Presidency[33] as also in Bijāpur;[34] they do all sorts of agricultural works with their own hands and with the help of their wives. Even the Sadas in Bangalore and Tumkur districts of the Princely State of Mysore are farmers. They were even soldiers earlier.[35] Other occupations of Jainas are: weaving (Gaḍiyas in Mysore),[36] cotton-printing (Bhāusārs in Barodā),[37] tailoring (Śimpis in Ahmedābād district and in Khāndesh),[38] goldsmiths (Sonārs in Khāndesh),[39] coppersmithy (Bogārs in Bijāpur and Hyderābād, Kasārs in Kolhāpur and Bhopāl).[40] There were also Jainas earlier in Kolhāpur who were barbers and washermen, but the members of this occupation have now ceased to be Jainas.[41]

If we now count Jainas, as it can be seen from what is said above, as persons belonging to all sorts of occupations and people from all the stratas of the Indian society, from Brāhmaṇas to Śūdras and the members of the fifth class (Pañcamas), it must be remembered that the whole religion gets its distinguishing stamp from the fact that the major part of their community is and was businessmen since centuries. Their peaceful disposition which disliked wars and upheavals on account of their religious and social interest made Jainas, from time immemorial, the protectors of the state; their wealth grew on account of their efficiency in business which they achieved through generations. It gave them economic power which assures them even now, in spite of their small numbers, quite a significant influence in the political and social life of India.

The number of Jainas belonging to the class of businessmen is so big because the members of the castes whose occupation was not in agreement with the precepts of Jainism, turned to commerce when they joined the community of Mahāvīra. But this does not mean that those who were converted became the members of the other castes; they adhered to their earlier caste. When thus such a person wants to marry or enter into marriage connection for his children, then he selects his bride or his son's, respectively husband of his daughter only from his old caste. Thus 'Seṭha Bhagvāndās Kevaldās who was known as a salesman of handwritten manuscripts was a dyer (Bhāusār) by caste. His forefathers had given up their original occupation which was forbidden by Mahāvīra and became businessmen when they were converted to Jainism. The family, however, continued to have connubial relationship with the Bhāusārs of Kheḍā; they were not Jainas, but Vaiṣṇavas.[42]

This fact illustrates most clearly a peculiar paradox which is caused by caste system in India: the followers of the Jaina-religion are compelled to marry the members of the other religious communities because their all-powerful code of the caste does not permit them to marry a person from their own community, but coming from a different caste.

3. STATE AND LAW

As Jainas had numerous kings and princes as the laymen of their church when their religion was in its prime and the teachings of the Tīrthaṅkaras had the status of an official religion in a number of kingdoms, they developed special ideas on the state and law and evolved them into a system. Their teachings mainly agree with the teachings of Hindu philosophers; it is, therefore, necessary here to mention the theories in detail which are laid down in the Jaina-Nītiśāstras. I shall, however, restrict myself to sketching the general basic features and to emphasize what is specially Jainistic.

Statecraft and law practices trace back, according to Jainas, to the first Tīrthaṅkara Ṛṣabha (compare p. 293) and they were further passed on by his son Bharata. It is in accordance with its royal origin when the political philosophy of Jainas equates the governance completely with the king. India's great Machiavelli Kauṭilya or Cāṇakya, whom Jainas also consider as their own, had taught in his "Arthaśāstra" that the "king is the state",[43] and describes him as the most important element and the combination of all the seven elements of governance [king, minister, land, fort, treasury, army (with its components: elephants, horses, cavalry and infantry) and the allies]; this tenet was also valid for Jaina-king. Power that is conceded to the king and the almost divine position he takes make him responsible for the good and bad of the land and the subjects. If he has to do justice to his lofty duty, he has to fulfil the five functions which Hemacandra mentions in a quotation as the five "sacrifices" of a monarch: he must punish the bad, honour the good, increase the treasury, be an impartial judge and protect the land from the enemy.[44] A ruler who has this ideal must show all the virtues; he should not be cruel and greedy, should shun excessive sensuous pleasures and avoid forbidden vices like dice-game and hunting.

If a king has to keep up order in the state and defend it against external and internal enemies, he has to follow completely *realpolitik*,* he may then try to fulfil, personally the duties of the Jaina religion. This is explicitly expressed by Somadeva when he says:

---

*Realistic national policy.

> "Lokāyata (materialism) is the best means of carrying out the business of *this* world. For, a king who has studied Lokāyata tries to weed out the 'thorns' of the empire (i.e. internal and external enemies).... One who is completely filled with sympathy, is not capable of keeping up the possession found in his hands even once .... Peace of mind towards an evil-doer is an embellishment of an ascetic, but not of a king. Woe to the man who does not have in his power to reveal both anger and friendliness! The one who does not courageously fight an enemy is dead, even when he is alive!"[45]

A king has to proceed in accordance with this theory with his ruthless energy and should not flinch from using even dubious means when the good of the state demands it. He has to use with clever thinking those of the six methods of politics which are in his interest against his neighbours in each case: peace, war, preparedness of attack, neutrality, double-game or alliance. Although a king is allowed to make use of violent means and although they are against the Jaina-principle of "Ahiṁsā" with respect to all beings, it may be pointed out here that force is to be used only in emergency when all other means of warding off the enemy have proved to be unsuccessful. If war cannot be avoided, it has to be seen that there is, as far as possible, little loss to human life and that unnecessary cruelty is avoided.[46]

Statesmanly wisdom which knows to use every means has to stand by the side of a king in his internal politics. The king has many adversaries—and a king has to be afraid of many of them since he is not sure of his life even in his own palace and has to ward off attempts of murder on the part of his relatives and descendants—if he cannot win them over by his goodness, he must make them harmless by cunningness or force. Since time immemorial, secret agents play a great role in Indian polity. They have to spy on the subjects at the order of the subjects at the order of the king and give him information on the attacks against his rule. A king is supported in his governance by his minister, by the commander of his army and by the officials. A great caution is needed while choosing them, and therefore, qualities are enumerated in their minutest details; the servants of the state are supposed to have them to know the duties in the interest of their master. One fault which must have been inextirpable among Indian officials appears to be corruptibility. Even Kauṭilya said:

> "As it is not possible not to taste honey and poison when it is on the tongue, it is not possible for the king's finance officer, not even to enjoy at least some of king's money....As it is not possible for the fish living in water to know whether they are drinking water, it is not possible for the king's employees to know whether they are taking money."[47]

A king normally inherits, gets by election or conquers by sword his rule. But there are several cases in Indian history that a capable minister restricts a weak monarch to a shadow-kingship and rules as an all-powerful "majordomo"* and then finally usurps the crown or that his descendants give to this powerful position its legal sanction. Jaina-stories describe a peculiar method of finding out a proper successor to the king who has died childless.[48] Five royal insignia are circulated, respectively carried in his capital and its surroundings, i.e. an elephant, a horse, a water-jug with the oil necessary for the anointing of the king, a Yak-tail and a sun-umbrella. If these insignia go past a man who is chosen by destiny to become the successor of the deceased king, then the elephant grunts, the horse neighs, the jug pours the oil on the chosen one, the Yak-tail fans cool air for him, the umbrella stands over his head. As soon as the bystanders know that a man is determined by these five expressions of the will of destiny (*pañcadivya*) to become their ruler, they hail him and make him their king.

---

*A man having charging a great household.

Like political science, jurisprudence of Jainas also agrees with the one of the Hindus in its main features. 18 cases of law are already distinguished in Manu's law-book. They are: 1. Recovery of debt, 2. Agreement of a contract, 3. Presentations, 4. Inheritance, 5. Border disputes, 6. Extracting wages, 7. Cancellation of buying and selling, 8. Disputes between masters and servants, 9. Deposits, 11. Sale of right to property, 11. Verbal injuries, 12. Breach of contract, 13. Sexual offences, 14. Wagers, 15. Theft, 16. Violence, 17. Assault and battery, 18. Marriage law. The individual clauses of law correspond in general with those of the Brāhmaṇa-law givers and they are obviously copied from them.[49]

But there are, of course, differences in individual cases. They are on account of the different points of view with respect to metaphysical questions. Thus, e.g. Jainas do not give any great significance to accepting the adoption of a son which the Hindus replevy because the Hindu belief that the son could stop the father from going into hell by offering the sacrifice to the dead is not shared by them. There are also other differences, like law of inheritance. Jaina-law-books like the *Bhadrabāhu-saṁhitā* give more rights to the widow than it is done by most of Hindu Dharmaśāstras. Thus a childless widow will have a free hand, according to the teachings of Jainas, with the property she had inherited from her deceased husband. She can even adopt a son without needing the agreement of the deceased husband, his legal successors or any other person. These rules have even today juristic significance and the Jaina-advocates have fought successfully in getting the peculiarities of their laws acknowledged by the courts. They also see to it that they are applied to their co-religiosists in place of the different rules of the Hindu-law.[50]

Transgressions of laws are avenged by the king or his officials by punishment (*daṇḍa*). The invention of punishment originates from Kulakaras, the patriarchs who lived in the period before the first Tīrthaṅkara Ṛṣabha. As there were disputes among the twins of the 3rd era of our world-period, Kulakaras found it necessary to inflict punishments to establish peace. Vimala-vāhana, the first of these patriarchs invented the punishment "hā-kāra"; this punishment was light like use of whip for a horse, but it was sufficient for the twins to feel ashamed and thus come back on the path of virtue. Even during the reign of the 2nd patriarch "hā-kāra" fulfilled its purpose, but the 3rd Kulakara found it necessary to introduce a more stringent punishment "mā-kāra" which was also sufficient during the rule of his successor. The 5th Kulakara and the two after him had to make use of the punishment "dhik-kāra" which was quite considerably stringent. (According to Digambaras, "hā-kāra" was used by the first 5 Kulakaras, "mā-kāra" by the next five and "dhik-kāra" by the last four.)[51] King Bharata was compelled to inflict four further punishments in order to control the worsening of the conditions that were constantly taking place all-around. They were: admonition, fastening to a particular place (*pillory*), imprisonment, cutting of one or several limbs. Added to these as the 8th punishment was withdrawal of the means of earning, etc.

It is in agreement with the religious character of the Indian law when in its law-books worldly offences are punished in the same way as those against the holy statutes of the moral world-order Hemacandra's *Arhannīti* contains, therefore, a special chapter dealing with the atonements (Prāyaścitta) which can be imposed on those who become guilty by taking food together with the people of impure castes or by other offences against the caste-order. Persons who make themselves ritually impure in this way have to atone themselves by worshipping the Jinas, by baths, fasting, pilgrimage, organization of a caste-meal, mild donations, etc. They have to face excommunication if they fail to do this.

II

Spirituality and Laymanship

1. THE CONSTITUTION OF THE COMMUNITY

Every Tīrthaṅkara founded a community (Saṅgha). It consisted of four Tīrthas, i.e. groups of worshippers, viz., 1. Sādhus, monks, 2. Sādhvīs, nuns, 3. Śrāvakas (listeners), laymen; and 4. Śrāvikās, laywomen. The spiritual organization of the Saṅgha is in the hands of monks; all other groups are subordinate to them. Monks and nuns get their livelihood from the pious donations of lay-followers and they are, thus, materially dependent upon them. The bond between the clergy and the laymen in Jainism is very close. The firm organization which Mahāvīra had given to his community assured for the laymen, from time immemorial, a decisive influence; this has hindered the rise of power-hungry priesthood taking interest in all worldly matters, and it could preserve the quality of monks with a certain restriction upon a definite level. The customary law of the Jaina-communities in Gujarāt and Rājapūtānā grants to laymen, to a very great extent, right to decide the choice, education and the conduct of life of the ascetics. G. Bühler compares in this respect the church-constitution of Jainas with the one of the Scotish Free Kirk.[52] A number of events in the recent times teach how strictly a layman keeps a watch on the life of the ascetic at many places. A Jaina-monk Jinasena appeared in Arrah in the year 1913 and begged for his livelihood from the local laymen. A few Jainas tried to know about his life before and found out that he was in reality not a proper monk and that his alleged spiritual position was only an excuse for leading a comfortable life. They had, therefore, to take action against the false Muni, and he could escape punishment only by taking a quick flight.[53] Mrs. Stevenson got acquainted with a Sādhu in Pāliṭāṇā who was wearing glasses with a golden frame. Since the monks are not allowed to possess any metal, the laymen, when they noticed this, declared that they would not consider him as an ascetic because he had broken the rule of the order.[54] Even an ascetic from the Tapā-Gaccha sect was not considered any more as belonging to the spiritual order by laymen because he travelled by train instead of wandering on foot. When once a Sthānakavāsī Sādhu in Rājkoṭ had bitten his Guru, he was immediately excommunicated. The laymen asked a tailor to come and asked him to stich normal man's clothes for the ex-ascetic, ordered him to wear them, bought a ticket for him to the place Ṭhān which was about 44 miles away and despatched him immediately. Although the former Sādhu repented his sin, he did not succeed in getting a pardon in Rājkoṭ; he had to leave the town.[55]

The supervision of laymen is not restricted only to common monks, but it is also extended to Śrīpūjyas or the chiefs of the orders. It has happened several times that laymen obstructed unworthy persons from climbing the throne (Gaddī) of the spiritual teacher, although they were selected in the prescribed manner. The Paṭṭāvalīs (lists of teachers) mention cases in which the Śrīpūjyas were removed on account of their bad behaviour by the Saṅgha—i.e. the executive body of the community. The interference of laymen is usually restricted to their own sects; Kharataras take care only of the Kharataras and the members of the Tapā-sects only of the Tapā-monks.[56]

But very often the control exercized by laymen over the life of monks is not so strict or practically does not exist. The indifference shown by laymen and their ignorance was often responsible that precepts for the ascetics were only little or not observed at all by the Yatis, and there came a complete worldliness of the clergy—an evil which could not be completely rooted out in spite of the reformative enthusiasm of pious men.

The influence which was and which is exercized by the dutiful monks on the religious life of laymen is quite significant. History has preserved for us the names of a number of excellent pastors who have guided the fates of wide circles of people and of powerful empires and shaped them in accordance with the basic principles of the Jaina-religion. Even now benevolent influences of great spiritual men are felt on the whole Jainism. Many Munis have considerably contributed in defending the faith of laymen in their battle against other religions by assisting them in their trials and tribulations, by giving them religious education and spiritual weapons; this could be maintained by Jainism of today which is beleagured around by opponents. The great respect which the Jainas of all stratas of society have shown to the excellent Sādhus, as it was done to Vijaya Dharma Sūri who died recently, clearly indicates what a strong personality is capable of doing. It is also seen from the complaints of far-sighted Jainas that small people, on the other hand, can exercise a bad influence on laymen by their fanaticism and their hostile narrow-mindedness with respect to every renovation. They hold many monks responsible for obstructing the path of progressive thoughts by their excessive conservatism and thus contributing to the decline of Jainism.

2. LAYMEN

A pious layman is obliged to take upon himself the "small vows" we have mentioned above on p. 228. This influences his whole conduct of life most strongly. He is not allowed to take food which would make him guilty of killing a living being, he is not allowed to eat either meat or honey, or certain plants like pumpkins, potatoes, onions, garlic, carrot and radish because several souls live in them; he should eat only fruits which are ripe. Alcoholic drinks are strictly forbidden and water which serves as a drink must be filtered and boiled before use so that there are no living beings in it when it is drunk. Meal must be taken before sunset because one could eat small animals along with the food by mistake on account of darkness. The religion puts restriction to a layman even with respect to the choice of occupation: professions like military service, hunting, fishing, agriculture, preparation and sale of weapons, of ivory works, of things where bones and hair are used, digging of ponds and wells, running of mills and machines, trade with animals and slaves, etc. are forbidden to him because they are likely to harm the living beings. These injunctions have never been fully observed because we come across Jaina-commanders in history and even now there are Jaina-agriculturists; but on the whole the effect of these injunctions is that a great majority of Jainas have turned to trade, particularly the trade in pearls, cloth and corns, but above all banking.

It is the duty of a layman to look after the maintenance of ascetics and religious institutions. They have always done full justice to this duty. The generosity of the well-to-do Jainas and their willingness for sacrifice has very often proved to be really great. They have not only constantly helped the numerous servants of the religion to lead a withdrawn life, but they have also built community houses and temples. It can be humanly understood that vanity and passion for fame had a strong share in the charity of great businessmen; it is seen from a remark in Mānavijaya's *Dharmasaṅgraha* that Jaina-teachers fought against the donations given out of worldly motives. This remark says that it is eight times better and more deserving to repair a ruined temple than to build a new one, because the one who pays for the repairs gets less public attention than the man who builds a new building.[57] Even now many temples are built by generous donors; but modern Jainas feel that here a wrong sense of charity prevails. For, often there are later insufficient means to preserve the temple and the cult in it, but often there is no need for new places of worship; it is said in a Jaina-Gazette that in a place like Arrah the number of cult-idols is greater than the adult male Jainas.[58]

The "Dānavīras" (heroes in giving), as the great donors are called by Jainas, have often given huge sums for public purposes of different sorts. Corresponding to the universal spirit of Jainism, the charity of the Śrāvakas is not only limited to human beings, but is also directed at animals. Jainas are used to buying a certain number of animals from butchers on festive days and set them free. The most peculiar institution of Jainas' protection of animals are the veterinary hospitals, the so-called Pāñjrāpols.

Pāñjrāpols accept animals of all types. Veterinary hospitals in Ahmedābād had, e.g. in the beginning of 1875: 265 cows and oxen, 130 buffaloes, 5 blind calves, 894 goats, 20 horses, 7 cats, 2 monkeys, 274 hens, 290 ducks, 2,000 pigeons, 50 parrots, 25 sparrows, 5 red kites and 33 other birds. The animals were either given by the owners or they were bought. The latter often happens through private persons who want to do good work and protect the animals from being slaughtered. Often an official of Pāñjrāpol appears in animal markets to save the animals from death with the help of available means. The animals are mostly reared in the home; grazing places are at the disposal of the cattle. Animals born in Pāñjrāpols are normally not sold. The cadavers of the animals dying in Pāñjrāpols are mostly given to the Dheḍs or sold; they immediately carry them and bury them after removing their hyde.

Almost all Pāñjrāpols, with the exception of the smallest, contain also an insectarium (Jivāt Khāṇa). This is supplemented in Ahmedābād by an official who carries a bag through the streets, particularly in the rainy season, when there are often stuffs which are rotten, and he collects in them mites and vermins. Corns and other things are kept in the space meant for the insects. A new space is made available at the end of every year; the old one is then closed for 10-12 years. When this period is over, it is believed that all life in it must have died; it is then emptied and its contents are sold as manure.[59]

3. MONKS AND NUNS

Monks and nuns are the persons who have renounced the world, knowing that all worldly endeavours are worthless, to lead a life dedicated to penance and religious meditation. The realization of the ascetic ideal demands a more keen observance of the five precepts meant for laymen, as also the observance of the duties we have listed on p. 231; their consequence is the warding off and the extermination of Karma. The organization of asceticism among Śvetāmbaras and Digambaras is different; it is, therefore, better that the two sects are considered separately. We shall begin with Śvetāmbaras, because they have a majority today (including Sthānakavāsīs) and because the source-material which is available on them is rich and holds the first place in its reliability.

According to the doctrine of Śvetāmbaras which is generally theoretically accepted, only those men and women are allowed to enter into a spiritual position who can look after themselves or whose parents, relatives or elders have permitted them to do it; besides they must be morally worthy and possess the necessary physical and mental strength to pursue the requirements of their profession.

The following 18 types of men cannọt be accepted in the order of monks: 1. boys under 8 years, 2. old men (they can only receive Saṁstāra, i.e. volunatary death by starvation), 3. eunuchs, 4. impotents, 5. handicapped, 6. sick (people) who are not grown for the difficulties of begging, etc., 7. thieves, 8. those who are persecuted by the king and the law, 9. those who are mentally ill, 10. blind men, 11. slaves who are bought, 12. those who are spoilt by passions and sensuous pleasures, 13. fools who cannot remember even once the names of the Jinas, 14. those who are in debts, 15. people of low births (sons of prostitutes, members of the castes of workmen which are despised) or of low disposition (murderers of Brāhmaṇas), 16. persons who have accepted certain obligations, but which they want to avoid by becoming monks, 17. servants, i.e. people who depend upon others by getting clothes and food, 18. persons who are not permitted to enter the order by their parents, guardians, superiors, etc.[60]

20 types of women are not allowed to become nuns, viz. the 18 which correspond to those of men we have just mentioned as also the 19th, i.e. those who are pregnant and the 20th, i.e. those who have yet to breastfeed the children.

But the most remarkable is the injunction against the persons who are inflicted by specially prominent infirmities, i.e. those who do not have hands or feet or other limbs of the body or those who are abnormal from their birth, like hunchbacks and dwarfs. The same rules apply to those who aspire to a higher degree of monkhood; thus someone who loses a hand or a foot after entering the spiritual status, cannot become Ācārya, etc. People having one eye are allowed into the order, but promotion to higher positions is closed for them.[61]

Asceticism, no doubt, demands renunciation of all possession, but Śvetāmbaras, allow ascetics to wear particular clothes consisting of a white (for Saṁvegīs ocher-yellow) upper and lower garment. The monk is usually provided with a few wooden (and not metal) dishes and pots which he uses to collect food and drink, a piece of cloth with which he filters water before drinking it, another piece of cloth which he often (Sthānakavāsīs do it constantly) wears in front of the mouth to obstruct gulping of air-creatures, a broom or a brush with which he sweeps the insects on his way so that he does not harm them and a (walking) staff. Idol-worshippers carry besides five shells or sandal-pieces, a book or something similar as a symbol for the absent teacher. Head is not covered; hairs are supposed to be plucked according to a strict rule, but now cutting replaces the painful pulling out (of the hair).

An ascetic must renounce all comforts. He should neither take bath nor should he brush his teeth; he must sleep on bare earth or on a hard ground; he should not kindle fire nor should he cook any food. He begs for his food from Jaina-laymen; he should not take alms from those who are not Jainas. Begging should be done only once a day and has to follow certain rules. Only those houses are to be visited whose doors are open and only that food is to be taken which the donor does not need or the food that is left-over, and not the food which is specially prepared for the beggar. The benefaction consists of rice, bread, milk-pudding, sweets and boiled water. Normally each monk does not beg for himself, but one of them does this work for others so that they can dedicate themselves undisturbed to their studies or to the exercise of penance. The food so received is brought to the Upāśraya and distributed there. Other provisions are to be taken by the ascetics only in a limited quantity; they should accept only one piece of cloth, one garment, one dish for alms, one broom or similar things necessary for their ascetic life and place them at the feet of their teacher (respectively, their superior); they should keep them only when they are permitted by him.

According to the strict doctrine of Mahāvīra, ascetics should live in a village only for one day and only five days in a city; later this rule was extended in such a way that they could stay at the most for a week in a village and a month in a city; some texts extend this stay to one, respectively two months. But during rainy season they must give up their wandering life and stay at one place so that they do not do any harm to living beings.

There are a number of regulations about the places where the ascetics are allowed to spend their night. The following passages from the old Kalpa-sūtra may give an idea about the precepts of this type which are meant for Śvetāmbara monks and nuns. I am giving them below in W. Schubring's translation:

> "If grains of rice or some beans, sesame, pulses, wheat, maize or yavayava are spilled, muddled up, mixed or scattered within a house-enclosure, then the monks or nuns should not stay there even temporarily. But when they notice that they are not lying scattered, etc., but arranged in heaps, piled up near the walls, covered or bonded with ash and cow-dung, then the monks and nuns can stay there in summers and winters....Monks and nuns should not stay even temporarily at a place if a jug containing rice-porridge or fruit-porridge or a jug with cold or warm pure water is within a house-enclosure or where light burns throughout the night or where

> torch flares. If one looks further for a house, but does not find any, then one can stay there for a night or two, but not any longer. One who still does it, gets a demotion and does penance that is required of him as a punishment for transgression of the rules."[62]

Monks and nuns live preferably in the Upāśrayas maintained by laymen. They serve as community-houses and also as constant shelter for the ascetics.

The life of monks and nuns is regulated to the minutest detail by a great number of precepts which are meant to protect them from immodesty and worldly disposition and to keep them to a life of abstinence which is dedicated to the exercise of penance and studies. The rules for nuns in parts are stricter than those for monks because they are the victims of temptation against which there is no protection. However, all these precepts have not been able to prevent the clergy from degenerating with the time. Many regulations were de facto no more in force and the old order began to shake. Thus, it happened that in spite of a great number of people who were ascetics, only less and less people could claim that they were genuine ascetics. This truth is revealed in the following verse (which is often quoted by Jainas themselves) which is ascribed to Cāṇakya (Kauṭilya):[63]

> "Every rock does not produce a precious stone,
> Every elephant does not possess a pearl,
> Every ascetic is not really an ascetic,
> And there is no sandal-tree in every forest."

It is very often explained from the circumstances which make the ascetics take to a spiritual path that many of them do not fulfil the demands made on them. In fact, only those should become monks who strive for salvation and want to run away from the chaos of Saṁsāra. But in practice many persons accept the initiation not so much out of pure motives; they consider that monkhood is a comfortable support offering them an opportunity of living comparatively, comfortably without trouble and work. But the recruits for the ascetic order do not come only from those who take to it voluntarily; for they would not be sufficient to fulfil the need for monks. "The need for the recruits is generally taken care of by the richer members of the community by buying boys in their tender age from their parents and handing them over to the Yatis for education. Illegitimate children of Brāhmaṇa-widows are preferred who can naturally be had cheaply and among whom one may presuppose favourable mental ability because the fathers mostly belong to the most educated caste in India. It is also not seldom that, particularly when high prices are demanded, children of poor Brāhmaṇas or Vāṇiās (merchants) are bought. In some cases, Yatis themselves are active and assure themselves of the followers by taking forsaken orphans or beg for the children of their coreligionists whom they like."[64] Nobody can reasonably expect that the persons who were made ascetics without feeling an inner urge to lead the life of a monk would observe the precepts very accurately; it is, therefore, not surprising that degeneration of asceticism had to set in on account of the rampancy of the practice of training children to become monks.

Śvetāmbara-monks of this type are mostly the so-called "Gorajīs" (now they are also called "Yatis"). They take the duties of a monk partially so lightly that they are not considered as real monks by many Jainas; the circumstance that they prominently consist of the people from the lower castes and of the illegitimate sons who were bought in their youth, contributes as little to secure for them social esteem, as the fact that they are generally less educated and, therefore, have only a negligible knowledge of the holy scriptures. They follow a very lax practice in observing the precepts. They do not wander about constantly, but stay only at one place, enjoy dainty food, sleep in beds, and occasionally they are guilty of breaking the vow of celibacy. Using all sorts of excuses they do not shy away from accepting money and carrying it on them, and today they give an excuse and say that Mahāvīra had prohibited them from possessing coins and not bank-notes. Their heads are administrators of great foundations which are inherited by their pupils. The sumptuous means they have enable them to appear pompously with sedans and servants. Since it is believed that Gorajīs know magic-*mantras,* they are feared by laymen so that they give them alms although their life does not agree with the rules meant for the ascetics.

Reformers who tried to get again recognition for the strict order opposed again and again the worldliness of monks. The efforts of Yaśovijaya (17th century) got these great significance among the orthodox Śvetāmbaras. He introduced an innovation that his followers, the Saṁvegī-Sādhus wear ochre-yellow clothes instead of the white so that they could be distinguished in their appearance from the "impure Yatis". The Sādhus are greatly respected on account of their strictness of morals; their number, according to Jacobi, is approximately 250.[65] The Sthānakavāsīs who are basically bent upon restoring the conditions at the time of the oldest communities also see to it strictly that their ascetics observe the precepts of their holy scriptures very accurately.

The nuns (Sādhvī) of Śvetāmbaras and Sthānakavāsīs wear a dress of the same colour like the monks. The shoulder-cloth is put over the head so that it covers the face. They are like ascetics; their hair is also plucked or cut like the hair of ascetics. Nuns constantly wander in twos and threes and live in special Upāśrayas which are under the supervision of mother-superiors. Their duty, above all, is to give religious instruction to laywomen. In contrast to the nuns of other religious communities, e.g. of Buddhism, Jaina-sādhvīs have always maintained a lofty moral status and they are, therefore, respected by all.

The clergy is differently organized among *Digambaras.* The ascetics must go naked among them because they are not allowed to possess anything, thus also clothes. But this practice cannot be strictly followed in the present circumstances. There are, therefore, today isolated Digambara ascetics who follow this practice; they live in solitude outside the cities in forests dedicating themselves completely to pious meditation.[66] Women practising penance in this manner do not exist because their going naked would be offending.

The practice of living naked in solitude was not strictly followed by Digambara-ascetics in the old period. Jinasena lets Ṛṣabha predict in *Ādipurāṇa* itself[67] (9th century A.D.) that a time would come when the Munis, united into communities, would not live in forests, and Guṇabhadra talks in his *Ātmānuśāsana* about ascetics who would live in the evil Kali-period in proximity of human dwelling, like wild animals which force their way in the night into villages.[68] Āśādhara talks in the 13th century about the Caityavāsī-Digambara-ascetics who went around naked like Arhats, but did not keep the vow strictly because they had firm dwelling places. Munis going about naked declined during Muslim-rule because Muslims persecuted naked Munis. Vasantakīrti who apparently lived in the 13th century, opined that the ascetics should carry a cloth around them when they are seen in the public. The followers of this practice, of Viśvapantha (universal path) form today a sect of Digambaras. The ascetics live in monasteries under the supervision of Bhaṭṭārakas. According to G. Bühler, the Bhaṭṭārakas take off their clothes at the meal-time and sit completely naked while a pupil rings a bell to keep the strangers from coming.[69]

There was a protest by the followers of the old strict practice against the teachings of Viśvapanthīs. These so-called "Terāpanthīs" [followers of the path of your (soul)], whose organization traces back to Paṇḍita Banārasīdās (17th century) dispute the justification of this innovation, do not acknowledge the authority of the Bhaṭṭārakas and consider the naked Munis living in jungle as the true ascetics.

There are, among Digambaras, also besides the naked monks, those who wear clothes; but they are not considered as complete ascetics, but only the laymen who have reached the highest of the 11 Pratimā-stages. They are divided into two groups, Kṣullakas and Ellakas (Ailaka). Kṣullaka wears a loin-cloth (Laṅgoṭī) and a three-yard long and one-yard broad piece of cloth over it. Ellaka.wears only a Laṅgoṭī. A bowl for alms and a whisk of peacock-feathers (instead of a brush) complete the outfit of both. They live in forests or *maṭhas*. Kṣullakas and Ellakas are allowed to eat only once during the day and they must beg for it mostly in the forenoon hours (between 10 and 11). A Kṣullaka of the three upper castes is allowed to eat the food which he has got in one house; a Śūdra may visit five houses one after the other, but has to give up his begging the moment he has got sufficient food-in a house; he then sits down there and takes his food where his daily quota is full. Ellakas follow the same precepts, but they can enjoy only one meal daily which comes from one and the same kitchen.[70]

Laymen who have reached the 7th Pratimā-stage or a higher one, but in any case persons who practise Brahmacarya act as pastors among Digambaras. They wear red clothes and are called Svāmīs, but do not practise the functions of Purohitas (priests) in the ceremonies taking place in a house or in temples.

The conditions in South India are peculiar. If the following information agrees with the facts, then a position of priesthood based on inheritance has been developed here. W. Francis makes the following notes on it in the "Gazetteer" of the South Arcot District:[71] "There are three classes of priests. Numerically biggest is the one of Arcakas (Vāḍyārs). They carry out the rites in the temples. Laymen cannot become Arcakas because they are a class in themselves. Laymen eat, no doubt, with the Arcakas, but there is no connubium among them; Arcakas, therefore, find it very difficult to find suitable brides for their sons, and often pay Rs. 200 to 300 for these. An Arcaka can climb to the next higher class of priests and become Annam or Annuvṛti (Anuvirati), a type of a monk(?) who can marry, but has to follow special precepts in the conduct of his life. These Annams can climb to the highest of these three classes and become Nirvāṇīs or Munis, monks who lead a solitary life without getting married. The monks cut their hair and wear red clothes; they carry a container of brass and a bundle of peacock-feathers; this is used to clean the place where they sit so that they do not harm the insects. All Jainas greet them in a respectful manner by "Namaskāra"; they are maintained at the cost of the communities....There is a high priest (Mahādhipati) at the top of Jainas; he is elected by the representatives of the biggest Jaina-villages. He travels around, surrounded by a retinue of followers, in a palanquin between the main places at the cost of the community, settles disputes among the castes and punishes and excommunicates people who get on the wrong side of the law. The control he has over his followers is very strict and it is in sharp contrast to the diminishing authority of many Hindu-gurus."

There are high priests of this type at different places. The high priest in the shrine of Kārkala was, e.g. Lalita Kīrti Bhaṭṭāraka Paṭṭācārya Variya Jayasvāmigaḷu in the year 1907. His festive costumes consisted of red- and gold-embroidered body-cloth, a red and golden turban and brush of peacock-feathers with a golden handle.[72]

There are also nuns among Digambaras, as we have already mentioned, but they are not "clothed in air". These Āryās (Hindī: Arjikās, called Aryāgaṇais in South India) are virgins and widows or women who have left their husbands. They observe 11 Pratimās (p. 229 f.) of lay-sisters; they pull out their hair with their own hands, wear a white Sārī and carry peacock-feathers.

III

Sects

1. SCHISM OF THE OLDER PERIOD

Jainas do not represent a united religious community, but are divided into a great number of sects. Splits among them have been the order of the day since the most ancient times. Śvetāmbaras know to report 8 schisms (Nihnava) which have arisen in the early history of the church.[73] The first two took place in Mahāvīra's times themselves. The first schismatic was his own son-in-law Jamāli. He proposed in contrast to the master his theory that an influence could be considered as over when it is completed. He did not admit that he committed a mistake and died, therefore, without getting redeemed.

The second schism came from Monk Tiṣyagupta. He refuted Mahāvīra's theory that the soul comprises all the atoms of the body, but allowed himself to be convinced finally of the fallacy of his views by a pious layman.

214 years after Mahāvīra's Nirvāṇa, Āṣāḍha's pupils proclaimed a "doctrine of indistinguishability" according to which ascetics and gods are to be treated without any distinction. This theory was proposed with respect to a peculiar event. Āṣāḍha had died suddenly one night

without anyone noticing it. Reborn as god, he immediately entered his earlier body. The pupils showed him the usual mark of respect in the wrong belief that they had before them their living teacher. But when Āṣāḍha who had become god left again the corpse and explained to his pupils their error, they claimed that one could never know whether somebody is an assiduous ascetic or a god. As they did not want to give up their heterodoxy, they were excommunicated from the community. Finally they were guided again to the correct view by King Balabhadra.

Six years later, Aśvamitra propagated a theory saying that all beings would disappear one day. Excommunicated on account of his mistake, he was later taught by a customs' officer and offered his apology.

Eight years later Gaṅga thought wrongly that two contradictory sensations, like hot and cold, are simultaneously possible. For this he was expelled, but he confessed his mistake and atoned for it.

While the last schisms concerned only minor points and ended with the final conversion of the heretics, the next one (6th) which took place 544 years after Mahāvīra's Nirvāṇa, was extremely significant. The monk Rohagupta opined that there is a third class of "Nojīva" (actually, non-life) besides the living ones (Jīva) and the lifeless ones (Ajīva). According to the opinion of Jainas, the Vaiśeṣika-system, the Brahmanic atomisticism, has emerged from this "Triassic-doctrine".

40 years later Goṣṭāmāhila claimed that the soul does not completely merge with Karma-matter, it is only touched by it, since otherwise its parting, i.e. its salvation would be impossible. He also taught that one should not take a vow of renunciation for a limited period, but for an unlimited period. His views were rejected in an assembly of the church; he was himself excommunicated because he did not retract from his stand.

The 8th great schism led to the splitting of the community into two sects, and it exists even today.

The legendary report of Śvetāmbaras on the origin of Digambaras says the following: A warrior Śivabhūti lived in the city Rathavīrapura. He had shown in a battle of local king that he was a brave warrior and was, therefore, honoured. He had become arrogant on account of this, roamed about dreaming and would come home after midnight or even later. His unfortunate wife who always waited for him in the night, told her mother of her sorrow. So she stayed there in the night, scolded him when he came home late and kept the door closed. In search of shelter he finally came to the only house whose doors were open, into the monastery, and became a monk. When he served notice to the king, he gave him a precious overcoat. The abbot asked him to return it; Śīvabhūti, however, did not listen to him. The abbot tore then the overcoat and made carpets for sitting from it. This angered Śivabhūti and he declared that he would roam about now on without clothes like Mahāvīra. He, therefore, undressed himself. His sister Uttarā wanted to emulate him, to the annoyance of the prostitutes in the town because they felt that their business would be at a disadvantage on account of it. Śivabhūti forbade the women from roaming about in nude and declared that no woman can attain Nirvāṇa. Thus, the Botika-heterodoxy came into existence in the year 609 after Mahāvīra's Nirvāṇa. All the Digambara-sects are based on it.[74]

But Digambaras explain the origin of schism differently. Their report is connected with the story of famine in Magadha (see p. 45). According to this, the monks who had not gone to Mysore and who had remained in Bihār strayed from the strict norms of Mahāvīra and did not want to give up their lax interpretation of the precepts. When Sthūlabhadra tried to bring them back to the right path, they murdered him. The disloyal ascetics formed immediately their own sect, the Ardhapālikas (perhaps: people who carry half rags). The monks of this community taught Candralekhā, the daughter of King Candrakīrti of Ujjain. When the princess married King Lokapāla of Valabhī, she called the Ardhapālikas to her new home. Her husband went to receive them. When he saw the monks coming who were "neither naked nor clothed", he turned back in anger. The queen then sent clothes to the ascetics, and now the ruler received them with honour. Since then, the Ardhapālikas kept up the habit of wearing clothes and they were named Śvetāmbaras.

Both reports on the origin by the two sects are tendentious. Each party is trying to project itself as the only true protector of the tradition and the adversaries as a heterodoxical new formation; each one of them wants also to trace back the foundation of the inimical community to an idle worldly reason. We have already considered above (see p. 45) the supposed actual causes of the split; we have also said there something about the differences in the teachings of the two sects.

2. SECTS OF THE LATER PERIOD

The great sects of Śvetāmbaras and Digambaras are both divided into a number of schools, orders and smaller sects. The causes of their origin and the differences between the two are quite diverse. Only few of them owe their origin to teachers whose views were different from those which were generally acknowledged; many came into existence purely on account of the fact that the pupils of a teacher or the monks of a place came together who felt that they belonged together as one group with respect of the others.

A number of Gaṇas "schools", Kulas "sub-classifications of schools" and Śākhās "branches" are already mentioned in the Kalpa-sūtra in which they were split. The inscriptions found in Mathurā give also names of numerous schools and their sub-classifications and thus confirm the information given in the *Kalpa-sūtra.* It is seen from inscriptions and literary sources that the conditions continued in the following period down to the present days. One can get a list of numerous such groups from careful compilation of epigraphical and other reports; but such a list can hardly include all schools which existed and still exist in Jainism, because some of them have been so insignificant that their names have not been preserved for us. One cannot exactly determine, as Jainas themselves say, the number of schools.[75] Thus, when it is said of Śvetāmbaras that there were 84 Gacchas, then it does not mean that there were really 84 Gacchas; what it means is that there were many Gacchas. (The number 84 plays a great role in India when it comes to enumeration.) It is not only from the enumerations themselves which often vary and in which the names of the few well-known schools are missing, but also on account of the fact that all these Gacchas trace back to the 84 pupils of Uddyottạna Sūri (937 A.D.) that the number 84 may not, after all, be correct. It is also true that new Gacchas came into existence in a later period, and that is why Nahar and Ghosh[76] mention over hundred of them in their list.

The number of Gacchas existing today is negligible. The most important Gacchas of Śvetāmbaras who worship idols are Tapā, Kharatara, Pāyacanda and Añcala. Among them there are reformed (yellow) and not-reformed (white) monks (Sādhus and Yatis, see p. 367); the number of the latter is considerably greater than the one of the former; the Yatis make the real majority of the order, and the Sādhus only a minority of the reformers.

H. Jacobi has described the organization of a Gaccha in accordance with the information given by Pannyāsa Gulab Vijaya in Ahmedābād. It is as follows:[77]

> "A great master, Bhaṭṭāraka, is at the head of a Gaccha (Bhaṭṭāraka is also called Śrīpūjya since the end of the 16th century). All the Yatis (monks) are

supposed to listen to him. He decided where the monks should live during the rainy season, and he alone can give the order of excommunication. The order consists of a number of groups of monks who come together around a master, Ācārya. The teacher, Upādhyāya (Vācaka, Pāṭhaka) who bequeaths the texts is under him; under him is the Paṇṇyāsa who is to supervise the ritual and the monks as far as they come into consideration. Lower than Paṇṇyāsa is Gaṇi who has studied up to Bhagavatī and who observes the external asceticism. All other Yatis are called Munis; those of them who have studied up to Mahāniṣītha are allowed to teach ascetic exercises to laymen."

An ascetic who has become a member of a Gaccha can go over to another under certain conditions. In this case he has to speak a special formula in which it is explicitly said that there is no prospect of some advantage to look for his admission to a new Gaccha.[78]

It does not appear to be necessary in the framework of this book to give the list of all well-known schools and sects;[79] I am, therefore, restricting myself to mentioning only the most important of them on which more precise information can be given. But unfortunately the material[80] at our disposal is quite scanty and, therefore, mostly only scanty and often inaccurate information can be given, and I must leave the responsibility for its correctness to my informants.

(1) Śvetāmbaras

(a) Idol-worshippers

1. *Upakeśa-Gaccha* traces its origin back to Pārśvanātha; one of his successors in guiding the community was Keśi (see p. 28). He associated himself with the reforms of Mahāvīra. The followers among the laymen are Osvāls.

2. *Kharatara-Gaccha* branched off according to one ver-

sion in the period after Uddyottana Sūri (till 937 A.D.). The first head of the Gaccha was then Vardhamāna Sūri (till 1031). His pupil Jineśvara, who was made master (Ācārya) in 1022, got the honorary title "Kharatara" (very sharp) because he remained victor in a battle of words with Surācārya, the leader of Caityavāsīs in a disputation in the court of King Durlabha of Anahilavāḍa in Gujarāt (1023 A.D.). It is said that his title was transferred to the Gaccha. According to another tradition, Jinadatta Sūri (1147 A.D.) is said to have been the founder of the Gaccha. The members of this Gaccha live mainly in Rājapūtānā and Bengāl; they are very few in the Bombay Presidency. The number of Sādhus is approximately 50-75 and those of the Sādhvīs 300. The Yatis are in great numbers; their Śrīpūjyas are highly respected by the followers of the Gaccha.

3. *Tapā-Gaccha* branched off after Uddyottana Sūri (till 937 A.D.). As Uddyottana had made his pupil Sarvadeva a Sūri under a fig-tree (Vaṭa), the name of the school at first was Vaṭa-gaccha. Jagaccandra (died in 1228 A.D.) was one of the successors of Sarvadeva. A king saw him doing penance (Tapas) according to an old practice and therefore, gave the school the name Tapā-gaccha. The Tapā-gaccha today is the most important of the Śvetāmbara-sects. Its followers live in Bombay Presidency, the Pañjāb, Rājapūtānā and Madrās. At present 400 Sādhus and 1,200 Sādhvīs belong to it and they are under 13 Ācāryas. Further, the number of Yatis who are obedient to Śrīpūjyas is very great. There must have been on the whole 12 "Gaddīs" (Thrones, i.e. seats) of these; the most senior Śrīpūjya is said to have lived in the princely state of Jaipur.

4. *Pārśvacandra (Pāścandra-)-Gaccha* is a branch of Tapā-Gaccha. The teacher Pārśvacandra belonging to Tapā-Gaccha (born in 1480 in Hamrīpur, died in 1555) left it in 1515 because he proposed a new doctrine on action and did not consider a number of works (Niryuktis, Bhāṣyas, Cūrṇis, Chedagranthas) as authoritative. The

sect has its followers today in Ahmedābād district. It is said that 8-10 Sādhus and 20-25 Sādhvīs belong to it, besides a large number of Yatis. Their Śrīpūjya has a seat in Bīkāner.

5. *Paurṇamīyaka-Gaccha* was founded by Candraprabha in 1102 A.D. He had proposed doctrines which were different from the ritual and he did not consider Mahāniśītha-sūtra as canonic. The sect was driven out by King Kumārpāla from his empire at the behest of Hemacandra. After the death of the two adversaries, Paurṇamīya Sumatisiṁha came to Anahilvāḍa and revived the school; it was then called Sārdha-(=half) or Sādhu-paurṇamīyaka (1180 A.D.). It appears that there are no more Sārdha-pauraṇamīyakas or Paurṇamīyakas.

6. *Añcala-Gaccha* (also called Vidhi-pakṣa) traces back its teachers to Uddyottana; its founder was Upādhyāya Narasiṁha, called later as Ārya-rakṣita Sūri (1157 A.D.). According to the tradition he had been a Paurṇamīyaka before. It is said that the blind Śrāvikā Nāṭī played a significant role in the origin of the Gaccha.

The name of the sect is derived from the practice that in it the seam (Añcala) of the garment can be used in place of mouth-cloth. Today 10-15 Sādhus and 30-40 Sādhvīs belong to the sect. The Sādhus do not have an Ācārya at the moment, but the Yatis have a Śrīpūjya. Śrīpūjyas are highly respected in the Añcala-Gaccha.

7. *Āgamika-Gaccha* was founded in 1193 by Śīlaguṇa and Devabhadra who were first Paurṇamīyakas and then Āñcalikas. They did not worship the Kṣetradevatās. The school of the Kaṭukas founded by Kaṭuka emerged in 1507 from this school. They were also called Munyaris (enemies of the ascetics) because the sect consisted only of laymen.

(b) Idol-Fiends

1. *Lumpāka (Loṅkā-) Gaccha* was founded in 1451 by Loṅka Śā who opposed idol-worship. (For details see p.

73.)

2. The Veṣadharas who have emerged from the Lumpākas get their name from their peculiar dress (Veṣa). They were established by Bhānaka in 1467 (or 1476); he came from the region of Sirohī. A branch under Rūpa split from them in 1511; the old group was called Nāgpurīya Veṣadharas, the new one Gujarātī Veṣadharas.

3. The *Vandhyas* are a sect of Veṣadharas which was founded by Bīja in 1513.

4. The *Sthānakavāsīs* (those living in community-home and not in temple) or Bistolas, mocked also as *Ḍhūṇḍiyās* (seekers), owe their origin to the reform of Lava, who was Vīra's son. He stood against the grievences which had spread among the followers of Loṅkā in the year1663 (compare p. 78).

5. The *Terāpanthīs* are a very strict sect which is hostile to idols. It was founded by Bhikham in Mārvār. Their name is said to have come from the number of originators of their community (*terah*=13). H. Jacobi writes on them:[81]

> "They try to let the conduct of life of the monks exactly agree with the precepts of the canonic scriptures and expect from them unswerving observance. In fact, I am told that Yatis belonging to this community died on their wanderings because they could not get water which the monks were allowed to drink according to their precepts although there was no scarcity of water. It is strange that the Terāpanthīs do not consider it to be their duty or even only a good work to save a being threatened by danger to its life; for, one must allow to let the Karma have its course. The most peculiar in this sect, which was so far almost completely unknown to us, is that there is a very strict spiritual regimentation among them. The head, the Pūjyajī Mahārāja, has a position which can be compared with the one

held by the general among the Jesuits: all monks owe him unconditional obedience and for that purpose they must sign a letter of guarantee every day. The sect is said to have 70 monks and about 210 nuns; for many widows prefer a spiritual status to the difficult fate of a widow. This is mainly spread in Western India; but the laymen of the Terāpanthīs are also found in all great commercial centres up to Calcutta."

(2) Digambaras

(a) The Great Schools

According to the tradition of Digambaras, the "Mūla-saṅgha" (i.e. the original community) was divided into 4 schools for practical reasons in Saṁvatsara 26 by the great teacher Arhadbalī (known also as Guptigupta or Viśākha). Their heads were four of his pupils. These schools were:

1. Nandī-saṅgha founded by Maghanandī. The school is said to have got the name from the fact that its founder had meditated under a fig-tree (Nandī) during the rainy season.
2. Sena-saṅgha, founded by Jinasena.
3. Siṁha-saṅgha, founded by Siṁha who is said to have spent the rainy season in the cave of a lion.
4. Deva-saṅgha, founded by Deva who had lived in a village belonging to a courtesan by name Devadattā.

Each one of these Saṅghas is further divided into several sub-schools. The monks affix certain words to their names; these indicate their affiliation to the concerned Saṅgha. These titles are among the first: Nandī, Candra, Kīrti, Bhūṣaṇa; among the second: Rāja, Vīra, Bhadra, Sena; among the third: Siṁha, Kumbha, Aśrava, Sāgara and among the fourth: Deva, Datta, Nāga and Tuṅga. The ascetics carry a fan of peacock-feathers and are greeted with the word "Dharmavṛddhi".

In contrast to the schools of the "Mūlasaṅgha" which are considered as orthodox, a few sects came up which depart from these in some points of religious practices. They are, therefore, considered as heterodoxical. The most important of them are the following:[82]

1. Drāviḍa-saṅgha (also called Dramila-saṅgha) was founded in Madurai by Vajranandī, a pupil of Pūjyapāda, apparently in the year 526 after Vikarma (583 A.D.?). The schism apparently took place on account of the dispute over the question whether one should eat certain plants; it is said that the followers of this school permit bathing in cold water and are engaged in commercial transactions.
2. Yāpanīya-saṅgha (also called Gopya-saṅgha) was founded by a former Śvetāmbara-monk Śrī-kalaśa in the year 705 after Vikrama(?) in the city of Kalyāṇa. The monks who are saluted with the word "Dharmalābha" believe that women can get salvation and that the Kevalīs can enjoy food; thus they agree with Śvetāmbaras in these points.
3. Kāṣṭhā-saṅgha, was founded by Kumārasena, a pupil of Vinayasena, in a village called Nandītaṭa in the year 753 after Vikrama(?) according to one version; but according to another version, it was already founded in the year 515 after Vikrama by Loha I, and on the basis of the following event. Loha had become critically ill in Hisār near Agrohā and had lost his consciousness. Thinking that he would die, his laymen vowed the oath of Saṁlekhanā. But Loha recovered again against expectation. When he was begging, the Śrāvakas refused him alms in view of the Saṁlekhanā-vow. So Loha went to Agrohā and converted King Divākara and 1,25,000 Agravālas to the Jaina-faith with the help of his sermon. They worshipped him as Ācārya and

supported him. His community was called Kāṣṭhā (wood) Saṅgha because the idols he used in his cult were wooden. The monks are saluted with word "Dharmavṛddhi" and carry a fan of cow-hair instead of peacock-feathers.

4. Mathurā-saṅgha, founded in the year 953 after Vikrama(?) by Rāmasena in Mathurā. The monks are welcomed with word "Dharmavṛddhi" and they do not carry any fan.

It appears that only the Kāṣṭhā-saṅgha of these four sects exists today.

(b) The Present Sects

The present Digambara-Jainas are divided into a larger number of sects which are different from one another in unimportant points of the doctrine, but also in a few important points of the ritual.

The two most important Digambara-sects of today are the Viśvapanthīs or Visapanthīs (Bispanthīs), as they are mostly called today, and the Terāpanthīs. We have already discussed their origin (see p. 81). The following are the main differences between the two sects: Viśapanthīs recognize Bhaṭṭārakas (p. 388) as spiritual leaders, install images of Kṣetrapālas, of gods like Bhairva, etc. in their temples, cover the idols with saffron, embellish them with flowers, offer them sweets, worship them with gifts in the night and wave lights in front of them. Terāpanthīs do not accept any Bhaṭṭārakas, do not install images of Kṣetrapālas, do not offer flowers or sweets to the idols, do not apply saffron to them, do not worship them in the night with offerings and lights, but restrict themselves to reciting Ārātrika-pāṭha.[83] According to J.L. Jaini, Viśapanthīs worship in sitting position and Terāpanthīs in standing position; Terāpanthīs sit only when they count the pearls of their rosaries while gently uttering the *mantras.*[84] It can be seen from all this that Terāpanthīs are a sect of reformists; they are against a number of rites which do not belong to Jainism according to their view. They have nothing to do with Terāpanthīs of Śvetāmbaras. The opposition between the Visapanthīs and Terāpanthīs is so great that they do not visit one another's temples.

Visapanthīs are in great numbers in Mahārāṣtra and Gujarāt and Terāpanthīs outnumber in Rājapūtānā, in Uttar Pradesh and Madhya Pradesh.

Other Digambara-sects of the present-day are: Teraṇapanthīs or Samaiyapanthīs; their community was founded by Taranasvāmī (1448-1515). They are hostile to the idols, but worship the 14 books of their founder (Granthas) by keeping them on the altar. Then there are Gumānpanthīs who take their origin from Gumān Rām (end of the 18th century); and finally the Totāpanthīs about whom there is no information.

REFERENCES

1. Samantabhadra, *Ratnakaraṇḍa-śrāvakācāra*, 120.
2. George Bühler, *Uber die indische Sekte der Jaina*, p. 36.
3. Hemacandra, *Pariśiṣṭhaparva*, 89-200.
4. Bühler, *ibid.*, p. 36. H. Jacobi knew a Parsi who was converted to Jainism.
5. Samuel Beal, *Si-yu-ki, Buddhist Records of the Western World*, London, 1906, I, p. 55.
6. Pullé, *GSAI*, I, 1887, p. 55.
7. A. Grünewedel, *Alt-kutscha*, Berlin, 1920, I, p. 10 and 12.
8. G. Bühler, *Ind. Antq.* 7, 1878, p. 28.
9. F. Buchanan, Particulars of the Jainas, *Asiatic Researches IX*, 1807, p. 208.
10. *Ādipurāṇa* 6, 183 ff.; 38, 3 ff. More in my treatise in the *Jacobi-Festschrift*.
11. Bhadrabāhu's *Kalpa-Sūtra*, Jinacarita § 17.
12. *Bombay Gazetteer* 4, p. 106.
13. *Jaina Gazette* X, No. 4, April 1904.
14. *Imperial Gazetteer of India*, 1907, I, p. 416.
15. J.L. Jaini, *Jaina Law*, p. 77.
16. *Census of India 1911*, XXI, Mysore, p. 177.

17. *Bombay Gazetteer* 7, p. 56.
18. Dr. Buchanan-Hamilton, *Transactions of the RAS,* I, 1824, p. 524 and 537 made us aware of this for the first time.
19. *Bombay Gazetteer,* 23, p. 280; they are partially selected from the Caturthas and Pañcamas (*ibid.*, 24, p. 135).
20. *Census 1901*, XIX, p. 66.
21. J. Tod., *Annals of Rājasthān,* 1832, II, 166.
22. J.N. Bhattacharya, *Hindu Castes and Sects,* Calcutta, 1896, p. 207 makes a distinction between "Srimals" and "Srisrimals" who are supposed to form a caste with the "Ossawals" and "Srimalis". The last ones, according to him, are members of a special caste and they cannot marry others.
23. H. Jacobi writes to me: "The Porvāls or Prāgvātas were not originally a "merchant's caste"; see Jacobi's edition of Haribhadra's "Sanata-kumāra-caritaṁ" (Munich, 1921), Introduction, p. X f., and the treatise of Kielhorn, Epigr. Indica IX, p. 151 cited here."
24. J. Tod, *Western India,* p. 465; Sir A. Baines, *Indian Ethnography,* Straβburg, 1921, p. 33.
25. *Bombay Gazetteer,* 9, 1, p. 97.
26. U.D. Barodia, *History and Literature of Jainism,* p. 50.
27. J.N. Bhattacharya, *Hindu Castes and Sects,* p. 205.
28. Cf. *Bombay Gazetteer* 9, 1, p. 97.
29. Sir A. Baines, *ibid.*, p. 34.
30. *Bombay Gazetteer* 9, 1, p. 73.
31. Syed Siraj ul Hassan, *Castes and Tribes of H.E.H. the Nizam's Dominion,* I, p. 259.
32. *Bombay Gazetteer* 4, p. 113.
33. *Ibid.*, 19, p. 58 f.
34. *Ibid.*, 23, p. 80 f.
35. *Census 1911*, XXI, p. 59.
36. *Ibid.*, p. 177.
37. *Bombay Gazetteer* 7, p. 67.
38. *Ibid.*, 17, p. 99; 12, p. 71.
39. *Ibid.*, 12, p. 71.
40. *Ibid.*, 23, p. 280 f; 24, 135; Syed Siraj ul Hassan, *ibid.*, p. 263.
41. *Bombay Gazetteer* 24, p. 135.
42. G. Bühler, *WZKM* 4, 1890, p. 324.
43. "Rājā rājyam" *iti prakṛtisaṁkṣepa* (*Arthaśāstra,* p. 325).
44. Hemacandra, *Arthan-nīti,* I, 44 (p. 9).
45. Somadeva, Nītivākyāmṛta, Bombay, 1887, p. 14 according to M. Winternitz, *Gesch. der ind. Literatur,* III, p. 529.
46. It can be deduced from the inscription 57 in B.L. Rice's "Inscriptions of Śṛavaṇa Beḷgoḷa" *[Epigr. Carnatica,* Vol. II, p. 145

(Banglore, 1889)] that the Jainas had even treated the art of warfare scientifically. In this 338 different cuts and thrusts used in a battle are distinguished.

47. Kauṭilya, *Arthaśāstra*, p. 69 f.; Winternitz, *Gesch. der ind. Literatur*, III, p. 512.
48. Joh. Hertel, *Das Pañcatantra*, Leipzig, 1914, p. 374; *Indische Märchenromane*, I, p. 76. King Nanda (p. 34) is said to have got the throne in this way (Bhandarkar, *Report*, 1883/85, p. 132).
49. Padmaraja Pandit, *A Treatise on Jain Law and Usages*, Bombay, 1886, Karnataka Press and J.L. Jaini, *Jaina Law: Bhadrabāhu Saṁhitā*, Arrah, 1916 give a brief survey on the Jaina law.
50. J.L. Jaini, *Jaina Law*. There are in it several examples.
51. Nemicandra, *Triloka-sāra*, 798.
52. G. Bühler, *Deutsche Revue* XIX, 1894, 4, p. 228.
53. *Jaina Gazette* IX, 11, November 1913, p. 8.
54. Stevenson, *Heart of J.*, p. 226 f.
55. *Ibid.*, page 211, note 2.
56. G. Bühler, *WZKM* 4, 1890, p. 326.
57. *Dharmasaṅgraha* I, p. 252a. That is why Samprati got 89,000 temples repaired and constructed only 36,000 new ones; Kumārapāla and Vāstupāla also acted similarly.
58. *Jaina Gazette* X, 1914, No. 4, p. 153.
59. *Bombay Gazetteer* 4, p. 114 f.
60. *Ācāradinakara*, p. 74 f.
61. *Ibid.*, 75 a.
62. W. Schubring, *Das Kalpa-Sūtra*, p. 50.
63. O. Böhtlingk, *Indische Sprüche* (2nd ed., 1873), No. 6523; used as a motto in Vidyāvijaya's "Ādarśa Sādhu" (Shri-Vijayadharmasūri-Jivanavṛtta)? Bhavnagar, 1918.
64. G. Bühler, *Leben Hemacandras*, p. 9, comp. p. 59.
65. Jacobi, *Archiv für Religionswissenschaft*, XVIII, 1915, p. 271. The Jainas gave me numbers which were quite divergent.
66. A Hindī-newspaper is trying to find out, at my request, the names of the Jaina-ascetics who wander about in nude. The names of the naked Munis given to me in a reply are: Śāntisāgara, Ādisāgara I, Ādisāgara II in Belgaum, Candrasāgara in Jhalrāpaṭan, etc.
67. *Ādipurāṇa* 41; cf. V. Glasenapp in the *Jacobi-Festschrift*.
68. According to the information given by Mr. Chhotelal Jain in Calcutta in his letter.
69. G. Bühler, *Ind. Antq.* 7, 1878, p. 28. The correctness of this information is disputed by the Digambaras in a letter; but a similar information is also available in Syed Siraj ul Hassan, *The Castes and Tribes of H.E.H. the Nizam's Dominions* I, p. 259 (Bombay, 1920).

70. Champat Rai Jain in *The Householder's Dharma*, p..69 f.
71. E. Thurston, *Castes and Tribes of Southern India*, Madras, 1909, II, p. 432 f. and 430.
72. *Ibid.*, p. 424. Even the High-priest of Śravaṇa Beḷgoḷa whom Sir Charles Eliot visited, wore a purple garment (Eliot, *Hinduism and Buddhism*, London, 1921, I, p. 117, note). The Digambaras are, therefore, also called today "Raktāmbaras" (wearing red-coloured garments).
73. E. Lehmann, "Die alten Berichte von den Schismen der Jaina" in *Ind. Studien* 17, 1885, p. 91 ff.
74. According to Devendra's Vṛtti on Uttarādhyayana-Sūtra,. transl. by Jacobi, *ZDMG* 38, 1884, p. 1 ff.; comp. Weber, "*Kupakṣa-kauśikaditya des* Dharmasāgara", *Sitzungsberder Berliner Akademie*, 1882, p. 796.
75. Written information given by Vijaya Indra Sūri.
76. *Epitome of J.*, p. 669 f.
77. H. Jacobi, *Archiv für Religionswissenschaft* XVIII, 1915, p. 270.
78. W. Schubring, *Das Mahānisīha-Sutta*, p. 82.
79. Miles, *Transact. of the RAS*, III, 358 ff. (some also Dalamaine, *ibid.*, I, 414 ff.) enumerates a great number of sects and sub-sects.
80. Particularly Dharmasāgara's "Sonne für die Eulen der Irrlehren", a controversial treatise written by a Śvetāmbara in 1573 (Weber, *Sitzungsber. der Berliner Akademie*, 1882, p. 796) serves as a source. This work deals with 10 sects, but does not take into account those which were not significant during the period of Dharmasāgara and obviously ignored those which came up latter. A Digambara-treatise like this is Devasena's "Darśana-sāra", which is said to have been written in 990 after Vikrama (1047 A.D.). There is also useful information in Guṇaratna's commentary on Haribhadra's "Ṣaḍdarśana-samuccaya". These informations were supplemented by the (scanty and inaccurate) datas in the reports of the "Census of India" and the Gazetteers, by the notices of Nahar and Ghosh and by correspondence which I owe to Ācārya Vijaya Indra and Mr. Chhotelal Jain.
81. *Archiv für Religionswissenschaft* XVIII, 1915, p. 272. Comp. also Appendix IV in *Census of India*, 1921, Vol. I.
82. Devasena's "Darśana-sāra" and Guṇaratna on Haribhadra's "Ṣaḍdarśana-samuccaya" IV, beginning.
83. According to a written information given by Vijaya Indra.
84. J.L. Jaini, *Ind. Antq.* 33, 1904, p. 330 f.

SECTION VI

Cult

A. General Part

1. PREREQUISITES AND OBJECTS OF THE JAINA CULT

Jainas refute the existence of a personal god who has created the world and who rules over it. They do not believe that the saints attaining perfection can interfere in the fate of human beings. They grant only a limited life span and limited power to the numerous Devas who rule in many heavens. And yet, their religion has a well-developed cult, a rich ritual and marvellous temples. The contradiction which a person familiar with the occidental systems of religion appears to see in this is cleared when one takes into consideration the peculiar spiritual attitude from which Jainas want to look at their cult.

The goal of all religious actions is to free the soul from all the impurity that is attached to it and from the Karma and passion and to establish it in its true, pure, spotless and blissful condition. All those many precepts, vows, mortifications, observances and rites prescribed by the Tīrthaṅkaras to the believers serve to attain this goal. It is true, many apply only to an individual, are meant for an individual and are to be realized as such by an individual. The psychological knowledge that an individual as a member of a community overcomes more easily the resistance in himself put up by imperfection and indifference with respect to religious observances, made Jainas, like the followers of other religions, take up their religious exercises jointly, systematically and keep up to certain norms. But this is known from experience that nothing spurs so strongly the enthusiasm of a believer as the example of a great man, whom an individual, as far as it is in his weak power, emulates, the one who is a shining example for all his efforts, what he hopes to achieve once later. He worships him as a master to whom he is dedicated in love with the whole fervour of his heart. The ideal of a Jaina which is not yet attained, but which can be attained, is the Perfect One who is detached from the world, who has overcome hatred and love and who has become omniscient by conquering all delusions. Such a man who has attained Nirvāṇa after destroying the whole Karma and whom, therefore, all beings serve, is alone a true god (Deva) because he is no more subject to the laws of existence:

> Only the omniscient whose fame has permeated the world,
> For, he has vanquished all passions and sins,
> One who has taught wisdom to all living beings,
> He alone is praised as god and the highest Lord.[1]

Such a person who has conquered the world and proclaimed salvation, whom even the heavenly kings approach with reverence, is alone worthy to be worshipped, the one who is, for the humanity, an example of a person who is detached from the world. He alone can guide humanity on its way to salvation. The one who has him constantly before his eyes, the one who is immersed forever in his endless virtues and merits, will be, thereby, himself promoted and elevated; he would thereby approach slowly but surely the condition which is peculiar to him; he would be like him and may hope finally to be identical with him. Just as the look of a beautiful woman awakens the feeling of love, the look of a friend the feeling of friendship, so the feeling of saintliness is awakened in the one who is busy in his thoughts with a Jina, or concentrates upon his image. His heart is purified by this feeling. By constant occupation with the sublime Arhats, his mind finally assumes their qualities, just like a crystal which reflects the colour of the object which is in its proximity.

Thus, according to the Jaina-theory, the worship of the Tīrthaṅkaras has no objective goal, but only a subjective one: the Tīrthaṅkaras themselves do not need any adoration because they are elevated above everything that is mundane, and a believer does not get any mercy through them because they do not pay any attention to the activity in the world in their blissful perfection; but the Jina-cult is beneficial and necessary for salvation because the one who accomplishes it, turns a new leaf in his life and is redeemed on account of it.

The view that is underlying here that one, who merges all his thinking with another one, experiences finally a great change in his nature, that he becomes similar to him or finally identical with him, is genuinely Indian; it is clearly expressed in the oft-quoted Vedānta-metaphor of a worm which finally becomes itself a wasp by constantly thinking of the wasp it has seen.[2]

The sublime basic idea of Jina-worship has, however, not remained preserved among all the Jainas in this its pure form. It is not sufficient for a common man to worship a Tīrthaṅkara and ask him for enlightenment, if he has to say at the end that the whole service dedicated to him is only a propaedeutic fiction which is supposed to promote the one who worships. He wants himself to talk with a blessed saint who is detached from the world as if talking to a king; he wants to pour out his heart to him, confess his sufferings and hopes to get from his mercy help even in the small and big wants of his life. And that is why worship made to the Arhats has often assumed the forms of the Hinduistic cult of gods in the popular Jaina-faith; the pious man offers flowers and other gifts to the Tīrthaṅkara and expects from him a corresponding *quid pro quo.* But the right-believing Jainas judge such a *do ut des** cult as an efflux of heterodoxy and they combat it.

All the Tīrthaṅkaras who appeared, appear and will appear in the different parts of the world are worshipped. But it is primarily obviously the 24 Tīrthaṅkaras who appeared in the Bharatavarṣa in our world-period are mainly worshipped; it is seen from the number of hymns and shrines dedicated to them that Ādinātha (Ṛṣabha), the first Tīrthaṅkara, Śantinātha, the 16th and the last three Neminātha, Pārśvanātha and Mahāvīra, are the most popular. Of the other Tīrthaṅkaras from the other parts of the world, Sīmaṅdhara, who now lives in Mahāvideha, enjoys, above all, a great respect.

Tīrthaṅkaras are the most prominent among the 5 "Parameṣṭhīs" or the chiefs of Jainism. Four others apart from them are: Siddhas or the Perfect Ones, Ācāryas or the masters, Upādhyāyas or the teachers and Munis or the ascetics. They are also given their due respect in the cult although their service is not so prominent as a result of the impersonal character which the worship of a group brings with itself. The most remarkable from among the individual persons belonging to this group are Bāhubalī or Gommaṭa, Ṛṣabha's son (we discussed his salvation on p. 295), then the Gaṇadharas, i.e. the pupils of the Tīrthaṅkaras, above all, Gautama. Then we have a number of saints of the later period who shared this honour on account of their piousness. Even the holy women belong to this category like the mothers of the Tīrthaṅkaras and the prominent nuns of the legends who (according to the view of Śvetāmbaras) attained salvation.

All the personalities discussed here so far to whom the Jaina-faith dedicates a cult are blessed beings; they are elevated above the life in the Saṁsāra. Jainas worship besides and beside them other supermundane persons who, however, do not possess the same level of perfection as these, but who show a great understanding

*I give you that you give.

for mundane life. We have to mention in this respect primarily the heavenly companions of the Tīrthaṅkaras, one Yakṣa (spirit) and one Śāsanadevatā (goddess of the Doctrine) who stand by the side of every Jina and, when they wandered on the earth, who reckoned with their orders. The names of the Yakṣas and Śāsanadevatās of the 24 Tīrthaṅkaras of the present world-period are partially different among Śvetāmbaras and Digambaras. They are (the number of the left corresponds to the one of the Tīrthaṅkara to whom these deities belong, thus 1. Ṛṣabha, 2. Ajita, etc., compare above p. 288):[3]

<table>
<tr><th></th><th colspan="2">Yakṣas</th><th colspan="2">Śāsanadevatās</th></tr>
<tr><th>Sl.No.</th><th>Śvetāmbaras</th><th>Digambaras</th><th>Śvetāmbaras</th><th>Digambaras</th></tr>
<tr><td>1.</td><td colspan="2">Gomukha</td><td></td><td>Cakreśvarī</td></tr>
<tr><td>2.</td><td colspan="2">Mahāyakṣa</td><td>Ajitabalā</td><td>Rohiṇī</td></tr>
<tr><td>3.</td><td colspan="2">Trimukha</td><td>Duritārī</td><td>Prajñāptī</td></tr>
<tr><td>4.</td><td colspan="2">Yakṣeśvara</td><td>Kālikā</td><td>Vajraśṛṅkhalā</td></tr>
<tr><td>5.</td><td colspan="2">Tumbura</td><td>Mahākālī</td><td>Puruṣadattā</td></tr>
<tr><td>6.</td><td colspan="2">Kusuma</td><td>Acyutā (Śyāmā)</td><td>Manovegā (Manoguptī)</td></tr>
<tr><td>7.</td><td>Mātaṅga</td><td>Varanandī</td><td>Śāntā</td><td>Kālī</td></tr>
<tr><td>8.</td><td>Vijaya</td><td>Śyāma</td><td>Bhṛkuṭī</td><td>Jvālamālinī</td></tr>
<tr><td>9.</td><td colspan="2">Ajita</td><td>Sutārakā</td><td>Ajitā(Mahākālī)</td></tr>
<tr><td>10.</td><td colspan="2">Brahmā</td><td>Aśokā</td><td>Mānavī</td></tr>
<tr><td>11.</td><td colspan="2">Manuja or Īśvara</td><td>Śrīvatsā (Mānavī)</td><td>Gaurī</td></tr>
<tr><td>12.</td><td>(Sura-) Kumāra</td><td></td><td>Caṇḍā</td><td>Gāndhārī</td></tr>
<tr><td>13.</td><td>Ṣaṇmukha</td><td></td><td>Vijayā (Viditā)</td><td>Vairoṭī</td></tr>
<tr><td>14.</td><td colspan="2">Pātāla</td><td>Aṅkuśā</td><td>Anantamatī</td></tr>
<tr><td>15.</td><td colspan="2">Kinnara</td><td>Paṇṇagā (Kaṇḍarpā)</td><td>Mānasī</td></tr>
<tr><td>16.</td><td>Garuḍa</td><td>Kiṁpuruṣa</td><td>Nirvāṇī</td><td>Mahāmānasī</td></tr>
<tr><td>17.</td><td>Gandharva</td><td></td><td>Balā</td><td>Vijayā</td></tr>
<tr><td>18.</td><td>Yakṣendra</td><td>Kendra</td><td>Dhāriṇī</td><td>Ajitā</td></tr>
<tr><td>19.</td><td colspan="2">Kubera</td><td>Dharaṇapriyā</td><td>Aparājitā</td></tr>
<tr><td>20.</td><td colspan="2">Varuṇa</td><td>Naradattā</td><td>Bahurūpiṇī</td></tr>
<tr><td>21.</td><td>Bhṛkuṭi</td><td></td><td>Gāndhārī</td><td>Cāmuṇḍī</td></tr>
</table>

	Yakṣas		*Śāsanadevatās*	
Sl.No.	*Śvetāmbaras*	*Digambaras*	*Śvetāmbaras*	*Digambaras*
22.	Gomedha	Sarvāhna	Ambikā	Kuṣmāṇḍinī
23.	Dharaṇendra (Pārśvayakṣa)		Padmāvatī	
24.	Mātaṅga		Siddhāyaikā	

The Yakṣas and the Śāsanadevatās are often depicted along with the Tīrthaṅkaraṣ to whom they belong. They have the appearance of the Brahmanic gods. Some of them even (like Brahmā, Kumāra, Kubera, Varuṇa, Kālī, Gaurī) share their names with them.

Further the 16 "goddesses of learning" (Vidyādevatās) are to be mentioned as the special Jaina-deities. Their names among Śvetāmbaras (according to Hemacandra[4]) are:

1. Rohiṇī 2. Prajñapatī 3. Vajraśṛṅkhalā, 4. Kuliśāṅkuśā, 5. Cakreśvarī, 6. Naradattā, 7. Kālī, 8. Mahākālī, 9. Gaurī, 10. Gāndhārī, 11. Savāstramahājvālā, 12. Mānavī, 13. Vairoṭyā, 14. Acchuptā, 15. Mānasī, 16. Mahāmānasikā.

The names of some of them agree with those of the Śāsanadevatās, particularly those in the list of Digambaras.

Peculiar to Jainas is the worship of Indras, i.e. of the kings of the gods of different heavens. Their number among Śvetāmbaras is 64,[5] and it is 100 among Digambaras;[6] but these numbers do not go along with those enumerated above on p. 269 when we discussed the cosmology.

The Jainas of today worship even a number of gods of the Hindu-pantheon. I shall give here a list of the most important ones. They are enumerated in the handbooks of ritual.

Indra, Agni, Yama, Nirṛti, Varuṇa, Vāyu, Kubera, Īśāna, Nāgas (serpent-gods) and Brahmā are enumerated in Vardhamāna Sūri's *Ācāradinakara* (p. 224b); a *mantra* of blessing in Sukhalājī's *Pañcapratikramaṇa* (p. 292) mentions 8 Lokapālas (guardians of the world): Soma, Yama, Varuṇa, Kubera, Indra, Āditya, Skanda, Vināyaka (Gaṇeśa). In *Ācāradhikaraṇa*(1) (p. 223a) different gods are connected with the houses of the moon: Bṛahaspati, Pitaras (Manes), Yoni, Aryamā, Viśvakarmā, Mitra, Jala, Viśvadevas, Viṣṇu, Vasus, Ajapāda, Ahirbudhnya, Pūṣā are mentioned besides those whose names have appeared here. Besides, there are the gods of the 9 planets: Sūrya (Sun), Candra (Moon), Maṅgala (Mars), Budha (Mercury), Guru (Jupiter), Śukra (Venus), Śani (Saturn), Rāhu and Ketu (Nodes), as also the genii of the signs of animal-circle and the houses of the Moon (Nakṣatras) and finally the patrons of the lands, cities and villages (Kṣetrapāla; Deśa-, Nagara- and Grāmadevatā).

Of the female deities we have primarily to mention the six goddesses Śrī, Hrī, Buddhi, Dhṛti, Kīrti and Lakṣmī; they live, according to the Digambara tradition, on the islands of the six big mountains of Jambūdvīpa.[7] Then Sarasvatī, the guardian of learning, and then numerous "mother-goddesses". Even every caste and every family has a patron-goddess (Jñātidevī, Kuladevī). The family deity of the Viśās Uśvas is, i.e. Uśādevī; her idol is at the entrance of the Hathisiṅgh's temple in Ahmedābād.[8]

Finally religious service is dedicated also to the holy animals, like the serpent-gods, holy trees, like those which are holy for the Tīrthaṅkaras, holy places and holy symbols. Even the temples, images and books are made an object of the cult.

The worship of the Hindu-deities—primarily Gaṇeśa, Skanda, Sarasvatī, the Mothers as also Bhairon and Hanumān—has got so much importance in the Jainism of today that the cult of the Tīrthaṅkaras has strongly receded behind it. Thus, the "Jaina Hostel Magazine" IV (1923) No. 2, p. 60 reports on Champat Rai Jain of Delhi, one of the most enthusiastic pioneers of the Jaina-doctrine: "Albeit being Jaina by birth, Mr. Champat Rai Jain, like many others, did not know anything about Jainism except the fact that there are 24 gods in it. There is no doubt that the religion of his family was

Jainism; but the family-head worshipped almost exclusively the Hindu-deity Hanumān whose temple he visited everyday, whereas he visited the Jaina-temple only thrice in the year on festive occasions." Similar information is given in Census-reports and the District-Gazetteers on the situations in different parts of the country. A strong Hinduization of the cult is seen everywhere and it is now fought with great enthusiasm by the enlightened Jainas.

The worship of the deities of different types, they may be of Hindu-origin or not, is essentially different from the cult of the Tīrthaṅkaras on account of the fact that these are pestered by all sorts of worldly wishes; this abolished the theory of the cult we have discussed above. Therefore, it can be given only a negligible value from the point of view of strict Jainism, particularly because all these Devas are not imperishable, redeemed beings, but only souls which are in possession of a significant, but limited authority for a long but limited period. Since the cult of the gods is little different in form and content from the one with which the Hindus surround their gods, we have not considered it in details in this book. Besides many Jainas oppose it.[9] We shall, therefore, restrict ourselves to speaking about the cult of the Tīrthaṅkaras.

A Tīrthaṅkara, like everything that exists, can also be considered from four points of view: Nāma, Sthāpanā, Dravya, Bhāva, (compare p. 174). Nāma-Tīrthaṅkara is thus what is called Tīrthaṅkara, Sthāpanā-Tīrthaṅkara is what is represented figuratively as a Tīrthaṅkara, Dravya-Tīrthaṅkara is a Tīrthaṅkara as such, irrespective of the condition in which he is, Bhāva-Tīrthaṅkara, a Tīrthaṅkara with respect to the actual Tīrthaṅkara condition. Accordingly, four types of the worship of a Tīrthaṅkara can be distinguished. By expressing or listening to the name of a Tīrthaṅkara, the figure of the prophet appears before the spiritual eye of the believer, and the feelings of reverence, holiness, etc. are evoked in the latter. The worship of the images enables one to imagine the Tīrthaṅkara mentally and brings the ideal of holy humanity closer to the mundane heart. The cult includes from the point of view of "Dravya" (substance) all souls which are predestined to become Tīrthaṅkaras in accordance with their nature, irrespective of the position they have now. It corresponds, thus, to the deference shown to a crown-prince as a later king. The reverence from the point of view of the actual condition (Bhāva) is, e.g. like the one that was shown to Mahāvīra by his contemporaries when he was alive.

The worship of the Jinas finds its practical expression in several ways. The common form of the cult is the so-called Bhāva-pūjā, i.e. meditating on a Tīrthaṅkara and his panegyric by singing hymns. While this type of worship is the only one which was taken up by the ascetics and considered by many sects as the only justified one, two further types are distinguished among the laymen of idol-worshipping Śvetāmbaras and Digambaras: Aṅga-pūjā: bathing, anointing and decorating the limbs of a Jina-idol, and Agra-pūjā: placing fruits, rice, sweets, lamps and perfumes *in front* of the idol of the holy saint. Besides these three, there are also other types of *pūjā*; we shall discuss them later in details.

But Jaina-texts mention the observance of the precepts laid down by the Jinas as the first and the foremost type of worship of the Tīrthaṅkaras; only the one who adheres to it can hope to improve his Karma or to let it vanish. The emphasis on the ethical factor and of the necessity of performance of certain moral duties are, as we shall see, extremely prominent in the Jaina-cult; this does not demand the observance of certain rites alone, but also includes atonement, vow and asceticism in sacral actions.

2. FORMS OF EXPRESSION OF THE DEVOTION

(1) Prayer, Hymn, Mantra

Prayer is the simplest form of devotion which is most commonly used in Christianity and in other religions. The believer converses with the god in it; he dedicates his worship to Him, he praises Him and shows his love and devotion, bares his sufferings to Him and hopes to get from Him salvation and rescue and merciful fulfilment of all sorts of wishes. But prayer, on the other hand, has no place in the right-believing Jainism; since a Jaina does not believe in a Tīrthaṅkara as a world-ruling god, he cannot invoke him and cannot expect from him an influence on his life and on the way of the world. There cannot, therefore, be, strictly speaking, any prayer in Jainism for this reason, and a Jina-worshipper can only restrict himself to praising the shining Arhat in his spotless purity in songs and sayings and by trying to emulate him. But as we have already remarked, this has not been adhered to in popular Jainism.

A number of songs and sayings serve the adulation of holy saints. The briefest form in which the devotion due to a saint is expressed is the "Parameṣṭhī-Mantra" that is composed in Prākṛta. It is repeated every day several times by every Jaina. It is:

"Namo Arihantāṇam, namo Siddhāṇam, namo Āyariyāṇam, namo Uvajjhāyāṇam, namo loe savva-Sāhūṇam!"

"Veneration to the Arhats, veneration to the perfect ones, veneration to the masters, veneration to the teachers, veneration to all the monks in the world!"

This form directed to the 5 "Parameṣṭhīs", i.e. the chiefs of Jainism consists of 35 syllables. It can be shortened in different ways to 16, 6, 5, 4, 2 or 1 syllable, viz.

"Arihanta Siddha Ā (y)iriyā Uvajjhāyā Sāhū"=16 syllables.

"Arihanta Siddhā" or "Arihanta Si Sā" or Om namo Siddhānam" = 6 syllables.

"A Si Ā U Sā" = 5 syllables.

"Arahanta" or "A Si Sāhū" = 4 syllables.

"Siddha" or "A Sā" or Om nhī" = 2 sayllables.

"Om" = 1 syllable.

The Mantra which is mentioned at the end plays a great role in the mysticism of all Indian schools. It is explained by Jainas as a contraction of the syllables A+A+Ā+U+M. The first A means the Arhats, the second A the Aśarīras (those who are bodiless), i.e. the Siddhas, the Ā the Ācāryas or the masters, U the Upādhyāyas or teachers and finally M the Munis (=Sādhus) or ascetics. The Parameṣṭhī-*mantra* is considered as the most significant and the most beneficial of all; a verse expresses it and it is often recited. Its translation is: "This homage dedicated to the five destroys all sins, it is the first blessing among all blessings."

While the Parameṣṭhī-Mantra is dedicated simultaneously to all the 5 groups of the heads of the Jaina-faith, other songs and sayings are dedicated to one or the other group or to the individual members of a group.

A number of hymns in prose and poetry are dedicated to the 24 Tīrthaṅkaras of the present period. One of the most famous used in the ritual is the so-called "Śakra-stava", the panegyric of Indras. It is also called "Namotthu nam" after its first words. In this all the Arhats are praised with all their titles as Tīrthaṅkaras, as Jinas and as Buddhas and honoured with a number of embellishing attributes. They are: "Lions among men, lotus-flowers among the best human beings, fragrant elephants among the best men, emperors of the four directions of the sky of the best law", etc. A Prākṛta-hymn beginning with the words Logassa" and composed in metrical form celebrates the Tīrthaṅkaras as the great men who bring enlightenment to the world and mentions their names in their chronological order. The later poets have paid homage to the 24 prophets exhaustively in Sanskrit and modern Indian languages by treating each one of them in one or several stanzas.

The other Parameṣṭhīs, i.e. the Siddhas, masters, Sādhus, Sṛtadevatās, Kṣetradevatās, Yakṣas etc. are also extolled in a similar manner, if not so often and so exuberantly. Even the shrines are appropriately glorified: the famous "Jam kiñci-Sūtra" praises all Tīrthas and Jina-images in the heaven, in the nether world and in the world of human beings, and the "Jāvanti ceiāim- Sūtra" all Caityas in the upper-, lower- and animal-world. Hymns and sayings are even dedicated to the Jaina-doctrine. Thus here a verse which is often used:

> "Propitious giver of benediction,
> Root of virtues I worship,
> The one which accomplishes pure faith,
> May the Jaina-doctrine blossom victoriously."[10]

Finally, there are also verses which give benediction to the whole world. One such is:

> "May the world get the very best,
> May everyone strive for the highest,
> May every mistake, every want vanish,
> And may humanity get happiness and peace."[11]

A number of phrases in prose are given in the ritual books which are supposed to bring forth mundane and supermundane welfare and keep away evil influences.

In contrast to the Mantras mentioned so far, whose words, whether they are in Sanskrit, Prākṛta or any other language, can be easily understood, there are others consisting of one or several syllables. They do not have any linguistic meaning, rather a meaning that can be understood only by the one who is initiated is attributed to them. The sound "Om" we have already mentioned belongs to these mystical syllables. We have already explained its meaning. Others are: hrāṁ, hrīṁ, hrūṁ, hraḥ, yaḥ, kṣaḥ, phuṭ, raṁ, rīṁ, rauṁ, raḥ, svāhā. Such syllables are very often used in a ritual; they are not only uttered, they are also written down; thus the following mantras are spoken in a Śānti-ceremony and they are written on the parts of the body mentioned in the following: " śrīm" on the head, "bhrūm" on the forehead, "hrīṁ" on the eye-brows, "hrīṁ" on the eyes, "aiṁ" on the nose,, "hrīṁ" on the ears, "hriṁ" on the neck, "hrūṁ" on the heart, "khrām̊" on the arms, "klīṁ" on the stomach, "haḥ" on the navel, "hvāṁ" on the organ of sex, "yaḥ" on the legs and "blūm" on the feet".[12]

(2) Meditation

Every Jaina should meditate at least once a day. This generally happens for 48 minutes in the morning, but many spend double to triple of this period in meditation or repeat them also in the afternoon and evening. The aim of this exercise is to isolate the mind from all the earthly desires and suffering and to put it in a state of unperturbed quietude and cheerfulness. This action which is technically called Sāmāyika can be taken up in solitude, at home, in an Upāśraya or a temple, alone with the face turned towards the north-east or in front of a Guru or an image of a Jina.

Reading a holy book or listening to a sermon can come in place of meditation.

While a Jaina-laymen dedicates generally only a brief period during the day to the meditation, the one who wants to progress in spiritual development to attain finally release from rebirths has to devote himself to meditation often and systematically.

The precondition for the success of meditation is indifference to everything that is mundane and a pure disposition. One who is meditating must be filled with friendliness (Maitrī) to all beings, wish good to all of them; he must cherish pity and sympathy (Kāruṇya) for those who are unfortunate and who are oppressed, take active interest (Pramoda) in the virtues of the saints and everything that is good and keep up complete impartiality (Mādhyasthya) even with respect to his opponents.[13]

The different types of meditations distinguished by Jainas are already discussed above on p. 236 f. Let us mention here practical examples of meditations which are given in the Jaina-texts.[14] Accordingly the following meditations are distinguished:

1. **Piṇḍastha-dhyāna**. One who is meditating tries to accomplish the transcendent nature of the soul by fixing his thought one after the other on certain images which are connected with the elements. The five "fixations" (Dhāraṇā) are:

(a) *Pārthivī Dhāraṇā*. One who is meditating imagines that the earth is a quiet, waveless ocean of milk. He imagines that in its centre there is a thousand-leaved, golden lotus of the size of Jambūdvīpa. There is a precious seminal capsule in the lotus which can be compared with a golden mountain, and in its centre there is a marvellous throne of silver, shining like the moon in an autumn night. He then thinks that he himself is sitting on the throne, completely quietly and detached, free from love and hatred and armed to bring down the Karmas.

(b) *Āgneyī Dhāraṇā*. One who is meditating imagines a shining, sixteen-leaved lotus growing out of his navel. There are 14 vowels of the Devanāgarī-alphabet (a, ā, i, ī, u, ū, ṛ, ṝ, lṛ, lṝ, e, ai, o, au) and the sounds aṁ and aḥ and the great Mantra "arhaṁ" in the seminal capsule. First a smoke comes out from the "ṛ" of the latter, then a sparkle and finally a burning fire. The flame grows continuously and burns the lotus-flower with 8 leaves in the heart. The leaves represent 8 Karmas. Then he imagines a flame of the form of a triangle with a Svastika on its top. This golden, shining and smokeless flame which is inextinguishable like the fire of the hell and which is found outside the body, is driven to it by the wind and burns it from outside, while the fire on the lotus makes it glow from inside. Finally the body and the lotus are completely consumed by fire, and only the ash remains.

(c) *Mārutī Dhāraṇā.* One who is meditating imagines that the ash that has remained from the fire is strewn by a big storm.

(d) *Vāruṇī Dhāraṇā.* One who is meditating imagines further that there is a huge cloud-burst with thunder and lightning and deluge which has inundated the whole cosmic space; the whole dust of his body is washed away by water.

(e) *Rūpavatī Dhāraṇā.* Finally he imagines that he is a pure spirit detached from the seven basic components of the physical body. Gifted with divine perfection, he sits, shining like the moon, on a lion-throne, and gods and demons bow before his majesty.

2. **Padastha-dhyāna.** This is a meditation on certain holy syllables (Mantra, compare p. 410 f.).

3. **Rūpastha-dhyāna.** This is a meditation which has a Tīrthaṅkara as an object. He is imagined as having all perfection, sitting on a throne, serving spirits fanning him with a Yak-fan while he is preaching the doctrine to the gods and human beings.

4. **Rūpātīta-dhyāna**. This meditation observes the real nature of the soul of the one who is meditating, imagines that it is purely spiritual, immaterial and similar in everything with the one of the Siddhas.

(3) Postures and Physical Exercises

A Jaina has to keep his body in definite positions while meditating. The purpose of this precept can be immediately understood: By taking a comfortable posture the one who is meditating should be able to shut off every thought of the body so that the mind can exclusively turn towards the supermundane. The posture of meditation is called Kāyotsarga (Kāya = body, utsarga =throwing from oneself) because detachment of the psychic from the physical should take place in it.

Generally it consists in the contemplating person sitting down with crossed legs and placing the loosely hanging arms on the lap. While doing this a formula is spoken in which a pious man says that he would like to rest now all the body functions to purify his soul. He has to abstain from all voluntary movements during the period he is practising Kāyotsarga; involuntary movement necessary for the body (like breathing, etc.) or which cannot be prevented (like blinking, coughing, etc.) are not considered as interruption of Kāyotsarga.

The mind can also be concentrated in other positions then in the usual sitting position. A meditating person can also do so while standing; then the arms are held stiffly downwards, the knees are pressed together, the feet kept about four fingers apart and the toes stretched forward. There are a number of other postures besides these two main ones; in their details they are different from those we have mentioned.[15] Great significance is given particularly to the position of hands. The gesticulations (Mudrā) play a great role in the cult, and the textbooks of the ritual include a great number of them which have to be used on certain definite occasions.[16]

A movement of the hand which is to be made before the beginning of Sāmāyika is the so-called Āvartana; a half-circle is made with the hands in front of the face from the left ear to the right one which is considered as an expression of respect shown to the Tīrthaṅkara or Guru.

A number of other body-movements are used in the cult; bowing, bending of knees and other similar movements are to be done according to the accurately fixed rules.

Finally the regulation of the breath (Prāṇāyāma) is also to be mentioned among the physical exercises. They are done by Jainas in agreement with the Yogis of the Hindus. There are, according to Hemacandra, 5 types of breath, and they are localized in the different parts of the body. "Prāṇa has its seat at the tip of the nose, of the body. "Prāṇa has its seat at the tip of the nose, in the breast, in the navel, at the tip of the large toe; Apāna in neck, back, sacrum and heels; Samāna in the joints, breast and navel; Udāna between the head and the breast; Vyāna in the whole skin.[17]" By regularizing breath, the circulatory system of the body gets purified and one can attain a complete control of the soul over the body.

It deserves to be emphasized that women, particularly nuns, are forbidden to do a number of physical exercises, particularly doing certain postures which are recommended to men[18] because they could excite sensuousness.

(4) Confession and Expiation

Repenting the sins committed knowingly or unknowingly forms an essential part of the devotional practices of Jainas. Great significance given to confession (Pratikramaṇa) is prominently seen in the fact that the totality of actions meant for the edification are also indicated as "Pratikramaṇa", and that the ritual books give to them heading "Pratikramaṇa".

The form of confession is very different. Confession consists in saying certain formulas in which the offences are systematically counted and a pious person expresses his repentance. At every daily meditation (Sāmāyika) a pious person has to say, "I come back from the sins committed earlier, I blame them, I repent them, I absolve myself of them." In a formula which is often used, and which begins with the words "Sāt-lākh"[19] the 84,00,000 different types of living beings are enumerated according to their classes (thus 7,00,000 earth-beings, 7,00,000 water-beings, etc., see above p. 251); a person who is confessing then, says that he is sorry, if he has harmed one of these beings with his mind, speech or body, or he allowed someone else to harm them or tolerated that someone else harmed them. This form to express general apology for the offence committed against the commandment of "Ahiṁsā" is the only possible one, for no one can know how many insects or elementary beings he has injured or killed while walking, even though as this is prescribed for the ascetics —he pays careful attention to the path. Another formula often used by Śvetāmbaras enumerates 18 sources of sin (*athārah pāpsthān*), as they are the infringement of the small vows (p. 228), passions, etc., and concludes with an affirmation of the repentance.[20]

Jainas know, beside this general confession, also an auricular confession (Ālocana) in which special sins are enumerated. A layman makes this confession before his Guru or some other monk, an ascetic before his superior. Frequency of the confession depends upon the piousness of an individual. Monks and nuns confess, of course, more often than a layman. Many laymen confess daily, others only fortnightly, every fourth month or once in a year. Confession of the last day of the year is the least what a Jaina has to do, but it is recommended that one should confess one's sins as often as possible so that the heaping up of the Karma can be prevented.

The Guru lays down certain expiations (Prāyaścitta) to the one who is confessing to atone for the sins committed by him. The expiation consists usually in fulfilment of certain cult acts, doing special acts of penance among other things. Expiations have a special significance in the orders of the monks. Here punishments meant for even the smallest offences are exactly laid down. If one does not clean his house or his clothes according to the precept, forgets to utter a formula, commits mistake while eating or studying, then he is disallowed eating of certain dishes or even taking certain number of meals. There are stricter punishments for a serious offence: One is not supposed to wish a monk for a certain period, if he has fallen into dispute; he ḥimself also should not speak. In certain cases, there is even a reduction of spiritual *ancienneté* (seniority), etc. A nun has to suffer more than a monk, a senior person more severely than a junior one.[21]

(5) Renunciation and Penance

A Jaina always declares while doing his daily Sāmāyika: "I renounce culpable activity. As long as I follow this observance I shall practise twofold renunciation in a threefold way—with mind, word and body. I shall not do anything that is culpable or get any such thing done by someone else." Soon on finishing the meditation, a pious man makes it his duty to renounce four types of diet (food, drink, fruits, spices, e.g. pepper); this "renunciation" (Pratyākhyāna) is extended to one or to several hours, to a whole day or even longer.

We have already mentioned while discussing the ethical teachings of Jainas that a layman has to keep himself away from a number of actions and that it is considered as meritorious when he takes a vow not to use certain things. Such "Vratas" are closely connected with the cult because they are often taken up in a solemn manner during festivals.

Jainas give extraordinary importance to Tapas. Its great value for the purification of soul and for the destruction of the Karma is a special peculiarity of Jainas since time immemorial, and this essentially distinguishes them from the Buddhists. Penance is done in form of fasting, and it has been developed into a perfect system. From giving up certain items of food, like favourite dishes one eats with great relish, to gradual restriction of the intake of food; from the momentary or periodical abstention from every food to complete renunciation which results in death by starvation, there are also many stages of different types of fasting which are given in the ritual books with all details and explained with the help of tables. What Jainas are able to achieve in fasting is shown by the example of a 47-year old ascetic Sundarlālјī who did not take any food for not less than 81 days in the year 1923 after he had fasted for 61, or

44 days in a row in the previous years.[22]

(6) Yoga

Yoga is a systematic combination of different physical and mental exercises done with the purpose of freeing the soul from everything that is material; its final goal is salvation. Jainas give also exceptional importance to Yoga like Hindus and Buddhists; it is the highest of all the religious observances, the best of all the trees, the biggest of all the precious stones, one wishes for oneself.[23] The Jaina-Yoga is in many points dependent upon the Brahmanic; the most significant Yoga-teacher of Śvetāmbaras, Haribhadra, quotes Patañjali extensively and emphasizes explicitly his agreement with him. But the Yoga of Jainas has been particularly developed in accordance with their metaphysical attitude and in connection with the doctrine of the three processes which promote salvation (p. 218), of the conditions of the soul (p. 211) and the Guṇasthānas (p. 221). I have discussed the nature of Yoga as practised by Hindus in my book "Der Hinduismus", p. 289-300; much of what is said there is applicable to the Jaina-Yoga; it is, therefore, sufficient here only to refer to it. I can restrict myself here to describing the doctrines which are peculiar to Jainas.

Just like meditation which can be worldly and withdrawn from the world (p. 234 f.), two types of Yoga are distinguished depending upon whether it has a worldly goal, connected with passions and binding of the Karma, or whether its goal is salvation, cessation of all instincts and the destruction of all Karmas. The latter, the true Yoga, consists in introspection, reflection, meditation, equanimity and thinking which stop the inflow of Karma. It has 8 parts: 1. self-restraint (Yama), i.e. not harming the other beings, truthfulness, abstention from stealing, chastity, abstention from taking presents; 2. Control (Niyama), particularly purity, contentment, asceticism, study and devotion to the masters; 3. Doing certain postures (Āsanas, p. 415); 4. Regulation of breath

(Prāṇāyāma, p. 416); withdrawal of sensory organs from the objects (Pratyāhāra); 6. Concentration, fixing of thinking on a definite point (Dhāraṇā); 7. Meditation (Dhyāna); and 8. Absorption (Samādhi).

Each of these parts finds its complete development in one of the 8 stages of "seeing" (Dṛṣṭi[24]) which represents a gradual development of the knowledge beyond the indifferent, dim "seeing" (Ogha-dṛṣṭi) of a common, indisciplined man. The seed of the Yoga is sown on the lowest stage, "Mitrā", by practising discipline; the enlightenment here is only negligible, like a straw-fire. Complete control is got in the second seeing "Tārā"; knowledge resembles here the fire arisen by burning cowdung. Enlightenment is compared with the fire of woodpieces in third stage "Bala" which is characterized by perfect experience in the right style of sitting; in the fourth, "Dīprā" characterized by complete regulation of breath; the knowledge corresponds to the shining of a torch. A person practising Yoga can "fall down"[25] from these first four "seeings" because the detachment of the soul from all that is mundane is too negligible in them to guarantee a lasting success; but this is not the case with the next four. Enlightenment grows here without interruption in these stages in which complete withdrawal of organs, concentration, meditation and absorption is achieved. It resembles the shining of precious stones on the fifth "Sthirā", on the sixth "Kāntā", shining of the stars, in the seventh, "Prabhā", the dazzling of the sun, in the 8th "Parā", it is like the cool and mild light of the moon. The last viewing, as its name suggests, is the highest; in it the Karmas vanish, knowledge, viewing, wandering and energy of the soul are concealed, and a complete knowledge is achieved and salvation assured.

Attaining mastery in Yoga is connected with gaining supernatural powers; a Yogī does not only purify his mind, but also but achieves transcendent capabilities of different types. Thus, e.g. his soul can sever its connection with the body and enter some other body. It is reported on the famous Digambara-teacher Kundakunda in an inscription that he could go four Aṅgulas above the ground to show that the matter does not adhere either to his soul or to his body.[26] But all these miraculous powers are not strived for by a wise man for their sake only; his aim is rather to free the soul completely from the matter, to destroy the Karma and to get salvation.

3. SPIRITUAL WELFARE

Among Jainas monks and nuns, mainly, of course monks look after spiritual welfare of a common man. By preaching and explanation of the scriptures, by edifying words and good example, by listening to confessions and fixing the expiations, they seek to support the members of the community in their moral and religious life. The gratitude shown by the pupils, whether they are spiritual people or laymen, whether men or women, to their Gurus (teachers) for the instructions they receive, knows no bounds. In the history, there are reports on many Jaina-rulers who distinguished and honoured their Gurus in an effusive manner and numerous legends know to narrate what a great reward those got in this world and the other world who showed due respect to their teacher and generally to those who had spiritual status. Deference to the teachers is especially made obligatory to all Jainas and it is emphasized in many ways in the cult. A layman expresses his respect to the teacher in nine ways: by throwing himself at his feet; offering him a seat on a higher place; washing his feet with water; while doing this moistening his own forehead with the same water; then praising him, wishing him, prosperity to his work of penance, and by keeping his own thoughts, words and works pure and by offering him suitable food.[27]

Worship of the teacher (Vandana) is one of the six

duties which have to be performed daily and this is done in connection with the Sāmāyika. We have talked above on p. 416 about the rite of Avartana which is often performed.

Worship of a Guru has a distinctive feature among the sects which are inimical to idols, because the cult which is otherwise focussed on the idols of the Tīrthaṅkaras is now focussed on Guru. But when it is said about the Dhuṇḍiyās in the census-reports and Gazetteers is that "they worship their gurus", they rightly and angrily refute this insinuation because they do not bring offering to their Gurus as some Hindu sects do (e.g. Vallabhācāryas) who worship their Gurus like gods.

Welfare of the ascetics is both private and public. The former tries to influence an individual, and the latter the community. One can have a sufficient idea about the first from what is already said; what remains, therefore, here is to consider the latter and to show how a teacher shares a spiritual word with his community.

George Bühler has given a lively description of an hour of instruction in a Śvetāmbaras-Upāśraya in Ahmedābād which is under a Tapā-school and which was built and supported by the family of Seṭha Maganbhāī Hathisiṅgh (1874).[29] I am giving below in brief in his own words what he said.

"When we entered, the room was approximately half-filled. The men stood or sat in the front close to the seat of the preacher, the women squatted at the back. Two monks, the Ācārya whom I knew and a novice stood behind a wooden railing. Both bowed politely. I greeted them with the greeting of the Jaina-laymen "vandum", "I respect (you)", and got the usual answer: "dharma-lābh", "profit of faith". The others who were present took little notice of me.....My guide invited me to take a seat on a cushion in front of an estrade and remarked loudly that I should correct the speaker if he makes a mistake. The Ācārya who then sat down on the Mañcha (see p. 440) with the crossed legs wanted to give in my honour a special lecture on the life of the prophet Vardhamāna. But I requested him to continue with the explanation of the scripture there where he had stood on the previous day. He agreed at once and began to read the second chapter of the first book from *Sūtrakṛtāṅga* (p. 112). While doing this he made use of a manuscript which he had placed on a small, polished wooden stand, the so-called Thui. He held only the page he was reading in his hand. At first he sang few verses of the text which was written in the old dialect, the Jaina-Prākṛta and in Vaitalīya-metre in the usual recitative style with the melody of the metre. Then followed the Tabā, a fairly literal translation into the local language of Gujarāt. He ended with grammatical and etymological, dogmatic and other relevant explanations, applications for use and illustrations from the legends of holy men. Many things in the explanations were rather farfetched....But in spite of all verbosities, he was able to go through ten verses of his text in a little more than one hour.

His lecture made a generally favourable impression. He was a well-built man in his thirties, with an intelligent and a sympathetic face; the closely cut hair and his white garment which lets him keep the right hand free, looked good on him. Many European preachers could have taken an example from the modulation of his voice, his gesturers and his changing expressions. Everything was measured, dignified and noble in these outward appearances to which the Jaina-monks give a great importance.

When the Seṭha asked him he stopped, and his companion hung immediately the mouth-cloth. Jaina-monks are supposed really to wear it always not to harm insects while breathing. He then began to recite the Bhaktāmara-Stotra (see p. 150)....This florid Sanskrit-poem always concludes the divine worship. It is more reeled off than recited with devotion. In all cases, wherever I heard it, it was given very little attention. Even now the people who had gathered got up even before it had ended and began to converse with one another. I said a few words of appreciation to the Ācārya in Gujarātī on his lecture and added in Sanskrit a few words of criticism on his grammatical and etymological remarks. He accepted all that amiably and while taking leave asked me to come soon again.....

The similarity of the Jaina hours of edification with those of the western folks is very great. But there is a significant difference in one point. The so-to-say familiar attitude an Indian shows with respect to his gods or to his pantheistic god is to be emphasized here. Here the feeling of unlimited reverence is missing, with which the western folks are filled during the divine service. This peculiarity is seen quite clearly in Seṭha Maganbhāī asking me to correct the preacher if he were to make a mistake. It would be completely against the feeling of a European to permit a person believing in another religion to interfere in the divine service at a sacred place—even if he were basically to feel little reverence for his preacher, like an aristocratic Indian merchant who has in him aristocratic or even royal blood, has for a monk whom he has bought from his parents, then got him educated by a teacher and now finally supports him."

4. ICONOLATRY

(1) Holy Symbols

Indians like to give a visible expression to their religious convictions with the help of external signs. Jainas also carry a symbol of their sects on the forehead like Śaivites who carry the "Tiryakpuṇḍra", i.e. 3 horizontal strokes of white ash on the forehead or the Viṣṇuites, the "Ūrdhvapuṇḍra", i.e. two strokes in the shape of U or Y produced from white loam with a black vertical one. Jainas put it in the centre between the two eyebrows in the form of heart, and they use a paste of sandal for it; this shows that the person believes in the "religion of the heart".

Objects used in prayer have also a symbolic significance. The holy thread (Yajñopavīta, Janeo), the three strands of which are supposed to symbolize the three constituents of prime matter, Sattva, Rajas and Tamas, among Brāhmaṇas, reminds one of the three precious stones (knowledge, faith, conduct of life) or three successions of the Tīrthaṅkaras in the past, present and the future world-periods, among Jainas. The 108 pearls of the rosary which Jainas let glide everyday at least five times through their fingers remind the believers of the 108 characteristics of the 5 Parameṣṭhīs (i.e. the 12 characteristics of Arhats, 8 of Siddhas, 36 of Ācāryas, 25 of Upādhyāyas and 27 of Sādhus).

Jainas, like believers in other religions, make use of other definite symbols and icons to be able to represent their Jaina-truths in symbols which can be perceived by senses. Svastika is the most important of all the symbols, the fylfot which plays a great role in so many religions. The Svastika of Jainas appears as below:

(c)
(b)
(a)

The real cross (a) is supposed to symbolize four stages of existence in which a soul can be born, the existence as god (above) and as a being from the hell (below), as animal (heraldic left) and as man (right). The three points over the figure (b) are the three jewels: right knowledge, right faith and right conduct of life; the crescent moon with a point over it (c) signifies salvation. The sign is extensively used in the cult because every worshipper, who enters a temple, arranges the rice he offers to the idol in the form of such Svastika.

Nandyāvarta is a sign which is related to Svastika.

Śrīvatsa is really a cowlick which the Tīrthaṅkaras carry on their breast. It also appears as Śrīvatsa-Svastika in the following shape:

Svastika, Nandyāvarta and Śrīvatsa are counted with eight "Maṅgalas" or signs of luck which are extremely popular in the iconography of Jainas.[30] The other 5 Maṅgalas are:

1. Vardhamāna, a powder box,
2. Bhadrāsana, a throne,
3. Kalaśa, a water jug,
4. Darpaṇa, a mirror,
5. Matsya-yugma, two fish.

The 8 Maṅgalas are often illustrated in the temples and also shown on the banners of the processions.

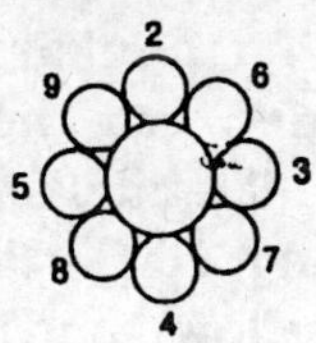

The wheel of the saints (Siddha-cakra) is a symbol which should not be missing in any of the Jaina temples. It has the shape of a lotus having eight leaves. The centre and the eight leaves are supposed to symbolize 5 Parameṣṭhīs and 4 virtues, and the centre signifies (1) Arhat, the uppermost leaf, (2) Siddha, the middle right, (3) Ācārya, the lowermost, (4) Upādhyāya, the middle on the left, (5) Sādhu. The other leaves symbolize: (6) knowledge, (7) belief, (8) way of life, (9) ascetcism. So much importance is given to the Siddha-cakra which is illustrated on a silver or a copper plate that a festival is arranged in its honour twice a year.[31]

Even the holy sounds are symbolically illustrated in the temples.[32] The syllable "Om" consists of a thick line of black stone which is bent and runs pointedly upwards and downwards with two lines running heraldically to the left from this and lying horizontally over one another. Of these, the upper one which intersects the black line is red and has a form of a rectangle, whereas the lower one has yellow colour. It joins the black line on one side and it is rounded off on the other. There is a yellow half moon over this sign with a black circular point over it. A sitting saint is depicted respectively on the point, the half moon and the three lines.

The sound "Hrīṁ" is illustrated by a conventional symbol which consists of several multi-coloured horizontal and vertical lines which are arranged in a definite form. There is a white half moon and a black circle over the figure. The images of the Tīrthaṅkaras are fitted in the individual parts of the figure, viz., both the black Jinas Munisuvrata and Ariṣṭanemi in the black circle, the two white saints Candraprabha and Puṣpadanta in the white moon, the two red Tīrthaṅkaras Padmaprabha and Vāsupūjya on the upper, red, horizontal line and the two blue prophets Malli and Pārśva on the blue vertical lines; the remaining 16 Tīrthaṅkaras who are said to have the golden (yellow) body colour are illustrated on the other part of the figure which is of yellow (golden) colour.

Footprints of the Tīrthaṅkaras or other holy persons serve as their symbols. They play the same role among Jainas as footprints of Buddha and Viṣṇu in the other religions of India.

Mystic diagrams which are dedicated to higher beings, e.g. Goddess Durgā or Bhairava are itched or set in plates of gold, silver, copper, in stone or piece of wood.

A more or less distinct cult is dedicated to the holy signs and symbols we discussed here. They are solemnly consecrated and partially worshipped in a similar way like the idols of the gods whom we shall discuss in the next section. But many of the signs and symbols are considered as substitute for the idols of the gods.

Jainas have represented not only supersensible beings and certain concepts by symbols, but also mundane persons. Thus, worship is made to a holy book in place of the absent teacher, and the monks of the idol-worshipping Śvetāmbaras have certain symbols as the representatives of their Gurus—the followers of Tapā-Gaccha have usually 5 Kauri-shells, the members of the Kharatra-Gaccha 5 pieces of sandal. They carry these on them. These "Sthāpanācāryas" symbolize five virtues: knowledge, faith, way of life, asceticism and energy (Vīrya).[33]

(2) Cult Icons

While all the types of the cult discussed so far are common to all Jainas, if not everywhere to the same extent, there are far-reaching differences of opinion among the different sects about the justification of the worship of the statues of Tīrthaṅkaras. While many Śvetāmbaras and Digambaras allow the iconolatry to full extent, Sthānakavāsīs reject it completely, and between these two extreme trends there are others who take a conciliatory position. The question whether the worship of the idols was taught by the Tīrthaṅkaras or not, has caused lively controversies and produced a whole literature. Therefore, before we take up the treatment of the idols and the cult dedicated to them, we must discuss briefly the pros and cons of iconolatry.

The followers of image worship, the so-called Dehravāsīs (i.e. those who stay in temples while doing religious practices) say that this is age-old. According to them, the first world-ruler Bharata constructed a temple which was shining with gold and jewels and installed in it 24 Jina-statues.[34] Pious people of all times followed in his example. A number of passages from the canon are quoted to prove that even Mahāvīra worshipped idols. Worship of the cult-objects is recommended because it diverts the mind from worldly life and its pleasures and worries and it directs one's attention to what is supermundane; just as the thoughts of a pious man are diverted from the reality when listening to the holy legends and turned to what is transcendent, the mind and the heart of the believer would also be purified and elevated by looking at the images of the perfect ones. Many events taught that the persons who were prepared for it got enlightenment by looking at the Jina-images; only "the oxen without horns and tails" could, therefore, advise against the use of such a significant means of salvation.

The opponents of iconolatry, the Sthānakavāsīs (i.e. those who worship only in community-houses and not in temples) maintain, on the other hand, that the cult of idols was not taught by the Tīrthaṅkaras. They dispute the genuineness of the holy scriptures in which iconolatry plays a great role (like; e.g. Mahāniśītha-Sūtra), and explain the passages in other canonic works considered by iconodules as examples of iconolatry, as later interpolations or they interpret them differently. They say that it is wrong to worship the world-renouncing Jinas in the same way as the gods who have thoroughly had the enjoyments of the world. Iconolatry contradicts completely the spirit of Jainism, the purpose of all worships is to free the mind from passion and Karma, and this can be achieved only from within, and not by offering flowers and fruits to lifeless images of the saints who are detached from the world. The magnificent ritual of the temples is not done to divert one's thoughts from the world, but the world fetters them more strongly to itself. It is besides wrong that the Pūjārīs wake up the silent idols of the Tīrthaṅkaras with the sounds of bells, music and dances from their serene peace in the belief that they themselves would get peace by doing this. Iconolatry, therefore, has no place in the old, genuine Jainism; it is distortion of the true doctrine and owes its origin to only the egoism of the selfish priests who desire to get worldly advantages for themselves at the cost of misled pious laymen.

We shall desist in the following from discussing whether iconolatry is valuable or otherwise for religious life; one cannot come at all to any universally valid judgement on questions of this type because the religious needs of human beings are personal and have to be much distinguished from one another. Criticism of the Indian iconolatry on the part of a Christian, that too of a Protestant missionary, is based mostly on a complete misunderstanding of its nature; its critics are put off by the abuses that are easily connected with it, and overlook completely the crux of the matter that is present in it. The apostles of Hinduism in the lands of the west, Premānand Bhāratī[35] and others have rightfully shown what a great help a sacramental cult-object is for a meditating person and pointed out how foolish it is, when the people, who themselves pursue an extended cult with the help of the flag of the country, picture of the monarch and photo of the beloved, campaign against idolatry. It is a different question, whether the worship of "Jina-bimbas" was peculiar to the most ancient Jainism or not.

This question cannot be decided at present from the archaeological point of view. The oldest illustrations of the Tīrthaṅkaras in figures which have come down to us, hardly reach out beyond the beginning of our Christian era. An inscription of King Khāravela in the Hāthigumphā-cave near Cuṭṭuck which can be dated to a time around 155 B.C. refers to an earlier period. It appears to emerge from this inscription that Khāravela had stolen the statue of "Agra-jina" (Ṛṣabha) from King Nanda and again installed it. One could conclude from it that Tīrthaṅkara-statues existed even during the dynasty of King Nanda (since 371 B.C.); it is even believed that Nanda's period could be dated to a century earlier.[36] This would mean that Jina-statues were worshipped even before the 5th century B.C. But all this is uncertain because the dating of the inscription is questionable.

Old texts dating from the period of the Tīrthaṅkaras or the most ancient community can give us a convincing proof for the presence of iconolatry during Mahāvīra's period. Most of the writings, however, which report on the worship of idols by the contemporaries of Vardhamāna or his predecessors, originate from a later period in which iconolatry was generally prevalent, therefore, prove nothing to show that it existed in the most ancient period of Jainism. It is also not different with the canonic writings. The edition of the holy books of Śvetāmbaras which is before us, comes, according to the tradition, from the year 980 before Vīra. In the chiliad which separates it from the period of the prophet, there was ample opportunity to make changes.

It is strange that in many of them, even in the passages from which one should really expect it, there is no mention of Jina-statues, although in a few, temples and idols of gods are mentioned. Others speak indeed of a worship of Tīrthaṅkara-statues, but give no precepts for the rites to be performed in their cult. A thorough examination of the individual passages of the canon in which there is a mention of "Padimās" and "Bimbas", shows that their chronological distinction is missing; a satisfactory solution of the question about the age of iconolatry cannot be had, till this is done.

What role Jainas have played in the history of plastic art is an important problem for research on Indian art. The idol-worshipping Jainas believe that the production of statues is devised by Jainas first and the other religious communities have learnt from them. The same view is held by the followers of Hindu-reformers who are hostile to idol-worship; but this is, of course, done with the intention of shifting the odium of idol worship to the heretics. The Sthānakavāsīs, on the other hand, presume that it is only an imitation of the Hindu examples when it comes to the production of Jaina-idols.

Even most of the European researchers tend to share this view. The production and the cult of the Tīrthaṅkara-statues were alien to the old community of monks and they were developed only on account of the need of the world of laymen by imitating the idol-worship of other religious communities before the beginning of our era. It is, of course, certain that Jainas have got a great significance for the artistic creations of Indians; but whether they have played a leading role, which Berthold Laufer ascribes to them,[37] needs a more extensive evidence.

The Jaina-statues are mostly produced from stone (preferably from marble) or metal. Occasionally 5 metals (Pañca-loha) were used for a statue in which silver often played a predominant role. The Tīrthaṅkaras are mainly depicted in the so-called "lotus-posture" (Padmāsana), i.e. the prophet sits erect with crossed legs; the toes of both the feet are in resting position, the soles are turned upwards, very close to the knee of the other leg. The hands lie on the lap, the right over the left. Jinas are often shown standing in meditation among Digambaras. Digambara-statues are completely naked, those of Śvetāmbaras wear ornaments of gold and precious stones. Among Digambaras, the eyes of Jinas are turned downwards; among Śvetāmbaras the eyes are open and they are made prominent by inserting a piece of glass or by jewels.

There are minutest rules as to how the individual limbs of a Tīrthaṅkara are to be reproduced and what should be their size. These rules are to be strictly observed by an artist who wants to make a statue. Accurate descriptions of the appearance of the Tīrthaṅkaras are given in the canonic literature. Thus in the Aupapātika-Sūtra[38] a detailed description of Mahāvīra is given, a description which appears almost like an instruction for a sculptor with its abundance of details it offers. I am emphasizing here a few details from it: Jina's hair of the head is soft like wool, black, curly, a chignon at the parting looking like a roof. The ears are long, symmetric and snug (attached) and the cheeks are fleshy. The nose is long like the beak of a Garuḍa, the lips fitting exactly upon one another. The breast shows the Śrīvatsa-sign, the spine not visible on the back. The navel is deeply set and resembles a whirlpool of waves. The hands show the following lucky signs: sun, moon, shell and Svastika. The thighs are well-grown like an elephant-trunk and the soles are tender like red lotuses.

All Tīrthaṅkaras have the same figures; most of them are to be distinguished only by their colour and the blazon (Cihna), which is affixed under their statues. Supārśva and Pārśva, on the other hand, are to be recognized at the first sight by heads of serpents which surround their top of the head like a baldachin.

The dimensions of Jina-statues are extremely different; from small figurines which are used in the house to the great cult-idols in temples and mighty sculptures hewed out from the rocks or freely standing figures, there is the whole range of nuances. Once a statue is finished by an artist, it must be blessed with the consecration to be able to serve as a sacramental cult-object. For this purpose, a priest (Guru) utters certain holy formulas about the statue at a point of time that is astrologically favourable, most preferably in the night; he touches it with a golden stick which is dipped in a silver container containing a mixture of ghee, honey, sugar and flour, and thereby opens its eyes. Then he whispers seven times a Mantra into the right ear of the idol and touches it several times with the hand.[39] Certain ceremonies are performed when the idol is installed in a shrine. More on it later.

Some Jina-idols are regarded as particularly sacred because they are attributed a supernatural origin. They are supposed to be self-existent or erected by the saints of a legend or found by a miracle. Thus an idol of Pārśvanātha which is worshipped in Sthambanaka (Cambay) was found as under: Saint Abhayadeva (11th century A.D.) once became ill on his pilgrimage to the holy shrines of Gujarāt. Jaina-doctrine appeared to him in the night in his dream and asked him to go to Sthambanaka to the bank of Sedhikā river, where he would find an idol of Pārśva in the midst of a thicket of Palāśa-trees and it would cure him from his illness. Abhaya dragged himself with great effort to Sthambanaka in the company of several pilgrims, but the idol was not found there. Finally the people noticed that a crow was constantly letting milk drip on a definite spot. The sage went to this place and composed there in the inspiration of the moment thiry stanzas of his panegyric "Jaya tihuyana". The goddess prevented him from reciting two further stanzas he had also composed, because he would have then got a great power over the gods. While the verses were being recited the idol of Pārśvanātha emerged slowly from the earth, where it had remained hidden for centuries, and pious people constructed a temple over it. It was consecrated by Abhaya.[40]

Legends of this type are narrated about a great number of idols of the Tīrthaṅkaras.

There is a whole series of the statues of the Tīrthaṅkaras in the temples, usually beside a big statue of "Mūlanāyaka", i.e. of the Tīrthaṅkara to whom the shrine is dedicated; but their dimensions are smaller. Even the persons of the legend who are close to the Tīrthaṅkara, like their mothers, are often represented in the temples by their statues or pictures. The worship of Gommaṭa or Bāhubalī (see p. 295), one of the sons of the first Tīrthaṅkara Ṛṣabha, is a special feature of Digambaras. The colossal statues of this prophet found in the different places of the west coast of India belong to the most remarkable creations of Jaina-art.[41] They are mighty, unsupported monoliths, which, visible at far distances, rule over the whole region. The biggest of these statues stands in Śravaṇa Beḷgoḷa (Mysore) on a mountain which is 400 feet above the place. It is 56½ feet in height and has a breadth of 13 feet at the hips. The material used is a huge granite block. Gommaṭa is depicted as he remained unmoved in meditation for one year. Wholly naked, the face turned towards the north, he stands erect on a pedestal in the form of an open lotus. His thighs are surrounded by two big ant-hills from which serpents creep out. Legs and arms are entwined by a creeper. According to a legend, the statue is age-old, erected by Bharata and even worshipped by Rāvaṇa. It is said that a merchant informed the minister Cāmuṇḍarāya of King Rājamalla about this statue which was forgotten and hidden in a mountain, upon which he took a pilgrimage with his mother and several companions to the hill Vindhyāgiri to look for the precious monument. Kuṣmāṇḍī, the Yakṣiṇī of Tīrthaṅkara Ariṣṭanemi, appeared to him in dream and showed him the place, where he could find it. Cāmuṇḍarāya split the mountain with a golden arrow, after which Gommaṭa's statue could be sighted. The minister got it uncovered and beautified artistically by sculptor. It was then solemnly consecrated and dedicated to the cult. Other sources report, on the other hand, that Cāmuṇḍarāya himself got the statues made for which an (invisible) statue erected by Bharata in Poṭaṇapura had served as a model. The name of the artist who made it was probably Ariṣṭanemi (Ariṭṭo Nemi); it was ready around the year 980 A.D.

Prince Vīrapāṇḍya of Kārkala got a similar representation of Gommaṭa made in 1432 in Kārkala (in South Canara). Timmarāja, probably a descendant of Cāmuṇḍarāya did the same thing in 1604 in Veṇūr (or Yeṇūr in South Canara). The statue in Kārkala is about 41, the one in Veṇūr 37 feet in height. Both resemble completely the one of Śravaṇa Beḷgoḷa, but the aesthetic effect of the one in Veṇūr is hampered by the fact that the face gets a grinning expression on account of the dimples in the cheeks. Another famous Gommaṭa-statue, which is only 20 feet in height, is on a hill 15 miles south-west of Mysore.[42]

Although these statues do not come up to the occidental concepts of beauty in idea and execution, all the European travellers agree that they are exceptionally impressive. "There is nothing greater and more imposing than this outside Egypt, and even there so far no known statue surpasses this in height", wrote Fergusson about the one of Śravaṇa Beḷgoḷa, and even today it is one of wonders of the world.

Besides the statues of the persons who are connected with the legends of the Tīrthaṅkaras, also those of the deities of all types are erected; they are closely or distantly connected with Jainism. There are idols of Yakṣas and Kṣetrapālas, of Indras and of the deities of directions, of the sky, of Gaṇeśa and Hanumān, of the numerous mother-goddesses, of planets and other heavenly powers. Even the statues of dead masters and teachers are erected and worshipped in a solemn ceremony.

Three dimensional representation of groups is also popular. In these, the Tīrthaṅkaras figure next to one another, or a Tīrthaṅkara with people who are worshipping him, surrounded by musicians, Caurī-carriers, etc.

Also reliefs of different types besides the sculptures serve to reproduce graphically the images of the Tīrthaṅkaras and the gods. Particularly the Āyāgapaṭas, the "memorial tablets" which were found in Mathurā are peculiar. They are these longish or rectangular stone-plates with an illustration of a Jina, a holy symbol like the Dharma-cakra, or a Stūpa which is surrounded by lucky signs and worshipping gods and men.[43]

Finally even paintings are used to embellish the temples and houses, as also to illustrate the books. The oldest remains of wall-paintings are found in a cave in Orissā.[44] Jaina-frescos from the 7th century A.D. were found by Jouveau-Dubreuil in Sittanavasal near Pudukoṭṭai in South India.[45] The most ancient book-illustrations are obtained in a manuscript of Kalpa-Sūtra from the year 1237; it is available in Pāṭaṇ.[46] W. Hüttemann[47] and Ananda K. Coomaraswamy[48] have appreciated the aesthetic qualities of the Jaina-miniatures. The Jaina-paintings illustrating the life of Tīrthaṅkras or similar other personalities or things have clearly the stamp of hieratic art; they are an expression of a religious spirit; they are symbols of a mythical happening. In their detachment from the world, they lack human interest which is seen in the frescos of Ajantā or in the works of Rājapūta art. The form that is sanctified by tradition and that reproduces the events in the history of the church has preserved them in their purity, and they have remained through centuries like unalterable templates. But the artists had freedom in dealing with the legends. Here they did not have to follow clearly defined rules which were prescribed for depicting the canonic history. The illustrations done under the influence of the Mogul-art to depict the story of Śālibhadra show Jainas as the masters in the reproduction of the eventful happenings in daily life. The contrast in interpretation, clothing, colour and other things between the Kalpa-Sūtra miniatures originated in the pre-Mohammedan period and the illustrations of the "Śālibhadra-Carita" influenced by Persian examples is of great interest for art-history.

The cult undertaken in front of the idols of the Tīrthaṅkaras is very complicated and in its details it is different for different sects. It begins mostly by bowing and making some movements of the body, by solemnly circumambulating (Pradakṣiṇā) the cult-image, by reciting Mantras and singing hymns. The real Pūjā (worship) consists in offering certain gifts; it is generally eightfold; it is put together from 8 actions, but they need not be followed in a certain order. They are:

1. Jala-pūjā, washing and sprinkling with water,
2. Candana-pūjā, applying sandal,
3. Puṣpa-pūjā, garlanding and covering with flowers,

4. Dhūpa-pūjā, kindling of pastilles,
5. Dīpa-pūjā, swinging of lamps,
6. Akṣata-pūjā, offering of rice,
7. Naivedya-pūjā, offering of sweets,
8. Phala-pūjā, offering of fruits like banana, cocoanut, orange, almond, etc.

There are still some other besides these main forms of the Pūjā, like unfirling the flag in honour of the cult-image, arranging dances with musical accompaniment before it, among other things.

5. PLACES OF THE CULT

The Jaina places of the cult are of different types according to their regulations. The so-called Upāśrayas ("places of shelter") are the centre of the community among all sects in which the orders of monks and nuns are the bearers of the religious life. These are the houses maintained by laymen serving as lodgings for monks and nuns. The Upāśrayas are usually two-storeyed, oblong buildings done in bricks and teakwood with a tiled roof; thus it is not much different from the houses of opulent Indians. The main room, a hall for preaching, is mostly in the first floor; a narrow staircase leads to the first floor. George Bühler who had visited such an assembly hall describes it as under: "It is about 30 feet long and about 15 feet broad. The ceiling which is not very high is supported by a few carved wooden-pillars; the walls are white-washed and the windows are provided with glass panes in the European manner and the ground is covered with mats and coir....An adjustable wooden railing with a little gate separates a small room very close to the door; there is the so-called Mañca, a long and broad wooden platform which is elevated 3 feet above the ground. This is the seat of the Ācārya, preacher, teacher, as also of the monks and pupils who assist them."[49]

There are, of course, carvings on the doors and on

the ledges; otherwise, there is neither a picture nor a sculpture in Upāśrayas. This is very remarkable; it is according to the regulations of the old Kalpa-Sūtra (1.20) that monks and nuns are not allowed to live in a house which has wall-paintings.

Jaina monks or nuns preach to their followers in the Upāśrayas, take confessions from them and give them religious instructons. But a real cult does not take place there; rather holy places of different types which are partially embellished with a great splendour serve this purpose.

The Jaina architecture has been developed in close contact with the Indian architecture in general. Like this, their monuments also were originated from a fairly later period. So far no monuments have been found which date back beyond two centuries B.C.[50] The reason that no buildings from older period have come down to us is probably to be found in the fact that Jainas, like the Indians in general, used earlier wood as a building material which obviously could resist the influence of the climate only for a limited period. It is true that this assumption of European research is contested by Jainas, and they claim, by pointing out to the tradition, that temples and palaces in stone have been built among them since time immemorial, that it has not only a high degree of probability in view of the conditions of the Indian past, but is also confirmed by the style of the architecture of the later period: the artistic stone pillars supporting the arches and the roofs of the temples, as also the endlessly fine filigreed marble-work in the inside of the shrines; this obviously comes from the ornamental work in wood which was later imitated in stone.

Jaina buildings have a great variety. A sort of sacral-constructions which appear to have been erected in the early period of Jaina-architecture, are the so-called Stūpas. A Ṣtūpa, as it is well-known, is a memorial monument which represents a relic or which was built as a reminiscence of an even in the religion's history. A Stūpa has a form of a hemisphere upon which there is a rectangular construction which is crowned by a sun-umbrella (the symbol of the rule). There is a passage around it so that one can walk around it; the whole thing is surrounded by a railing with gates to the four directions. Construction of a Stūpa was special fashion among Buddhists; they kept the mortal remains of deceased saints inside them. Therefore, one thought of attributing all the Stūpas to the Buddhists without any exception. But since the period A. Führer found a Jaina-Stūpa near Mathurā, and one more was found in Rāmnagar, it is confirmed that Jainas have also made use of Stūpas although the service to the relics is alien to them. As it is shown by E. Leumann for the first time, Stūpas are already mentioned in the Śvetāmbara-canon.[51] G. Bühler thinks that even the word *Caitya* did not mean originally a temple, but a memorial monument erected in an honour of deceased teacher. It is said of some Caityas which are mentioned in the canon that they are provided with a Chattra, i.e. a sun-umbrella, and this applies to a Stūpa and not to any other shrines.[52] A relief was also discovered in Mathūra in which a Stūpa is depicted which is worshipped by Kinnaras and Garuḍas or Suparṇas.[53]

Tombs of Śrīpūjyas or other important monks come in place of the Stūpas during a later period. They were called "Chatrīs" in Rājapūtānā and resembled cenotaphs of the Rājapūta-princes. According to an inscription in Pāliṭāṇā, the Pādukās (wooden sandals) of the famous Hīravijaya (p. 74) were buried near the temple of Ādīśvara in a shrine after he starved himself to death. There are numerous tombs of the Digambaras in Śravaṇa Beḷgoḷa.

Among the temples of Jainas, the cave-temples are the most ancient and most colossal. The technique of carving rocks to create in them the places of the cult and houses for monks appears to have come up in the 5th century A.D. It is possible, it arose by the influence of alien examples: it was in practice in Egypt from time immemorial and was taken over to Persia since the 6th century, where the tombs of Darius and his successors were carved out from the rocks by Naksh-i-Rustam and Persepolis.[54] Since the period of Aśoka who got the caves constructed in the 12th and the 19th year of his rule in the Barābar-rocks (16 miles to the north of Gayā in Bihār), caves have been dug out for cult purposes in different parts of the Gangetic planes for over thousand years. Jainas also competed with Buddhists and Hindus in making brittle rock useful for sacral purposes. The most famous Jaina caves are in Udayagiri in Orissā (around 150 B.C.?) in Bādāmi in Bijāpur district (around 650 A.D.) and in Ellora near Aurangābād (9th-10th century A.D.). Most of them consist of several smaller or larger halls with forecourts. They show rich sculptural decoration, beautiful pillars and numerous sculptures of the Tīrthaṅkaras and divine beings of different types. Very remarkable in this respect particularly is one of the 5 Jaina-Grottos of Ellora, the so-called Indra-sabhā which has a beautiful statue of Mahāvīra besides other statues, and there is a statue of Indra in its veranda. It is a piece of Indian sculpture which is most often reproduced.

The open temples erected by Jainas to show respect to their Tīrthaṅkaras are more in number and besides also artistically more valuable than cave-temples. The bigger temples consist mostly of an open hall (Maṇḍapa), a closed assembly-hall (Sabhā-maṇḍapa) and an enclosure which is the holiest of all (Garbhagṛha) in which there is the main idol. Arch-halls and cells in which there are statues of Tīrthaṅkaras surround this. The whole construction is covered by domes. The actual holy area is demarcated by a yard mostly of a rectangular form, which is surrounded by rest-houses for pilgrims. Most Jaina-temples, both from the north and the south (the so-called "Bastīs"), are laid out in similar manner; they may then be different in style and type of construction.

The "four-faced" (caturmukha) temples, i.e. those with four gates, each leading to one or several Tīrthaṅkara-statues are popular both in the north and the south.[55]

There are also temples in South India which have an altogether different form. The peculiar Bastīs of Mūḍbidri in South Canara resemble with their double or tribble slanting roofs Nepali(an) temples or Chinese towers; the copying from the works of wooden architecture is quite obvious. The other type of sacral-buildings which are peculiar to the south are the so-called Beṭṭas, i.e. the buildings which are open above and on the sides. They surround the statues of Gommaṭa in Śravaṇa Beḷgoḷa and other places.

In front of many temples there is a pillar (Mānastambha) built in a colossal monolith which is richly decorated. There is often a flag-post (Dhvaja-stambha), mostly of wood and covered with copper, between the pillar and the shrine.

The Jaina-temples owe their origin almost exclusively to the donations coming from rich donors. The generosity of laymen is revealed in these by the splendour of embellishment and the preciousness of the material that is used; Jainas have indeed constructed their buildings in marble. Jaina community is numerically strong. But it has by far a great number of shrines. Not only all great cities in which Jainas live have one or several temples, often much more than the need would demand it, but there are several places which are overcrowded by temples. Places which have become true temple-cities. Khajurāho in Madhya Pradesh, Ābū in Rājasthān, Śatruñjaya and Girnār in Kāthiāvāḍ, are the most famous examples of this type. The impression which these temples have on a visitor is described as overwhelming. The visitor thinks that he has come into a magical world when he wanders from shrine to shrine and the Tīrthaṅkaras smile at him in their solemn quietude from the countless aedicules.

The inner Jaina-temple also evokes similar feelings. One who enters the umbrageous coolness of the marble shrines from the dazzling brightness of the dusty day, believes to feel in himself the effect of the remote, quiet peace of the Jinas who are enthroned there. The perfect beauty and symmetry of the pillars and arches which have made up these buildings have as much solemn effect as the perfect serenity which rests in these halls. It is true that all temples are not equally artistically perfect, and the artlessness and the overladen colourful pomp, particularly of modern buildings which have become a fashion, in the masterly works of architecture, also in those which do not belong to the Jaina church, disturb the feelings of devotion.

The temple contains an idol of the Mūlanāyaka, i.e. of the Jina who is considered as a patron, as also the figures of other Tīrthaṅkaras and of the genii and gods serving them. There are also idols of deities borrowed from Hinduism (this is, in any case, not approved by all Jainas), like Hanumān, Bhairon, "mothers" etc. The arrangement consists of a number of things which are used in holy actions; these include a box for alms (Bhāṇḍāra), a wooden table, a tripod, a bell, containers for incense as also pots of different types.

The temple service is mostly done by the Pūjārīs, ministrants, who are paid by the community for their work and have a share in the offerings that are given. They are either Brāhmaṇas or they belong to other castes like Baniyās (merchants), Mālīs (gardeners), Kuṇabis (farmers), Baroṭas (bards), etc. While Digambaras employ ministrants who are Jainas, Śvetāmbaras employ people who do not at all believe in the Tīrthaṅkaras for whose honour they have to perform the holy acts, but they have to be vegetarians and are not allowed to take alcohol. Occasionally, individual rites are performed by pious Jaina-laymen who undertake this task of performing a work which is religiously meritorious. Considerable sums are paid for the right to perform individual ceremonies. In big temples, so many laymen think That it is an honour to show their religious fervour. That the privilege of this or the other Pūjā is regularly auctioned by the ministrants to the one who offered the most. In these auctions generally a certain number of Sers (name of a weight) of ghee is offered; but in reality no ghee is actually given; its cost is paid in rupees. Also not the prevalent cost but the cost that was valid many years ago.

Only those persons who are pure in every respect are permitted to participate in the cult. That is why, the worshippers take a bath and put on special clothes before they perform a holy action. These clothes are kept in the front room of the temple. They consist of a loincloth (Dhotī) and a shoulder-piece (Uttarāsana); other things needed for the ritual are a piece of cloth for the mouth, cloth for sitting and a brush. The holy thread (*janeo*) is worn only at the time of the Pūjā by those who have right to wear it. The worshippers avoid carrying anything in the pocket because the things which are used in the temple should not be used for mundane purposes.[56] The worshipper, as a part of the preparations needed before performing holy actions, wears certain signs on the forehead and the ears with a yellow powder and draws lines on the arms, in the midst of the chest and around the neck.

There are daily performal three services in the shrine. They consist mainly in eightfold worship (Pūjā) of the Jina-idols; we have already described it above on p. 439. The idols are washed only once; the other rites can be as often repeated as one likes. While the three types of Pūjā in which the object of the cult is touched (washing, anointing, garlanding), can be carried out only in the holiest place (Garbhagṛha) by persons who have taken their bath and have special clothes on, the other ceremonies can be performed in the hall by people without putting on special clothes and even by women.

There are pantomimes in many temples on festive occasions. They consist mainly in half a dozen boys singing and dancing with the accompaniment of drums and other instruments. The boys carry a costume used in a play and first dance together, then in the groups of twos and then they walk under the gates formed by the hands of their co-players. Singing the hymns in front of the idols of Tīrthaṅkaras and bowing before them conclude every act of performance.[57] It is noteworthy that (at least among Śvetāmbaraś), women, even widows, are allowed to take an active part in the cult.

6. SORCERY AND DIVINATION

Jainas share a belief in the existence of numerous supermundane intelligences with Hindus and followers of other religions. These can interfere in the fates of the individuals or all; they may help them or hamper them in their progress. These beings have, of course, only a limited power; they are themselves subject to the eternal laws of the world and liable to Karma and rebirth; but they occupy now a position as a consequence of their deeds in an earlier existence. They are in a position that they can be noticed by people in a pleasant or unpleasant manner. They cannot, of course, harm holy men who have freed themselves from the bonds of the world, but all others depend upon them in their happiness and sorrow, and therefore, they see to it that they take a right position with respect to them and that they are favourably disposed to them.

Cult and sorcery easily merge into one another among all peoples; among Jainas it is more so difficult to draw a line of separation because the worship of the deities originating from Hinduism—particularly when it is compared with the cult of the Tīrthaṅkaras—has a strongly magical character. For, when a Jaina worships Gaṇeśa or Mother-goddesses, hẹ does not, in fact, do it to purify his self, but to dispose them favourably towards him and to get mundane or supermundane things with their help. We have already discussed the worship offered to the deities, and we can, therefore, restrict ourselves here to speaking only of magical actions; spirits of the lower order are their object.

The stars, particularly the 9 planets (sun, moon, as also the two nodes Rāhu and Ketu are reckoned along with the five which are visible to the naked eye), the 12 signs of the zodiac and 28 houses of the moon (Nakṣatras) take the first place among the heavenly powers which influence life on the earth. The position they have at the time of the birth of an individual exerts a dominating influence on the fate of the newborn; the planetary constellation is otherwise also of great significance and that is why astrologically favourable moments are to be chosen for all important rites like initiation, marriage, consecration as an ascetic, etc. The astronomy and astrology of Jainas corresponds, no doubt, in many basic features to the one of Hindus, but it is different in some essential points (compare p. 265). Like all Indians, Jainas also, when they accept that the stars have a determinative influence on their life, don't think that it contradicts their belief in Karma; siderial hours and Karma are in profound harmony with one another, and the astrology makes it to some extent possible to read the Karma of a being from the stars. Corresponding to this view, Jainas also know to indicate the Nakṣatra for the five great periods in the life of each one of their Tīrthaṅkaras with which the moon was then in conjunction. Jaina-astrologers also link the individual planets with the 24 Jinas, and to be more precise, they have linked the Sun with the 6th, Moon with the 8th, Mars with the 12th, Mercury with the 13th, 14th, 15th, 16th, 17th, 18th, 21st and 24th, Jupiter with the 1st, 2nd, 3rd, 4th, 5th, 7th, 10th and 11th, Venus with the 9th, Saturn with the 20th, Rāhu with the 22nd and Ketu with the 19th and 23rd. The constellations are worshipped by reciting Mantras and offering benefactions; one tries to neutralize unfavourable effects coming from them with the help of suitable rites of appeasement.

While the idea of the power of stars is generally recognized in the writings of Jaina-theologians and to that extent can be considered as legitimate, the belief in the influence of ghosts is more a part of popular belief and it is not generally approved by the Jainas who are philosophically inclined.

The idea that all sorts of evil spirits (Bhūtas) can cause harm to human beings is generally spread, particularly among women and the uneducated. Particularly Jakhiṇs (Yakṣiṇīs), i.e. ghosts of deceased women, become dangerous for children. If a child is ill, then it is presumed that the illness is to be attributed to the influence of the dead first wife of the father, and then one promises to place her metal image along with the house-idols and worship it. If the child recovers, then the vow is fulfilled; a few married women are invited when the image is installed and they are given food and presents. All sorts of sufferings and diseases are caused on account of ghosts of all sorts even among adults. Priests are called to pacify them. They try to drive the ghosts away by magic-*mantras*, burning of incense, applying ash to the patient, with amulets and by other magical methods. The danger caused by Bhūtas is prophylactically fought by pleasing the ghosts by offering them gifts on certain days, by giving water to the trees in which they may be living or by performing other rites.

Other popular views which Jainas share with the members of other religions, is the belief in evil eye. Evil eye is peculiar to many people from their nature; its cause may have different reasons. It appears among those in whose eyes some blood fell when the umbilical cord connecting them with the mother's body was cut.[58] Particularly people who become conspicuous by their beauty or wisdom or who are particularly lucky are exposed to the attacks of evil eye. The influence of evil eye is most effectively fought by the use of something that is black;

thus a black thread is bound to the ornaments of a woman who is festively dressed, a black spot is painted on the cheek of a pretty child, etc. The practice of fixing a lemon to the turban of the bridegroom or the Sārī of a bride has a similar purpose. Thus, the sweetness of their happiness is mixed with something that has a sour taste. Fever among children is usually ascribed to the influence of an evil eye; a pot-filled with ash, salt, corns, mustard and other ingredients is kept under the bed of the sick person to get cure. Once the suffering is removed, the contents of the pot are poured out at a crossing.

Besides these magical ideas and practices we have mentioned here, there are countless others among Jainas, but we cannot enumerate them here. Jainas are generally considered as particularly conversant in practice of black magic. James Tod calls them "Vediavān or Magi of Rājasthān" and remarks that often a charge is made against Jainas that they deal with sorcery.[59] Similar charges were also made against Jainas in South India as can be seen from *Madurā-sthala-purāṇa*, the annals of the temple of Madurai.[60]

Divination is closely connected with sorcery. We have already discussed the most significant of all the augural sciences, i.e. astrology. Besides this, there are many other devinations which are more or less developed. The belief in omens of all sorts is widely spread. Objects and beings a traveller meets on his journey are often mentioned in the Jaina-stories; they have all the favourable and unfavourable portents.[61] The most remarkable of the auspicious are dreams. Nine types are distinguished according to their origin: Those which owe their origin to worry, illness, an experience, the nature of the one who has a dream, to something that is heard or seen, to a religious work or to a sin, and those upon which is based an advice given by god or some other higher being. Dreams of the first six types are meaningless, but the last three mentioned indicate good or bad consequences. Of the meaningful dreams, 72 are particularly remarkable, 30 of them are the so-called *great dreams.* They proclaim the birth of great men.[62] We have already mentioned on p. 275 f. the 14 (respectively 16) dreams which precede the birth of a Tīrthaṅkara; the birth of other "famous men" and of great rulers or sages is predicted by individual dreams among these.

In contrast to these dreams which predict something pleasing, there are others which predict evil. Thus, Candragupta is said to have seen 16 dreams which predicted the famine in Magadha which lasted for 12 years.[63] Bharata's 16 dreams which predicted the fall of the Brāhmṇa-caste are famous.[64]

B. A Special Section

1. RITES FOR LAYMEN

(1) The Daily Rites

A layman has to perform a number of rites from the morning to the evening. When he gets up from his bed in his last night watch, he chants the Parameṣṭhī-Mantra and dedicates himself to pious thoughts. He has then to fulfil "6 necessary duties" (Āvaśyaka). They are:

1. Sāmāyika, devotion lasting 48 minutes which is dedicated to the inner self-communion with a vow to keep oneself away from all evils.
2. Caturviṁśatijinastuti, panegyric of 24 Tīrthaṅkaras.
3. Vandana, worship of Guru.
4. Pratikramaṇa, confession.
5. Kāyotsarga, remaining in a particular posture (see p. 415) by which one should aim at freeing the mind from the physical.
6. Pratyākhyāna, taking a vow to renounce certain pleasures.

The Āvaśyakas are fulfilled either at home or in an Upāśraya, and that too in the morning, noon and evening, and even more often. Visit to an Upāśraya is connected with listening to a sermon.

While among Sthānakavāsīs, participation in public cult is restricted to visiting an Upāśraya, the followers of idol-worship take part also in temple-cult, at least once a day, in many cases, even more often.

Meals—quite pious people are satisfied with only one—have to be taken before nightfall, and they have to be preceded by prayers, and if possible, by donations to ascetics or the needy.

When a Jaina goes to bed in the night, he utters again pious sayings and is engrossed in pious thoughts, till he falls asleep which is beautified for him by lucky dreams as a reward for good works.

Even the Vedic fire-sacrifices were performed by many Jainas under the influences of Hindus; three fires should be kindled in the morning, at the noon time and in the evening, according to *Ādipurāṇa* (47.348) as a memory of the cremation of Ṛṣabha's mortal remains.

(2) Rites on Special Occasions

The whole life of a pious Jaina from his first to the last breath is accompanied by holy actions. Jainas share many of these rites with Hindus; they have been even partially borrowed from them. The individual ceremonies differ with different sects and regions in many respects; they are not even performed in the same manner at all the times. We are trying in the following to give only an approximate idea of the most important observances which are common among Śvetāmbaras, without going into the details of the differences.[65]

The first rites which are connected with the life of a man are performed before his birth. When the mother is five months pregnant, a Brāhmaṇa is called, who performs the ceremony of *Garbhādhāna* (conception). In this, a pregnant woman who has taken her place on the left of her husband and whose garment is bound to his, is sprinkled with consecrated water and she is blessed by the chanting of Śāntidevī-stotra and holy Mantras. In these Mantras which are chanted here, the heavenly powers are called upon to protect the mother and child from demons, wild animals and all sorts of sufferings and grant them happiness and prosperity.

The *Puṁsavana*-ceremony takes place in the 8th month of pregnancy. Its aim is to get male progeny. In this the Guru sprinkles the expectant mohter who has worn new clothes with consecrated, perfumed water on a day which is favourable for the birth of a boy in the 4th night-watch under a starry sky; same thing is repeated at daybreak. In the Mantras chanted on this occasion, the soul gone into the womb of the mother is wished an easy birth and a hope is expressed that it may turn out to be the happiness of the parents and the honour of the family. Coins and sweets are distributed in this ceremony.

The pregnant woman then goes soon to the house of her parents and looks forward to her confinement. Once the expected child is born, its umbilical cord is cut, and mother and child are bathed. An astrologer prepares the horoscope of the young citizen of the earth. The Guru burns sandal and bilva-wood and puts the ash mixed with mustard and salt in a bundle, sayings directed to Ambikā are chanted seven times in which this goddess is called upon to protect the child. Then a piece of iron, red sandal, otter's-hair among other things is put into the bundle; then it is tied with a black thread to the hand of the child by the oldest female member of the family.

On the 3rd day after the birth, the Guru, after he has worshipped the image of the sun, guides the beautifully bedecked mother with the child she carries in her arms into the Sun. He shows them the Thousand-rayed Lord of the day, while he implores him for happiness. In the evening, the nectar-giving king of the stars, the Moon, is shown and worshipped in a similar fashion. This sacrament is called Sūryendu-darśana.

The Kṣīrāśana-ceremony takes place on the same day.

In this the suckling as drinks milk from the mother's breast. The Guru wishes it health and long life by chanting a Mantra.

In the night of the 6th day after birth, the Guru performs in the house of birth the Ṣaṣṭhī-saṁskāra the solemn worship of 8 Mothers: i.e., of the tutelary goddesses Brahmāṇī, Māheśvarī, Kaumārī, Vaiṣṇavī, Vārāhī, Indrāṇī, Cāmuṇḍā and Tripurā. They are called upon to come and stay with the help of Mantras and pleased by the offerings of perfumes, flowers, incenses, lamps, rice and sweets. The same thing happens then with Ṣaṣṭhī, protectress of children. Then women whose husbands are alive spend the night with the mother without sleeping. The next morning, the Guru lets the Mother-goddesses go with the words: "Sublime ones! Goodbye! Hail to you!" Then he sprinkles the child with the consecrated water and blesses it.

The mother becomes impure on account of the birth. The impurity disappears after a number of days; this number is different with different castes: it is 10 days among Brāhmaṇas, 12 among Kṣatriyas, 16 among Vaiśyas and 1 month among Śūdras. Once this period is over, the mother and the child and the other member of the family take a bath and they are declared as pure by the Guru (Śucikarma-saṁskāra).

The name-giving (*nāmakarṇa*) takes places on the same day or after 2 or 3 days. All members of the family gather for this ceremony, and the Guru appears along with an astrologer. The astrologer then explains the horoscope which is written down on a paper in clean handwriting; the ascendant and others of the 12 heavenly houses are worshipped by the relatives by expending 12 gold, 12 silver and 12 copper coins, 12 betel-nuts, 12 fruits and 12 cocoanuts, and the 9 planets are offered 9 each of these things. Then the Guru whispers into the ear of one elderly aunt the name of the child which is fixed after taking concern of all the members of the family. All then go to a temple. Here the mother and the child worship the Tīrthaṅkaras; then the aunt announces the name of the child in front of the Jina. This is followed by some other rites. The ceremony can also take place in front of the Jina-image in the house where the birth took place.

The name-giving with such a pomp takes place very often only for the first son; it is done in a simple form for later male children, and the girls get their name from the mother without much ado.

The Jainas prefer first names which have a connection with the persons of their holy legends, like Rikhabdās (Ṛṣabhadās, servant of Ṛṣabha). Ajitaprasāda (blessed by Ajita), etc. As it is with Hindus, the names are common which indicate plain things, like Dhoṇḍu (Marāthī) "stone", Kaḍappa (Kannaḍa) "forest". The purpose of this peculiar practice is to divert the evil demons with the help of these names so that they do not do any harm to the bearer of the name.

The "*offering of food*" (Annaprāśana) takes place for a boy in the 6th month of birth, and for a girl, in the 5th month. After the Guru has performed some rites, the mother feeds the child something from the food that is dedicated to the family goddess.

The Guru takes up the solemn *piercing of the ear-holes* (Karṇavedha) when the child is 3, 5 or 7 years old. The holy action takes place after due worship of the Mother-goddess, and its purpose is, as it can be seen from the chanting of the Mantras at that time, to prepare the ears to listen to the teachers of the Jaina-religion.

Then follows—not at a particular time—the Cūḍākaraṇa, i.e. *cutting of the hair.* After the Guru has worshipped the Mother-goddesses, a barber cuts the hair by removing all of them. He lealves in the middle a tuft of hair for boys belonging to the upper three castes.

The most important event between birth and marriage

is *Upanayana*, the acceptance by the teacher, a sort of an initiation of the young man. The Upanayana takes place only among the male members of the upper three castes; among Brāhmaṇas, it is in the 8th year, among Kṣatriyas in the 11th and among Vaiśyas in the 12th year after Garbhāddhāna. Śūdras are not allowed this ceremony which finds its visible expression in the wearing of the holy thread. A boy to be initiated has to take bath few days before this ceremony and rub himself with sesame-oil. His hair is cut on the festive day itself. An altar with a Jina-idol upon it is erected in fornt of the house. After the Mantras have been recited and circumambulations have been performed, the pupil is initiated. Then he falls to the feet of the Guru and says, "Revered one, I am without a caste, without right conduct, without Mantra, without virtue, without Dharma, without purity, without Brahma; teach me my duties with respect to gods, Ṛṣis, fathers and guests (i.e. ascetics)." During the chanting of the Mantras, he is then provided with a girdle of Muñja-grass and the holy thread; this is prepared from gold among Brāhmaṇas and from cotton among Kṣatriyas and Vaiśyas. After this, the Pañcaparameṣṭhī is whispered into his ear three times. Then follows the initiation as a Brahmacārī. For this purpose the pupil is dressed with a garment of bast and he is given a stick of Palāśa-wood. In a conversation with the Guru, he is taught the duties he has to do and the vow he has to keep. After this he goes for begging. He gets gifts in the houses of some Jainas he visits.

The period which the initiated one has to spend with the Guru as a pupil, is maximum 8 to 16 years among Brāhmaṇas, 10 to 16 years among Kṣatriyas and 12 to 16 years among Vaiśyas. But the apprenticeship is not generally kept up; it is reduced to a few days or to one day. Leaving the pupilage is effected by a ceremony called "Vratavisarga" (delivery from the vow). The pupil puts down the stick, the clothes of a penitent and the girdle, receives instruction and is blessed. This is followed by a ceremony of the "gifting a cow" (Godāna), in which the initiated one offers a beautifully embellished cow or something else as an honorarium to the Guru. Then he distributes clothes, food, containers, etc. among monks.

Among the Śūdras there is a different ceremony instead of Upanayana or the thread-ceremony. It is called *handing over of the upper garment* (Uttarīyaka-nyāsa) in which also Mantras are chanted, instructions given and gifts presented.

The beginning of study (Adhyayana) is reckoned as the 13th sacrament. It is performed under certain formalities. The pupil takes his place on a seat of Kuśa-grass on the left side of the Guru in a temple or under a Kadamba-tree. The Guru whispers the Sārasvata-Mantra thrice into his right ear. Then he is led in a solemn procession to an Upādhyāya, who then begins the lesson. He teaches to Brāhmaṇas Āyurveda (medicine), then the 6 Aṅgas, the lawbooks and the Purāṇas, to Kṣatriyas medicine, archery, politics and the knowledge necessary for one's sustenance (Ājīvikā),[66] to Vaiśyas the lawbooks and prudence and to the members of the other castes the knowledge that is proper for them.

The 14th sacrament, "marriage" (Vivāha)[67] is the most significant for the society. This is allowed to be contracted only among persons who belong to the same caste, but to a different Gotra. Already when the children are in their tender years, the parents look around for a suitable bride. If something proper has been found, then the two families start negotiations, and the horoscopes of both the partners are compared to find out whether they suit each other. Once these negotiations end satisfactorily, official visits take place, presents are exchanged. Mostly several years pass between the engagement and marriage; the latter takes place these days when the bridegroom is 15 years old and the bride 12 years. An astrologer is consulted to fix the date of marriage; he suggests a favourable constellation under which the marriage can take place. Then rites are performed in the houses of the parents of the bridegroom and the bride to worship the idols of the Mother-goddesses, of Ṣaṣṭhī Gaṇapati, Kandarpa and the Kulakaras (see p. 292). A day before the marriage, the bridegroom and the bride have to take bath in their respective houses, rub their body with oil and perform other propitious ceremonies.

On the day of the marriage, the bridegroom who is splendidly bedecked rides to the house of the bride on a horse or an elephant, surrounded by an escort of friends and relatives who sing songs in his honour Brāhmaṇas march at the head of the procession; they recite Mantras to combat bad planetary influences (Grahaśānti-mantra). After performing a number of rites, the bride and the bridegroom sit next to each other, and their hands are tied together with a saffron-coloured thread; hope is expressed in the Hastabandhana-mantra chanted here that they would be united for ever.

In the mean time, a rectangular pavilion of wood and an altar is erected on the yard or in front of the house of bride's father. Fire is kindled on the altar. After several ceremonies, the bride and the bridegroom go around the fire several times. Then the bridegroom holds the hand of the bride, when again Mantras are recited. After the marriage is thus celebrated and presents distributed, the Guru takes the couple into the house of the bride's mother, where again some rites are to be performed and gifts to be distributed. The couple again visits once more the pavilion, where again some rites are performed and goes into the bedroom where the two are supposed to spend the night together. Here the young couple worships the god of love, the two enjoy milk and rice together and abandon themselves to the pleasures of love. Again on the next day, some ceremonies are to be performed and gifts to be given. Marriage is connected with the organization of numerous festivities and banquets which go on for days. The costs of performing marriage with everything that goes with it, are quite significant; they are mainly a burden to the bride's father who is compelled to make arrangement for the expenditure which is beyond his means.

The number of ceremonies performed during marriage is exceptionally great; we could therefore state briefly only what is the most important. A number of popular customs, which vary from region to region, are connected with it; besides, the influence Hindus upon Jainas plays its role in the ritual that is described here. In actual practice it is much more strong than the textbooks would admit it. Therefore, one who takes the troubles of comparing the individual description of the marriage with those of the eye-witnesses,[68] will come across a muddle of rites which have not been dealt with here.

Human happiness becomes a receptacle of fortune and it bears fruits in this and the other world only then when the man succeeds in fulfilling the pious vows. These "Vratas" are reckoned as the 15th sacrament and considered as the most important of all. They are different from all we have discussed so far in two essential respects: While those are administered by a house-priest (Gṛhya-guru), i.e. a Jaina-Brāhmaṇa or a Kṣullaka, a vow can be taken only with the help of an ascetic, a Nirgrantha-guru Yati; and while the formulas used in the other Saṁskāras are composed in Sanskrit, those used for taking the vow are mostly in Prākṛta because they should be understood by the men and women of all castes. The Vratas and Pratimās laymen have to fulfil are discussed above on p. 228 f. The assumption of duties which these presuppose takes place in accordance with an exactly fixed ritual. A layman goes to an ascetic and expresses his wish to him to take a vow for a certain period to a certain extent, and worships the Tīrthaṅkaras, Śrutadevatās, etc. with gifts and circumambulations. Then he receives instruction and solemnly vows to avoid certain things for a fixed period (days, weeks, months, years, and even for the whole life), to travel only up to a certain limit or possess money, etc. One who has vowed to do a certain thing has to remind himself of it several times everyday and atone for his failure.

The "last sacrament" (Antyasaṁskāra) that is given to a pious Jaina is the cremation. When someone is in his death-bed, his relatives give him spiritual consolation; his Guru is called to give him consolations, recite Mantras to him and make him recite them. When death approaches, a pious man vows not to take any solid or liquid diet and renounces all worldly desires. He makes donations to the religion, to its servants and to the poor and finally dies concentrating all his thoughts on the five Parameṣṭhīs.

The dead body is put down on the ground, washed, anointed with perfumes and new clothes are put on it. Then it is put on a bier and carried by four near relatives on the shoulders to the place of cremation. A pyre is kept ready there. It is placed on a stone to prevent the destruction of other living beings. The pyre is kindled with the fire that is brought from the house of the deceased. Once the corpse is reduced to ash, the mourners return home. Then the ash is thrown into a river by a near relative on the third day, while the mortal remains are buried near a consecrated place. [Pyramid-shaped tomb is often erected over it later. A pot of water (Kalaśa) made of stone is placed over it. Then the survivors go to a temple and worship the Jina-images, and to an Upāśraya where a monk gives a sermon to them on the ephemerality of all that is worldly.

The relatives become impure for ten days on account of the death in the family. Celebrations for the dead (Śrāddha), as they are practised by Hindus, do not take place among right-believing Jainas.

If the deceased person leaves behind a widow, her bangles are broken, she must put down her ornaments, should not wear any more the sign of luck on her forehead, must dedicate her life to penitence by renouncing worldly pleasure and should never marry again.

The rites we have discussed here are the most important in practice today among idol-worshipping Śvetāmbaras, but there are several differences in different regions and among different sects. The ceremonies of Sthānakavāsīs differ from them in many respects, particularly in their practice of not using the Jina-idols. Similar Saṁskāras are practised by Digambaras. *Ādipurāṇa* (Chap. 38) enumerates 20 holy rites to be performed for a pious layman till his death. The first sacrament is "Garbhādhāna"; it is done to a young woman before the married life begins for her. Then follow the ceremonies *Prīti, Suprīti, Dhṛti* and *Moda* which are performed for a pregnant woman in her 3rd, 5th, 7th and 9th month with the purpose of achieving healthy growth of the embryo. *"Priyodbhava"* takes place at the birth of the child; 12 days later the *"name giving"*; 3 or 4 months later the first *"going out"* (Bahiryāṇa) of the mother and child, and immediately after this the *"Niṣadyā"* -rite, in which the newborn is solemnly put down on a bed. The *first food* (Prāśana) is given to the child in the 7th or 8th month; a year later the "Vyuṣṭi" celebration is done by inviting relatives. Boy's hair are cut for the first time soon thereafter. He is then initiated into the secrets of the alphabet (Lipisaṁkhyāna-saṅgraha) in his fifth year. He is girded with the holy thread at the age of 8 or later, and then he goes to a Guru for learning, when he takes the vow of observing celibacy, not to use a raised bed, etc. On completion of apprenticeship (12th to 16th year), he is freed from this vow (Vratāvartana), and he can marry. There are further celebrations through special rites: the attainment of independence in the caste (Varṇalābha), the practice of right conduct in the family (Kulacaryā) and achievement of position as a layman (Gṛhīśitā) which is generally respected and preferred.

Special events in the family demand special rites. If a man or a widow *adopts* someone, then he or she has to fetch first a written permission of the parents of the one who is to be adopted given in the presence of witnesses, show it to his or her relatives and get it attested by an official of the king by putting his seal. After the legal side of the matter has been settled, a festival of religious character is organized. Male and female relatives are invited and entertained with songs and dances. Then all the participants go to a temple, where different rites are performed and gifts distributed. Then a meal is arranged which is followed by birth-ceremony. The father of the one who is to be adopted gets then a diadem, a cocoanut and several coins. Once giving and taking of these things is over, it is considered that the process of adoption is over, and the adopted son steps to the right of the real son of the parents who have adopted him.[69]

The promotion of a man to a high position is also celebrated by certain ceremonies. The textbooks of the ritual give extensive instructions for the consecration of the king, the festive introduction of a minister, field marshal, governor, district officer, school teacher, etc.[70]

2. RITES FOR ASCETICS

(1) The Daily Rites

When a monk wakes up in the last hour of the night (at about 4 a.m.), then he should recite the Parameṣṭhī-Mantra and get up from his bed. He then goes out of the house to relieve himself. On return he meditates and thinks of the sins he might have committed in the night, like unintended harm to small living beings, etc. When it gets light, he looks for the insects on his body, clothes, room and puts them at a safe place. He then studies, teaches, writes, copies books. Then he goes to a temple and worships there the Tīrthaṅkaras by bowing before the idols, circumambulating them and by reciting hymns and meditating. A monk cannot perform any of the types of the Pūjā (see p. 439) performed in temple; he does not also put on a special dress in temple like a layman; his cult is rather spiritual and introspective. He then returns to his house where he meditates.

He goes out around 10 a.m. to beg for food and drink. On returning from his round, he confesses his sins which he has committed on his way by harming living beings. After chanting the Mantras, he takes the food he got by begging. The utensils are washed after the meal. After an hour's rest he studies or teaches. Insects are again searched around 3 p.m. Another begging round is done around 4.30 p.m. which is again followed by a confession, chanting of Mantras and meals. Meals have to be finished before sunset. Nothing can be taken, even water, during darkness. No light is burnt in Upāśrayas. After the ascetic has dedicated himself to pious meditation, he recites the Parameṣṭhī-Mantra and other pious Mantras and goes to bed (latest around 9 p.m.). The first part of the night should be devoted to pious conversation, the second to rest and the third to contemplation.

The hourly plan[71] sketched here is common among idol-worshipping Śvetāmbaras; it varies in individual things among Śvetāmbara-nuns and ascetics of other sects.

(2) Rites on Special Occasions

Like the life of a layman, that of a monk and nun is

also interwoven with a number. of rites. The first rite takes place before their entry into ascetic life and the last shortly before and after the death. The particular ceremonies in practice among particular sects and orders are very different; besides they involve such a great number of details that it is not possible to treat them in full here. I am, therefore, restricting myself to mentioning only some of the rich material and beginning with the ascetic-rites of Śvetāmbaras.

The path on which a Jaina comes to enter into a spiritual position is very different, as we have shown it above on p. 372 f. The usual is, or should be, that he is induced by a sermon of an ascetic to become introspect, and then he takes a considered decision to dedicate himself completely to renouncing the world. A man who has the will to do this, turns to a monk with the request to prepare him for asceticism. If he thinks that he is right for it, then he accepts him as a pupil and makes him finally an ascetic by organizing a solemn initiation-ceremony. But many times, the entry into the rank of a homeless penitent happens in a different manner. Sometimes the one who wants to renounce the world, may awake to the knowledge of the futility of all that is worldly and become an ascetic without any human help and without receiving instruction from any one. This is, e.g. the case with the Tīrthaṅkaras who become Yatis as "Svayambuddhas" as the Jainas always emphasize. But then, and as we have already remarked on p. 377 above, it is quite often that children enter the spiritual status. Boys who have been educated in their tender age to become monks. They have thus a long process of training while others have to complete in a very short time. All this, of course, needs a differential treatment.

According to Vardhamāna Sūri's *Ācāradinakara*, someone who, after getting the permission of his parents, his wife, his son or his superiors, wants to dedicate himself to the life of a monk, becomes first a Brahmacārī. The ceremony consists in reciting sayings and Mantras, in taking the vow of fulfilling the duties of self-discipline. The pupil remains in this stage for a period up to 3 years; he still has the tuft on his tonsured head and also the holy thread. If he can show patience, he can become a Kṣullaka, otherwise he returns to the status of a householder.

The second prestage of becoming a monk is the status of a Kṣullaka. A Brahmacārī becomes a Kṣuallaka by a special initiation (Dīkṣā). Even here special formulas are recited and the duty of keeping 5 important vows is fulfilled. The future ascetic remains in the Kṣullaka-stage up to 3 years. His conduct during this period should be one of the preparatory stage of complete self-discipline (Sāmāyika-caritra). During the period as a novice, he has to study the holy scriptures and pass a number of examinations which show that he is mature for the great initiation as a monk. If he does not pass this examination, he returns to the status as a householder.

The real life as a monk begins only with the performance of the Pravrajyā-ceremony. It consists of a number of rites of different types. It can be seen from the letter of Ācārya Vijaya Indra Sūri who wrote to me that the festivities and celebrations connected with it can go on for a long period. He wrote to me on 10th November, 1923 from Belanganj, Agra that he was busy with initiating Sādhu Himāṅśu Vijaya and that the completion of the ritual would take 27 days and after it is over, the new monk would need still one more week to keep a certain vow.

The initiation of a monk is done on a day which is astrologically favourable, and it is celebrated with the pomp of a marriage; the costs needed for this are borne the one who is renouncing the world or by his relatives, if they have the means, otherwise they are borne by the laymen through contribution. The pupil is fetched from the paternal home in a procession by festively dressed men and women accompanied beating of drums and songs. He is brought in a palanquin or on a horse-back to the place, where the solemn event is supposed to take place. A saint, mostly an Ācārya, awaits him there to initiate him, on occasions even an Upādhyāya does this work. It is either a place away from the town with a holy tree, or an open place in front of the house of the Guru. An altar and an imitation of Samavasaraṇa (see p. 278) is erected there. Pūjā of God takes place in front of this in the presence of numerous ascetics and laymen of both sexes. In this the Samavasaraṇa is circumambulated, hymns are sung and holy sayings are chanted. Then the pupil takes off his clothes, his ornaments, his holy thread (if he has one) and puts on the garments of a monk. He himself pulls off a slock of hair or lets the Guru or someone else do this painful ordeal. After the chanting of the sayings and formulas, he vows to fulfil the duty of complete self-discipline and gets a new name (among Śvetāmbaras, it has to agree with his earlier name). Then Vāsa-ointment is rubbed on to his head. After going round the Samavasaraṇa, the new Sādhu bows to the Guru and the monks. Nuns, laymen, men and women who are present for the ceremony bow to the new Sādhu.

The initiation of a monk or a nun is performed differently among Terāpanthīs. H. Jacobi who was present for such a ceremony in Ladnū writes to me: "Both (the persons to be initiated) were married people, and not pupils or novices; the scene was played in front of a caravanserai (Dharmaśālā), in front of which there was an open place. A staircase of, say, height of a man, led to the entrance of the Dharmaśālā. There were terraces on both the sides of the staircase; the Ācārya and Yatis sat on the one to the right, and nuns on the left. Then the couple which was beautifully dressed was led. She stood completely veiled beside the nuns, he on an even ground in front of the Ācārya. A Pradakṣiṇā (circumambulation) was made around the place. The elder brother of the person to be initiated stood behind him and gave the written consent of the family to the Ācārya. The Ācārya recited quite fluently a formula, after the people in the immediate surrounding had become quiet to some extent. Then the monk bent down his head which was shorn but for a tuft of hair, and the Ācārya pulled all his hair in five jerks and the monk did not flinch even once. The monk bowed before the other monks and seated himself as the last in their row; the nun was led to the other nuns. She had to bow down before the Ācārya when he spoke, before the initiation of the monk was taken up."

A sermon generally concludes the initiation which is followed by some more rituals. The actual act lasts only for 4 hours, but throughout the day later a number of celebrations have to take place and duties of different types to be fulfilled.

The spiritual *Ancienneté* of the monk is calculated from the conclusion of the initiation ceremony. The stage he has reached thereby is called Chedopasthāpanā. By doing penance, uprooting of all passions and by severing all connections from all that is worldly, he is able to climb from here to the three higher stages of his life. The ascetic has to perform a number of duties to achieve this; they are imposed upon him by his Guru. There is a great number of precepts on them. If they are neglected, the consequence is punishments and atonements of all sorts, thus, e.g. reduction of the spiritual *Ancienneté* can be imposed.

The promotions taking place within the Saṅgha, thus when a monk is made reader (Vācaka), teacher (Upādhyāya) or master (Ācārya), give an occasion for celebrations. The rites to be performed on these occasions are circumambulation of the Samavasaraṇa, recitation of the hymns and the sayings, applying Vāsa, etc Initiation of an Ācārya is particularly solemn. The dress to be put on by him is consecrated in the night before the celebration; then two seats are put up, on one of them the Guru sits, while on the other a bundle of Akṣa is kept. After a number of celebrations, chanting of the sayings and the Mantras, the Guru whispers into the ear of the one who is becoming master 3 times the "Sūri-Mantra" and gives in his hand the Akṣa-bundle. Then he gives him a new name (This is mostly the inversion of the earlier name which precedes the title Sūri, thus, e.g. the new name Indra Vijaya is Vijaya Indra Sūri). The new Ācārya then sits on one of the seats and is worshipped by the Guru and all those who are present, and he is praised in lively verses as the harbringer of the Jaina-doctrine, the one "who shatters the mountain of Saṁsāra with a thunderbolt". The initiation of the master is followed by sermons and celebrations of a religious nature, and the laymen perform them in a festival lasting for ten days.

The mode of death to be aspired by an ascetic is Saṁlekhanā, i.e. the voluntary death from starvation. The Saṁlekhanā should be done after 12 years of extremely severe asceticism in such a way that the ascetic wanting to die goes to a mountain, sits there under a tree and does not move any of his limbs till the death comes on account of the want of food. But this form of Saṁlekhanā can seldomly be carried out. Most of the monks (as also laymen) are satisfied with taking a vow on the death-bed in the presence of the master, teacher or ascetic that they would abstain from taking any food. This happens after the dying person sits down with crossed legs on a seat of grass, with his face turned towards the north-east, and has worshipped the idol of a Jina that is brought there and the Tīrthaṅkaras and the deities extolled by chanting of sayings and hymns. The dying person then requests all the living beings to pardon him, if he has done to them something bad, as he also pardons all who have done to him something bad. Then he repeats the five important vows and promises not to take any solid or liquid diet. Amidst the recitation of sayings or holy texts, the pious one who has performed Saṁlekhanā goes to the heavenly world, assured that he would attain salvation in a later birth which cannot be attained by him in the present bad era in our part of the world. A man who, thus, dies a voluntary death "in the state of ecstasy (Samādhi)", is held in high esteem by Jainas, and the pious people go to him with a belief that his merciful proximity would help in wiping out the Karma, as if to a place of pilgrimage.

If a monk dies, his dead body is cremated with pomp. The monk and the pious laymen fast on that day and listen to the sermons on the ephemerality of the earthly life.

The special rites for initiation and at the time of death of a nun, at her dedication of Pravartinī, Mahattarā, etc. resemble those of the monks we have discussed here.

Digambaras follow their own ritual in organisation of their asceticism. The change over from a layman to a monk and the successive attainment of higher position are characterized by special ceremonies. The Ādipurāṇa (38) enumerates the following stages through which a holy man goes: First comes for a layman Praśānti, giving up the attachment to the objects of senses and the preference for religious study, etc.; this is followed by his leaving the house, after he has given the earnings; one third for pious purposes, one third for the eldest son and remaining one third for other children. The pious man then is initiated first to become Kṣullaka; as such he still wears clothes. As he progresses, he gives up these and attains "Jinarūpatā". After distinguishing himself in fasting, penance and studies, he becomes a Guru; if he climbs further, he becomes head of the community that is divided into four parts. This person seeking salvation does not keep to the position till he dies, but hands it over to his pupil so that he can completely devote himself to penance and meditation once he is relieved of the burden of the office. In meditation and by abstaining from taking any food, he gets the "Saṁlekhanā"-death which procures for him rebirth in a heaven of gods.

3. TEMPLE-RITUAL

(1) Daily Rites

The rites to be performed in Jaina-temples are multiferous. Enumeration of all ceremonies of the cult in shrines would fill a whole book. I shall, therefore, restrict myself to giving a brief description of the main rites performed in a temple in Gujarāt in the morning, at noon and in the evening. The description given on p. 191 ff. of J. Burgess in the *Indian Antiquary* 13 (1884) serves me as guide.[72]

The morning service begins around 6.30 a.m. The Pujārī who has taken a bath, or who has, in any case, washed the five main parts of his body, mouth, hands and feet, opens the temple. On entering the consecrated hall, he speaks "nissahi" or "nissarahi", and it means that he goes out of the world and leaves all that is worldly behind. Then he cleans the temple and the idols. A lamp is kept on the right of the idol of the Tīrthaṅkara and on the left a container for incense and they are kindled. Then the nine limbs of the Tīrthaṅkara (the big toes, knee-joints, hand-joints, shoulders, top of the head, forehead, neck, breast and the navel) are smeared with Vāsa-powder by the Pujārī, which is a nicely smelling paste consisting of sandal, camphor, ambergris, musk and saffron.

Then a Svastika-mark (see p. 426) is drawn on a small table in the temple-hall; fruits are placed on the Svastika and sweets (Naivedya) on the crescent moon. Then the Pujārī takes the tag of his upper garment (which is worn in a way like the holy thread of a Brāhmaṇa) between his hands, dusts the ground with it and utters a

Mantra. Then he "bows with the five limbs" (Pañcāṅga-praṇāma) by touching the ground with both the kness, both the palms and the forehead. He then goes round the idol thrice and then sits before it in the Yoga-mudrāsana-posture. Then after requesting the Tīrthaṅkara through a saying to permit him to say a prayer called Caityavandana, and giving himself the permission in place of the saint with an "iccham", he sings this hymn in which he implores the Tīrthaṅkara (e.g. Śāntinātha) for blessing. He then chants a number of other panegyrics and Mantras by changing the position of the body each time in accordance with the precept. At the end of the Pūjā he rings the "bell of victory" (Jayaghaṇṭā) and leaves the shrine with the words "āvissahi" which indicates his return to the world.

The second Pūjā begins around 10 a.m. The Pujārī has to take his bath before. In this he washes, with his face turned towards the east, 10 Kakāvalis, i.e. 10 limbs; their Indian names begin with K, viz, ears, joints of hands and feet, armpits, neck and loins and dries his body with a clean white towel. He then enters the temple with a pot of water in which he washes his feet before entering the hall. After drying his feet on the mat outside, he enters the shrine with the words "nissahi". He folds his upper-garment (Uttarāsana) eight times, binds it over his mouth so that the idol is not defiled by his breath.

On entering he washes the stone on which the holy powder is prepared, prepares a new one, puts it in a container and goes into the sanctum sanctorum (Garbhagṛha). Here he removes the flowers of the earlier Pūjā and removes the dust from the idol of the Tīrthaṅkara with the help of a brush of peacock-feathers (Mayūra-puccha). Then he dips a piece of cloth in water and wipes with it the idol to remove the sandal-paste. If saffron sticks to some place, then he cleans the idol with a brush (Vālakuñci) prepared from the roots of nice smelling Uśīra-grass (Andropogon muricatun). After cleaning the idol, he prepares the "nectar of five" (Pañcāmṛta), a mixture of milk, curds, ghee, water and sugar. The preparation is put in a container called "Kalaśa" which is somewhat like a tea-pot without handle. The Pañcāmṛta is poured over the idol, followed by clean water which was in another Kalaśa. Sanskrit Mantras are chanted while doing this. The Pujārī then takes three different clothes (Aṅgaluhaṇa) and dries the idol with them thrice. Then he washes the throne of the idol and then after washing his hands he applies the sandal to the nine limbs of the idol while reciting Mantras.

Now follows the worship with flowers (Puṣpapūjā). The Pujārī takes flowers from a pot which he has brought with himself and strews them over the idol and puts a garland round its neck. While reciting the sayings he performs the worship with incense and lamps. Then after fanning the idol with a Yak-fan, he goes into the hall, draws a Svastika on a table and offers on it rice, fruits and sweets. This is followed by the singing of hymns and ringing of the victory-bell. Then the Pujārī departs from the shrine with the word "āvissahi".

The evening Pūjā is simple. It begins between 5 and 6. The Pujārī enters the temple with a "nissahi", kindles the lamps, burns the incense (Dhūpapūjā). Then he does the Āratīpūjā by swinging a lamp with five wicks in front of the idol. Then an oil-lamp (Maṅgaladīpa) is moved one way and the other way in front of the idol. While doing this, instruments like drum, bells, etc. are played. After the chanting of Mantras, the Pujārī rings the victory-bell and leaves the temple with "āvissahi".

What is written here gives generally an idea of the manner in which the Pūjā takes place in a Jaina-temple. There are many difference in the details. Thus, the kindling of the lamps in front of the idol and its worship after the darkness sets in is common only among the

Śvetāmbaras; Digambaras do not worship in the night, but only kindle the lamps in the temple to read the holy scriptures.[73]

(2) Rites on Special Occasions

The installation and dedication of a cult-idol requires a number of ceremonies. The rites are different in details among the two creeds and their sects; they are also different for different idols, because the idols of the Tīrthaṅkaras are to be treated differently from those of the Śāsanadevatās, gods, planets, etc. Finally there is also difference in nature and purpose of the idols: those which are used in the house of a believer for his worship, are dedicated in a different manner from those which are installed in temples; then for the idols in temples, the rites are different for the idols which are so big that they cannot be moved from the place, from those which are smaller and which can be comfortably transported. The ritual works of Jainas contain numerous detailed precepts on all this; we shall deal in the following only with the most important ones.

The installation (Pratiṣṭhā) of a Jina-idol requires extensive preparation. First the place where it is to be installed, is to be cleaned in a wide area. Dirt lying around, excrement, bones, hair, nails, teeth of living beings of all sorts are to be removed. Then an astrologically favourable time for the performance of the ceremony is to be fixed. If this is not possible, a moment has to be fixed in which all the heavenly bodies are favourable. Then the rites are to be performed which neutralize the influences of evil stars. Further all the ascetics and believers living in the surroundings are to be informed about the ceremony and to be suitably invited. The idol is cleaned before the beginning of Pratiṣṭhā and brought to the place where it is to be installed. All the necessary things like pots and utensils, water, herbs and other things are carried to the temple for the solemn ceremony (when dancing and music can be arranged); an altar is erected in the shrine, and benediction rites are performed in the house of the donor of the idol.

Before the installation ceremony, Dikpālas, the patrons of the directions of space are worshipped after their cult-images are installed. Then four jugs of precious metal are placed on all the sides of the idol and four beautifully bedecked girls powder the thousand herbs which are to be used for washing and anointing the idol.

The dedication of the idol is done by an Ācārya, a Pāṭhaka, a Sādhu, a Jaina-Brāhmaṇa or a Kṣullaka, but all these cannot perform the same ceremonies. The person conducting the ceremonies is called "Pratiṣṭhā-Guru"; four "Snātrakāras" are supposed to help him.

The holy act begins with a cake called "Bhūtabali" prepared from a Bakula-plant among other things being kept in the directions. The spirits of all sorts, Bhūtas, Pretas, Piśācas, Gandharvas, Yakṣas, Rākṣasas, Kinnaras, Vetālas, are requested to accept the offerings in the formulas which are uttered at that time. Then the Śāsanadevatās and other deities are worshipped immediately after by reciting hymns and sayings, then the idol to be dedicated is washed with water which is mixed with all sorts of ingredients, anointed with consecrated sandal, decorated with garlands of flowers and consecrated by touching its individual parts. A big festival lasting for eight days follows the Pūjā with its different Mantras and offerings; the donor has to entertain the participants at a feast. The hospitality and the pomp shown on the occasion of the installation of the idol involves quite an expenditure, so that now only few persons are in a position to bear them, and the complete execution of all Pratiṣṭhā-ceremonies and everything that goes with them is no more common these days as it was in the past.

Rites, like those for the installation of Jina-idols, take place at the consecration of statues of different deities, of the Yantras (plates with mystic symbols), of holy banners, etc.; even the dedication of the temple is done in a similar fashion.

The dedication of the cult-image can be renewed from time to time. Thus, e.g. the famous statue of Gommaṭa in Śravaṇa Beḷgoḷa is washed again anew after the lapse of certain number of years with Pañcāmṛta (milk, curds, ghee, honey, water), anointed and showered with flowers, fruits, etc. The last such celebration took place in 1925; big structures were erected to reach the top of the mighty monument. The pouring of holy liquids was done by numerous Jaina-laymen who were sold this right after the payment of a considerable sum of money.

On special occasions, flags with different emblems are hoisted for the purpose of the cult. The Ādipurāṇa mentions 10 types of flags; 108 pieces of every type, i.e. 4,320 flags were hoisted in each of the 4 directions in the honour of Ṛṣabha. This practice of "Pālidhvajas" is common even today.[74]

One of the types of worship of the Tīrthaṅkaras is the organization of a huge chariot-procession (Rathayātrā). Such a procession should take place at least once in a year; but these Yātrās have today lost much of their significance, which they had earlier when powerful kings were the followers of Jainism, and that is why the textbooks of rites refer with great penchant to the chariot procession of the world-rulers Mahāpadma (see p. 312 f.), Samprati and Kumārapāla which are glorified in the literature of Jainas.[75] In these festivals, the idols of the Tīrthaṅkaras, which were washed and anointed, were driven with a great pomp amidst jubilation of the people, on beautifully embellished shining chariots which were pulled by elephants and horses.

4. FESTIVAL DAYS

The holiest festival of Jainas is Paryuṣaṇa ("the rainy season"). It has this name because in accordance with Mahāvīra's[76] precepts it should begin when a month and twenty days of the rainy season are over, i.e. at a point of time, when monks and laymen have time to devote themselves to their religious obligations. Among Śvetāmbaras of today, it begins usually on the 12th day of the second half of the month of Śrāvaṇa (July-August) and ends with the 4th day of the first half of the month of Bhādrapada, although 70 days (till the 14th day of the first half of Kārttika) are considered as a holy period.[77] This festival consists primarily of fasting. Śvetāmbaras should really fast for the whole period of eight days, but this precept is not strictly followed, and many of them fast only for a day or two; but all abstain from food and drink on the last day. Particularly the keeping of the Poṣadha-vow (see p. 229) is made a duty, and a layman lives like a monk. Those who observe Poṣadha, are engrossed in meditation or studies in Upāśrayas or in solitude for 24 hours. During the holy week no work is done, and everyone goes to the community houses; where sermons are heard and holy scriptures are read. It is Kalpa-Sūtra among Śvetāmbaras. The 5th day is celebrated by Śvetāmbaras as a conventional birthday-festival of Mahāvīra and they organize a procession. (It is said that Mahāvīra was actually born on the 13th day of the first half of the month of Caitra.) Saṁvatsarī, the last day of Paryuṣaṇa, which is at the same time the last day of the Jaina-church, is spent by making a great confession; its purpose is that no sin be carried over to the next year. Every Jaina should reconcile on this day with those with whom he had quarrels. Since this is generally not possible orally, Jainas have a practice of writing letters to the acquaintances who are staying away, ask them for pardon for the annoyance caused, which they believe to have caused them intentionally or unintentionally (compare. p. 153).

Siddha-cakra-pūjā, the worship of the holy wheel, is the most significant festival next to Paryuṣaṇa that is particularly peculiar to Jainas. This takes place twice in a year, in the month of Caitra (March-April) and in Āśvina

(September-October) and lasts for 9 days from the 7th day till the full-moon day. The Siddha-cakra in the temple is worshipped by holding solemn ceremonies during this period. The wheel is brought on one of these days to a pond and washed there (Jalayātrā). Special types of fasting have to be observed in this festival.[78]

Let us mention, of the other festivals, the Śruta-pañcamī which is celebrated by Digambaras on the 5th day of the first half of Jyeṣṭha (May-June) to remember the day on which Kundakunda began to write his canon of the Jaina-doctrine.[79] Jñāna-pañcamī on the 5th bright day of Kārttika (October-November) is dedicated to sacred knowledge; the holy scriptures are worshipped on this day and cleansed of dust and insects. Mauna-Ekādaśī, on the 11th bright day of Mārgaśīrṣa (November-December), is spent in meditation and in keeping the vow of silence. The day is connected with the life-stories of several Tīrthaṅkaras. The 14th bright day of Āṣāḍha (June-July) indicates the beginning, the 15th bright day of Kārttika (October-November) the end of the rainy-season, of the Caturmāsya. Jainas fast on all full-moon days, and pious Jainas fast more or less strictly on 5 to 12 days in every month.[80]

A great number of days are dedicated to the memory of the events in the lives of Ādinātha, Pārśva, and other Tīrthaṅkaras and are correspondingly celebrated.

Among the festivals which Jainas share with Hindus, the most significant is Divālī on the 15th dark day of the month of Kārttika (October-November). Hindus celebrate Divālī mainly by illuminating the houses and the streets in honour of the goddess of Fortune, Lakṣmī. Jainas celebrate it to remember Māhavīra's Nirvāṇa; it is said that the kings who were his followers, organized a great general illumination in the night in which he died.[81] On this day, sweets, so-called "Laḍḍūs" are offered in the temples, and the pilgrimage to Pāvā on this day is considered as most beneficial. However, on account of the influence of Hindu-customs, the festival is celebrated by most Jainas more as one which is dedicated to luck and riches than as one which is dedicated to the memory of the saint who had attained salvation. Special rites are performed on two days which precede the new-moon day; on the first, women polish their ornaments in honour of Lakṣmī, and on the second, they leave sweets on cross-roads as a protection against spirits. But on the actual day of the festival, the book of accounts is made an object of the cult. For this purpose, the word "Śrī" is written by a Brāhmaṇa in it, then a coin and a leaf of a creeper is put on it and a lamp is swung in its honour. At the end, red powder is sprinkled on it, after which the Brāhmaṇa and the Jaina eat sweets. Then the book is kept open for a few hours; when it is closed, it is uttered: "Lakṣa-lābha, lakṣa-lābha", i.e. may it bring a hundred-thousandfold profit!

Jainas have borrowed a few other Hindu-festivals, but with a different significance. Thus, Gaṇeśa-caturthī for them, the birthday of the elephant-headed god of prosperity on the 4th day of the first half of Bhādrapada (August-September) is dedicated to Gautama as the master of the Gaṇas, i.e. to the main pupil of Mahāvīra, and the 9 days before the Daśaharā-festival in the month of Āśvina (September-October) are dedicated to Bharata.[82]

Jainas celebrate a number of festival days in accordance with the Hindu-customs, e.g., the Holī-festival in spring, the festival of the goddess of small-pox, Śītalā, etc.

5. SHRINES AND PILGRIMAGES

The worship of Tīrthaṅakaras, Pūjā in front of their idols and the proper celebration of the festival days bestow particularly a great religious reward in this and the other world, if it is done at places which are considered holy. Jainas also share the conviction deeply rooted in all the Indians that there is a great number of holy places on the consecrated ground of Bāratavarṣa, by visiting which one can look forward to effects which promote salvation and destroy sins. Hindus have given the name "Tīrtha" to the holy places which pilgrims coming from distant places visit. The word "Tīrtha" means access, a street, particularly to water, a channel, a ford near water, a pond, a bathing place.[83] From the meaning "bathing place", the word got among Hindus the meaning "holy place, place of pilgrimage" because most important shrines are near a holy river or sea to whose waters expiatory power is attributed. The term "Tīrtha" was also then transferred in earlier period to other shrines which do not have the characteristic of bathing places; thus, Tīrtha is a place which opens the passage to the crossing of the stream of metempsychosis. Among Jainas the word is especially used in the latter sense because the holy places of Jainas are not bathing places. In contrast to Hindus, orthodox Jainas do not believe that holy rivers have power to destroy sins. They consider that this belief is madness and they have placed it on the same level as other pointless religious acts held in high esteem by Hindus like widow-burning or throwing oneself down from the peak of mountain.[84]

For Jainas, Tīrtha is a place which became holy by a Tīrthaṅkara staying there for a long period, particularly where a Tīrthaṅkara was born, took the initiation into monkhood, attained knowledge or went into Nirvāṇa. Further, Tīrthas are places where other saints lived or attained perfection or where there are famous cult-objects.

The number of Jaina-Tīrthas is exceptionally large; a complete list cannot be made because many of the shrines which were famous earlier have fallen into oblivion today as a result of the decline of Jaina-faith during the last centuries and because many Tīrthas are not in the same renown among the members of all sects; a few communities which want to bring reform dispute completely the justification of the belief in the power of holy places. And besides, the .strong process of Hinduization that is going on in the Jainism of today, has made Jainas visit Hindu pilgrim-centres which have, in fact, nothing to do with the Jaina-religion and in which a connection with Jainism, if any is only too loose and is artificially established.

On page 28 of the prayer-book "Pañca-pratikramaṇa" which is usually used by Śvetāmbaras and published by Paṇḍita Sukhalāl "few Tīrthas of today" are mentioned. They are: Śatruñjaya, Girnār, Tārāṅga, Śaṅkeśvara, Kumbhāriyā, Ābū. Rāṇakpur, Kesariyājī, Bāmanvārā, Māṇḍavagarh, Antarīkṣa, Makṣi, Hastināpura, Allahābād, Banāras, Ayodhyā, Sammetaśikhara, Rājagṛha, Kākaṇḍī, Kṣatriyakuṇḍa, Pāvāpurī, Campāpurī. Few more are mentioned elsewhere in the book: Satyapurī, Bhṛgukaccha (Bhadoch), Muharī (p. 25), Aṣṭāpada, Varkān, Jirāvalā, Khambāṭ (p. 172), Gajapada, Vaibhār, Sonāgiri, Citrakūṭa (p. 249): This enumeration, of course, takes into consideration mainly those Tīrthas of the North which are visited by Śvetāmbaras. In the South India, there are a number of Digambara-shrines like Śṛavaṇa Beḷgoḷa, Padmāvatī, Gommaṭagiri near Mysore city, and there are numerous others. With this plethora of the places of pilgrimage,[85] it is unnecessary here, of course by taking into consideration the space available to us, to go into each one of them. I can do it all the more, as I have discussed a number of Jaina-Tīrthas in my book *Heilige Station der Hindus, Jainas und Buddhisten.* I shall, therefore, restrict myself to speaking only briefly on few of the most important ones.

A number of the most famous Jaina-shrines are on the mountains. The Aṣṭāpada (Kailāsa) in the Himālayas is considered as the place where the first Tīrthaṅkara, Ṛṣabha, had attained salvation. All his successors (except Vāsupūjya, Ariṣṭanemi and Mahāvīra) attained Nirvāṇa on the Sametaśikhara. This mountain, which is now mostly referred to as "Mount Pārasnāth" after the 23rd Jina, Pārśvanātha, is situated in district Hazāribāgh of

Bihār state. Thousands of Śvetāmbaras and Digambaras climb this every year to worship in the numerous temples which are on its peak. The 22nd Tīrthaṅkara, Ariṣṭanemi, got salvation on mountain Girnār (Raivataka) in Kāthiāvāḍ. Mount Śatruñjaya ("Victory over the enemy") where many saints are said to have got their salvation, lies in the same region, not far from the city of Pālitānā. This is considered by most of Jainas as the most beneficial of all the Tīrthas. "By only touching the Śatruñjaya great sinners could get the heavenly pleasures, and the people who accomplished good deeds, attained salvation in a short time....With every step one comes nearer to the Śatruñjaya-mountain, one is absolved of all the sins whose consequence is thousands of Koṭis of births."[86] Girnār and Śatruñjaya are famous for their beautiful temples. But this is true, above all, of the holy mountain of Rājapūtānā, Mount Ābū. The most beautiful temples, mighty magnificent buildings of white marble, are situated on this mountain which is near the place Dilvārā, and they were built by the banker Vimala Śā and the brothers of Tejapāla and Vastupāla in the 13th century.

Of the other shrines which deserve primarily to be mentioned are those in which Tīrthaṅkaras ended their life, e.g. Campā (now Bhāgalpur) in Bihār, where the 12th Jina, Vāsupūjya, attained salvation, and Pāvā in the same region, where Mahāvīra died and where his footprints and those of his pupils Gautama and Sudharmā are to be seen.[87] The old city of Rājagṛha in the same district is visited often by pilgrims on account of many reminiscences which are connected with the life of Mahāvīra and the 20th Tīrthaṅkara, Munisuvrata. Cities in which Jinas were born, like Banāras, Ayodhyā, Hastināpura (56 miles North of Delhi) and Kuṇḍa, are also the goal of pious pilgrims.

A number of places owe their fame to the statues of the Tīrthaṅkaras and saints which are there, and it is said that they have a miraculous influence. We have already mentioned some of them on p. 435 f.

If someone wants to begin a pilgrimage to a Tīrtha, then he has to prepare himself properly for the holy work by fasting and meditating, etc. In the journey itself, he has to do a number of observances; so he has to take food only once during the day, sleep on the ground, remain celibate and walk only on foot. If these rules are not followed, then the pilgrim loses a part of the transcendental reward which is beckoning him. Thus the reward got through a journey made in a vehicle is only half of the reward he earns by walking on foot. On reaching the place of pilgrimage, a pilgrim devotes himself to pious exercises, worships the Tīrthaṅkaras in individual temples and makes sumptuous donations for religious works. Certain actions promise an excellent reward in many places. Thus, e.g. in Śatruñjaya, the believer has to ascend and descend the thousands of steps, which take him up to the mountain, 99 times and circumambulate the shrines in a definite order. If this happens in the right manner, what takes three months' time, and when the pilgrim who has not eaten or drunk anything on the last day, finally reaches the main temple, then the priests there put an idol of the Tīrthaṅkara on a silver throne under a baldachin in the yard. Then the pilgrim offers eleven times the eightfold Pūjā, while hymns are sung and the boys dance ritual dances. The performance of these ceremonies which are very expensive promises an excellent reward.[88]

If someone is not in a position to undertake the pilgrimage himself, then he can still get its reward, by enabling others to go on pilgrimage, by making preparations for them, giving them money for the journey, accommodates them on the way or promotes them otherwise. But it is particularly rewarding, when someone goes himself on a pilgrimage and also lets others make the journey at his cost. Jainas narrate about the pious kings and statesmen who were followers of their religion that they undertook such "Tīrthayātrās" with a large number of their retinue.[89] Thus, it is said of the minister Vāstupāla that when he visited holy places, not less than 4,500 carts, 700 palanquins, 700 chariots, 1,800 camels, 2,900 servants, 3,300 bards, 450 Jaina-singers, 12,100 Śvetāmbaras and 1,100 Digambaras accompanied him.[90]

REFERENCES

1. Quotation from "Yogaśāstra" (in Nyāyavijaya's *Jaina-darśana*, Vol. 1 of the series *Dharma-nīti-granthāvalī*, Ahmedabad 1920), p. 48.
2. Śaṅkara, *Aparokṣānubhūti* 140, *Ātmabodha* 49.
3. J.G. Bühler, *On the Indian Sect of the Jainas*, Engl. ed. by Jas. Burgess, London, 1923, Appendix, p. 66 ff. The names among the Śvetāmbaras as given in Hemacandra's *Abhidhāna-cintāmaṇi* (Yaśovijaya Granthamāla 41) I.44.
4. Hemacandra, *ibid.*, II, 153 f.
5. *Ācāradinakara*, p. 223b.
6. According to a verse which is oft quoted and which is printed on p. 3 of the English translation of *Dravyasaṅgraha*, the number comes in the following manner: 40 Indras of Bhavanavāsīs, 32 of Vyantaras, 24 of Kalpa-vaimānikas, 2 of the Jyotiṣkas (viz. Sun and Moon), 1 of human beings and one of animals.
7. *Ādipurāṇa* 38. 226; Umāsvāmi, *Tattv.* III.19
8. Burgess, *Ind. Antq.* 13, 1884, p. 276.
9. Cf. e.g. Nemicandra's *Ṣaṣṭi-śataka* 82 (in *Prakaraṇa-ratnākara*, Vol. II) in which the worship of Gaṇeśa is disallowed.
10. *Pañcapratikramaṇa*, p. 295.
11. *Ibid.*, *Ācāradinakara*, p. 225b.
12. *Ācāradinakara*, p. 228a.
13. Hemacandra, *Yogaśāstra* IV, 177 ff.
14. Subhacandra's *Jñānārnava* (Text and transl. in Ghoshal's edition of *Dravya-saṅgraha*, Appendix p. LIX· ff.; cf. Hemacandra's *Yogaśāstra* VII-XII, Bhandarkar, *Report* 1883/84, p. 110-112).
15. A number of postures are mentioned in Hemacandra's *Yogaśāstra* IV. 123 ff. (transl. by E. Windisch, *ZDMG* 28, 1874, p. 257.
16. *Ācāradinakara*, p. 114 a.
17. Hemacandra, *Abhidhāna-cintāmaṇi* (verse transl. by Böhtlingk and Rieus, 1107 ff.).
18. Schubring, *Das Kalpa Sūtra*, 5, 22 f.

19. *Pañcapratikramaṇa*, p. 18.
20. *Ibid.*, p. 80.
21. Schubring, *Das Mahānīsiha-Sutra*, p. 84.
22. *Jaina Gazette* XX, January 1924, p. 24.
23. Haribhadra, *Yogabindu*, 37.
24. The word "Dṛṣṭi" means right knowledge that is connected with the right belief (*suśraddhayā saṅgata eva bodho dṛṣṭiḥ*).
25. Haribhadra, *Yoga-dṛṣṭi-samuccaya*, 19.
26. Rice, *Epigr. Carnatica* II, p. 39, 162.
27. Samantabhadra, *Ratnakaraṇḍa-śrāvakācāra*, 113.
28. *Imperial Gazetteer*, Oxford, 1907, I, p. 417.
29. *Deutsche Revue* XIX, 1894, 4, p. 299 f.
30. *Anupapātika-Sūtra* §§ 10. 49; Hemacandra, *Abhidhāna-cintāmaṇi*, p. 191.
31. V.R. Gāndhī, *Jain Philosophy* , p. 88 f.
32. J. Burgess, *Ind. Antq.* 32, 1903, p. 464.
33. *Dharmasaṅgraha*, I, p. 210a.
34. R. Fick, *Eine Jainistische Bearbeitung der Sagara-Sage*, p. 13.
35. v. Glasenapp on him in *Der Hinduismus*, p. 441.
36. Jayaswal, *JBORS* III, p. 465; comp. also M.J. Mehta's Introduction to *Adhyātma-tattvāloka*, p. XV f.
37. B. Laufer, *Dokumente der indischen Kunst*, I: *Citralakṣaṇa*, Leipzig, 1913, p. 8 ff.
38. *Aupapātika-Sūtra* § 16 (I owe the references to a manuscript of Dr. W. Hüttenmann looked up by me).
39. The rites are described with all details in *Ācāradinakara*, Chap. 33.
40. P. Peterson, *3 Report*, 1887, p. 25.
41. Inscription No. 85 in Rice's *Epigr. Carnatica* II, 153 gives an enthusiastic description of Gommaṭa of Śravaṇa Beḷgoḷa.
42. *Jaina-Gazette* XX, January, 1924, p. 30.
43. G. Bühler in *Transact. of the IXth congress of Orientalists*, 1893, p. 219.
44. A.K. Coomaraswamy, *Jaina Paintings and Manuscripts*, p. 32.
45. Jouveau-Dubreuil, *The Pallava-painting*, Pudukottai, 1920.
46. Nahar and Ghosh, *Epitome of J.*, p. 696, 706 (also illustration on it).
47. W. Hüttenmann, *Miniaturen zum Jainacarita*, Baessler Archiv., 1913.
48. A.K. Coomaraswamy, Notes on Jaina Art, *Journal of Indian Art*, No. 127, London, 1914; *Catalogue of Indian Collections in the Museum of Fine Arts*, Boston, Part IV: *Jaina Paintings and Manuscripts*, Boston, 1924.

49. *Deutsche Revue* XIX, 1894, p. 229 f.
50. The buildings recently discovered in the Panjab and Sindha which are thousands of years old, belong apparently to a different culture, and, therefore, they are not taken into consideration here.
51. In *Rājapraśṇīya-Upāṅga.* See E. Leumann, *Transact. of the VIth Intern. Orientalist Congress,* Part III, Sect. II, p. 498.
52. G. Bühler, *WZKM* 4, 1890, pp. 327 f.
53. G. Bühler, *WZKM* 5, 1891, p. 179.
54. Sir J.H. Marshall in *Cambridge History of India,* I, p. 634.
55. E: Hultzsch, *Annual Report on Epigraphy,* Madras, 1900-1901.
56. *Bombay Gazetteer* 9, 1, p. 112.
57. *Census 1901,* XVIII, Baroda, p. 150.
58. *Bombay Gazetteer* 24, p. 139.
59. J. Tod, *Annals and Antiquities of Rājasthān,* London, 1832, I, p. 518.
60. Cf. ref. 44.
61. Jñānasāgara's *Ratnacūḍa* (Joh. Hertel, *Indische Märchenromane* I, p. 117).
62. *Ibid.,* p. 103 ff.; there also a brief theory on dream.
63. Cf. Rice. *Epigr. Carnatica* II, p. 4.
64. *Ādipurāṇa* 41; Comp. v. Glasenapp in the *Jacobi-Festshcrift.*—Comp. further the chapter "Aberglaube und Zauberei" in v. Glasenapp, *Der Hinduismus,* p. 369-377 on Sorcery and Dīvination. Much of it what is said there also applies to Jainas.
65. What is described in the following is based mainly on Vardhamāna's *Ācāradinakara.*
66. Ājīvikā-śāstra is in *Ācāradinakara,* p. 31 a with an ironical comment as the doctrine of love, utility and worldly wisdom (Nīti).
67. According to Padmaraj Pandit's *A Treatise on Jain Law and Usages,* p. 9, the Jainas (like the Hindus) distinguish 6 different forms of marriage. The *Brāhma*-marriage consists in the daughter being given by the father to the bridegroom; in a *Gāndharva*-marriage, a king marries a girl without any ceremony on the basis of their mutual consent; in *Svayaṁvara,* a princess chooses her husband; in *Rākṣasa*-marriage, a king robs a girl from the vanquished enemies and marries her; in the *Āsura*-marriage, a man marries a girl on payment of certain sum of money to her parents (it is said to be permitted only to the Kṣatriyas); in the *Paiśāca*-marriage, a king takes home a girl coming from the same or other Gotra by force. The regular form of marriage is the first because marriage is defined as giving over of a daughter by her father to a bridegroom in the presence of Fire-god. A

man may, according to the same text, marry again, if his wife is ugly, barren, has a bad conduct, quarrelsome, irreligious or sick. But even though these reasons could not be given, polygamy was always permitted.

68. The descriptions of the marriage originate from earlier times in Haribhadra's *Samarāicca Kahā,* in Dhanavāla's *Bhavisattakaha* and other similar poetic works. For the present time, one may compare *Bombay Gazetteer* 9, 1, p. 101; 15, 1, p. 234; 24, p. 141; Stevenson, *Heart of J.*, p. 195 ff.; J. Burgess, *Ind. Antq.* 13, 1884, p. 280; Syed Siraj ul Hassan, *Castes and Tribes of H.E.H. the Nizam's Dominions,* I, p. 261 ff.
69. Bhadrabāhu-Saṁhitā, *Dāyabhāga* 40 ff. (J.L. Jaini, *Jaina Law,* p. 40 ff.).
70. Even elephants, horses, bulls, etc. are solemnly dedicated by a Guru (*Ācāradinakara,* p. 383b).
71. *Ācāradinakara,* p. 127b; Stevenson, *Heart of J.*, p. 228; Comp. *Uttarādhyayana-Sūtra* 26.
72. Cf. *Bombay Gazetteer* 9, 1, p. 110 ff.; Stevenson, *Notes,* p. 86 ff. *Heart of J.* p. 250 ff.
73. J.L. Jaini, *Ind. Antq.* 33, 1904, p. 332.
74. *Ādipurāṇa* 22, 219 ff.; Pathak, *Ind. Antq.* 14, 1885, p. 104 ff.
75. Ratnaśekhara, *Śrāddhavidhi,* p. 163b f.
76. *Kalpa-Sūtra,* see *SBE* 22, p. 296.
77. There is a difference of opinion amog few sects about the main day of the festival. Some celebrate it on the 5th day of Bhādrapada, others on the 4th. The practice of celebrating the 4th day is supposed to trace back to Kālakācārya (see p. 50) who wanted to make it possible for the king to participate in the festical, as he was to take part in some other celebration on the 5th day (Stevenson, *Heart of Jainism,* p. 76).
78. See for more details in Nahar, *Epitome of J.*, p. 673 ff.
79. This legend is narrated in *Jaina-Gazette* XX, 1924, p. 104.
80. See *Ind. Antq.* 13, 1884, p. 196 for more information on festival days.
81. *Kalpa-Sūtra, Jinacarita* 128 (*SBE* 22, p. 266)
82. *Bombay Gazetteer* 22, p. 118.
83. O. Böhtlingk, *Sanskrit Wörterbuch in Kürzerer Fassung.*
84. Samantabhadra, *Ratnakaraṇḍa-śrāvakācāra* 22; Comp. Amitagati, *Dharmaparikṣā* XVII, 34 f.
85. A great number of Tīrthas are described in Jinaprabha Sūri's *Tīrthakalpa.* This work began to appear in 1923 in the *Bibliotheca India,* Calcutta.
86. *Ātmaprabodha,* p. 78b.

87. P.C. Nahar. *Tirtha Pawapuri. Extracts from Visitor's Remark Book*, Pawapuri, 1925.
88. Stevenson, *Heart of J.*, p. 254.
89. Cf. the information on Vikramāditya in *Śrāddhavidhi*, p. 165b.
90. Kathavate in his introduction to Someśvara's *Kīrttikaumudi*, p. XVI.

SECTION VII

Conclusion

I

The Position of Jainism in the History of Religions

Repeated attempts have been made from most different angles to classify morphologically the numerous religions of mankind. If one tries to incorporate Jainism into the most familiar systems, then one can characterize it somewhat as an atheistic, anthropocentric, spiritual and ethical religion of salvation having a world-denying, quietistic tendency. The expression "atheistic religion" appears to be a contradiction in itself to a person who is familiar only with the occidental forms of religion. But it is wrong. It may be then that the word "religion" in its original meaning denotes a connection between man and god ("*vinculo pietatis obstricti deo et religati sumus*", Lactanitius, Institut. IV, 28), or it may not, but today the word has, in any case, got a meaning which does not accept the thought of god as an integral component of religion, otherwise a number of most significant forms of beliefs which are generally given the name religion would be outside its conceptual sphere (like Buddhism, Chinese forms of religion, etc.). There is no doubt that from the point of view of the European theology, Jainism is to be considered atheistic because it is not polytheistic, deistic, theistic, pantheistic or theophanic; the expression "atheism" can be applied to it in the same sense as it is applied to Arthur Schopenhauer's system which has strong religious impulses. But when Jainas themselves object to their religion being considered "atheistic", they are justified from their point of view. For, from the approach an Indian has towards the problem of god and which is altogether different from the one a Westerner has, only that person can be considered in India as an atheist, who denies the divine nature of the Self or (as in Buddhism) of that what exists after the disintegration of the Self or who denies the existence of the redeemed saints who have attained the supermundane, divine condition of Nirvāṇa. Jainism, if it is seen from this angle, is decisively not atheistic, and Jainas are justified, when they think that they believe in god, for they believe in salvation that potentially exists in the soul (although it can finally be realized only by the one who is capable of getting it), and worship the persons who have obtained freedom, like the Tīrthaṅkaras, as their leaders, as their "gods" (Devas).[1]

II

Jainism and the Indian Religions

Jainism has all the characteristic features of the Indian religions in the historical as well as morphological context. Like Hinduism and Buddhism, the focus of its metaphysics is the doctrine of Karma, rebirth and salvation; its concepts of the hells, the divine and the human world, of the periodical course of the world-history and the regular appearance of the harbingers of salvation agree in their basic features with those of the other two religions, and the forms in which its social and cultural life is expressed are essentially the same as those of the other two religions. But this is natural because all the three religions, Hinduism, Buddhism and Jainism, have grown from the same root, have blossomed next to one another for centuries and have influenced one another most intensively.

1. JAINISM AND HINDUISM

The points of agreement between Jainism and Hinduism are extraordinarily extensive. In social and cultural life—and this is a determining factor in Hinduism—there is very little difference between a Jaina and a

Hindu. An average Jaina does not differ so much more from an average Hindu than his sectarian brother. A sectarian follows certain special customs, but otherwise act according to the usual standards in the conduct of his life. G. Bühler has already pointed out that the precepts of Jainism on the conduct of life agree in many respects with those of the Hindu Dharmaśāstras. "The Jainas have", he says, "directly borrowed a great number of rules from the Brahmanic lawbooks. The occupations forbidden to Jaina-laymen are almost totally those, which the Brahmanic law forbids to a Brāhmaṇa, when necessity compels him to live like a Vaiśya,[2] and further he reminds us of parallel passages from Manu's Lawbook and other works in Jaina-writings. The social and ritual practices of Jainas are mainly like those of Hindus who do not eat meat and drink alcohol; they are different inasmuch as Jainas emphasize more strongly the principle of "Ahiṁsā", and that is why do not eat or drink anything, etc. after darkness falls. The most important differences with respect to the rituals consist in the Jainas not giving any significance to bathing in the holy rivers and cremating their ascetics (and not burying them as the Hindus are used to do), in not offering sacrifices to the dead and in their not burning the widows. All these social and ritual differences are relatively negligible, as they concern things which are not contrary in any way to the idea of cleanliness even of the most fastidious Hindu. Hindus, therefore, do not generally consider Jainas today as followers of a different religion, but merely devotees of a new Hindu sect.[3] It was already mentioned above on p. 357 that many castes have Vaiṣṇavas and Jainas as their members. Most of Jainas on their part do not consider Hindus as devotees of an alien faith. Many have declared in the Census that they are Hindus, worship Hindu-gods, celebrate Hindu-festivals (p. 477) and engage Hindu-Brāhmaṇas in their temple-pūjās (p. 356). Jainas have come closer and closer to the general Hinduism in the last centuries; if this process were to continue at this rate, then one can expect a complete merger of Jainism in Hinduism. Educated Jainas have also become conscious of this danger, and they emphasize what distinguishes Jainas from Hindus (like, e.g. the right of inheritance) and plead for the preservation of all those practices which are specifically peculiar to Jainism.

But the differences between the *teachings* of Hindus and Jainas are greater. Jainas do not recognise the Veda. For them, the works of the Smṛtis and the other authoritative texts of Brāhmaṇas are not authoritative. They have a different tradition and their own holy scriptures. But above all, Jainism differs from Hinduism in its having a well-defined dogmatic system which is accepted as true by all who belong to the Jaina-community, at least in its important points, whereas Hinduism does not put forward any dogmas which are unconditionally binding to all its followers. It rather accepts a real chaos of most different views simultaneously as equally valid. In view of this exceptional diversity of views, one can naturally speak of the doctrines of the Hindus as such always only with certain reservations. Once can be only sure of those which are shared by the majority of Hindu philosophers. If we compare these doctrines, as I have tried to outline in my "Hinduismus", with those of Jainas, then we find remarkable differences: Most Hindus believe in a God (Īśvara) who has created the world and who rules over it, but Jainas do not; the Hindus let the world be created and perish in periodic alteration, the Jainas consider that it cannot be created and destroyed; for the Hindus, the gods mostly are the heralds of the true eternal religion (Brahmā teaches it to the mortals at the behest of Īśvara), the Jainas let their noble men, the Tīrthaṅkaras discover it themselves and spread it further; for Hindus gods can get salvation. According to Jainas gods cannot get salvation. It is rather the primary right of human beings. Gods, have to be reborn on the earth as beings and practise asceticism there, if they want to attain salvation; Karma is for Hindus an *adṛṣṭa,* an invisible power, for Jainas, it is a complex of fine particles of matter, and Karma infects their souls; for many Hindus, salvation can be achieved through divine mercy, as a consequence of evident and sincere resignation towards Īśvara; for Jainas, only through the incessant work on one's own self; for most of the Hindus, there is no limit to the capability of salvation, Jainas make a distinction between *bhavyas* and *abhavyas* (p. 217); for most of Hindus, salvation consists either in the eternal stay of the soul in the paradise of Īśvara or in complete merger with the universal soul, for Jainas, it is in the unperturbed actionless peace of the omniscient on the peak of the universe. Finally, and above all, Jainism has a number of concepts which are alien to the metaphysical systems of the Hindus (like the substances Dharma and Adharma, Leśyās, Guṇasthānas, etc.), it has an independent epistemology and dialectics (Syādvāda) and uses terminology which is peculiar to it alone.

It would be beyond our scope to compare here the metaphysical doctrines of Jainas with those of six orthodox "Darśanas; it may, therefore, be just sufficient to point out that Jainism is closest to the Nyāya-Vaiśeṣika-system insofar as both teach atomism as well as the perpetration of the soul. It shares atheism with Sāṁkhya and also the conception of salvation as and perfect isolation of the transfigured soul. Otherwise, there are comparatively few agreements between the specific views of Jainas with those of the classical systems.

Jainism has learnt and borrowed a great deal in the course of time from the philosophy of the Brāhmaṇas —e.g. from yoga and tantrism (p. 406 f.)—in spite of its independence and differences. Isolated attempts are made to final similarities with the Vedānta and to merge the Hindu concept of god with the belief in the Tīrthaṅkaras.

There appears to be a close relationship between the cosmography of Jainas and the one of Brāhmaṇas. It is no doubt peculiar—F.O. Scharder has drawn my attention to this fact—that the heavens of the gods of Jainas have partially Brahmanic, partially Viṣṇuite names (Brahmaloka, Sahasrāra, Acyuta, etc.).

The Brahmanic legends have exerted significant influence on the Jaina-hagiography. Jainas have borrowed the stories of Sagara, Paraśurāma, heroes of Mahābhārata and Rāmāyaṇa and many others and reworked them in accordance with their taste. They, of course, do not concede this and explain that the form in which they bequeath the stories is alone genuine and authentic and the Brahmanic form of old legends is a later falsification.[4]

Jainas share the same view with Hindus with respect to various opinions, conceptions, institutions and practices. But everywhere, they claim priority and consider that Hinduism has emerged from Jainism. Jainas hold this viewpoint since time immemorial; their ancient world-history teaches that human beings have been brought to heterodoxy and animal-sacrifices by distorting the meaning of the genuine "Vedas" proclaimed by Bharata,[5] and even now, Jaina-philosophers hold this view when they write like Champat Rai Jain: "Hinduism in its very inception was an offshoot of Jainism."[6]

Although this claim is not supported by historical facts, as also it has found no followers among those who are outside Jaina-circles, it is not completely wrong inasmuch as Jainism has doubtlessly influenced Hinduism in many respects. It is quite possible that Jaina-ideas are evident in the older scriptures of the Hindus, in the Upaniṣads and in the Epics, but the research on this is in such a preliminary stage that nothing definite can be said for the time being. The presumption of J. Hertel that there are closer connections between the Muṇḍaka Upaniṣad and Jainism does not appear to me to be well-founded; the view of Jainas on Brahmaloka and

Salvation which Hertel mentions are too different from those of the Upaniṣad to be fit for comparison with one another; more significant is the similarity of the individual technical terminal logies.[7] One can certainly prove Jaina-influence on the Hindu sect-practices. The strong propagation which the principle of "Ahiṁsā" got in its advocacy of vegetarianism, above all in Viṣṇuism, in its opposition to bloody sacrifices, is indeed, to a great extent, a merit which it shares with Buddhism. Even other influences of Jainism have found their way in Viṣṇuism. Jina is considered as an Avatāra of Viṣṇu.[8] It is taught in *Padma-Tantra* I, 1, 44 ff. that Viṣṇu as Ṛṣabha proclaimed the Ārhataśāstra.[9] Ṛṣabha is called an incarnation of Viṣṇu in Bhāgavatapurāṇa V, 3 ff. and XI, 2, as also in other holy works of Viṣṇuism; but what is narrated about Ṛṣabha's life, agrees only partially with the Jaina-legend, but the fact that Ṛṣabha plays a role in a Viṣṇuite work is all the same remarkable.[10] Of the philosophical systems of Vaiṣṇavas, the Brahma-sampradāya of Madhva (1199-1278 A.D.) shows clear traces of Jaina-influence, a situation which becomes clear without much ado, when it is realized that Madhva lived in South Canara, a region in which Jainism was a ruling religion for centuries. As I have shown in my book "Madhvas Philosophie des Vishnu-Glaubens", p. *27 and *31, it is not improbable that Madhya's doctrine of predestination, hierarchy of gods, etc. have been developed under the influence of the views of Jainas.

Jainism has also influenced the Śaivite-systems. G.U. Pope[11] thinks that the doctrine of Śaiva-Śiddhānta of the three fetters (Pāśa) or impurities (Mala) which estrange soul from its true nature is reminiscent of Jaina-ideas. Although what this scholar gives as an evidence for his theory is not correct on account of insufficient knowledge of Jainism, one cannot easily deny the influence of the Karma-theory of the Jainas upon the doctrine of Āṇava-, Karma- and Māyā-mala; but the problem needs further examination and clarification. The presence of

Jaina influence on the doctrine and the cult of the Liṅgāyats is also probable,[12] but more about this can only be confirmed, when this sect is made the object of scientific research. The same thing is also perhaps true of the Alakhgīrs in Rājapūtānā, of whose founder Lāl Gīr, Sir George Grierson says that his teachings have so many things common with those of Jainas.[13]

Even in recent period, Jainas do have significance for the spiritual life of Hindus: Dayānand Sarasvatī (1824-1883), the founder of Ārya Samāja, was influenced, as J.N. Farquhar has shown,[14] probably by the example of Sthānakavāsīs, who had assumed a prominent position in his native place Taṅkārā (in Kāṭhiāvāḍ), to condemn iconolatry, and Jaina-ideas must have certainly influenced Mahatma Gandhi, the leader of the Indian nationalists, when he proclaimed "non-violent civil disobedience". Although Mahatma Gandhi was a Vaiṣṇava. It can be proved that he was under a strong influence of Jainism when his mother made him take a vow before a Jaina-Sādhu Becarajī that he would abstain in the occident from meat, alcohol and women, before he went on his journey to England for his studies.[15]

2. JAINISM AND BUDDHISM

The question whether between Jainism and Buddhism there is a historical connection has occupied the mind of scholars who are studying Jainism since it became known in Europe. Jainas themselves believe that Buddhism is a heterodoxy which was propagated by a defected Jaina-monk. According to one version, the ascetic Buddhakīrti from Pārśva's school saw, when he had devoted himself to penance on the bank of the river Sarayū, how a dead fish was washed away by water at the place where he was sitting. He then thought that it could not be a sin to eat the fish since it was without a soul, and ate it. This act of his is said to have been the cause of schism from which Buddhism emerged. According to another report, another pupil of Pārśva, Maudgalyāyana, is said to have founded Buddhism as an expression of hatred against Mahāvīra; Buddha, Śuddhodana's son, was named god in it.[16] The view that Buddhism has emerged from Jainism was held also individually by European scholars (Colebrooke, Prinsep, Stevenson, Editor Thomas). They base their theory upon the fact that the name of one of the pupils of Mahāvīra was Gautama, and then they identified him wrongly with Gautama Buddha.

Buddhists, on the other hand, consider that Jainas are heretics and charge that they had stolen the basic tenets of the doctrine from Buddha's books.[17] Even many European research workers of the previous century were of the view that Jainas were a Buddhistic sect. While the older Indologists like H.H. Wilson and Th. Benfey presumed that Jainism "emerged from Buddhism at a time when it was in a state of degeneration",[18] the others like Chr. Lassen let it originate from Buddhism in the 1st-2nd centuary A.D., or like Weber, already in the first century of Buddhism. H. Jacobi has conclusively established the invalidity of all hypotheses which seek to let one religion derive from the other and has convincingly demonstrated that the agreements existing in the two forms of faith, do not bring even a trace of evidence to say that both have only one origin.

But it is a fact that Jainism and Buddhism are similar to one another in many respects. The fact emerges most clearly beacause Brahmanic writers often mix them with one another. There is a perfect agreement between the two in many points: both deny the authority of the Vedas and fight against the Brahmanic rule of the priests and the Brahmanic sacrificial practices. Both deny the existence of the highest personal god, but worship a number of saviours appearing at certain points of time. Their external forms are similar to those of the Hindus in many things (sculpture, Stūpas and Caityas).[19] Both give their prophets the same honorific name

(Arhat, Buddha, Jina), ascribe to them the same characteristics of beauty and provide them with the same signs and symbols, a fact which roused Hiuen Tsiang's interest.[20] Both recognize a number of Cakravartīs (world-rulers) and ascribe to them the same attributes. Both the doctrines advocate the principle of Ahiṁsā and proclaim in parts the same ethical commandments; among both, the orders of monks and nuns are the backbone of the community. The idea of the similarity of the two is strengthened by the fact that their prophets, Mahāvīra and Buddha, were contemporaries and worked in the same region of Bihār and that in the life-history of these two men, the same places and persons are mentioned, and a few people who were close to these founders of religions, had accidentally the same names because these names were a fashion at that time among the Kṣatriyas of Magadha (The name of Mahāvīra's father was Siddhārtha, this was also Buddha's name as a prince; the name of Mahāvīra's wife was Yaśodā, Buddha's wife, Yaśodharā, etc.).

All these agreements in the individual points of the doctrine conditioned by place and time, in the social organization and in many superficial things are, however, not able to mislead us with respect to the elementary difference between the two religions, particularly in the most essential aspects. Jainisms and Buddhism have not only different holy scriptures and different history and tradition, but at their root, they have, above all, altogether different philosophical views. Like the systems of Brahmanic philosophy, Jainism teaches the existence of eternal, immaterial souls which, as long as they are bound to the matter, wander about in Saṁsāra. The main principle of Buddhism, on the other hand, is that there is no "ego", no soul. What one calls self, I or soul is, according to it, not of a constant dimension but a "Santāna" of momentary "Dharmas", a chain of very different elements of existence which all exist only for a moment and, when they have disappeared in the next, are replaced by facsimiles of their self. This doctrine of the non-existence of ego, which was for Buddhist the most essential characteristic of their religion,[21] is, of course, in very sharp contrast to the concept of monads of soul which is held by Jainas. From the different operational points, one comes across further great differences in the fundamental concepts of the systems, in epistemology, in ethics, in the doctrine of Karma, and above all, in the doctrine of salvation. For a Jaina, Nirvāṇa is reached when the soul has removed all the material particles polluting it with the help of spiritual discipline and when its true, spiritual nature is about to become manifest. Then the soul climbs to the peak of the world and remains there forever as a purely spiritual, individual, blissful being which is provided with all the supermundane capabilities. Buddhism, on the other hand, considers that salvation is only then possible, once the painful, ephemeral "immaterial" character of the ego has been recognized, when the 5 groups of psychophysical existence (Skandha), do not enter into a new connection and the Dharmas attain a state of quietude. Otherwise they come together to form a new (apparent) individual after the death of a being on account of the power of Karma.

Of the other differences in the essential points of the doctrine, let us mention the one which concerns the concept of sin. Jainism considers that objective proof is decisive, and therefore, acknowledges the sins committed without knowing, whereas Buddhism presupposes the presence of criminal will in the sinner for a sinful action.[22]

The difference in the social organization is of profound significance for the fate of the two religions. The "Saṅgha" the community, comprised only two classes of persons among Buddhists: monks and nuns; laymen were outside it, and although monks and nuns depended upon them for their subsistence, they had no influence on its management and they were comparatively only loosely connected with it in their religious and ritual life. But Jainas, on the other hand, consider that the "Saṅgha" is "fourfold" because laymen and laywomen are also included in it besides monks and nuns. The Jaina-laymen have an important position in the "Saṅgha" as its integrated part and have extensive rights, thus, e.g. control over the conduct of ascetics (see p. 368). The relationship between the clergy and the laymen has a great significance for the future of the two religions. It suffered in Buddhism, because the tie between the "Saṅgha" and the laymen was too loose. When the Buddhistic monkhood degenerated, when it could not offer resistance to the attacks of the orthodox counter reformation of Brāhmaṇas and when it succumbed to the gruesome blows of fanatic Muslims, Buddhism disappeared from the Indian subcontinent, and the laymen became Hindus because they did not have any deeper interest in their Buddhistic clergy. Jainism owes, on the other hand, its existence even today in India to its organization. Of course, it has suffered with the changing times, but its monkhood has not been so much degenerated as the one of Buddhists, and its faith has asserted itself in its home till the present-day despite the attacks of Hindus and the persecution by Muslims.[23]

Although Jainism and Buddhism, as we have seen, are two religions which have originated independently of one another, they blossomed next to one another in so many lands and for so long that it must be considered as obvious that they have not been without any influence on one another. Despite their uniqueness and their mutual hostility, one religion may have borrowed from the other many superficial things, particularly in iconographic and social respect. Unfortunately, we do not almost have reliable research works on this mutual influence; such reseach works so far are not without difficulties because it cannot at all be confirmed in many cases, where there is really a borrowing from another religion, or whether both religions hostile to the Vedas owe their origin to a common heritage of Hinduism. In individual cases, on the other hand, we can bring a positive evidence to show who has been the lender and who the borrower. Thus, it is quite clear, e.g. that, as H. Jacobi has shown,[24] the Buddhistic concept of the "Āsravas", of the "influences" of the outside world which influence the thinking of unfavourably, must have emerged from the Jaina-concept of "Āsrava", because only according to the Jaina-philosophy an actual "inflow", viz. of Karma-matter into the soul can take place. On the other hand, one does not need any elaboration, that there are Buddhistic influences in Haribhadra's "Yogabindu" (271, 4), when the Tīrthaṅkaras are named there Bodhisattvas.

III

Jainism and the Non-Indian Religions

Jainas, as a result of their commercial activity, were in constant touch with the believers of foreign religions who had settled in India, but the spiritual exchange, as it appears, was restricted essentially to the linguistic and cultural field and crossed over only little to the religious. Albrecht Weber tried to find out agreements between the legends of Greeks and Indians, particularly of Jainas and presumed that here it is a question of "secondary similarities belonging to the bare-historical period and based on the Homeric and occidental legends which came over here, i.e. thus, just of the adoption and the borrowing of the latter". But what this scholar has brought as evidence for his theory in his treatise "Ahalyā-Achilleus"[25] and elsewhere, can hardly be considered as convincing.

It is possible that Parseeism has influenced Jainism. One could, e.g. think—H. Jacobi has drawn my attention to this—that the doctrine, according to which a figure emerges from the *shoulder* of an ascetic in Tejas-Samudghāta (see p. 201 f.), has originated in imitation of the Iranian legend of Sohak.[26] Nothing is known about the Parsee-influence on Jainism so far, but one Parsee himself told me that it is probable.

It is, an interesting question, whether Jainism has influenced Manichaeism. W. Bang[27] has compared the 3 Guptis (p. 231), i.e. the correct regulation of the activity of the body, speech and mind with the three Manichaean "seals" *(signacula)* of hand, mouth and thought and pointed out further to an agreement that the south is considered by both Jainas and Manichaeans as a place of darkness. But both would, and if at all, show not a Jaina, but Indian influence, for in both cases it concerns common Indian ideas. Very interesting is the agreement emphasized by O.G. von Wesendonk in the distinction between "electi" and "auditores", or between "*sādhu*" and "*śrāvaka*" (listener).[28] But it can be said only after finding out more similarties, whether Manichaeism was influenced by Jainism.

Islam, which is in closest spatial contact with Jainism since centuries, has exerted a great cultural influence on it. Numerous Persian-Arabic words have intruded in the vocabulary of Jainas, even the one of the Indians in general, particularly that of the north and west and have become part of the language. But above all, the Jaina-art, especially architecture and painting, has got a different form under the influence of Islamic examples, but unfortunately, not always to its advantage. The Jaina-architecture, on its part, had a stimulating influence on the Mohammedan art, but such an adoption was not in any case a normal adaptation, but an actual transportation by the use of the parts of the destroyed Jaina-temples for the building of mosques, or by rebuilding Jaina-shrines into Islamic shrines by making some architectural changes.

From the point of view of religion, Islam has influenced Jainism in one respect in a remarkable way: it has doubtlessly indirectly caused the rise of anti-iconolatry movement of Loṅkā Śā and also directly assisted in Viṣṇuism the emergence of sects which fought against the cult of idols. On the other side, Islam has also been influenced by Jainism because Indian Mohammedans, particularly the converts from Indian religions, maintained many Indian views and customs. An examination of this historically interesting point would be a grateful task for a person doing research on Islam.

It is possible that the influence of Jainism on Islam has crossed the Indian borders. A. Frhr. v. Kremer has shown in his comprehensive treatise that Arabic poet and philosopher Abu-l-'Alā (973-1058), usually called by the name Abu-l-'Alā al-Ma'arrī; a name given to him after his native place Ma'arrat an Numān, has developed his unique ethical doctrines perhaps under the influence of Jainas. The peculiar, quite un-Islamic life style of this man is described by A. v. Kremer in the following manner: "Abu-l-'Alā ate exclusively plants; he even refused to take milk because he felt that it was a sin to take away from the young animals milk of their mother's breast. In fact, he wanted, if he could, to wean himself from taking any food. He even despised honey; he thought, it was wrong to rob the honey from the bees which they have collected so diligently. For the same reason he thought that the eggs should not be eaten. In his food and clothes, he lived like a genuine despiser of the world: 'My dress is of (uncoloured) wool, not green or yellow or red-brown, and my food is such that everyone despises it.' He wears only wooden shoes, because the ones of leather are illegally got because it is a sin to slaughter the animals and to utilize their hyde. Elsewhere he praises wandering about in nude, when he says, 'The summer replaces for you a complete dress.'[29] How strictly he followed the precept of Ahiṁsā, is clear from his saying: 'It is better to let a fly live than to present a dirhem to a beggar.'"

The preference for nudity, mercy even for vermins, vegetarianism and above all, the warning against eating honey[30] show Jaina, particularly, Digambara, influences. It can be easily believed that Jaina-merchants must have visited a great commercial centre like Bagdad, where Abu-l-'Alā spent the major part of his life and the poet came in contact with them. It can be seen from many writings of Abu-l-'Alā that he knew many Indian customs. He mentions the practice of Indian ascetics of not cutting the nails. He praises the custom of creamation when he says: "See, how Indians burn their dead; it is better than the long torments! If I am burnt, there is no need to worry about the hyaenas which creep to the dead body in the night, and also not about ill-treatment and sacrilege. Fire is better than the camphor which we sprinkle over the dead, it removes every bad odour better." Abu-l-'Alā admired the Indian ascetics who threw themselves into the flames of the pyre. But this way of dying is considered by Jainas as "mad asceticism" which is common among heretics. They praised, on the other hand, death from starvation as the right way of dying. The saying of Abu-l-'Alā that he would like to give up food, if he could, suggests he also knew about "Saṁlekhanā" (p. 468), but he was too weak to carry it out. From what is said, it appears to be possible that Abu-l-'Alā had come in contact with Jainas and adopted partially their ethical views. But the metaphysical ideas, on the other hand, which are the basis of his poems, do not show any closer connection with Jainism, and as it can be deduced from it that he did not believe in metempsychosis.

There is no influence of Jainism on Judaism and Christianity. Individual agreements, like the parallel to the story of Solomon's judgement (p. 300) or to the simile of the three merchants,[31] show naturally as little influenc as the tradition that Mahāvīra and Jesus, each one had 12 disciples of whom one was a traitor (Gośāla, Judas).

Although Jainas must have come in contact with Christians much before the discovery of sea-route to East India—it is well-known that there were Christian communities, particularly in the south of the subcontinent even centuries before the arrival of the Portugese—the Christian influence on Jainism can become evident only since the last decades: the Jainas of the present times have adopted the methods of religious propaganda used by Christian missions, like distribution of tractates, organizing congresses, creation of welfare-bodies, youth-unions, etc. Recently Jainas have tried to make use of the Bible for their purposes. Starting from the thesis that "the creed of the Tīrthaṅkaras furnishes the only platform where all other creeds may meet and be reconciled to one another",[32] Champat Rai Jain finds in the 4th Chapter of the revelation of St. Johannes veiled references to the 24 Tīrthaṅkaras. etc.[33]

We have seen so far that the contacts between Jainism and Iranian, Mohammedan and Christian religions were very negligible; and much of what was brought as evidence remains, besides, problematic for the time being. But even if further researchers should succeed in ascertaining closer connections and vouchsafe for them, it would concern always only isolated details which would be insignificant with respect to the whole of these forms of faiths. For, Jainism was born wholly from the Indian mind, and its basic concepts, like those of Hinduism and Buddhism, are separated by a world from those of the religions of the occident and of the Near East. Not only are the traditions and the historical prerequisites of the Indian systems completely different from those of the religions of the west, but also the view upon which they are built reflect an altogether different spirit. Three points are significant here:

Life in its essence is suffering for an Indian, whether he be a Hindu, a Buddhist or a Jaina. That is a fact which changes nothing, and nothing changes it. No great progress can ever remove the suffering, no going into the heavenly worlds in which there is pleasure and happiness can banish suffering to which even the ephemeral gods are subjugated. All existence is suffering, because it is without peace, without rest, because actions are performed in it and Karma is produced. A Westerner, on the other hand, does not see at once suffering in the life on the earth, but also a source of joy. This does not apply only to Greeks, Zoroastrians,

Muslims and Moderners, but also to the pious Christian of the Middle Ages. For him, the world is no doubt a Valley of Sorrow in its present state. But this state exists only for a fleeting duration because at the end of the times, the Son of Man will appear in the glory of his Father on the clouds of the heaven and bring about the resurrection of the body. Then a new earth will be born, and it will be an unalterable abode of justice and holiness.

An Indian thinks timelessly. The world exists for him since eternity and in eternity: he considers (like Jainas) that it cannot be created and destroyed, or, when he believes in the creation and destruction of the world (like Hindus), then they are for him not unique events, but events which periodically recur. So also salvation is possible for him at any time, if the conditions for it are fulfilled; it is not bound to a definite, historical event. Zoroastrians and Mohammedans teach a drama of the world which takes its course once. A Christian believes in a world-process which is restricted in time; it begins with the creation from nothing and the Fall, reaches its turning points in the sacrificial death of Christ and ends finally with the Doomsday and the eternal Kingdom of Christ. A moderner believes in development and progress, and even there, where a pessimistic basic idea is revealed, as in the case of Eduard v. Hartmann, the course of the world is historically interpreted as an account of the Passion of the unknown god who fights his way from unblissfulness to blissfulness.

An Indian sees salvation in the suppression of the individual. A Jaina, who has freed his soul from everything that is material, becomes thereby a pure spirit which misses everything that is personal; a saint resembles others completely: they are different only in their blazons placed near their feet. A pious Hindu, whom Īśvara's mercy redeemed, becomes will-less reflexion of god; the Vedāntī, who recognized Brahma, sinks in the absolute;

for a Buddhist, the delusion of the idea of ego is extinguished in the state of Nirvāṇa. A Westerner, on the other hand, does not want to lose his individuality, but to improve it, may be then in this life, or in a higher one. He sows a perishable seed to reap imperishable fruit. Personality is for him the highest happiness of the children of the earth.

·The preceding observtion reveals a deep-rooted difference between the Western and the Indian thinking. It is a fact that there are hurdles between the two, and attempts have been made to remove them. But these cannot bridge the anti-thesis that exists between them. Both are equally entitled types of human experience, both have developed with historical necessity and will continue to exist, so long as forces live which called them into existence. The Western *weltanschauung*, as also the Indian—both have proved their justification for existence by existing for chiliads of years. It is, therefore, idle to quarrel about the higher value of the one or the other. But it is necessary to emphasize their difference, because only the one, who fully acknowledges the exceptional features of each one of them, will be able to appreciate both the ideals of life in their unanimity and one-sidedness.

REFERENCES

1. Cf. the verse above p. 402 and in Haribhadra's Ṣaḍdarśanasamuccaya, 45 f.
2. G. Bühler, *Über die indische Sekte der Jainas*, p. 38.
3. Cf. the testimonial of Paṇḍita Bāl Candra Śāstrī, *Census, 1911*, XXII, Rājapūtānā, p. 103, transl. in v. Glasenapp, *Hinduismus*, p. 19 f.
4. Mironow, *Die Dharmaparīkṣā des Amitagati*, particularly p. 47 f.
5. v. Glasenapp has narrated in his essay in the *Jacobi-Festschrift*, in accordance with the "Uttarapurāṇa" (67, 212 ff.) the legend of the origin of animal sacrifice which is said to have been introduced by the scholar Parvata in the period of the Tīrthaṅkara Munisuvrata.

6. Champat Rai Jain, *The Practical Path*, p. 230.
7. Joh. Hertel, *Muṇḍaka Upaniṣad*. Kritische Ausgabe, Leipzig, 1924, p. 65 ff.—*Nāsaketarī Kathā, An Old Rājasthānī Tale* published by Charlotte Krause teaches that the Jainas have reworked on their part the stories in the Upaniṣads for their purpose.
8. *Ahirbudhnya Saṁhitā* (ed. M.D. Rāmānujācārya, Adyar, 1916, 33, 18).
9. F.O. Schrader, *Indroduction to the Pāñcarātra*, Adyar, 1916, p. 113.
10. L. de Milloué, "Etude sur le mythe de Vrisabha" (*Annales du Musée Guimet*, Vol. X, p. 413 ff., Paris, 1887).
11. G.U. Pope, *The Tiruvāçagam*, Oxford, 1900, p. LXXXVI..
12. J.N. Farquhar, *Religious Literature of India*, New York, 1915, p. 104.
13. *ERE* 1, p. 278.
14. J.N. Farquhar, *Modern Religious Movements in India*, New York, 1915, p. 104.
15. Although the name Gandhi is also not rare among Jainas (cf. above p. 88 f.), M.K. Gandhi was not a Jaina, but a Hindu, in fact, a worshipper of Viṣṇu. This is clear from the confession of his faith ("Young India", 26th Oct., 1921), but this is explicitly expressed by him and with all clarity in an article published in U.S. Tank's *Some Distinguished Jainas* (2nd ed., 1918, p. 74) in which it is said: "By birth I am a Vaishnavite....I have derived much religious benefit from Jaina religious works as I have from scriptures of the other great faiths of the world. I owe much to the living company of the deceased philosopher Raichand Kavi who was a Jain by birth." Thus, what Romain Rolland has said on Gandhi in his "Mahatma Gandhi" is accordingly to be corrected.
16. Mironow, *Die Dharmaparīkṣā des Amitagati*, p. 47.
17. Beal, *Se-yu-ki* I, p. 143.
18. Th. Benfey, "Indien" in Ersch and Gruber's *Allg. Encyclopädie der Wissenschaften und Künste*, Leipzig, 1840, II, 17, p. 206.
19. Sir Charles Eliot, *Hinduism and Buddhism*, London, 1921, I, p. 119, draws attention to the similarity of Jaina-temple in Pāliṭānā and the shrines of Burmese Buddhism.
20. Beal, *Si-yu-ki*, I, p. 145.
21. Cf. the quotation in v. Glasenapp's *"Hinduismus"*, p. 30 note.
22. L. de la Vallée Poussin, *The Way to Nirvāṇa*, Cambridge, 1917, p. 67; A.B. Keith, *Buddhhist Philosophy*, Oxford, 1923, p. 203.
23. A.F.R. Hoernle, "Annual Address 1898" *(Proceedings of the Asiatic Society of Bengal*, 1898, p. 45).
24. *ERE* 7, p. 472.
25. *Sitzungsberichte der Berliner Akademie*, 10th Nov., 1887.
26. Graf Schack, *Heldensagen von Firdusi* (2nd ed., Berlin, 1865),

Introduction, p. 61.

27. W. Bang, "Manichaeische Laien-Berichtspiegel", *Muséon* XXXVI, Louvain, 1923, p. 131.
28. O.G. von Wēsendonk, "Über georgisches Heidentum" in *Caucasica*, Fasc. i, Leipzig, 1924, p. 39 f.
29. A. Frhr. v. Kremer, "Über die philosophischen Gedichte des Abul ala Ma'arry," *Sitzungsberichte der Wiener Akademie* CXVII, Vol. 6 (1889).
30. Amitagati, *"Subhāṣita-saṅdoha"* XXII.
31. *Uttarādhyayana-Sūtra* 7, 14 f. = Matth. 25. 14 and Lu. 19, 11; comp. H. Jacobi, *SBE* 45, p. XLII.
32. Champat Rai Jain, *Confluence of Opposites*, p. 375.
33. Jainism has not exerted so far, by any stretch of imagination, an influence on occidental literature which Buddhism has in the newer times.

    The first and the only narrative work dealing with Jainism which I have come across is Ludwig Fahrenkrog's "Dschain Mahawira" (4th Book of *Gott im Wandel der Zeiten*), Leipzig.

Abbreviation used in the References

ERE	=	Encyclopaedia of Religion and Ethics, ed. by J. Hastings
GSAI	=	Giornale della Società Asiatica Italiana
Ind. Antq.	=	Indian Antiquity
J	=	Jainism
JRAS	=	Journal of the Royal Asiatic Society
JBROS	=	Journal of the Bihar-Orissa Research Society
RAS	=	Royal Asiatic Society
SBE	=	Sacred Books of the East
Tattv.	=	Tattvārthādhigama-Sūtra
WZKM	=	Wiener Zeitschrift für die Kunde des Morgenlandes
ZDMG	=	Zeitschrift der Deutschen Morgenländischen Gesellschaft

Bibliography

The following three lists contain as a rule only the books and treatises which have appeared in independent works and which deal exclusively or mainly with Jainism; more literature is mentioned in references. While in the list of works in Indian languages only those are mentioned which were used in this book; all more important translations and treatises in European languages have been included in the other two.

1. WORKS IN INDIAN LANGUAGES

(Works marked with * contain also the translation of the text in a European language)

Ācārāṅg-Sūtra (Āyāraṅga), 1. Śrutaskandha, Text, Analyse und Glossar von W. Schubring, Leipzig, 1910—Abhlgn. f.d. Kde. des Morgenlandes, Bd. 12, No. 4.

*Amitagati, Subhaṣitasandoha, Sanskrit und Deutsch heraus, von R. Schmidt, Leipzig, 1908.

Amritacandra Sūri, Puruṣārtha-siddhyupāya in "Sanātana-Jiana-Granthamālā", Vol. I, Bombay, 1905.

—Tattvārthaśāstra, *ibid.*

Aupapātika-Sūtra, erstes Upāṅga der Jaina, Vol. I (eins): Einleitung, Text und Glossar von E. Leumann, Leipzig. Abh. f.K. d.M., 1883.

Die Āvaśyaka-Erzählungen, herausge, von E. Leumann, Heft 1. Leipzig, 1897, Abhdlgn. f.d. Kde. des

Morgenlandes X, 2.
Bhadrabāhu, Kalpa Sūtra, Ed. by H. Jacobi, Leipzig, Abh. f.K. d.M., 1879.
*Bhadrabāhu Saṁhitā, Jaina Law, Text with translation and notes by J.L. Jaini, Arrah, 1916—Library of Jaina Literature, Vol. IV.
Bhāṣāpūjāsaṅgraha, Bombay, 1922.
Bhāvadeva Sūri, Pārśvanātha Charitra, ed. by Pandit Hargovinddas and Pandit Bechardas, Benares, Veer-Era 2438.
Cāritrasundara Gani Acāropadesh, Bhavnagar 1909-1911—Ātmānanda Granthamālā, 35.
Devasena, Darśanasāra, herausgegeben von Nāthūrām Premī, Bombay, 1920.
Devendra Sūri, Karmagrantha (1-5 with the commentary of the author, 6 with the commentary of Malayagiri), Bhavnagar, 1909-1911.
Dhanavāla, Bhavisatta Kaha, Jaina-Legende in Apabransha, mit Einleitung, herausgegeben von H. Jacobi, München, 1918.
Dharmaghoṣa Sūri, Samavasaraṇastava, Bhavnagar, 1910, Atmānanda-Granthamālā, No. 1.
Guṇabhadra, Ātmānuśāsana in "Sanātana-Jaina Granthamālā", Vol. I, Bombay, 1915.
—Uttarapurāṇa, Sanskrit-text with Hindi-translation of Lālārām Jain, Indore, 1918—Syādvāda Granthamālā 8.
Haribhadra, Dharmabindu, Ed. by L. Suali, Fasc. 1. Calcutta, Lib., Ind. 1912.
—Samarāicca Kathā, Ed. by H. Jacobi, Vol. 1, fasc. 1-8, Calcutta, Lib., Indi., 1908-1923.
—Ṣaḍdarśana-samuccaya with comm. of Guṇaratna, Bhavnagar, Vīra-S. 2444, Jaina-Ātmānanda-Granthamālā 49.
*—Sanatkumāracaritam, Eine Jaina-Legende in Apabhransha (in Transkr.), mit Grammatik, Übers,

und Glossar herausgegeben von H. Jacobi, München, 1921.

—Yogabindu ed. by Luigi Suali, Bombay, 1912, Devchand Lalbhai Jain Pustakoddhar Fund 12.

Hemacandra, Abhidhānacintāmaṇi, Ed. by Hargonddas and Bechardas, Part I-II, Bhavnagar, Veer-Era, 2441-46—Yasovijaya Jaina Granthamālā 41-42.

*—Herausg., Übers. und mit Anm. begleitet von O. Böhtlingk und Ch. Rieu. St. Petersburg, 1847.

—Arhannīti, Ahmedabad, Vīra 2432.

—Sthāvirāvalī Carita or Prishishtaparvan, Ed. by H. Jacobi, Calcutta, Bibl. Ind., 1891.

—Triṣaṣti-śalākāpuruṣa-caritra, Vols. 1-9, Bhavnagar, 1905-1909.

*—Yogaśāstra, herausg. und und Übers. von Ernst Windisch. ZDMG 28(1874), p. 185 ff. (Leipzig, 1874).

—Yogadṛṣtisammuccaya, Calcutta, 1907 ff. Bibl. Indica.

Jinalābha Sūri, Ātmaprabodha, Ed. Hiralal Hamsaraja, Jamnagar, 1914.

Jinaprabha Sūri, Tīrthakalpa: a treatise on the sacred places of the Jainas, Ed. by D.R. Bhandarkar and K. Sāhityabhūṣaṇa, Fasc. 1. Calcutta, Bibl. Ind., 1923.

Jinasena, Ādipurāṇa, Sanskrit-text with Hindi-transl. of Lālārām Jain, Indore—1916 Syādvāda-Garnthamālā, No. 4.

*Kalpa Sūtra, Die alte Sammlung jinistischer Mönchsvorschriften, Einleitung, Text, Anmerkungne, Übersetzung und Glossar von W. Schubring, Leipzig, 1905.

Malayagiri, Karmaprakṛti-ṭīkā (commentary on Karmaprakriti of Śivaśarmā), Bombay, 1913 Seṭha Devchand Lalbhai Jain Pustakoddhar Fund Series, No. 17.

—Pañcasaṅgraha-ṭīkā, Mūlakarttā Śrī Candraśimahattara, Ed. by Hirālāl Hamsarāja, 4 parts in 2 volumes, Jamanagar, 1910.

Malliṣeṇa Sūri, Syādvāda-mañjarī. Benaras, Vīra 2438, Yashovijaya-Jaina-Granthamālā 30.

Mānavijaya, Dharmasaṅgraha, 2 vols. Ed. by Naginbhai Ghelabhai Javeri, Bombay, 1915—Setha Devchand Lalbhai Jain Pustakoddhar Series, No. 26.

*Nemicandra, Devva-Saṅgaha) (Dravya-Saṅgraha) with a commentary by Bramhadeva, Ed. with translations, notes and an original commentary in English by Sarat Chandra Ghoshal, Arrah n.d. with 11 illustrations.

—Gommaṭasāra with a Sanskrit-commentary of Keshavavarni and Abhayacandra and a Hindi-commentary of Todar Mallji, 2 Parts: Jivakāṇḍa, Karmakāṇḍa, introduction, register, etc. (Calcutta), Year not mentioned.

—Trilokasāra with a gloss by Todarmalljī, Bombay, 1918.

Nemicandra Sūri, Pravachana Sāroddhār, Part I: with the commentary by Siddhasena Sūri, Ed. by Anand Sagar Sūri, Bombay, 1922—Devchand Lalbhai Jain Pustakoddhar Fund, No. 58.

*Nyāyavijaya, Adhyātma-tattvāloka, The Spiritual Light, with Gujarati transl. and explanatory notes, Transl. into English general notes by Motichand Jhaverchand Mehta, 1920 (place not mentioned).

Padmarāja Pandita, A Treatise on Jain Law and Usages (with Sanskrit text), Bombay, 1886.

Pañcapratikramaṇa, *do Sukhalālji-kṛt Hindī-anuvād aur ṭippaṇī ādi sahit*, Ātmānanda-Jaina-Pustaka-Pracāraka, Agra, 1921.

*Prabhendu, Samādhi-śataka, with commentary by Prabhā candra, trans. into English with notes by Manilal N. Drivedi, Aḥmadabad, 1895.

Prakaraṇaratnākara, Ed. by Bhīmasinha Mānaka, 4 vols, Bombay, 1876-1888.

Ratnaśekhara, Śrāddhavidhi with the commentary of the author, Bhavnagar, 1917—Jaina Ātmānanda-Grantharatnamālā, No. 48.

Samantabhadra, Āptamīmāṅsā with commentary of Vasunandī in "Saṅātana-Jaina-Granthmālā" I, Bombay, 1905.

*—Ratnakaraṇḍa-Śravakācāra or the Householder's Dharma, Text and English translation by Champat Rai Jain, Arrah, 1917.

*Sidhasena Divākara, Nyāyāvatāra, the earliest Jaina work on pure logic. with Sanskrit text, commentry, notes and English transl. by S. Ch. Vidyabhusana. Arrah, 1915, Library of Jaina Literature, Vol. II.

*Śāntisūri, Jīvavicāra, Ed. et trad. par A. Guerinot, Paris, 1902, Journ. As., 1902.

*Umāsvāmī Ācārya, Tattvārthādhigama Sūtra- a treatise on the essential principles of Jainism, Prākṛta text, with introduction, transl., notes, commentary in English by J.L. Jaini, London, 1922—Sacred Books of the Jainas, Vol. 2.

Umāsvāmī, Tattvārthādhigama Sūtra, Sanskrit text with Bhāyshya ed. by Keshavlal Premchand Mody. Calcutta, Bibl. Ind. 1903-1905.

*—Tattvārthādhigama Sūtra, Eine Jaina-Dogmatik, Übersetzt und erläutert von H. Jacobi, Leipzig, 1906, *ZDMG* 60 (1906).

Uttarādhyayanasūtra, being the first Mūlasūtra of the Śvetāmbara Jainas; ed. with introduction, critical notes and commentary by J. Charpentier, 2 Vols. Upasala, 1922—Archives d'Etudes Orientales, publ. p. J.A. Lundell, Vol. 18, 1-2.

*Uvāsagadasāo or the religious profession of an uvāsaga, Ed. in the original Prākṛta with the Sanskrit comm. of Abhaya Deva and an Engl. transl. with notes by A.F.R. Hoernle, Calcutta, Bibl. Ind. 1885-1890.

Vardhamāna Sūri, Acāradinakara, 2 Parts, Bombay, 1922-23.

Vavahāra-und Nisīha-Sutta, Herausgegeben von W. Schubring, Leipzig, 1918.

—Abh. f. d. Kunde des Morgenlandes, Bd. 15, No. 1.

Vijayadharma Sūri, Jaina-tattva-jñānam, Bhavnagar (approx., 1917).

Vinayavijaya, Lokaprakāśa, ed. Pandit Hirālāl Haṁsarāja, Jamnagar, 1910.

*—Naya-Karṇika, a work on Jaina logic. Ed. with introd., English transl. and critical notes by M.D. Desai, Arrah, 1915, Lib. of Jaina Lit. Vol. III.

Yaśovijay, Pratimāśataka-grantha with the commentary of the author, 1920. Place not mentioned—Shrīman Muktikamala Jaina Mohanamālā Pushpam 7. Jacobi H. Ausgewählte Erzählungen in Māhārāshtrī. Leipzig, 1886. Jain, Banarsi Das, Ardha-Magadhi Reader, Lahore, 1923.

2. TRANSLATIONS

Comp. also in the first list those marked with*:

Amara Sūri, Ambada-caritra, See Krause Ch., in list 3.

The Antagada-Dasāo and Anuttarovavaiya-Dasāo, Transl. from the Prakrit by L.D. Barnett, London, Royal Asiatic Society, 1907—Oriental Translation Fund, New Ser., Vol. 17.

Hemacandra, Ausgewählte Erzählungen aus Hemacandras Pariśiṣṭaparvan, deutsch von J. Hertel, Leipzig, 1908.

Hemavijaya, Kathāratnākara, das Märchenmeer, Eine Sammlung indishcher Erzählungen, Deutsch von J. Hertel, Bd. I-II. München, 1920.

Jaina-Sūtras, Transl. from the Prākṛta by Hermann Jacobi, 2 Vols.—Sacred Books of the East 22, 45, Oxford 1884, 1895.

Jinakīrti, Campaka-śreṣṭī-kathānaka und Pālagopāla-kathānaka, See Hertel in list 3.

Jñānasāgara, Ratnacūḍa, See earlier.

The Kalpa-Sūtra and Nava Tatva, two works illustrative of the Jain Religion and Philosophy. Translated from the Māgadhi by J. Stevenson, London, 1848.

The Kathākoça, a treasury of stories, Transl. fr. Sanskrit Mss. by C.H. Tawney, W. Appendix containing notes, by E. Leumann, London, 1895—Oriental Transl. Fund, New Series, No. II.

Merutunga Ācārya, The Prabandhacintāmaṇi or Wishingstone of narratives, Transl. from the original Sanskrit by C.H. Tawney, Calcutta, Bibl. Ind., 1901.

Siddharṣi, Upamitibhavaprapantschā kathā, d.i. Eine Erzählung, in der das menschliche Leben in Vergleichen dargestellt wird. Verdeutscht von Willibald Kirfel. 1. Band, Buch 1-3. Leipzig, 1924. Indische Erzähler, Band X.

Yogindra Ācārya: Paramātma-prakāśa, Transl. by Rickhab Dass Jain, Arrah, 1915—Library of Jaina-Literature, Vol. 1.

3. TRACTS IN EUROPEAN LANGUAGES

Barodia, U.D. History and Literature of Jainism, Bombay, 1909 (Bhandari, Kesarichand), Notes on the Sthanakwasi or nonidolatrous Shwetambar Jains. By "Seeker", 1911.

Bloomfield, M., The Life and Stories of the Jaina Savior Parçvanatha, Baltimore, 1919.

Bohn, W. Die Religion der Jaina und ihr Verhälthins zum Buddhismus, München, 1921.

Bühler, G. Über das Leben des Jainamönches Hemacandra, des Schülers des Devacahandra aus der Vajrashākhā, Wien, 1889.

—Über die indische Sekte der Jaina, Wien, 1887.

—On the Indian Sect of the Jainas translated from the German, edited with an outline of Jaina Mythology by Jas. Burgess, London, 1903.

Chand, Sri Prem (late name Nanak Chand), Mithya Khandan containing the Origin of Jainism, Publ. by late Diwan Kirpa Ram Sahib, Ludhiana, 1914.

Charpentier, J., The History of the Jainas, Cambridge History of India, Vol. I: Ancient India, p. 150-170, Cambridge, 1922.

Coomaraswamy, Ananda K., Catalogue of the Indian Collection in the Museum of Fine Arts, Boston, Part IV: Jaina Paintings and Manuscripts, Boston, 1924.

Desai, Mohanlal Dalichand, Srimad Yashovijayaji (A Life of a Great Jain Scholar), Bombay without date.

Farquhar, J.N., An Outline of the Religious Literature of India, Oxford, 1920.

Fick, R., Eine Jainistische Bearbeitung der Sagara-Sage, Keil, 1888.

Gandhi, Virchand R., Speeches and Writings collected and edited by Bhagu F. Karbhari, Vol. I: The Jain Philosophy, Bombay, 1911.

—The Karma Philosophy, Bombay, 1913.

—The Yoga Philosophy, Bombay, 1912.

Garr, B.L. Samayika, or a way to equanimity, Arrah, 1918.

Glasenapp, H.v. Die Lehre von Karman in der Philosophie der Jainas nach den Karmagranthas dargestellt. Leipzig, 1915.

Guérinot, A. Essai de Bibliographie Jaina, Avec planches hors texte. Paris, 1906—Annales du Musée Guimet, Bibliothèqued'Etudes, tome 22.

—Repertoire d'Epigraphie Jaina, précédé d'une esquisse de l'histoire du Jainisme d'après les inscriptions, Paris, 1908—Publication de l'Ecole Française de l'Extrème Orient, Vol. X.

Hertel J. Indische Märchen, In "Die Marchen der Weltliteratur, herausgegeben von Friedrich v.d. Leyen und Paul Zaunert", Jena, 1919.

—Pantschākhjāna Wārttika, Eine Sammlung volkstümlicher Märchen und Schwänke, Vollständig verdeutscht, Leipzig, 1923—Indische Erzähler, Bd. 6.

—Indische Märchenromane I: Kaufmann Tschampaka, Pāla und Gopāla, Ratnaschūda, Vollständig, verdeutscht, Leipzig, 1923—Indische Er. 6.

—On the Literature of the Śvetāmbaras of Gujarāt, Leipzig, 1922.

Hüttemann, W. Die Jñāta-Erzählungen im sechsten Anga des Kanons der Jinisten, Straβburg, 1907.

Jacobi H. "Jainism" in "Encylopaedia of Religion and Ethics", ed. by J. Hstings, Vol. VII, p. 472.

Jain, Champat Rai, The key of knowledge, 2nd ed. revised, Arrah, 1919.

—Confluence of Opposites, 1921 (place not given).

—Immortality and joy, Arrah, 1919.

—Nyaya, the science of thought, Arrah, 1916—Library of Jaina Lit., Vol. VIII.

—The practical path, Arrah, 1917.

—Sacred philosophy (The Jaina Siddhānta), Allahabad, n.d. (approx. 1918).

—What is Jainism? 3rd rev. ed. Arrah, 1919.

Jaini, M.C., Life of Mahavira, Allahabad, 1908.

Jaini, R.D., An Insight into Jainism, Pamphlet No. 1, Meerut, n.d.

Jhaveri, H.L., The First Principles of Jain Philosophy, London, 1910.

Kirfel, W. Die Kosmographie der Inder, Bonn und Leipzig, 1920.

Krause, Ch. Prinz Aghata, Die Abenteuer Ambadas, Vollständig verdeutscht, Leipzig, 1922—Indische Erzähler Bd. 4.

Lala Banarsi Dass, A Lecture on Jainism delivered before the Dharma-Maha-Mahotsava or Great Religious Assemblage at Muttra, Agra, 1902—Jain Itihasa Series, No. 1.

Latthe, A.B., An Introduction to Jainism, Bombay, 1905.

Leumann, E. Die Nonne, Ein neuer Roman aus dem alten Indian, München-Neubiberg, 1922.

—Buddha and Mahāvīra, München, Neubiberg, 1921.

Meyer, J.J., Hindu Tales, Engl. transl. of Jacobi's "Ausgewählte Erzählungen in Mahārāṣṭrī", London, 1909.

Mironow, N. Die Dharmaparīkṣā des Amitagati, Ein Beitrag zur Literatur und Religion sgeschichte des indischen Mittelalters, Leipzig, 1903.

Nahar, Puran Chand and Ghosh, Krishnachandra, An Epitome of Jainism, Calcutta, 1917.

Pertold, O., The place and importance of Jainism in the comparative science of religions, Bhavanagar, n.d.

Ramaswami Ayyangar, M.S. and B. Seshagiri Rao, Studies in South Indian Jainism, Madras, 1922—Vizianagram Maharaja's College Publ., No. 1.

Schubring, W., "Jinismus" in "Licht des Ostens", herausgegeben von Maximilian Kern. Stuttgart, n.d.

—Das Mahanisīha-Sutta (Abhdlg. der Preuβ. Akademie.), Berlin, 1918.

Stevenson, Mrs. Sinclair, Notes on Modern Jainism, Oxford, 1910.

—The Heart of Jainism; with an introduction by G.P. Taylor, London, 1915.

Sunavala, A.J., Vijaya Dharma Sūri, His Life and Work, with a prefatory note by F.W. Thomas, Cambridge, 1922.

Tank, U.S., Dictionary of Jaina Biography, Part I: A. Arrah 1917—Library of Jaina Literature, Vol. VII.

—Some Distinguished Jainas, Agra, 1918 (2nd ed. by Jaina historical studies, Delhi, 1914).

Tessitori, L.P., Vijaya Dharma Sūri, A Jain Ācārya of the Present Day, Not dated, No place name.

Thornton, D.M., Parsi, Jaina and Sikh, or some minor religious sects of India, London, 1898.

Vinson, J., Légendes bouddhistes et djainas, trad. du Tamoul, Paris, 1900.

Warren, V.R., Jainism in Western Garb, as a solution of life's great problems, Madras, 1912, 2nd ed. Arrah 1916—Library of Jaina Literature, Vol. VI.

Warren, S.J., Les Idées philosophiques et religieuses des Jainas, traduit du Holladais par J. Pointet, Paris, 1887.

Weber, A., Über des Çatrunjaya Māhātmyam—Abh. f.d. Kde des Morgenlandes I, 4. Leipzig, 1858.

—Über ein Fragment der Bhagavatī. (Abhdlg. der Preub. Akademie), Berlin, 1866, bis 1867.

Winternitz, M., Die buddistische Literatur und die heiligen Texte der Jainas (Geschichte der Indischen Literatur. 2, Band.), Leipzig, 1920.

Illustrations

TITLE-PAGE: ŚĀLIBHADRA'S MARRIAGE

Śālibhadra was a virtuous wholesale dealer living in Rājagṛha during Mahāvīra's period. Moved by the knowledge that the world is ephemeral, he left his 32 wives, became ascetic and died finally the death of a wise man, i.e. from starvation.

The Śālibhadra legend is the most popular narrative of the Jaina-literature and is available in different forms. Compare on this Bloomfield, *Journal of the American Oriental Society* 43 (1923), p. 257 ff. in which an analysis of Pradyumna Sūri's reworking is given. The story has been commonly illustrated; A.K. Coomaraswamy, *Catalogue of the Indian Collections in the Museum of Fine Arts, Boston, Part IV: Jaina Paintings and Manuscripts* (Boston, 1924); reproduced on the plate XXIII ff. are a number of miniatures from a manuscript of the Hindi-version of Jinasiṁha Sūri (around 1621) which was written in Kaśangarh in the year 1793. The miniatures published by me here for the first time come from another manuscript of "Śrī Śālibhadra-Dhannā-caupaī" which I borrowed from Vijaya Indra Sūri.

The picture illustrates how Śālibhadra's marriage with his 32nd wife was performed and how his other 31 wives hold one another's hands to express their joy. The rites shown correspond to the rites which are common today; compare. p. 457 f.

BLACK PLATES AT THE END OF THE BOOK

Plate 13. Statue of Tejupāla and his wife Anupamā (see p. 59) in a temple on Mount Ābū. Both figures are holding garlands to be put on a Jina-statue. It appears that they are carrying the mouth-cloth around the neck; the worshippers bind it around the mouth in the cult not to soil the idol by their breath.

Plate 14. Earth-map (comp. p. 253 ff.). Original in Brooklyn Institute Museum, Brooklyn, New York.

Plate 15. World in the form of a woman (comp. p. 250). From a manuscript of "Saṅgrahaṇī-Sūtra" of Candrasūri in the Museum für Völkerkunde in Berlin.

Plate 16. Mahāvīra preaching in his Samavasaraṇa; gods, animals and human beings are hurrying to listen to him. Miniature (in the original size) in the manuscript of "Śrī Śālibhadra-Dhannācaupaī" (comp. p. 527).

Plate 17. King Śreṇika with his entourage, Miniature as in No. 16.

Plate 18. Jaina monks and nuns:

1. Ācārya Vijaya Dharma Sūri, the famous Śvetāmbara-Sādhu (1862-1922), comp. 84 ff.

2. Punaśrī, a Śvetāmbara-Sādhvī of Kharatara-Gaccha. She died around 1918 leaving behind about 80 nun-pupils.

3. Cārukīrti Paṇḍitārya Varya Svāmī, the high-priest of the Digambaras in Śṛavaṇa Beḷgoḷa.

4. Preaching monks with the mouth-cloth, Ahmedābād.

Plate 19. Master Vijaya Dharma Sūri (comp. plate 18) with his monks, among them his later successor Vijaya Indra Sūri, surrounded by Jaina-laymen.

Plate 20. Miniatures from the manuscript of the "Jinacaritra" (*IC* 23, 647) in the State Museum of Ethnology in Berlin. The copies were drawn by Mrs. Marg. Hüttemann and published and described by Wilhelm Hüttemann in his essay "Miniaturen zum Jinacaritra" (in: *Baessler Archiv* IV, Heft. 2. 47 ff.).

1. Hariṇaigamaiṣī transfers Mahāvīra's embryo to Triśalā's womb (comp. p. 324).

2. Above: Tīrthaṅkara Ariṣṭanemi (recognizable by the conch, his blazon which is seen on the border of his throne) in the crescent moon (Symbol of salvation, comp. p. 426 f.).

Below: A Tīrthaṅkara in Samavasaraṇa (comp. p. 278 and the plates 8 and 16).

3. The 8 lucky signs (Maṅgala, p. 427). The water-jug is in the centre of the whole picture, mirror on the left (of the observer) in the upper row and the throne in the right; in the middle area powder-box on the left, two fish on the right and in the undermost section, three diagrams next to one another: Śrīvatsa (developed in an ornamental form to an octangle filled by a lotus-flower), Svastika and Nandyāvarta).

4. Propitious dream-images which prophesize (according to the Śvetāmbaras) the birth of a Tīrthaṅkara (p. 275 f.). The following are given in an order: elephant, bull, lion, crowns, Goddess Śrī, flag, vase, lotus-pond, ocean, palace of gods, heap of jewels, fire. (The two images of dream, Sun and Moon, are missing here as they are illustrated in another picture of the manuscript.)

Plate 21. Siddhacakra as "Yantra" on the left (of the observer) and as "Maṇḍala" on the right. Comp. diagram on p. 426 for clarification. The 5 Parameṣṭhīs are illustrated in the Yantra. The names of 4 virtues figure in Devanāgarī-script at the appropriate places. The individual areas are written on in the Maṇḍala with the Mantras like "Om, Hrīṁ, Śrī, 'rhaṁ", followed by obeisance to each of the 5 Parameṣṭhīs or the 4 virtues which the relevant leaves symbolize, and finally a remark on the colour of the relevant area. The colours are: 1. white, 2. red, 3. yellow, 4. blue (green), 5. black (darkblue), 6th to 9th. white.

Plates 22-23. The blazons of the 24 Tīrthaṅkaras of the present world-period as depicted by Śvetāmbaras. This is from a copy of a multicoloured painting in Indian Institute in Oxford made by Mr. A.E.L. Rost.

The numbers in the upper left corner of each one of the squares refer to the numbers of the Tīrthaṅkaras whose order is shown by the table on p. 288.

The blazons according to Śvetāmbaras are: 1. bull, 2. elephant, 3. horse, 4. monkey, 5. curlew, 6. red lotus with six leaves, 7. Svastika, 8. crescent moon, 9. fish (Makara), 10. śrīvatsa, 11. rhinoceros, 12. buffalo, 13. boar, 14. falcon, 15. thunderbolt, 16. antelope, 17. ram, 18. Nandyāvarta, 19. water-pot, 20. tortoise, 21. blue lotus with five leaves, 22. conch, 23. serpent, 24. lion.

The same symbols are also common among Digambaras except for some differences: 9. cancer, 10. Ficus religiosa, 11. Garuḍa, 14. bear, 18. fish, 21. Aśoka-tree (9 and 21 not always).

The small squares above the individual symbols on the plate 22-23 are filled in the original with the colours of the Tīrthaṅkaras. The colours of the Tīrthaṅkaras (according to Śvetāmbaras are: 1—5. golden (yellow), 6. red, 7. golden, 8-9. white, 10-11. golden, 12. red,

13-18. golden, 19. blue (green), 20. black (dark-blue), 21. golden, 22. black (dark-blue), 23. blue (green), 24. golden. Among Digambaras, 7th has the blue (green) and the 19th has the golden (yellow) colour.

Plates 24-27. The Tīrthaṅkaras with their Yakṣas and Yakṣiṇīs as visualized by Digambaras in the Kannaḍa-regions of South India (copied from Jas. Burgess, "Digambara Jaina Iconography", *Ind. Antq.* 32 (1903), p. 459 ff.). Burgess got the pictures from the Archaeological Survey in Southern India with the help of Alexander Rea). Since the Tīrthaṅkaras, except Supārśva and Pārśva, resemble one another, but for their blazons, only Supārśva and Pārśva, and as an example of the others, Ṛṣabha and Padmaprabha (mentioned by mistake as Sumatinātha in *Ind. Antq.*) are drawn to save space. The remaining figures depict Yakṣas (on the left of the onlooker) and Yakṣiṇīs of the Tīrthaṅkaras in their usual order (comp. p. 405). A symbol next to every Yakṣa and Yakṣiṇī (Śāsanadevatā).

The symbols of the Yakṣas are: 1. bull, 2. elephant, 3. peacock, 4. elephant, 5. Garuḍa, 6. bull, 7. lion, 8. Haṁsa, 9. tortoise, 10. lotus, 11. bull, 12. peacock, 13. cock, 14. crocodile, 15. fish, 16. bull, 17. peacock, 18. peacock, 19. elephant, 20-21. bull, 22. tower or temple, 23. tortoise, 24. elephant.

The symbols of the Yakṣiṇīs are: 1. Garuḍa, 2. stool, 3. Haṁṣa, 4. Haṁsa, 5. elephant, 6. horse, 7. bull, 8. bull, 9-10-11. bull, 12. serpent, 13. serpent, 14. Haṁsa, 15. lion, 16. peacock, 17. peacock, 18. Haṁsa, 19. Haṁsa, 20. serpent, 21. crocodile, 22. lion, 23. Haṁsa, 24. Haṁsa.

On the plate 27 below: Sarasvatī, Goddess of Learnedness, next to her, Brahmayakṣa (another illustration above No. 10). On the side: the symbols for OM (p. 411 and 428) and Hrīṁ (p. 428).

Plate 28. Digambara-statue of the 23rd Tīrthaṅkara Pārśva (in the possession of Brooklyn Institute Museum, Brooklyn, New York). Pārśva in Kāyotsarga-position is surrounded by six figures; the two upper ones are Tīrthaṅkaras (probably Ṛṣabha, Śānti, Ariṣṭanemi and Mahāvīra) and the two lower ones, Indra and Indrāṇī with Yak-fan and lotus.

The two colourful plates at the end of the book are reproductions of the two pages of the "Jinacaritra" manuscript of the Museum of Ethnology in Berlin we have mentioned above under No. 10. The Prākṛta-text is written in a most artistic Devanāgarī-script. The hole in the middle is for a thread (compare p. 105 f.). Each one of the two pages (leaves) is decorated with a splendid miniature.

The picture on Fol 44 depicts Mahāvīra, when he is tearing off his hair in the process of becoming monk. Indra is behind him.

The miniature on Fol 53 shows Mahāvīra's predecessor Pārśva with the characteristic diadem formed by seven serpent-heads.

Both miniatures are described in detail by W. Hüttemann in his essay we have mentioned under plate 20.

Index

Index is restricted only to the most important names, words and references to avoid letting its scope swell to include all sorts of things. As a rule, names of the persons and the things which figure only in enumerations, like holy places p. 55 f., 480 f., unions and periodicals p. 86 ff., 152 f., canonic works p. 109 ff., 121 ff., Karma-types 185 ff., types of Siddhas p. 238 f., mountains and rivers 259 ff., hells p. 253, classes of gods 263 ff., names of the gods 405 f., wishing trees, p. 290 f., Kulakaras p. 292 f., patriarchs p. 332, Tīrthaṅkaras of the past p. 343 f., of the future p. 336, Yakṣas, Śāsanadevatās and Vidyādevīs p. 405, authors and works of biography p. 517 ff., etc. are not included.

The numbers refer to the pages in the text, those indicated by "P" refer to the numbers of the plates.

Plate 1: Ṛṣabha, the first Tīrthaṅkara
(Śatruñjaya)

Plate 2: A Temple on the Śatruñjaya mountain

Plate 3: A Temple on the Śatruñjaya mountain

Plate 4: A Temple on the Satruñjaya mountain

Plate 5: Neminātha Temple, Girnār

Plate 6: A Temple on Mount Ābū

Plate 7: Interior of a Temple on Mount Ābū

Plate 8: Mahāvīra's Procession

Plate 9: An Idol of a Tīrthaṅkara
(Mathurā)

Plate 10: Female Genii
(Mathurā)

Plate 11: Gommaṭa Monolith in Śravaṇa Beḷgoḷa

Plate 12: The Tīrthaṅkara Candraprabha

Plate 13: Tejaḥpāla and Anupamā

Plate 14: Map of the Earth

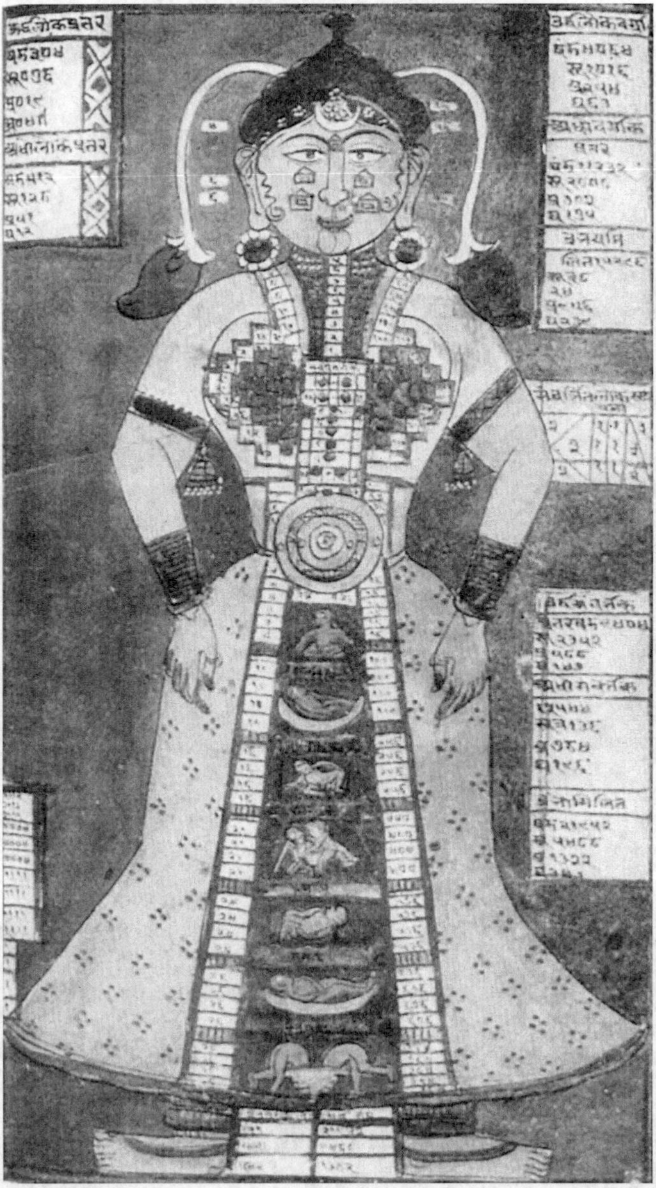

Plate 15: The World in the Form of a Woman

Plate 16: Mahāvīra preaching in the Samavarasaṇa

Plate 17: King Śreṇika with his retinue

1. Master Vijaya Dharma Sūri (Śvetāmbara)

2. Nun Punaśrī (Śvetāmbara)

3. Digambara Cārukīrtīpaṇḍitāryavarya Svāmī

4. A monk preaching with a piece of cloth in front of his mouth (Ahmedābād)

Plate 19: Master Vijaya Dharma Sūri with his monks, surrounded by Jaina-laymen

1. Hariṇaigamaiṣī transferring Mahāvīra's embryo into Triśalā's womb

2. Above: Ariṣṭanemi in the crescent moon
Below: A Tīrthaṅkara in the Samavarasaṇa

3. The 8 lucky signs

4. Ominous Dreams

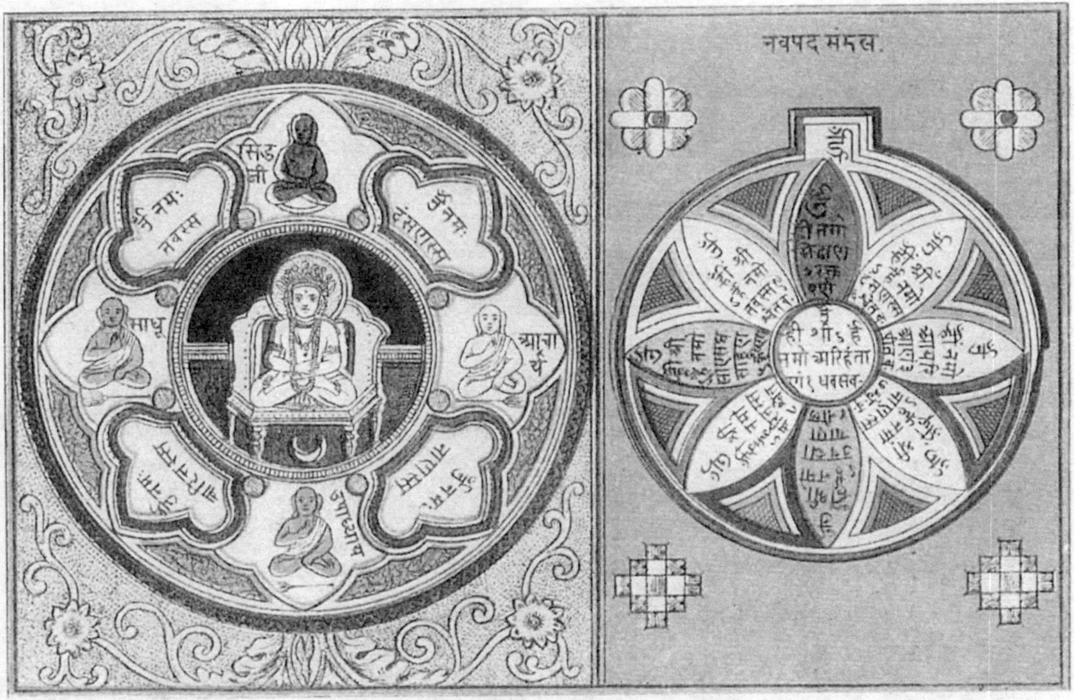

Plate 21: Siddhacakra

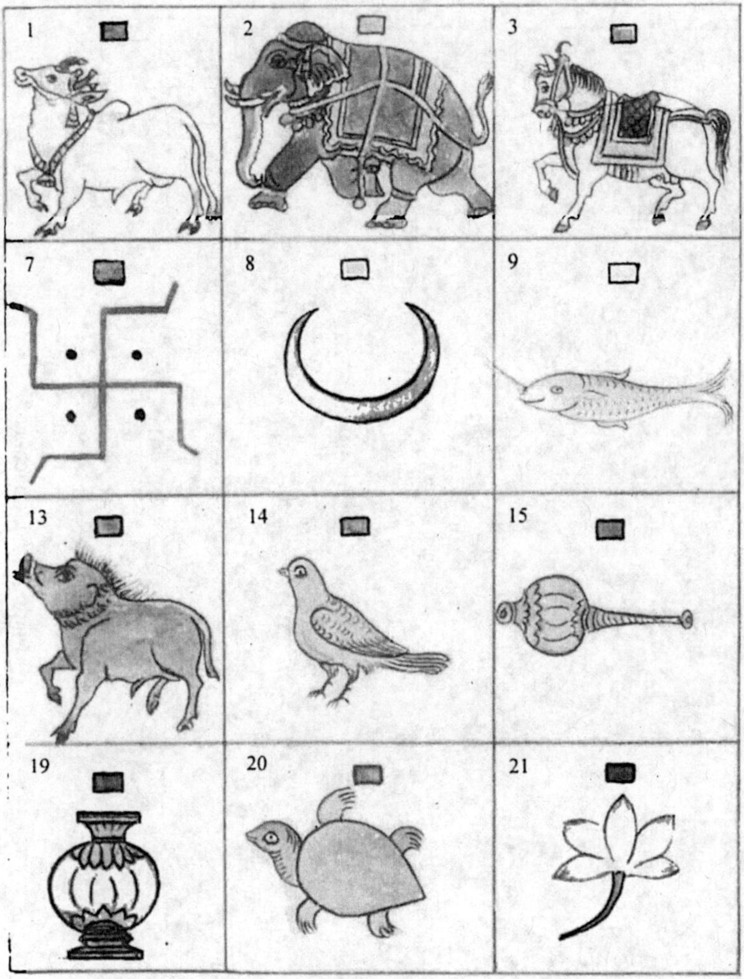

Plate 22: The Blazons of 24 Tīrthaṅkaras
(Śvetāmbara)

Plate 23: The Blazons of 24 Tīrthaṅkaras
(Śvetāmbara)

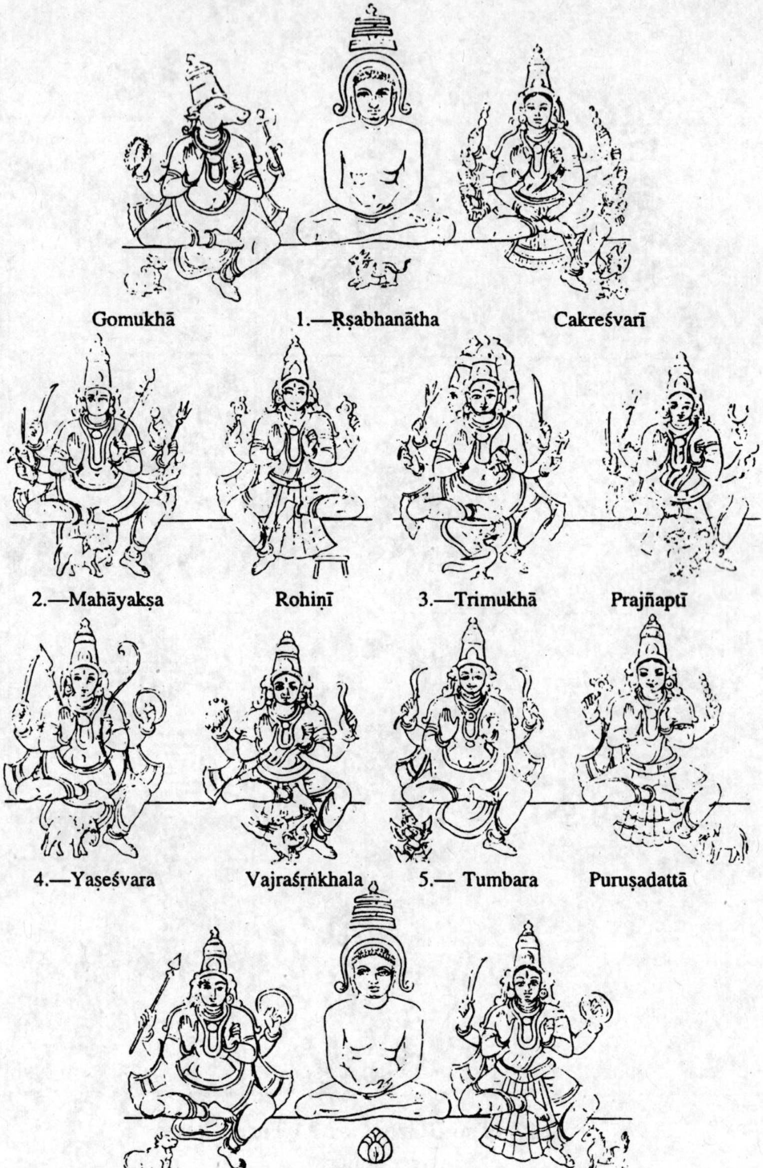

Plate 24: The Yakṣas and Yakṣiṇīs of the Tīrthaṅkaras (Digambara)

Varanandī 7.—Supārśvanātha Kālī

8.—Śyāma (Vijaya) Jvālamālinī 9.—Ajita Mahākālī

10.—Brahmeśvara Mānavī 11.—Īśvara Gaurī

12.—Kumāra Gāndhārī 13.—Ṣaṇmukha Vairoṭī

Plate 25: The Yakṣas and Yakṣiṇīs of the Tīrthaṅkaras (Digambara)

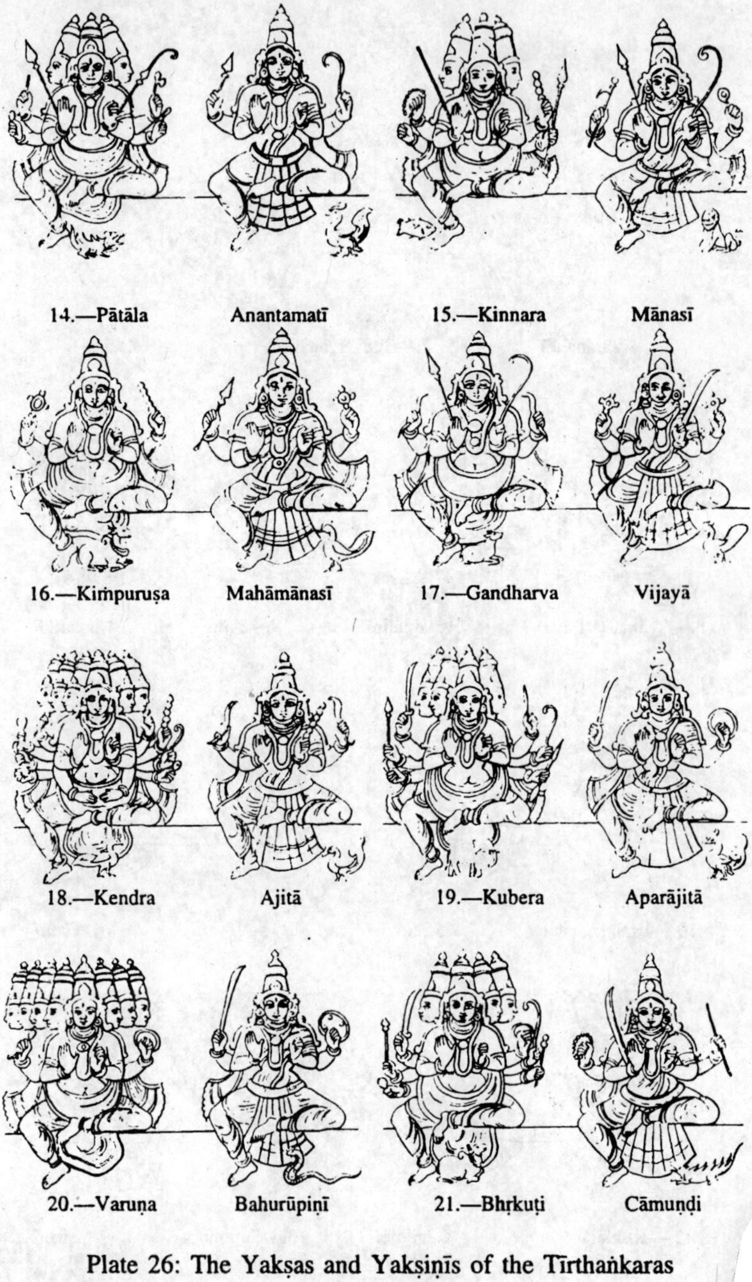

Plate 26: The Yakṣas and Yakṣiṇīs of the Tīrthaṅkaras (Digambara)

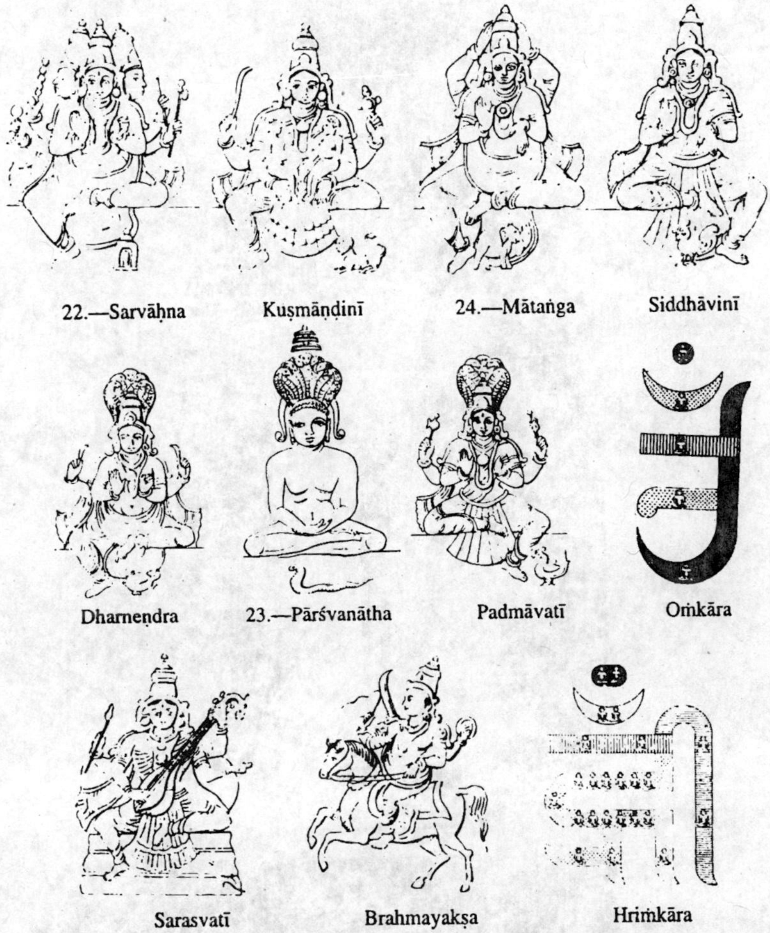

Plate 27: The Yakṣas and Yakṣiṇīs of the Tīrthaṅkaras (Digambara)

Plate 28: Pārśva